*This book is dedicated to the people
who personally gave their precious time,
to teach this author
the wonders of astrology.*

*Alphabetically, they are:
Larry and Gail Adams, Santos Bonacci,
Donna Cunningham, Pearl Foster,
Ronnie Grishman, Ed Kajkowski, Marwayne Leipzig,
Joanne McEvers, Maggie Nalbandian,
Marc Robertson and Carol Wickenkamp.*

ISBN: 978-0-9614627-2-7
Library of Congress Catalog Number: 2019900382

*Photo image in cover circle by Matheus Bertelli
licensed under Creative Commons Zero (CC0)
Proofing/Editing: Loretta Anderson, Elena Pilieci*
~~~

© 2019 by William Schreib
Published by Starry-Eyed Productions
1019 11th St., Lewiston, Idaho 83501
All rights reserved. No part of this book may be used
or reproduced in any manner whatsoever, without
written permission of the copyright owner,
except in the case of brief quotations
embodied in critical articles and reviews.

TABLE OF CONTENTS

History on How Celebrity Portraits was Created	1
As Above, So Below	2
4 Seasons & the 12 Step Creative Process	3-6
How Seasons & Planets fit into the chart	7
Considerations that create altered states	8
The Zodiac's Impact on the Physical Body	9
Decans of the Zodiac Signs	10
Key Lights of the Personality: The Sun Sign	11
The Moon Sign Bob Dylan and George Carlin demonstrate the difference between the Sun and Moon	12-13
The Ascendant	14
Mercury	15
Venus (Effects of Venus Rulership defined)	16-17
Mars (Effects of Mars on three Aries Sun Signs)	18-19
Opening Discussion	20

The Celebrity Portrait Collection
Capricorns

Introduction to Capricorn: 21-23   Page

Triple Capricorns: James Earl Jones & Zooey Deschanel
Page

Mel Gibson	24-25	Robert Duvall	36
Jared Leto	26-27	Kevin Costner	37
Kati Couric	28-29	Betty White	38
Maggi Smith	30-31	Ted Danson	39
Denzel Washington	32	Jim Carrey	40
Nicholas Cage	33	Muhammed Ali	41
Jude Law and Bradley Cooper	34-35	Orlando Bloom	42

 Aquarius

Introduction to Aquarius: 43-45
Double & Triple Aquariuses: Sarah Palin and Gene Hackman

	Page		Page
Tom Selleck and Alan Alda	46	Arsenio Hall	55
Paul Newman	47	Jennifer Aniston	56
Elijah Wood	48	Oprah Winfrey	57
Mia Farrow	49	Justin Timberlake	58
Tom Brokaw	50	Ellen Degeneres & Chris Rock	59
Geena Davis	51		
Carole King	52	Joseph Gordon-Levitt	60
James Spader	53	John Travolta	61
Garth Brooks	54	Nathan Lane	62

 Pisces

Introduction to Pisces: 63-65
Johnny Cash & Vanessa Redgrave

	Page		Page
Albert Einstein & Edgar Cayce	66	Gary Sinise & William H. Macy	77
Emily Blunt	67	Billy Crystal	78
Drew Barrymore	68	Queen Latifah	79
Dakota Fanning	69	Elizabeth Taylor	80
Alan Rickman	70	Alan Greenspan & Rupert Murdoch	81
George Harrison	71		
Bruce Willas	72	Ron Howard	82
Glenn Close	73	Steve Jobs	83
Steve Irwin	74-75	Daniel Craig	84
Bon Jovi	76		

Aries

Introduction to Aries: 85-87
Triple Fires Marlon Brando & Lucy Lawless are restrained by their Earth Mars

	Page		Page
Alec Guinness & Evan McGregor	88	Alec Baldwin	96
William Shatner, & Leonard Nimoy	89	Russell Crowe	97
		Reba McEntire	98
Celine Dione	90	Sarah J. Parker	99
James Woods	91	Emma Watson	100-101
Rachel Maddow	92	David Letterman	102-103
Gloria Steinem & Hugh Hefner	93	Al Gore	104
James Franco	94	Elton John	105
Lady Gaga	95	Robert Downy, Jr.	106

Taurus

Introduction to Taurus: 107-109
Triple Fixed Signs: Kate Hepburn & George Lucas

Cate Blanchett	110	Al Pacino	121
Daniel Day-Lewis	111	Kirsten Dunst	122
Candice Bergan	112	Barbra Streisand	123
Mark Zuckerberg	113	Tina Fey & Stephen Colbert	124
Adele	114-115		
George Clooney	116	Jay Leno	125
Cher	117	Jessica Lange	126
Michael Moore	118	Craig Ferguson	127
Renee Zellweger	119	Michelle Pfieffer	128
Jack Nicholson	120		

Gemini

Introduction to Gemini: 129-131
Juliette Lewis & Gene Wilder share Gemini Suns and Ascendants

Michael Fox	132	Venus Williams	141
Bob Dylan	133	Anderson Cooper	142
Johnny Depp	134	Bill Moyers	143
Ian McKellen	135	Mike Myers	144
Liam Neeson	136	Clint Eastwood	145
Joan Rivers	137	Nicole Kidman	146
Donald Trump	138	Natalie Portman	147
Neil Patrick Harris	139	Paul McCartney	148-149
Marilyn Monroe	140	Angelina Jolie	150

Cancer

Introduction to Cancer Traits: 151-153
Ross Perot & Karen Black: Two Crabs with New & Full Moons

Courtney Love & Liv Tyler	154	Forest Whitaker	163
Harrison Ford	155	Meryl Streep	164
Dali Lama	156	Willem Dafoe	165
Arianna Huffington	157	Lady Diana Spencer	166
Robin Williams	158	Jesse Ventura	167
Will Ferrell	159	Sylvester Stallone	168
Della Reese	160	Benedict Cumberbatch	169
Kathy Bates	161	Jane Lynch	170-171
Tom Hanks	162	Tobey Maquire	172

 # Leo

Introduction to Leo: 173-175
Double Leos Hulk Hogan and Patrick Swayze show traits of the Lion

3 Film Directors	176	Martha Stewart	185
Joan Allen	177	Sandra Bullock	186
Halle Berry	178	Barrack Obama	187
Charlize Theron	179	Amy Adams	188
Lisa Kudrow and "Friends"	180-181	Jennifer Lawrence	189
		Hilary Swank	190
Robert DeNiro	182	Bill Clinton	191
Whitney Houston	183	Steve Carel	192
Sean Penn	184	Dustin Hoffman	193
		J.K. Rowling	194

 # Virgo

Introduction to Virgo: 195-196
Triple Virgo Lyndon B. Johnson and Double Virgo Agatha Christie

Sean Connery	197	James Coburn	207
Mark Harmon	198	Richard Gere	208
Keanu Reeve & Adam Sandler	199	Jane Curtin	209
		Pink	210-211
Cameron Diaz	200	Amy Poehler	212-213
Dr. Phil McGraw	201	Jeff Foxworthy & Jack Black	214
Colin Firth	202		
Jimmy Fallon	204	Charlie Sheen	215
Melissa McCarthy	205	Tyler Perry	216
Lily Tomlin	206		

Libra

Introduction to Libra: 217-219
Double Libras Barbara Walters & Jimmy Carter show traits of Libra

Kate Winslet	220	Susan Sarandon	230
Hilary Duff	221	Sigourney Weaver	231
Kelly Ripa & Fran Dreshler	222	Yo-Yo Ma & Jason Alexander	232
Hugh Jackman	223	Bruno Mars	233
Gwyneth Paltrow	224	Deepak Chopra	234
John Lennon	225	Paul Simon	235
Christopher Reeve	226	Julie Andrews	236
James Caviezel	227	Michael Douglas	237
Tim Robbins	228	Will Smith	238
Matt Damon	229		

Scorpio

Introduction to Scorpio: 239-241
Photos of four Scorpios show body language of Scorpio

Whoppi Goldberg	242	Joni Mitchell & K.D. Lang	251
Leonardo DeCapiro	243	Martin Scorcese	252
Emma Stone	244-245	Maria Shriver	253
Roseanne Barr	246	Bill Gates	254
Condoleezza Rice	247	Julia Roberts	255
Matthew McConaughey	248	Goldie Hawn	256
Ryan Gosling	249	Anne Hathaway	257-258
Walter Cronkite & Dan Rather	250	Jodie Foster	259
		Danny DeVito	260

♐ Sagittarius

Introduction to Sagittarius: 261-263
Joe Dimaggio and Caroline Kennedy show the traits of the Centaur

Jon Stewart	264	Jeff Bridges	274
Bruce Lee	265	Don Johnson	275
Scarlett Johannsen	266	Steve Buscemi	276
Steven Spielberg	267	Kiefer Sutherland	277
Bette Midler	268		
Ben Stiller	269	Sarah Silverman	278
Tina Turner	270	Brad Pitt	279
Jake Gyllenhaal	271	Taylor Swift	280
Julianne Moore	272	Miley Cyrus	281
Britney Spears	273	Jane Fonda	282

The Dance of the Seasonal Lights .... Page 283

Astrological Cross References

Here, portraits are cataloged to provide insights into the common astrological components and arrangements in our subject's charts. This should help the reader to discover how astrology defines deeper layers in the human personality.

Content Defining Character & Appearance

You may want to read these portraits first, to start your lessons in astrology:

Contributions of 12 signs (in chronological order)...... pg. 3-6

Explanation of Cardinal Cross
Mel Gibson 24

How the author learned to recognize the key components in a chart: Goldie Hawn 256

How the Hemispheres work:
Taylor Swift 280

Portraits That Describe Ways to "Guess A Rising Sign"

Maggie Smith	30	Gwyneth Paltrow	224
Oprah Winfrey	57	Jason Alexander	232
Steve Irwin	74	Will Smith	238
Alec Baldwin	96	Rosanne Barr	246
Hilary Swank	190	Goldie Hawn	250
Mark Harmon	198	Jake Gyllenhaal	271
Dr. Phil McGraw	202	Tina Turner	270
Melissa McCarthy	205	Steve Buscemi	276
Jeff Foxworthy	214		

How components define "The Voice"

Daniel Day-Lewis	111
Adele	114
Cher	117

Other Astrological Influences that Affect One's Nature

Portraits Describing Body Type & Language

How It Works 9
Cher 117
Nicole Kidman 146
Natalie Portman 147
Will Ferrell 159
Lisa Kudrow 180
Yo-Yo Ma 232
Emma Stone 244

Fixed Stars physically effect the body
Hugh Jackman 223

Discussions on Decans of Components

Explanation of Decans 10
Bob Dylan/ G. Carlin 13
Jude Law and
Bradley Cooper 34
Ted Danson's Moon 39
Elijah Wood 48
James Spader 53
Russell Crowe 97
Cate Blanchett 110
Johnny Depp 134
Liam Neeson 136
Neal Patrick Harris 139
Bill Moyer 143
Forest Whitaker
and Tom Hanks 162

Sylvester Stallone 168
Charize Theron 179
Sean Penn 184
Colin Firth 202
Jimmy Fallon 204
Pink 210
Tyler Perry 216
Kate Winsett 220
Condi Rice 247
Ryan Gosling 249
Anne Hathaway 257
Julianne Moore 272
Jeff Bridges 274
Don Johnson 275
Steve Buscemi 276

Common Combinations of Modes and Elements

Portraits with Key Lights in Same ELEMENT:

FIRE
Celine Dion 90

EARTH
Candice Bergan 112
Sean Connery 197

AIR
Kate Winsett 220

WATER
Arriana Huffington 157
Robin William 158
Walter Cronkite 250
Joni Mitchell 251

People Lacking an Element in their Charts:
~To compensate for a missing Element, it often becomes obvious~

NO FIRE
Keannu Reeves 196
M. McConaughey 244

NO EARTH
Oprah Winfrey(?) 53
Rachel Maddow 88
Marilyn Monroe 131
Liam Nelson 132
Tobey McGuire 168
Condleeze Rice 243
Martin Scorcese 248
Bette Midler 264

NO AIR
Celine Dion 90
Keannu Reeves 199
Dan Rather 250
Julia Roberts 255
Bruce Lee 265

NO WATER
Surprisingly, all of our subjects have at least one of their components in a water sign.

Portraits with Key Lights in the SAME MODE:

TRIPLE CARDINAL
Mel Gibson 24
Jared Leto 26
Maggie Smith (?) 30
Katic Couric 28
Courtney Love 154
Liv Tyler 154
Harrison Ford 155
B. Cumberbatch 169
Kate Winsett 220
Fran Dresser 222

Susan Sarandon 230
Yo-Yo Ma 232

TRIPLE FIXED
Candice Bergan 112
Kirsten Dunst 122
Jessica Lange 125
Halle Berry 178
Whoppi Goldberg 242
Martin Scorcese 252
Maria Shriver 253

TRIPLE MUTABLE
Ian McCkellan 135
Liam Neson 136
Pink 210
Charlie Sheen 215
Ben Stiller 269
Julianne Moore 272
Jeff Bridges 274
Steve Buscemi (?) 276

The next five pages list portraits of individuals who share Common Moon Signs and Ascendants
PLUS miscellaneous common arrangements

Celebrities Who Share Common Moon Signs

Aries

Jared Leto	26
Katie Couric	28
Alan Alda	46
Chris Rock	59
Ellen DeGeneres	59
Steve Jobs	83
Daniel Craig	84
Celine Dion	90
Kate Blancett	110
Daniel Day-Lewis	111
Anderson Cooper	142
Bill Moyers	143
Angelina Jolie	150
Benedict Cumberbatch	169
Whitney Houston	183
Lily Tomlin	206
Pink	210
Bill Gates	254
Kiefer Sutherland	277

Taurus

Geena Davis	51
Billy Crystal	78
William Shatner	89
Elton John	104
Robert Downey, Jr.	106
Mark Zuckerberg	113
Michael J. Fox	132
Bob Dylan	133
Meryl Streep	164
Bill Clinton	191
Cameron Diaz	200
Dr. Phillip McGraw	201
Colin Firth	202
Jane Curtin	209
Sigourney Weaver	231

Gemini

Jim Carrey	40
James Spader	53
Evan McGregor & Alec Guinness	88
Reba McEntire	98
Stephen Colbert	124
Barack Obama	187

Gemini Moons Continued:

Jennifer Lawrence	189
Jeff Foxworthy	214
Hugh Jackman	223
Gwyneth Paltrow	224
Jason Alexander	232
Rosanne Barr	246
Goldie Hawn	256
Jake Gyllenhaal	271
Tina Turner	270
Julianne Mooore	272

Cancer

Robert Duvall	36
Edgar Cayce	66
Emily Brunt	67
Drew Barrymore	68
Leonard Nimoy	89
Mike Myers	144
Courtney Love	154
Harrison Ford	155
Sean Penn	184
J. K. Rowling	194
Keanu Reeves & Adam Sandler	199
Melissa McCartney	205
Yo-Yo Ma	232
Paul Simon	235
Condoleezza Rice	247
Dan Rather	250

Leo

Ted Danson	39
Tom Selleck	46
Joseph Gordon-Levitt	60
Dakota Fanning	69
Queen Latifah	79
James Franco	94
Michael Moore	118
Renee Zellweger	119
Kirtsten Dunst	122
Barbra Stressand	123
Venus Williams	141
Clint Eastwood	145
Paul McCartney	148
Tom Hanks	162
Forest Whitaker	163

Leo Moons Continued:

Willem DaFoe	165
Jane Lynch	170
Halle Berry	178
Charlize Theron	179
Amy Poehler	212
Bruno Mars	233
Maria Shriver	253
Julia Roberts	255
Taylor Swift	280

Virgo

Betty White	38
John Travolta	61
Steve Irwin	74
Candice Bergen	112
Jack Nicholson	120
Jay Leno	125
Michelle Pfieffer	128
Ian McKellen	135
Natalie Portman	147
Dalai Lama	156
Arianna Huffington	157
Amy Adams	188
Dustin Hoffman	193
Sean Connery	197
Mark Harmon	198
DeePak Chopa	234
Matthew McConaughey	248
K.D. Lang	251
Jodi Foster	258
Steve Buscemi	276

Libra

Mel Gibson	24
Nicholas Cage	33
Jude Law/Bradley Cooper	34
Alec Baldwin	96
Tina Fey	124
Sylvester Stallone	168
Tyler Perry	216
Kate Winslet	220
Kelly Ripa	222
Emma Stone	244
Anne Hathaway	257

Scorpio

Name	Page
Orlando Bloom	42
Elijah Wood	48
Nathan Lane	62
George Harrison	71
Liz Taylor	80
Gloria Steinem	93
Lady Gaga	95
Mark Zuckerberg	113
Craig Ferguson	127
Will Ferrell	159
Lisa Kudrow	180
Jimmy Fallon	204
Julie Andrews	236
Will Smith	238
Whoppi Goldberg	242
Bruce Lee	265
Scarlett Johansson	266
Steven Spielberg	267
Bette Midler	268
Don Johnson	275
Miley Cyrus	281

Sagittarius

Name	Page
Kevin Costner	37
Carole King	52
Jennifer Aniston	56
Oprah Winfrey	57
Justin Timberlake	58
Albert Einstein	66
Alan Greenspan & Rupert Murdcoch	81
Emma Watson	96
Adele	114
Liam Neeson	136
Joan Rivers	137

Centaur Moons Continued:

Name	Page
Donald Trump	138
Neil Patrick Harris	139
Nicole Kidman	146
Jesse Ventura	167
Martha Stewart	185
Richard Gere	208
Charlie Sheen	215
Hilary Duff	221
Christopher Reeve	226
James Caviezel	227
Tim Robbins	228
Danny Devito	260
Jon Stewart	264

Capricorn

Name	Page
Mia Farrow	49
Tom Brocaw	50
Bon Jovi	76
Ron Howard	82
Sarah Jessica Parker	99
David Letterman	98
Al Gore	104
Candice Bergan	112
George Clooney	116
Cher	117
Johnny Depp	134
Liv Tyler	154
Hilary Swank	190
Fran Drescher	222
Matt Damon	229
Susan Sarandon	230
Michael Douglas	237
Ryan Gosling	249

Aquarius

Name	Page
Denzel Washington	32
Muhammed Ali	41
Arsenio Hall	55
Glenn Close	73
Bruce Willis	72
Russell Crowe	97
Jessica Lange	124
Marilyn Monroe	140
Diana Spencer	166
Tobey Maquire	172
Joan Allen	177
Sandra Bullock	186
John Lennon	225
Britney Spears	273

Pisces

Name	Page
Paul Newman	47
Garth Brooks	54
James Woods	91
Rachel Maddow	92
Hugh Hefner	93
Robin Williams	158
Della Reese	140
Kathy Bates	161
Robert DeNiro	182
Steve Carrell	192
James Coburn	207
Jack Black	214
Walter Cronkite	250
Joni Mitchell	251
Martin Scorcese	252
Ben Stiller	269

Miscellaneous Odds & Ends

Relationship Between Venus and Mars

Name	Page
Steve Irwin	74
Martha Stewart	185
Barack Obama	187
Amy Adams & Jennifer Lawrence	188

Links of Destiny/Nodes

Name	Page
Dali Lama	156
Daniel Day-Lewis and Abraham Lincoln	111
Kirsten Dunst	122

T-Squares to Pluto

Name	Page
Pink	210
Jon Stewart/Bruce Lee	264

Effect of MARS

Portraits that discuss Mars (and a list of the Mars placements of many celebrities) are featured on the last index page.

Effects of Component Placement in Houses

Name	Page
Rachel Maddow	92
James Franco	94
Lady Gaga	95
Adele	114
Nicole Kidman	146
Natalie Portman	147
Arianna Huffington	153
Courtney Love and Liv Tyler	154
Jane Lynch	170
Tyler Perry	216
Deepak Chopra	234

Celebrities Who Share Common Ascendants (ASC)

Aries

Chris Rock 59
Joseph Gordon-Levitt 60
Ron Howard 76
Alec Guinness 88
Barbra Streisand 123
Joan Rivers 137
James Coburn 207
John Lennon 225
Yo-Yo Ma 232
Bette Midler 268

Taurus

Mia Farrow 49
Dakota Fanning 69
Billy Crystal 78
Queen Latifah 79
Dave Letterman 102
Cate Blancett 110
Halle Berry 178
Sigourney Weaver 231
Dan Rather 250
Miley Cyrus 281

Gemini

Garth Brooks 54
Drew Barrymore 68
Alan Greenspan 81
Lady Gaga 95
Reba McEntire 98
Sarah Jessica Parker 99
Michelle Pfieffer 128
Jesse Ventura 167
Sandra Bullock 186
Amy Adams 188
Charlies Sheen 215
Matthew McConaughey 246
Ben Stiller 269
Julianne Moore 272

Cancer

Mel Gibson 24
John Travolta 61
Nathan Lane 62

Cancer Ascendants Continued:
Albert Einstein 66
Glenn Close 73
Rachel Maddow 92
Adele 114
Cher 117
Angelina Jolie 150
Liv Tyler 154
Dalai Lama 156
Jane Lynch 170
Joan Allen 171
Lisa Kudrow 180
Cameron Diaz 200
Barrack Obama 187
Lily Tomlin 206
Joni Mitchelll 251
Bill Gates 254
Julia Roberts 255
Steven Spielberg 267

Leo

Betty White 38
Muhammad Ali 41
Justin Timberlake 58
Edgar Cayce 66
Celine Dion 90
James Woods 91
Al Gore 104
Robert Downey, Jr. 106
Michael Moore 118
Jack Nicholson 120
Kirsten Dunst 122
Tina Fey 124
Jessica Lange 126
Johnny Depp 134
Donald Trump 138
Marilyn Monroe 140
Mike Meyers 144
Meryl Streep 164
Tobey Maquire 172
Christopher Reeve 226
Will Smith 238
Emma Stone 238
Martin Scorcese 252
Tina Turner 270
Jake Gyllenhaal 271

Virgo

Kevin Costner 37
Ted Danson 39
James Spader 53
Bruce Willis 72
Steve Jobs 83
Hugh Hefner 94
Emma Watson 100
Candice Bergan 112
Mark Zuckerberg 113
Renee Zellweger 119
Will Ferrell 159
Della Reece 160
Kathy Bates 161
Tom Hanks 162
Forest Whitaker 163
Charlize Theron 179
Steve Carell 192
Keanu Reeves 199
Kelly Ripa 222
Tim Robbins 228
Paul Simon 235
Julie Andrews 236
K.D. Lang 251
Jeff Bridges 274
Don Johnson 275

Libra

Jared Leno 26
Katie Couric 28
Denzel Washington 32
Geena Davis 51
Carole King 52
Jennifer Aniston 56
George Harrison 71
Bon Jovi 76
Ewan McGregor 88
Craig Ferguson 127
Venus Williams 141
Anderson Cooper 142
Courtney Love 154
Harrison Ford 155
Benedict Cumberbatch 169
Bill Clinton 191
Kate Winslet 220
Fran Drescher 222

Scorpio

Jim Carrey	40
Leonard Nimoy	89
Gloria Steinem	93
James Franco	94
Clint Eastwood	145
Nicole Kidman	146
Natalie Portman	147
Arianna Huffington	157
Robin Williams	158
Martha Stewart	185
Mark Harmon	198
Colin Firth	202
Richard Gere	208
James Caviezel	227
Michael Douglas	237
Walter Cronkite	250

Sagittarius

Nicholas Cage	33
Jude Law & Bradley Cooper	34
Robert Duvall	36
Tom Brokaw	50
Arsenio Hall	55
Liz Taylor	80
Elton John	105
Steven Colbert	124
Bob Dylan	133
Ian McKellen	135
Liam Neeson	136

Sagittarius Continued:

Diana Spencer	166
Sylvester Stallone	168
Sean Penn	184
Jennifer Lawrence	189
Hilary Swank	190
Jane Curtain	209
Pink	210
Goldie Hawn	256
Anne Hathaway	257
Jodie Foster	258
Danny DeVito	260
Bruce Lee	265
Scarlett Johansson	266

Capricorn

Tom Selleck	46
Alan Alda	46
Paul Newman	47
Elijah Wood	48
Ellen DeGeneres	59
Rupert Murdoch	81
Daniel Day-Lewis	111
Candice Bergan	112
Dustin Hoffman	193
Sean Connery	197
Susan Sarandon	230
Kiefer Sutherland	277
Sarah Silverman	278
Brad Pitt	279
Taylor Swift	280
Jane Fonda	282

Aquarius

Orlando Bloom	42
Steve Irwin	74
William Shatner	89
Russell Crowe	97
Adele	114
Jay Leno	125
Michael J. Fox	132
Bill Moyers	143
Willem DaFoe	165
Barrack Obama	187
J.K. Rowling	194
Amy Poehler	212
Hilary Duff	221
Matt Damon	229
Whoppi Goldberg	242
Rosanne Barr	246
Condoleezza Rice	247

Pisces

George Clooney	116
Paul McCartney	148
Whitney Houston	183
Dr. Phil McGraw	201
Jimmy Fallon	204
Gwyneth Paltrow	224
Jason Alexander	232
Bruno Mars	233
Deepak Chopra	234
Ryan Gosling	249
Steve Buscemi	276

Life Cycles, Progressions & Outer Planet Transits

Moon, Rising & Sun Sign define Passages of Life

Drew Barrymore	68
Dakota Fanning	69
Emma Watson	100
Kirsten Dunst	122

Progressions

Katie Couric	28
Nicholas Cage	33
Emily Blunt	67
Paul McCartney	148
Britney Spears	273

Transits of Jupiter

James Coburn	207

Transits of Uranus and/or Pluto

Intro to these planets	3-4
Garth Brooks	54
Arsenio Hall	55
Square in Earth Signs	67

Transits of Saturn

Maggie Smith	30
Kevin Costner	37
David Letterman	102
Mark Zuckerberg	113

Placement & Transits of Neptune

Celine Dion	90
Adele	114
Arianna Huffington	157
Neptune Signs of Four Motion Picture Directors	176

Arianna Huffington	156
Michael Douglas	237
Jodie Foster	258
Britney Speers	273

Al Pachino	121
Sandra Bullock	186
Britney Spears	273
Don Johnson	275

Pink	210
Neptune's "Sign Shift" and Hollywood trends	216, 233
Tyler Perry	216
Michael Douglas	237

Placement of Mars

Observe the physical metabolism of these celebrities and you will see the nature of their MARS in their actions.

Effect of MARS
The Mars Effect 18
Mars Placement
for three celebrities 19
Mars of Gary Sinise and
William H. Macy 77
Rhythms of Mars with
Neil Patrick Harris 139

Placements of MARS

Aries Mars:
Katie Couric 28
Bradley Cooper 34
Kevin Costner 37
Daniel Craig 84
James Woods 91
Gloria Steinum 93
Russell Crowe 97
Clint Eastwood 145
Angelina Jolie 150
Paul Simon 235
Emma Stone 244
Kiefer Sutherland 277

Taurus Mars:
Muhammad Ali 41
Carole King 52
Gary Sinese 77
Queen Latifah 79
Celine Dion 90
Reba McEntire 98
Meryl Streep 164
Jane Lynch 170
Charlize Theorn 179
Robert DeNiro 182
Jennifer Lawrence 189
Jeff Foxworthy 214

Gemini Mars:
Daniel Day-Lewis 111
Barbra Streisand 119
Al Pacino 121
Tina Fey 124
Meryl Streep 164
Steve Carelll 192
Sean Connery 197
Tim Robbins 228

Cancer Mars:
Alec Guiness 88
Leonard Nimoy 89
Robin Williams 158
Tom Hanks 162
Halle Berry 178
Keannu Reeves 199
Richard Geer 208

Jane Curtain 209
Pink 210
Miley Cyrus 281

Leo Mars:
Robert Duvall 36
James Franco 94
Candice Bergan 112
George Clooney 116
Cher 117
Michael J. Fox 132
Mike Myers 144
Clint Eastwood 145
Paul McCartney 148
Harrison Ford 155
Willem Dafoe 165
Melissa McCarthy 205
Richard Gere 208
Sigourney Weaver 231
Goldie Hawn 256
Jodie Foster 258
Bette Midler 268

Virgo Mars:
Chris Rock 59
Sarah J. Parker 99
R. Downey, Jr. 106
Johnny Depp 134
Joan Rivers 137
Venus Williams 141
Princes Dianna 166
Sly Stallone 168
B. Cumberbatch 169
Barrack Obama 187
Amy Adams 189
Cameron Diaz 200

Libra Mars:
Maggie Smith 30
Jon Bon Jovi 76
Bill Macy 77
Anderson Cooper 142
Dalai Lama 156
Liza Krudrow 180
Bill Clinton 191
Jimmy Fallon 204
Gwyneth Paltrow 224
John Lennon 225
Matt Damon 229
Jason Alexander 232
Michael Douglas 237

Scorpio Mars:
Jennifer Annison 56
Michelle Pfieffer 128

Liam Neeson 136
Neil P. Harris 139
Dr. Phil 201
Charlie Sheen 215
Susan Sarandon 230
Leonardo DeCaprio 243
Martin Scorcese 252
Danny Devito 260
Bruce Lee 265
Taylor Swift 280

Sagittarius Mars:
Geena Davis 51
Arsenio Hall 55
Ellen DeGeneres 59
Ron Howard 82
Evan McGregor 88
Lady Gaga 95
Cate Blanchett 106
Jack Nicholson 120
Jack Black 214
Christopher Reeve 226
Julie Andrews 236
James Caviezel 227
Ryan Gosling 249

Capricorn Mars:
Jim Carrey 40
Orlando Bloom 42
Mia Farrow 49
Steve Jobs 83
Michael Moore 118
Lily Tomlin 206
Rosanne Barr 246
Julia Roberts 254
Anne Hathaway 257
Steven Spielberg 267
Ben Stiller 269
Jake Gyllenhaal 271
Brad Pitt 279

Aquarius Mars:
Hugh Hefner 93
Alec Baldwin 96
Adele 114
Amy Poehler 212
M. McConaughey 248
Scarlett Johannson 266
Jane Fonda 282

Pisces Mars:
Jared Leto 24
J. Gorden-Levitt 60
Emily Blunt 67
Alan Rickman 70
Glen Close 73
Elton John 105
Marilyn Monroe 140
Tina Turner 270
Steve Buscemi 276

Make this book a Multi-Media Experience

It is suggested that readers view the charts of celebrities, when their portraits discuss the following points:

◆ **Complex Aspects of Planets**

◆ **Planet Transits or Progressions**

◆ **Placements of Components in Houses**

Since each portrait has limited space (and the details are often briefly described), it is believed that "the viewing of a subject's chart" will make the information easier to understand.

Data on thousands of celebrities can be found at:
www.astrotheme.com *or* **www.astro.com/astro-databank**

View our *Subjects* on Video

This book's collection of photos displays the physical characteristics of the twelve Zodiac Signs, primarily the expressions we see in their Suns, Moons and Ascendants. These photos capture the look of our subject's expressions, but the energy in which they express themselves can not be demonstrated in a still photo. Therefore, we suggest that readers go to the internet and view videos on any subject that piques their interest.

We also suggest that the reader try to view the celebrity on a TV talk show, or in a situation where the true mannerisms of their three key components will likely be accurately presented—since they are being themselves and they are NOT playing a role.

Cross Reference the Signs in our Index....

After the initial viewing, this author encourages the reader to use the index list that was featured in the opening pages. There, you can compare Sun Signs who share the same Moon, or see people who share a common Ascendant or Mars. There is also a cross reference list to show portraits that discuss specific astrological phenomenons (i.e., Decans, Saturn transits, dominate Modes, Elements, etc.)

Test your observations on your friends....

With all this, you will likely discover how the cycles of Nature (as captured in one's astrology chart) define your character, as well as those of your family and friends. In time, you may be able to guess the signs of people that you meet—and perhaps help them to discover their true self, so that they can become what Nature intended them to be.

Visit our website at
Astro-Visions.com
Seeing is Believing!

A Historical Overview
on the creation of *Portraits of Personality*

In 1995, *DELL HOROSCOPE*'s Editor-in-Chief Ronnie Grishman replied to my submission for a monthly article in "The World's Leading Astrology Magazine". She liked my idea of showing the astrological features of a celebrity with a collage of facial photos. This *Celebrity Snapshots* column debuted in January of 1996 (in the Capricorn issue of the magazine). This may have been an omen, since this author is a Capricorn.

With this, I began the task of creating a new article—every month for over two decades! In these years of regimented research, my knowledge of astrology grew steadily, as I discovered how this ancient language was able to diagram Nature's creative process—while it also showed us how these cycles of changing lights and colors affected human attributes.

Graphic Layout and Content Grows

Initially, I assumed my column would be just a description of the physical traits of the Sun, Moon and Rising Signs. After all, it had taken me nearly twenty years of studying faces to "see what I was seeing", when I submitted the idea to Dell Horoscope. However, after a few years of submissions, I began to find subjects who did not fit the expected traits of their key components. This impelled me to research other influences—i.e., the aspects and transits of the luminaries and planets, the impact of the rulers of the signs, the effects of progressions, and even the simple degree changes in one's components. It became clear that all of these acquired insights had to be presented in a different manner—and they had to follow a plan! (*Damn right, I'm a Capricorn!*) That plan inspired the creation of this book.

Bringing the Collection Together

It soon was clear that these portraits had to be presented in groups of Sun Signs—and they had to be assembled in an order that would illustrate common chart components or planet configurations. With this, the reader could then observe a particular Sun Sign—perhaps examine one with a Libra Moon and compare that with the following person who has a Libra Ascendant. Other groupings would include portraits that shared strong Saturn or Pluto influences, etc.

The first step was to find new facial photos, ones that would describe the unique features in each subject—as well as the similarities between one portrait and the next. Naturally, this text also had to reflect this author's advanced understanding of astrology—and provide a needed tread of continuity to the dialogue.

To this end, new portraits were created to fill perceived holes in the presentation—and since most of my subjects were noticeably from my generation, I added some younger faces to provide insights to a new era of budding astrologers.

To finalize the "grand plan", a cross-reference list was added in the index of this book—so readers could research Sun Signs who share common features (like perhaps a Virgo Moon or Aries Rising). I also listed links to portraits that shared material on certain planetary transits, progressions, decans, etc.

With that, I hope this book helps readers to recognize that the colors and qualities in Nature's daily and seasonal lights are ingrained into our being—and with this understanding, we all can become closer to the divine process that made life possible on planet Earth.

William Schreib

As Above, So Below
When humans evolved from hunters into farmers, they learned to observe the cycles of Nature, so they could tend their flocks and gardens. With their close connection to "Mother Gaia", they recognized that Earth's yearly cycle of seasons were unfolding in a regimented pattern of operation—and they appeared to move in synchronicity with the stars in the Heavens. With this, the language of astrology was born.

The Modal Patterns of the Seasons
When ancient astrologers looked to the South, they saw that the Sun, Moon and stars were moving clockwise, as they rose in the East and set in the West. (This was primarily due to the Earth's daily West to East rotation). Later, they discovered that—in a month's passage of the Sun—a different constellation (Zodiac sign) would appear on the eastern horizon. Also, in every 3 month period, they saw that the Sun would turn in a new direction at each of the four **Cardinal compass points**. There, the signs *Aries, Cancer, Libra* and *Capricorn* were in the east—to start the four seasons in the year.

In the middle month of each season, the signs of *Taurus, Leo, Scorpio* and *Aquarius* were observed behind the Sun. At these points, all things appeared to be "caught in the middle" and placed on hold—to manifest the essential contributions of each season. The ancients named these signs the **Fixed Signs** of the Zodiac.

In the final month in each season, the Go-and-Stop actions of the previous two modes are "mixed together", when *Gemini, Virgo, Sagittarius* and *Pisces* appear in the East. These **Mutable Signs** create the alterations, to prepare for the new season ahead.

When these three modes are repeated in each of the four seasons, their respective stretching, holding and twisting forces shape all of the states of being on this planet.

Shifts in Polarity Bring 4 Elemental States of Being
Those stargazers felt these shifts in polarity—in the daily tides and in the Sun's movement from one sign into the next. They sensed the expansive/masculine force, when the Sun entered a **Fire** or **Air** sign. When the Sun entered a feminine sign, they could feel the solidifying force of **Earth** and the liquefying energy of **Water**. They believed that everything in the Universe could be catalogued into one of these spiritual, physical, mental and emotional states of being.

In Combination, They Define the 12 Zodiac Signs
With their Earth-centered view, (i.e., **Tropical Astrology**)—these ancient wizards were able to illustrate how these twelve combinations of 3 Modes and 4 Elements reflected the patterns that they saw in each of the Zodiac Signs. These signs defined the system, that orchestrated Nature's 12 step process of creation!

Amazingly, these scholars also observed that these "heavenly qualities" were present in the expressive natures of their friends and family. Furthermore, they not only defined the impact of the 3 key lights (a person's Sun, Moon and Ascendant)—they also were able to identify the affect of the long-range cycles of the planets. With this, they recognized that "the patterns above, were being replicated below"— a concept that is now supported by the latest discoveries in quantum physics and cosmology.

The ancients believed that the Sun was circling the Earth. However, the fixed Sun was actually being circled by the Earth. Still, when they faced south, the Sun would always rise on the eastern, left side of the horizon—and **Spring** would always begin with ***Aries** behind the morning Sun. Every month, a different sign would rotate clockwise, to bring its light into the "upper southern sky". What they saw is what follows:

*In this age of Aquarius, the constellation of Aries is not behind the Sun at the Spring Equinox. See page 11.

Spring

(In the Southern Hemisphere, it's FALL)

The Season of Self Discovery

It is time to recognize the true nature of our being.

When the Sun rises over the Eastern horizon, the building light sweeps away the darkness.

① **Cardinal Fire: Aries**
② **Fixed Earth: Taurus**
③ **Mutable Air: Gemini**

♈ March 21 to April 19
Life is reborn at the Spring Equinox

① ARIES: *Explore a new adventure*

On the first day of Spring, life awakens as the Sun rises above the Equator. Here, light and dark are in balance, but the Cardinal Fire of Aries* is building—to light the path ahead. This inspires all individuals to begin their personal journeys of self discovery!

With this awakening, the seeds from Nature's past endeavors are carried forward, as individuals take action—to bring new creative formations to the Earth.

♉ April 20 to May 20
Mid-Spring delights arouse the senses

② TAURUS: *Slow down and smell the roses*

In mid-Spring, the fixed force of Taurus contains the fire of Aries, but the warmth is bringing the Earth its most productive month of physical growth. In this garden, the five senses are aroused, to seek the resources that will give the body physical strength.

With a strong body, one can perform the work, that will grow and enrich the gardens of Nature. With this effort, Nature rewards the contributors with an abundant and substantial array of riches.

♊ May 21 to June 20
At Spring's end, think of the possibilities!

③ GEMINI: *Study the content of your perceptions*

At Spring's end, the swirling winds are feeding a massive mix of data, to stir the senses of Taurus! In this interplay of opposing polarities, the generated electricity activates the two sides of the bicameral mind. This enables all sentient beings to analyze these sensed bits and pieces, and then group them into the larger concepts—that will enable them to understand and interact with their surroundings. With this, Spring's lessons of Self Discovery are complete.

Summer

Feel the warmth around you!

Find your place, in your surroundings.

After the Sun reaches its highest point in the sky, it begins its downward journey into night.

④ **Cardinal Water: Cancer**

⑤ **Fixed Fire: Leo**

⑥ **Mutable Earth: Virgo**

June 21 to July 22
The light peaks at the Summer Solstice

④ CANCER: *Find a place to call home*

When the Sun begins its downward journey to the equator, the shift into feminine polarity instills an urge for individuals to gather their previous desires, senses and thoughts together—so that they can form the emotional base, that will instill a feeling of comfort.

With the finding of this home, individuals find the confidence to begin the interaction with their surroundings—so that they can gather in the treasures that they will need, to sustain their families.

July 23 to August 22
Shine in the glow of Midsummer's light

⑤ LEO: *Celebrate the glory of your creations*

In the masculine light of Leo, it's time to move further from one's home, strut about the neighborhood—and find a place to play! Why not? The glowing light of midsummer is showing individuals the grandeur in their surroundings—as it sparks a desire to create a more magnificent world. With these creative visions, individuals find the confidence to place themselves on center stage—so that they inspire others to serve their magnanimous cause!

August 23 to September 22
Everything works, when we serve others

⑥ VIRGO: *Work it out & make things perfect*

At Summer's end, it's time to make Leo's vision a reality! To do this, individuals need to perfect their personal physical and mental skills—so that they organize the offerings of Nature into the new arrangements, that will make future harvests more bountiful.

In this cool Virgo light, individuals perform the "work" that will be of a service to others. When others contribute to this effort, we all will be prepared to face the chilly seasons that lie ahead.

Autumn
(In the Southern Hemisphere, it is Spring)

Recognize the significance of others

Reach out to others. Create relationships and communities.

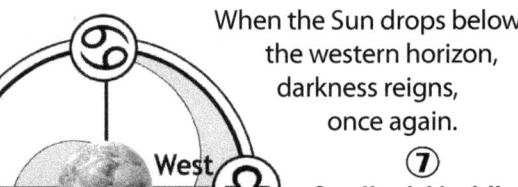

When the Sun drops below the western horizon, darkness reigns, once again.

⑦ Cardinal Air: Libra
⑧ Fixed Water: Scorpio
⑨ Mutable Fire: Sagittarius

 September 23 to October 22 •————————•
Fall's light brings balance and harmony

⑦ LIBRA: *A time to recognize the other half*

At the Fall Equinox, the Sun brings the serene light of Libra drops takes us into the darker half of the year. In this "other hemisphere", the light-of-self is fading with the dimming Sun. Now, individuals must learn to share their ideas and deeper feelings with others.

Here, the enriched Venusian sensations of Libra inspire the artful creations and selfless aspirations, that will make this world a more beautiful and peaceful place to live.

October 23 to November 21 •————————•
In the dark, Nature's secrets are revealed

⑧ SCORPIO: *Hold on to all things that feel good*

In the darkness of mid-Fall, resources are hard to find. To survive, all of us must trust our instinctual feelings—so that we can discard all things of little worth, and hold on to what is truly meaningful.

With these values, others will find trust in our personal insights, and share them with others. This sharing of feelings is rejuvenating, for it links individuals to the **One Source of Power**—the one that connects everything in the Universe.

November 22 to December 21 •————————•
At Autumn's end, the possibilities are endless

⑨ SAGITTARIUS: *Free yourself from attachments*

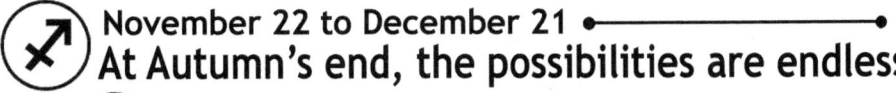

In the last month of the year, it is the darkest of times, but optimism still prevails—for our feelings has affirmed that a divine process is in operation, to support the creative desires of everyone!

We see it in the contributions of others, and in the centuries of human effort that have given us the acquired wisdom, to raise our standard of living. These advancements have all come with our gained understanding of Nature—the master teacher who shows us the way.

Winter

Unify the parts & complete the process

Unite all people to become stewards of the Earth

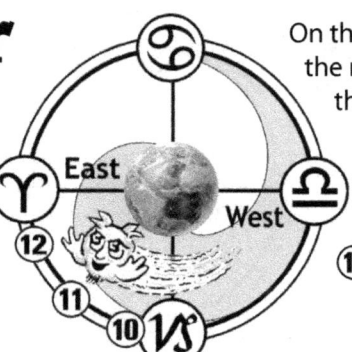

On the darkest day, and on the midnight of everyday, the light of the Sun begins to rise again.

⑩ **Cardinal Earth:** Capricorn

⑪ **Fixed Air:** Aquarius

⑫ **Mutable Water:** Pisces

♑ December 22 to January 19
Things are looking up at Winter's Solstice
⑩ CAPRICORN: *The rising light shows the way*

When the Sun begins its upward movement in the sky, all beings are driven—to set new goals for the New Year ahead (**Capricorn**). With their inventive reformations (**Aquarius**) and the transformational imagination of **Pisces**, our future dreams will become a reality.

It is Capricorn, who uses the "lessons of the ages" to orchestrate future goals. The wiser goats become the teachers, who pass this knowledge on to others—so that everyone can do their part to build a better world.

♒ January 20 to February 18
Midwinter manifests grand resolutions
⑪ AQUARIUS: *Invent a whole new concept*

In the crystal clear light of midwinter, all past-planted seeds are quickened by the melting snow. Here, the fixed force returns, to meld the resolutions of Capricorn (and the hopes of every individual) into a newly invented conceptual whole—one that will revolutionize the collective consciousness of humanity. This creates the social changes that will bring a brighter future.

These changes are finalized in the universal solvent of water.

♓ February 19 to March 20
At the end of Winter, the dream is complete
⑫ PISCES: *Imagine that Everything is possible*

At winter's end, the waters are flowing again—to loosen all firmly held beliefs. Now, all beings are free, to let go of all attachments, so that they can flow with the greater currents of destiny.

With this release, all past contributions are passed forward—to be used and transformed by the imaginations of others! With this creative input from many individuals, all dreams are possible!

These aspirations are activated next month, in the fiery light of **Aries**.

How "Seasons & Planets" fit into the Chart

From their spot on Earth, ancient star gazers viewed the heavens, as they faced the southern sky. This placed South at the top of their charts, and East on the left side.

Every month, a different Zodiac Sign would appear in the East, and then move clockwise in the sky. To capture this movement, the 12 Signs were listed in counter-clockwise order. As they rotated CW, these 12 spokes would clock the yearly rise and fall of the Sun.

The seasonal qualities in each of these 12 months defined the nature of each of these chart segments. These "Houses" were given their own planetary or luminaries rulers.

Lower Hemisphere: Where the Personal Planets Shine

When **Aries** sits in the East, the Equinox equally lights both halves of the Earth. This is what is shown in the illustration.

When the **1st Quadrant (Houses 1, 2 and 3)** moves CW over the equator, it is the season of **Spring**. Here, the light of the Sun (*the light-of-self*) is building. It is time to explore the "Self Discovery" lessons of *Aries, Taurus* and *Gemini* and their respective ruling "personal planets": Mercury, Venus and Mars.

Three months later, **Cancer** sits in the East, as **Houses 4, 5 & 6** begin to fill the UL quadrant. When complete (with Spring's Houses in the in UR quadrant) the upper sky is completely filled with the white light of **Summer**.

Here, the Moon, Sun and Mercury enable all beings to feel *(Cancer)*, appreciate *(Leo)* and interact *(Virgo)* with their surroundings.

The Upper Hemisphere: Recognition of Other

When the Sun drops below the western horizon, the **Libra** Sun sits in the East. Here, the signs in the **3rd Quadrant (Houses 7, 8 & 9)** begin the transition from *personal to transpersonal awareness*. This act of "relating to other" begins with the weighing judgements of **Libra**. These relationships

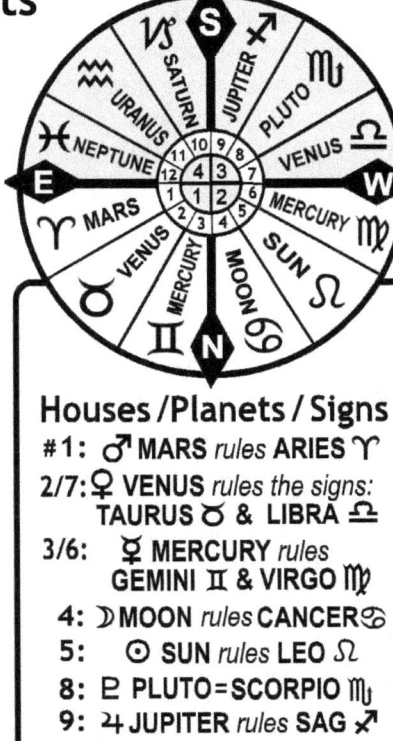

Houses / Planets / Signs

- #1: ♂ MARS *rules* ARIES ♈
- 2/7: ♀ VENUS *rules the signs:* TAURUS ♉ & LIBRA ♎
- 3/6: ☿ MERCURY *rules* GEMINI ♊ & VIRGO ♍
- 4: ☽ MOON *rules* CANCER ♋
- 5: ☉ SUN *rules* LEO ♌
- 8: ♇ PLUTO = SCORPIO ♏
- 9: ♃ JUPITER *rules* SAG ♐
- 10: ♄ Saturn *rules* Capricorn ♑
- 11: ♅ Uranus *rules* Aquarius ♒
- 12: ♆ Neptune *rules* Pisces ♓

reveal the hidden values of *Scorpio* and wisdom of *Sagittarius*.

This "recognition of other" is signified in the duel rulerships of Venus and Mercury. Venus rules Houses 2 and 7; Mercury rules Houses 3 and 6. Save for these two, all of this hemisphere's rulers consist of the outer (non-personal) planets.

In **Quadrant 4 (Houses 10, 11 & 12)**, the Earth is at its lowest point below the horizon. On this **Winter Solstice**, the Sun begins its upward climb—to complete the steps of integration, that will enable life to perform its needed physical tasks *(Capricorn)*, manifest inventive resolutions *(Aquarius)* and imagine the prophetic dreams of *Pisces*.

Factors That Create Altered States

Every chart component is rarely a pure form of its sign of residency, since its form and nature are often altered by: (**1**) Its House of placement within the chart— (**2**) Its aspects to other chart components— (**3**) the transits of other heavenly bodies to itself—and (**4**) its own progression through time.

Houses, Planet Transits and Progressions

The 12 Houses in a chart each represent one of the months in a year, or the home of one of the Zodiac signs. (*The previous page shows how Houses fit into the chart*).

The **Ascendant** is determined by the Zodiac sign that was rising on the eastern horizon at one's time of birth. The becomes the **1st House** in the chart.

At one's birth, the two luminaries and eight other planets are each planted in one of these Houses. This placement tells us the area in one's life where a specific component is "doing its thing." For example, the House in which your Sun is placed at birth becomes the main stage—where your solar light fully shines!

When **Transiting Planets** enter a certain House, or hit a component, the character of this transiting planet alters everything that it touches. Major and long lasting changes usually come from the slow-moving outer planets.

When **Uranus** transits a House, expect a breakup or rearrangement in that area of your life. (I.E., Uranus' transit of the 7th House can spark up or destroy a marriage).

In contrast, transiting **Saturn** stabilizes the activity in its House of occupation. This task master brings the substantial lessons, that will make one's goals achievable.

The forces of the other outer planets support this process of building and disassembly. **Jupiter** expands the reach of everything it touches, while **Neptune** weaves them back into a unified whole. The life-long cycle of **Pluto** regulates everything from a person's inner biological clock to "The Rise and Fall of Civilizations".

These cycles constantly revolve, as the small and giant cogs (COGnitives) in the cosmic wheel register the passage of time. Somehow, ancient observers discovered that everything progresses *forward* one day (or one degree) for every year of its existence. Astrologer Marc Robertson noted that these Progressions can best be seen in the Moon, since it changes signs every 2.5 days. Thusly, a person's Moon will progress into a new sign or House every 2.5 years. When this happens, one often experiences an attitude change in their emotional being, or a major event in one's life. (*See index for the 5 portraits that discuss progressions*).

Aspects and Angles Bring Additional Changes

When one waveform overlaps another, they intersect at different points. The angle of interception (i.e., aspect) pulls or pushes the waves up or down—or closer and further apart. Conjunctions, sextiles and trines blend one waveform with another, to enhance common waveform qualities. Squares and Oppositions are the points in the circle, that are maximum distance from each other. They define the area, in which their forces will be distributed.

Each of the luminaries and planets have their own vibration or waveform quality, as does each Zodiac sign. When one shares a common condition with another, the waves resonate, harmonize and reinforce each other. This affinity is called "rulership." The effects of these rulerships can usually be observed in one's personal components: The Sun, Moon, Ascendant, Mercury, Venus and Mars.

The Zodiac's Impact on the Physical Body

Amazingly, ancient astrologers discovered that the cycles of the stars were altered the biorhythms in our bodies. Their early observations of these rhythmic patterns was originally based on the cycles of the "7 original planets". In modern terms, six of these closely match the physical, mental, emotional, spiritual, aesthetic and intuitive biorhythms. The 7th cycle is the hourly or daily cycle of one's hourly Circadian rhythm.

In 2010, this hourly effect was confirmed by a group of "seasonal biologists", who claimed that "the biorhythms in the body all start at zero at a child's moment of birth—and they all change with the turning of the seasons." This "time of birth" is markedly close to what the ancients defined as one's Rising Sign or Ascendant. *(The Ascendant is described on page 14).*

Body Language of the Signs

Notably, these ancients also recognized that different areas of the body were being affected by the planets and signs. With this, they declared that each sign would rule a different part of the body. This ridership starts with the *head and eyes* of Aries, the sign that signifies an individual's awakening of consciousness. This rulership follows the order of the signs as it moves downward in the body.

In the wheel below, you can see how the full body fits into this Zodiac circle. Note how the head aligns with Aries, the neck and shoulders with Taurus, the lungs with Gemini, etc. The cycle ends at Pisces, where the magic meridians in the feet connect to all of the other parts in the body!

In the upcoming introductions to each of the signs, the body language of each is illustrated, as it shows how each specific body part is energized by its ruling sign. This empowerment in a certain body area changes the dynamics in the body and therefore, the expressive mannerisms of the individual.

When all of these body areas are in sync with Nature's rhythms, the body functions well—as it maintains a state of perfect health.

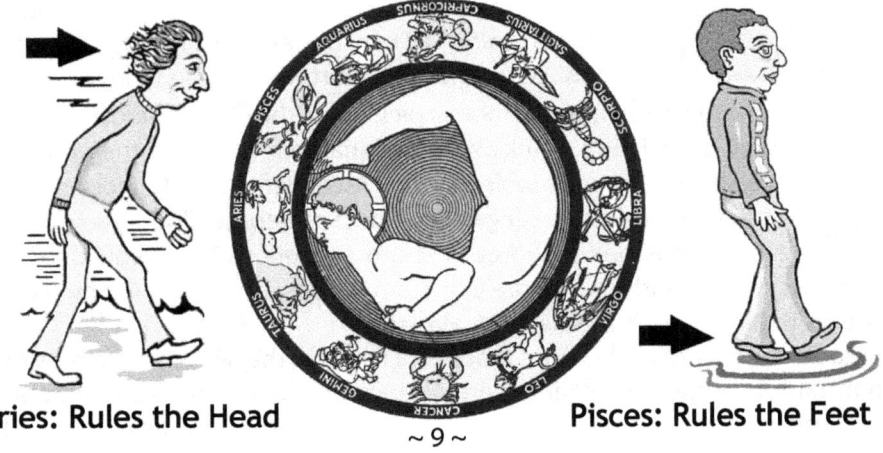

Aries: Rules the Head **Pisces: Rules the Feet**

Decans of the Zodiac Signs

Another interesting insight by the ancient astrologers was their ability to see the patterns and physical changes within each 10 degree segment (or decadent) of every sign. Each decan shows traits of one of the cardinal, fixed and mutable versions of the sign's parent Element. The *First Decan* of every sign matches the mode and element of "its making." The *Second Decan* (10 to 19 degrees) injects the qualities of the next mode in the Element. The *Third Decan* (20 to 30 degrees) displays the traits of the final sign in that Element. *(See the index, to view a list of portraits that discuss the decans of celebrities).*

This concept is illustrated best with the sign Taurus, since its Fixed Earth gives us "the most physically stable sign of the Zodiac." When the Sun is in a decan other than the first, the expected change in appearance is fairly easy to see.

Decans of the Sign of Taurus

Jessica Lange's Sun is in the first decan of Taurus and therefore, she shows the holding pattern of Fixity. This gives her the square jaw and skull, the broad flat eyebrows and the bovine eyes of fixed Earth. In her movie roles, she often showed the stubborn determination of her fixed Sun.

Audrey Hepburn has a 13° Taurus Sun, thusly it is in the second decan (or the Earth sign that follows Taurus—Virgo). Here, Taurus' raw sensuality appears more delicate and meticulous. Hepburn also has the long face, the mutable features and the lanky body and protective stance of the Virgin.

Cate Blancett 27° Sun is in the Earth decan that follows Virgo: Capricorn. Here, the sensuality of Taurus appears cooler and paler, as Cate's steely eyes and high-set cheek bones suggest the qualities of a cardinal driven goat. *(Her portrait is on page 108)*

Discover the Effects of the Decans

This idea of decans became clear, when this author was researching for new subjects on the wonderful astrology site of astrotheme.com. You can do the same by going to their front page. Look for *Celebrity Search* on the upper left. Click tag: *By Astrological Positions*. Then, under *Planet in Sign*, chose the Sun sign. We suggest you start with "Sun in Taurus."

As you look at Astrotheme's thumbnail pics, guess the decans before you look at the degree of their Sun. Think about their natures, as well as their physical appearance, since you may be fooled by their Ascendants. Jack Nicholson fit the fixed image we see in Jessica Lange. Virgo decans George Clooney and Adele show the meticulous look of Audrey Hepburn. The serious "empire builders" like Mark Zuckerberg and Tina Fey are Capricorn decans. They show the high goat cheeks that we see in Cate Blancett. Have fun!

Modern astrologers conclude that every notch in the 360° circle creates recognizable changes. This changes are captured in several books on the Sabian symbols. Naturally, this is a subject that goes beyond the range of this work.

The Yearly Cycle of the Sun

This image shows the Earth in its counter-clockwise orbit around the Sun. On the circle's eastern point, we see the Earth moving into the season of **Spring**. On this Equinox, the Sun is in **Aries**. The graphic also shows why the Sun is behind the Sun—in the opposite sign in which the Earth is placed!

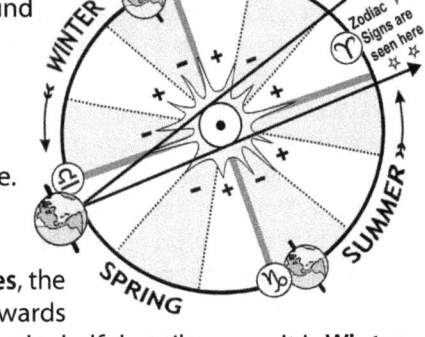

What is significant here is the Earth's fixed 23° polar axis tilt. When the Earth moves around the Sun, different halves of the planet are angled towards the Sun. This creates the four seasons, and it is why the season in the northern hemisphere is the opposite of the one in Earth's southern hemisphere.

When the Earth crosses the Equator at both of the **Equinoxes**, equal portions of the Earth are lit by the Sun. At the **Solstices**, the hemisphere that is at its maximum tilt towards the Sun is experiencing **Summer**'s light. In the half that tilts away, it is **Winter**.

About 4,000 years ago, the constellation **Aries** was seen behind the morning Sun. Today, because of the *Precession of the Equinox*, **Aquarius** is behind Spring's morning light—to bring the Earth the *Age of Aquarius!* In Tropical Astrology, the first day of **Spring** (in both hemispheres) will always be on the day that the Sun crosses the equator to enter that half of the Earth.

The Sun Sign
Projection of Radiant Energy
Self-Expression, The Creative
Spirit, Leo and the 5th House

The Key Light in Human Personality

The Sun is Earth's source of light. It is the governor of the seasons, agriculture and the guardian of herds and flocks. One's Sun Sign qualities become apparent when individuals **project** the radiant glow and color of the elemental and modal qualities, that were present at their moment of birth. The Sun is considered to be the most important factor in one's horoscope.

The other components in a person's chart will write the script, design the set and perhaps direct the movie—but the Sun is the light source that lights up one's creative desires, so that they can project their movie out to others!

The Sun is the light of all creation, and the ruler of Leo and the 5th House—the place where creative visions come into the light. The House where one's Sun is placed often indicates the area of creativity, where one's Sun will shine at its brightest.

⊙ The Sun rules Leo ♌ Leo rules 5th House

The heart is the part of the body ruled by the sign of Leo. This fits, since the heart (like the Sun) is the source that provides fuel for life on this Earth.

When individuals age, the nature of the Sun Sign tends to become more defined and expressive, since they have learned to create *their heart's intent*. The intent of each of the Sun Signs is explored in the opening of each portrait collection.

The Monthly Cycle: ☽ The Moon Sign

Reflection of Light, Reactive Energy, Collective Subconscious, Emotional Memory, Nurturing Mother, Cancer, 4th House

In the dark of night, the Moon reflects the light of the Sun. The amount of reflection varies with the lunar phases; Its color changes every 2.5 days, when the Moon enters a new Zodiac Sign.

Previously, it was suggested that the Sun is the projector in one's personal movie theater. Therefore, the Moon is the silver screen, that reflects "the light in our surroundings".

Our Moon Signs define how we absorb and internalize all external stimulus—and how we emotionally respond—as we feed our feelings back out into our surroundings. It is our Moon that defines the bubble in which we place ourselves, so that we can establish a sense of security, and a place of comfort to call home.

These reflections often indicate what a person finds to be emotionally dear, and it therefore shapes the content of what will become one's favorite memories.

The character of your lunar reactions is often defined by the Element of your Moon Sign. If your Moon is in Earth, you may tend to react slowly, precisely or deliberately—as we would respectively expect from Taurus, Virgo and Capricorn.

If your Moon is in a water sign, your emotions may shift with the tides, penetrate unknown depths, or drift with the currents of Providence. Respectively, these feelings are felt in the signs Cancer, Scorpio and Pisces.

In contrast, a Fire Sign Moon (in Aries, Leo or Sagittarius) can bring explosive responses, an expansive and glorified sense of self—or an unrestrained exuberance!

With the Air signs, emotions are expressed in windy swirls of words, in well balanced and thoughtful arrangements or in inventive, but firmly held beliefs. (Gemini, Libra and Aquarius). These lunar expressions are illustrated in the faces of our portraits.

☽ Moon rules Cancer ♋ Cancer rules 4th House

At the Summer Solstice, the Sun is at its highest peak, as it enters Cancer (the sign ruled by the Moon). Here, the Sun begins its journey down to the Equator, to bring the Earth a six month period of waning light. With this powerful polar switch to femininity, the cardinal forces pull us downward. There, on the ocean's floor, we find the Cancer Crab, seeking shelter from the turbulent tides—and the comfort of a home! These desires for personal security are magnified for all of us, when the Sun is in Cancer.

The nature of this "comfort zone" is determined by the sign in which one's Moon is placed. The House of placement shows the area where individuals find emotional comfort. The sign on the 4th House shows how one relates to the home. (For example, those who have Aries on the 4th House are rarely home).

The 28 day lunar cycle regulates the Emotional Biorhythms of all humans. Thusly, the Moon's phase (and its movement from one sign to another) alters the transitory emotions of humans everywhere. Watch how the emotional impulses of the public match the sign in which the Moon is transiting. And as to its phase, just ask any police officer about the effects of a Full Moon.

The difference between the Sun and the Moon:

Here we look at two celebrities with swapped Suns and Moons. This allows us to demonstrate how their Sun Signs are seen in their self-projections—and how their emotional reactions are seen in the reflected light of their Moons.

The sign of any luminary can often be determined by observing the facial flesh. Its force (or vibrational nature) usually shows the Element in which it is placed. Meanwhile, the pattern of this activity often indicates the Mode of the sign.

With these subjects, we have Gemini and Taurus luminaries. Thusly, we see the opposing vibrational frequencies of Air and Earth—and the contrasting patterns of Mutability and Fixity.

Bob Dylan
May 24, 1941 / 9:05 P.M. Duluth, MN

 **Gemini Sun
Taurus Moon**

When Dylan projects the mercuric light of his Sun, his hands and fingers fly about, as he expresses the stream of words running through his head. In the process, one brow and eye rises above the other as the mouth and chin skews in the opposite direction. What we are seeing are the facial moldings of Mutability.

When Dylan reacts to others, the Fixed Earth of his Taurus Moon alters his facial features. In addition, the chatter stops, as the electricity of his Sun grounds to Earth. In this moment of serenity, the offset features disappear, as Dylan's eyes fix onto the outer substances, that are intruding on his inner comfort zone. These rigid and stubborn reactions are more obvious, when Dylan becomes highly emotional.

(See Bob's full portrait on page 133)

George Carlin
May 12, 1937 / 11:43 A.M. Bronx, NY

 **Taurus Sun,
Gemini Moon**

Carlin's Sun and Moon are the reverse of Dylan's. Therefore, they provide a similar mix of energy—but in different layers of his personality.

Carlin reveals the sensual and fixed nature of his Sun, notably when he is relishing the "stuff" in his life. Listen to how his deep voice becomes noticeably anchored, as he tries to describe the things that have real value.

When George's emotions are aroused, his voice elevates in pitch, as his mercuric reactions rise to "stir up the dust"—to give words to his astute and reality-based observations. This is what made him a comedy legend.

Centaur Energies also present

Our subjects both have Fire Ascendants. Dylan's is in Sagittarius, while Carlin's is in the Centaur decan of Leo. Underneath the flesh, both share the long-faced bone structure of a horse.

ⓐˢᶜ *The Daily Cycle:* The Ascendant

First House, One's Window to the World, Physical Container & Mask

With Earth's daily rotation, the primal light changes with every passing minute, on every spot on this planet. At any time, the Sun is rising on a specific place on this globe—to light up the ascending path and awaken a new day of anticipation!

In each day's morning light, astrologers saw a different constellation rising in the east. From this, they could calculate the sign "that was rising" at anyone's time of birth.

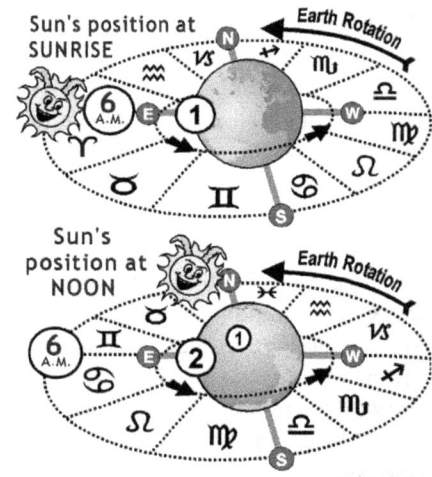

Here, we illustrate what is seen in the daily rise and fall of the Sun, as portions of the Earth turn from day to night. The graph shows how the Earth's CCW daily rotation gives the appearance that the Sun is moving in a clockwise direction, when in reality, it is fixed and not moving.

The top drawing shows **Aries Rising at** 6 A.M., or sunrise. Thereafter, *the Sun remains in Aries*, but (in the passing of roughly every two hour period), another sign appears on the eastern horizon.

The lower image shows the Sun at high noon, when **Cancer rises** in the East! If born around sunset, one's rising Sign will be Libra, etc. In a normal 24 hours day, it is easy to estimate one's Ascendant, but at higher latitudes, long days or nights make the intervals irregular and more difficult to calculate.

The Individualized View, seen in Morning's Light

As we look through this window to the east, we awake in the NOW, where the Circadian rhythm of a new day begins. It is here where all of the biorhythms of newborn children begin at "zero". That is why the Rising Sign defines the starting point and the 1st House in any chart.

The Ascendant is the chart component that pinpoints the physical spot on Earth, where one is born. This may be why the Rising Sign strongly influences the shape of the underlying bone structure (the densest part of the body). These bones greatly shape one's physical appearance, one's body type and the "physical mask" that makes a first impression on others.

You'll see the effect of the Ascendant when one's facial flesh is not animating its solar or lunar qualities. Resting in repose, the face takes on the contours of the underlying formations of the skeletal structure.

Focused Light Creates Viewable Form

In our movie analogy, the Sun and Moon were the projector and the screen. The Rising Sign is the lens thru which light is transmitted. This lens focuses light into viewable form and defines the image. It may have its own colored filter, or a different depth of focus. Jupiter on the Ascendant would create a very wide angle lens. Pluto would make it microscopic, etc.

This Rising Sign creates the cross that divides the chart into four quadrants. When planets transit into the different quadrants on this cross, they can change the nature of what we perceive, as well as the directional course we take in life. This is the "cross that we bear."

The Three Personality Planets

Previously, we showed how the seasonal Sun, the tides of the Moon and the daily Circadian Rhythms dictate three of the biorhythmic cycles in the body. Here, we show how the orbits of the planets **Mercury, Venus** and **Mars** regulate the other creative functions in the human character.

MERCURY The Messenger, The Thinking Process, Conception of Ideas

In ancient times, Mercury was the Winged Messenger of the Gods, the source of the thoughts and words that enabled humans to acquire and communicate knowledge and ideas. It is symbolically represented in the Caduceus.

The body's intellectual biorhythm waxes and wanes in a 33 day cycle. Ancient astrologers decreed that the planet Mercury was the regulator of the mind. Its sign of placement determines how one analyzes the world, and how once cerebrally "processes this incoming data".

In our movie analogy, Mercury's sign indicates the speed of your movie camera, or how fast your hard drive collects data.

Persons with a **Fire Sign** Mercury will often judge and analyze the opinions, desires and thoughts of others. People with Mercury in **Earth Signs** analyze the physical content in their world with their senses, while **Water Signs** ponder the relationships between spirit and matter. **Air Signs** are figuring out how these judgments, sensations and feelings interact with each other.

In our movie analogy, Mercury's sign indicates the frame speed of your movie camera, or how fast your hard drive collects data.

The closest planet to the Sun is Mercury, therefore it can only be a limited distance from the Sun. About half of the people will have their Mercury in the same sign as their Sun; Such people (without any major Mercury aspects) will usually find that the cadence of their thoughts match the expressive natures of their Suns. However, Mercury can also be in one of the signs on either side of the Sun, both of which will be of a difference Polarity, Mode and Element than the Sun. People with this arrangement have a noticeable distinction between "the way they think" and the manner in which they articulate their solar expressions. Their minds will likely run *slower or faster* than their Sun's capability to express the needed language. This can have its magical consequences. Pisces Albert Einstein had his Mercury in Aries. It allowed him to clear away the clutter and see universal relationships in their purest and simplest state.

Mercury: The Ruling Planet of Gemini & Virgo

The mutable signs of Gemini and Virgo are both ruled by Mercury. Gemini's masculine force of Air communicates ideas by assembling thoughts into larger and more complex concepts. In contrast, the feminine Earth Sign Virgo attempts to break the complex ideas of Gemini into smaller increments. Gemini's thinking process is inductive; Virgo is deductive.

VENUS ♀

Sensual Arousal, Feminine Attraction, Aesthetic Enhancement of Matter, The Anima, What Makes You Happy!

Venus takes us beyond Mercury to move us one step closer to lovely Earth. With Mercury, we learned to comprehend the data, that was gathered from our senses. Now, it is time to arrange the material we perceived—and create ways to advance our personal enjoyment.

Venus was the ancient Goddess of Love. Her essence was captured in *The Birth of Venus*, a painting by Sandos Botticilli (circa 1486). The cropped view on the right shows how she represents the two Venus-ruled signs of Taurus and Libra.

The Birth of Venus, a painting by Sandos Botticilli

In Venus' rulership of Taurus, the raw and lusty world of our senses is activated. As the figure on the left shows, the Goddess Venus is emerging from the sea, naked but firmly connected to her new found physical environment. This material connection is symbolized in the feminine polarity and fixed Earth of **Taurus**.

There also is a more complex side to Venus—i.e., the state created in one's mind by the input from one's Taurus' senses. This stimulation activates the masculine drive of Venus' other-ruled sign: **Libra**. The painting shows Venus, fully wrapped in her artful and material creations. They are providing the physical comforts, desired by Taurus.

In contemporary terms, Venus is Carl Jung's Anima: The magnetic and feminine function that attracts the Animus—the masculine projections of others *(See Mars, page 18)*. These components can run in either direction, regardless of gender.

Venus also defines the nature of our business associates, partners and intimate relationships. Venus is the regulator of the 43 day Aesthetic Biorhythm, that determines the up and down rhythms of one's creative impulses.

Design the Sets and Direct Your Movie!

With Mercury's script in hand, it's time to utilize the collaborative skills of your Venus and let your "Art Director" create the final sensual effects in your movie!

Your main directorial vision may be an expression of your lifelong solar desires, but when the creative calls are made—be they the tone of the actor's voice, the coloring of the light, or the composition in the frame—your final artistic choices are often determined by the nature of the sign in which your Venus is placed.

Not sure of someone's Venus? Check out their rooms and clothing. Lots of oceanic blues and purples suggest a love of water. If yellow or light shades of blue appear, their Venus is likely in Air. Reds and oranges indicate Fire. Brown and Green tones are the stuff of Earth. These different frequencies (or colors) reflect the vibrational differences in the Elements. The House where Venus is placed indicates the area of your life where "your artistic urges desire to create harmony."

When Venus forces run strong in one's chart, it clearly alters one's artistic temperament and creative direction. To illustrate this, we look at two Venus-empowered celebrities.

Aquariuses: Harry Styles and Taylor Lautner

In full solar projection, these lads both show the buoyant optimism of their airy Aquarius Sun Signs. However, these men were picked because **both of their Moons and Rising Signs** are in one of the Venus-ruled signs of Libra or Taurus. These two subjects show us how the masculine and feminine expressions of Venus can alter one's physical appearance and personality.

Libra reigns in Styles' chart

Harry Styles is a singer and song-writer of the popular band *One Direction*. He was born February 1, 1994, 12:06 A.M., in Redditch, UK. This gives Harry a Libra Moon and Ascendant. His Moon accounts for his cheerful emotional reactions, while his Ascendant masks and calms his erratic solar impulses.

With his Aquarius Venus conjoined his Sun (and both trine his Libra Moon), the charm is enhanced. Likely this is why so many of the band's fans consider him to be the group's most likeable member, as well as the mind behind its musical compositions. (Harry was the one who came up with the band's name; He also wrote many of the lyrics for the band's songs.)

When the cardinal forces of Libra are activated, the cubical and compacted features of Harry's Aquarius Sun are stretched out to the sides. The sideways sweep pulls the eyes into an almond shape—as it spreads the cheeks to create his wide and cheery smile. With his abundance of air, and an Aquarius Mars, it's no wonder that Harry has a tendency to flutter and float about, when he performs on stage.

Taurus reigns with Lautner

Taylor Lautner (born February 11, 1992, 11:47 A.M., Grand Rapids, MI) is recognized for his role in the *Twilight Saga* films. There, the mental electricity of air (that we saw in Harry Styles) is hidden. Instead, we see a person who appears introverted and anchored. His Moon and Rising Sign are placed in the fixed Earth of Taurus.

Notably, Lautner's rising and lunar lights are opposed by forboding Pluto (in the water sign of Scorpio). This opposition adds an aura of mystery to his intensely fixed persona. This is likely why the producers of the *Twilight Saga* films cast him in the role as the werewolf Jacob Black.

At the age of 12, Taylor became the Junior World Champion in Black Belt competition. Unlike Styles, Lautner's creative impulses are more physical than mental. This can be attributed to his Venus' conjunction with the warrior planet Mars (in Capricorn), and their trine to his Ascendant and Moon. This Capricorn Mars gave him the cardinal drive and discipline to hone his physical and motor skills.

With his fixed and earthy Ascendant, the vaporous qualities of Taylor's Sun are anchored in stone. This also gives him Taurus' unique bovine features, i.e., his wide nostrils, cubical forehead and the sturdy jaw.

MARS ♂

Physical Drive (Metabolism), Masculine Projection (The Animus) What Makes You Angry!

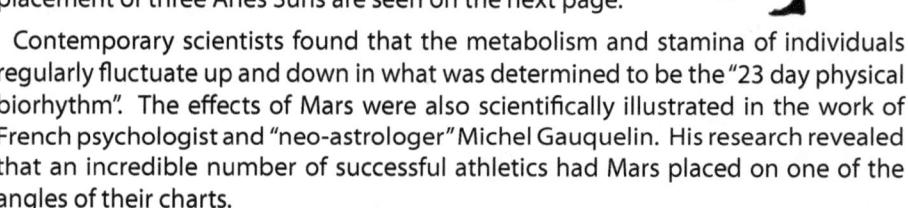

If Mercury shows how we think, and Venus shows how we arrange our thoughts to create something of value—Mars would then show the nature of the physical activity that we perform, when we participate in a creative project.

With their observations, ancient astrologers saw that the cycles of Mars appeared to affect the muscular capability, motor control and physical drive of people. They also concluded that the sign of one's Mars would determine the quality of a person's physical metabolism. Some folks run at higher speed, but they don't have the torque, power or endurance of others. Others have strength, but little finesse, etc. The effects of the Mars placement of three Aries Suns are seen on the next page.

Contemporary scientists found that the metabolism and stamina of individuals regularly fluctuate up and down in what was determined to be the "23 day physical biorhythm". The effects of Mars were also scientifically illustrated in the work of French psychologist and "neo-astrologer" Michel Gauquelin. His research revealed that an incredible number of successful athletics had Mars placed on one of the angles of their charts.

The Red Planet is associated with the blood in our veins, which carries the oxygen and iron that gives us physical strength. It is also the adrenaline that flows *when we are angry*. On another level, Mars indicates the penetrating force of the Animus, the masculine personality component described by Carl Jung. This Animus suggests the physical energy that one projects outward to attract the feminine Anima (Venus) of others.

The best way to determine people's Mars is to watch them in action, as they perform physical work. Don't take the first impression—or any of their attempts at communication. Watch them for several minutes and observe how they perform their physical tasks, as they move about. Is it a holding pattern, meandering or a straight forward push (Fixed, Mutable or Cardinal?). Do they move with the intensity of fire? Are their actions sludgy, liquid or do they dissipate like air? Put the mode and element together, and you'll likely identify the sign of an individual's Mars.

Mars is the Ruler of Aries & Ancient Ruler of Scorpio

The ancients saw that Mars appeared to be more forceful and controlled in the signs of Aries and Scorpio. Thusly, Mars became the ruling planet of Masculine Aries and its feminine side was ruled by the water sign of Scorpio. Later, with the discovery of Pluto, it became the new ruling planet of Scorpio.

The House in which one's natal Mars is placed may indicate the area in one's life where one expends a great deal of physical energy, and the product of this "work" will depend on the sign in which Mars is placed.

Some say that Mars' House placement often indicates the hour in the day when one's physical biorhythms are at their peak. Others say that your physical energies are rejuvenated when Mars enters the 8th House. This is beyond the scope of this book.

A list of the Mars placement of several of our portraits are listed in the Index

The Impact of Mars:

The Moon and Sun reveal the force and the nature of one's expressions and emotional reactions. However, as mentioned earlier, the placement of the rulers of these luminaries often alters the nature of their expression.

Since our three subjects all have Aries Suns and Mars is Aries ruling planet, these three comedians give us an opportunity to observe how the sign in which their Mars are placed alters their creative drives and metabolism.

Eddie Murphy
Mars in Cancer
4/3/1961, Brooklyn, NY

In ancient times, Murphy's Aries' Sun and Scorpio Moon were both ruled by Mars. With this doubling of martian forces, Eddie became recognized for his abrasive nature. We saw it in his many boisterous characters on *Saturday Night Live*, and in his array of action films.

However, with his Mars in Cancer (trine his Moon), there was a softer side to his nature, as we saw in his SNL parody of *Mr. Roger's Neighborhood*, and in his films *Shrek, Dr. Doolittle, Nutty Professor* and *The Haunted Mansion*. In these films, Eddie's family friendly Mars made him a top box office star in a new genre of entertainment. Oddly, after doing these family films, Eddy attempted to reboot his action-comedy career with the film *The Adventures of Pluto Nash*. It was a box office dud.

Paul Reiser
Mars in Gemini
3/30/1957, New York, NY

With his Sun, Moon, Mercury and Venus in Aries, you would expect Reiser to be an archetypal Aries. True, he is highly directed and successful at initiating his own projects, but when at work, his actions show the energy and mercuric drive expected from his Gemini Mars. From his first role in *Diner* to his ever questioning dialogue in his TV show *Mad About You*, Paul has found his soul's physical expression, exploring and describing the comic dichotomies that he sees in the world before his eyes.

Martin Short
Mars in Libra
3/26/1950 Hamilton, Canada

Martin's Mars is in Libra, opposing his Sun and squaring his Moon in Cancer. Quixotic Uranus sits on his Moon and his Venus (the ruler of Libra) is placed in Uranus-ruled Aquarius. With these hard angled aspects, the cardinal forces run strong in all directions, while the Uranus connection gives him a quirky and erratic nervous energy.

In *The Three Amigos* and *Father of the Bride* Martin presented characters who always attempted to be charming and friendly. In his TV show *Prime Time Glick*, his character was grating and unnerving. This unpleasantness is likely due to his Mars square to his Moon and Uranus.

It's time to reveal the evidence!

In this opening, we showed how the cycles and patterns in Nature's seasons are captured in the language of astrology. Now, with a multitude of celebrity facial images, we will display evidence, to show how these various degrees of astrological lights (and planetary aspects) shape our attributes and character.

For the novice, it may be difficult to understanding the mechanics of astrology. That is why we suggest the reader refer back to the introduction and review the 12 signs that were briefly presented in chronological order on pages 3 to 6. This may help the reader to understand each sign's place in the circle, and what task they contribute in Nature's 12 Step Process of Creation.

As noted in the introduction, these portraits are positioned in a manner that will show common traits—be they the Sun, Moon or Ascendant. In some, a running narrative ties nearby portraits together, but the layout has its limits. Therefore, the reader is encouraged to peruse freely through the portraits and regularly cross-check them in the index.

As you progress thru these portraits, you will notice that there is often little discussion on complex aspects. This is due to limited space and the fact that it is difficult to explain their subtle influences. However, many provide enough visual evidence to show the physical impact of the aspects and the planets.

This seeing of these "planetary influences" tells us that there is something more encompassing than *Tropical Astrology* occurring here—for these pictures give us hints that *Everything is connected in a Unified Universe!* Astrology may be the language, that will enable humanity to find the answers to this long pondered question.

The lessons apply to all

At any moment, hundreds of individuals are born with the same "cognitive nuggets". However, some will face difficult upbringings and circumstances. Many will fail to recognize their potential—while others will be far more successful than what could ever be imagined. Then, there are those individuals, who will only be recognized by their families or by the communities they served. If all of us were celebrities, none of us would have even *15 seconds of fame*!

Here, we will show individuals whose actions brought success, as well as failure. This shows that our WILL has an overpowering effect on the actions that we take. None of this is ordained by the stars! With that, this book will attempt to provide insights into the "process", so that individuals can learn to flow in synch with the **Pulse of Nature**—and master the gifts they were given.

With all of these considerations,
it is time to take the lessons from the past,
pass them forward—and begin a new journey of discovery

~~

It all begins at the Winter Solstice,
when Nature's clock starts another cycle of building light
with the Cardinal Earth of Capricorn.

♑ Capricorns

	Page
Introduction to Capricorn	
Two triple Capricorns	
James Earl Jones, Zooey Deschanel	21-23
A look at the Cardinal Cross	
Mel Gibson	24-25
A master at manipulating his Mars	
Jared Leto	26-27
A Look at Progressions and Saturn Transits	
Maggi Smith	27-29
Kati Couric	30-31
Libra Ascendants and Moons	
Denzel Washington	32
Nicholas Cage	33
Sagittarius gallops onto the field	
Jude Law, Bradley Cooper	34-35
Robert Duvall	36
Kevin Costner	37
A mix of all three Modes	
Betty White	38
Ted Danson	39
Jim Carrey	40
Fixed Air carries us into the next sign of Aquarius	
Muhammed Ali	41
Orlando Bloom	42

Capricorn ♑ December 22 to January 19

Aim high, as you climb to achieve your goals!

Feminine Polarity, Cardinal Earth

At the Winter Solstice, it is the shortest day in the year. Still, hope is high, for the higher knowledge of the **Sagittarius** Archer have shown us that a "Divine Process of Creation is in operation". And it all starts here on Earth, when the Sun begins its climb in the sky, to bring another round of building light—and a New Year of creative opportunity!

These portraits begin here, for **Capricorn** symbolizes the starting point in Nature's many cycles. It can be the midnight in a day, the phase of a New Moon, the start of a season—or the angle of an orbiting planet. This is why your Capricorn friends have a fascination with "process" and an acute sense of the progressions in time.

At the end of all cycles, the lessons of the past must not be discarded. To grow, past experiences need to be passed forward and integrated into the next level of creation. This is the task of the chart's **4th Quadrant**: the 3 months in the **Winter Season**.

It is our Capricorn teachers who pass these valuable lessons on to others, so that the intuitive resolutions of **Aquarius** and the prophetic dreams of **Pisces** can become a reality. In the Spring (when the Sun enters **Aries**), many individuals will be inspired to use these lessons to pursue a new creative adventure!

Mythically, this evolutionary process is symbolized in the Sea Goat. Its lower body is the tail of a fish; The upper half is the goat, whose hinged legs (i.e., knees) enabled life to climb upward onto the land—to build a higher state of physical existence!

It is the femininity of Earth that integrates all of the elements—to build new forms on the physical plane. These creations are rendered by the fixed Earth of **Taurus** and refined by the sign of **Virgo** (the mutable sign in the Earth trinity). These constructive efforts are elevated to the next level, when the cardinal force of Capricorn returns.

These goats are the task masters, who constantly observe the actions of their fellow citizens, as they evaluate how they are contributing to their communities, cities and the nation. They also know that when these citizens work together, things will get better with time! Perhaps that's why so many of these goats live to ripe old ages.

Sadly, some of these souls can become overwhelmed by human foibles and failed institutions—and with this, they lose all sense of hope and direction. Some become insufferably cynical, miserly and obsessed with power. However, many will find faith in humanity once again, when they realize that their fellow beings share the same hopes and wishes. This optimistic lesson is formed in the socially conscious mind of **Aquarius**, the "Next Step of Integration" in this quadrant of the wheel.

♄ Ruling Planet: Saturn (Also traditional ruler of Aquarius)

Saturn is the last planet we can see with our natural senses. Therefore, it is the planet that is associated with the limitations of physicality. Saturn's 28 year cycle represents the key passages in an individual's life—where each quarter cycle brings the "seven year itch" that compels many to move on—in a new direction!

Saturn is associated with the teeth, joints and bones (the solid structure that shapes our bodies). It is also the crystallization in the joints that comes with aging. Positive Saturn traits include perseverance and self-discipline. Negatively, Saturn brings restriction, bitterness and cynicism.

Capricorn Physical Traits:

The features of a goat are prominent in Capricorns! Note how the wide-set eye socket bones pull the eyes and eyelids to the sides of the face—back and upward from the large, drooping snout. All the while, the high-set cheek bones make a depression below the eyes, as they angle the lower half of the face forward.

This gives the goat a somber and serious appearance. Other common features include a large upper lip plate, a thin upper lip and a recessed, but broad based chin.

James Earl Jones 1/17/1931, 7:10 A.M. Arkabutla, MS
Zooey Deschanel
1/17/1980, 6:57 A.M. Santa Monica, CA

Since their Suns, Moons and Ascendants are all in the sign of Capricorn, James and Zooey clearly show the force of Cardinal Earth in their outward expressions, inner reactions and stoney masks. All the while, the deep resonance of Earth is heard in their voices.

In her Emmy nominated TV role in *New Girl*, Zooey's gravely voice made her stand out from the others. As heard in his voicing of Darth Vader in Star Wars, James' voice echoes from the bowels of the Earth.

Body Language of Capricorn

The Cardinal Earth forces of Capricorn are contained and centered in the knees—the part of the body ruled by this sign. At these joints, the bony knees point to the front, as the lower leg turns sharply to the back, to plant the feet firmly on the ground. Step by step, the feet are cautiously placed, as the knees pull these goats forward—to climb the rocky paths to the mountains above.

The resulting body mechanics send the butt to the back and this tilts the upper torso and head forward. This angle points the head down to the ground. Consequently, the eyes appear be aimed upward, so that the goat can see the craggy peaks that lie ahead.

This body rulership greatly influences this creature's physical features, as Saturn's constraining energies reduce the size of the goat's body parts. The torso and shoulders are noticeably undersized, and the extremities are often thin and short.

Capricorn rules the knees

The Four Cardinal Directions

Ancient astrologers believed they lived in "the center of the Universe", for their eyes saw that all things were running "clockwise around the Earth". In the **Spring**, they saw the stars of **Aries** in back of the Sun, when the Sun was rising over the eastern horizon. When **Cancer** was there, the upper sky was at its brightest on the **Summer Solstice**. In **Autumn**, it dimmed back into balance, when **Libra** was rising in the East. In **Winter,** the stars of **Capricorn** were seen in back of the Sun. These four seasonal starting points create the Cardinal Cross in the chart.

These sky watchers also noticed that when the Sun transited one of these points, all of those who were born in a Cardinal Sign would appear to emulate the directional drive of their Cardinal Suns.

On the horizontal plane, the fire of **Aries** charges from back to front. This force is spread equally to both sides by the Cardinal Air of **Libra**.

On the vertical axis, the forces of **Cancer** draw us to the bottom of the sea. **Capricorn** turns it around, with the New Year's upward climb of Light.

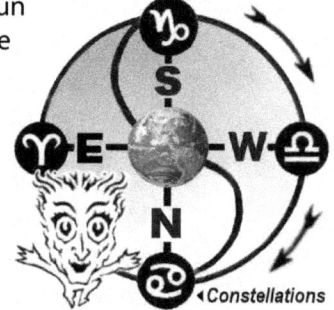
◄ Constellations

We begin with **Mel Gibson** and **Jared Leto**, two goats who have their three key lights in cardinal signs! They show us how these well-aimed cardinal forces stretch our facial features in the four compass directions.

♑ Mel Gibson 1/3/1956, 4:45 P.M. Peekskill, NY
Sun in Capricorn (The Upward Climb of Earth)

In 1996, Mel Gibson was the *first* subject in this author's *Celebrity Snapshots* column, and he was the only celebrity to appear for a second time in the magazine, when this author realized how his components explained Cardinal forces. It is appropriate that he is also the first one in this updated collection.

Gibson's critical successes have been Capricorn in nature. In *The Road Warrior* we saw a bitter goat struggling against a lawless society, instilling his own form of order. Gibson soon moved on, to become producer, director and star of the historical *Brave Heart*. There, he played the steely-willed warrior who lead Scotland's upward battle for independence.

As Mel's career progressed, he created an increasingly array of serious films that reflected his strongly held beliefs and values. This was seen in *Patriot, The Passion of Christ* and *Apocalypto*. In the latter film, he questioned religion's influence on indigenous cultures.

Fortunately, many of Mel's films were not always so serious, for he had the Cardinal Air and Water of his Moon and Rising signs that allowed him to star in several romantic and family roles.

Ascendant: Cancer (The Downward Flow of Water)

When a component is placed in the feminine sign of Cancer, the cardinal waters rise up from below, to gush to the surface. This surge of emotions often swells the facial flesh and enlarges the eyes. Soon, it will slowly recede, to carry the crab back to its base of comfort, on the bottom of the ocean.

This internal/downward forces pulls the crab's eyes low on the face, down below the broad delta on the brow—centering these features between the moonbeam temples. This Ascendant also gives Gibson the large torso and body shell of a crab, with its short appendages and undersized legs.

Mel's Cancer Ascendant gives him the caring persona of Cardinal Water. This liquid mask was apparent in the damp-eyed emotions of *Forever Young* and in the comedic romantics of *Bird On A Wire* and *What Women Want*. This family oriented Cancerian window likely accounts for Mel's first marriage and large family of 7 children. However, these moody emotions (and his abrasive and chilly Sun) brought the actions that ended his marriage, and this may have precipitated the alcoholic rants that loss him the favor from his fans and supporters.

Moon in Libra
(The Side-to-Side Spread of Air)

As the opposing sign to Aries, Libra disarms the forward charge of the Ram, by pushing its energy off to the sides —in a horizontal direction! Such patterns are seen, when Gibson activates the light of his Libra Moon.

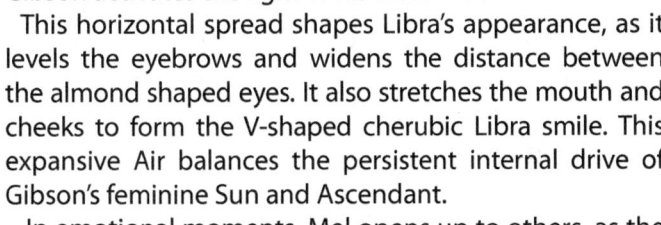

This horizontal spread shapes Libra's appearance, as it levels the eyebrows and widens the distance between the almond shaped eyes. It also stretches the mouth and cheeks to form the V-shaped cherubic Libra smile. This expansive Air balances the persistent internal drive of Gibson's feminine Sun and Ascendant.

In emotional moments, Mel opens up to others, as the protective mask of his Cancer Ascendant evaporates. In the subsequent interaction with other, Gibson's breezy lunar energy injects a needed lightness into his heavy solar demeanor. In these moments, he also becomes surprisingly chatty.

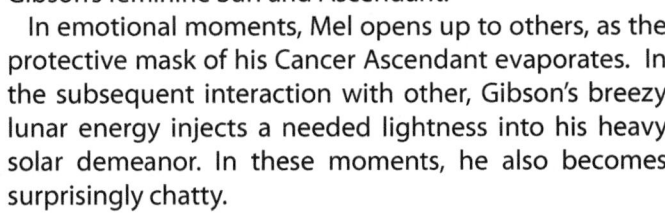

Gibson's lunar nature was seen in his reactions with Danny Glover in *Lethal Weapon* and in his charm laden role as *Maverick*. In these films, Mel was easy going, emotionally sociable and likeable. These qualities made him a star!

Note: Though attempts were made to keep the list in balance, this Capricorn section contains only 3 women portraits. This is due to the lack of birth times on many female celebrity goats.

Here we look at another triple Cardinal Sign: one with his Moon in Aries and a Libra Ascendant. (Most "Midnight Born Capricorn Suns" usually have Libra Rising).

With this, we will also take our first look at the effects of Saturn (Capricorn's ruling planet), examine the impact of Mars (the ruling planet of Aries), and then show how planetary aspects can alter a person's personality and creative nature.

Jared Leto

12/26/1971
12:00 A.M.
Bossier City, LA

Jared Leto has five chart components in fire and five in Air—and his earthy Sun and water Mars are the only feminine components in his horoscope. Still, he appears very grounded for someone who has only one component in Earth. This can be attributed to Saturn—the ruling planet of Capricorn.

Saturn is the nearest planet to Jared's Midheaven and what the public sees here is a hard working goat, who appears to be obsessed with orchestrating and maximizing every thing that he does in his career(s). Notably, Saturn also makes harmonious aspects to his Ascendant and Mars. This adds a coolness to his persona, as it keeps his physical energies "stable and controlled".

Fortunately, Saturn is in Gemini—and this gives Leto strong verbal skills, as it adds an electrical and exuberant quality to what could be a dour personality. Saturn's opposition to Neptune (and trine to Venus) gives him a gift for creating unique images and illusions. Leto is a musician, actor, director, businessman, philanthropist and activist.

♑ Sun in Capricorn

The two left photos show several of the physical traits of Capricorn. Note the broad cheek bones and how they rise high on the side of the face, to push the beady eyes just under the bushy brows. These wide-set cheekbones and the deep-set eyes account for the serious appearance we see in most people with strong Capricorn (or Saturn) in their charts.

Jared's Sun forms a T-square with his late degree Pisces Mars and his cardinal Rising Sign. This angle gives him a distant and hard edged appearance. This intensity is heightened by the other aspects to his Moon and Ascendant.

Moon in Aries

Rising Sign: Libra

With an Aries Moon trine his Jupiter, Jared's emotional reactions are markedly expansive and assertive. In contrast, when his luminaries are in repose, Jared's Libra Ascendant often presents its soft Venusian eyes and pleasant smile to the world. Shockingly, as we saw in Jared's portrayal of The Joker in *Suicide Squad*, this mask can also be quite disturbing. Pluto conjoins his Ascendant.

With his Mercury in Sagittarius (sextile to Uranus and trine his Moon), Leto has a gift for creating an inventive array of inspired ideas! This is apparent in his music, in his band's videos and in his socially-conscious documentaries.

Mars Controls Physical Drive & Metabolism

Jared's ability to submerge himself in his film performances can be attributed to his Mars' placement in the mutable water sign of Pisces. This is the sign that is ruled by Neptune, the planet of illusion. This sign is not known for having strong physical strength, but Leto's Mars is in the last degree of Pisces. It is in the act of *becoming Aries*—and he is driven to achieve his art, by making phenomenal changes in his physical body!

In his 2000 role in *Requiem for a Dream*, Jared lost 28 pounds to portray the mental and physical degradation of a drug addict. This performance gained him his first acclaim as a serious actor. In 2007's *Chapter 27*, Leto went the opposite direction, gaining 67 pounds to submerge himself in the bloated delusions of Mark Chapman, John Lennon's killer. In 2013, he transformed his back-to-normal physique once again, losing 30 pounds to play a transgender AIDS patient in *Dallas Buyer's Club*. (This role won him an Oscar for Best Supporting Actor).

Jared's ability to make these changes in his physical appearance are likely a product of his transformational Neptune's trine to Mars—and its opposition to form shaping Saturn. This gives Leto the discipline to regulate his metabolism to make his incredible physical alterations.

(**Robert De Niro** has similar aspects. Read about the physical changes he made in *Raging Bull* on page 163).

The Amazing Cycles of Saturn

In long established careers, it is possible to use the cycles of Saturn to make a reasoned guess on unknown components in one's chart.

Maggie Smith

12/28/1934, 10:10 P.M.?
Ilford, England

Saturn is the ruler of Capricorn and its transit often indicates the ups and downs one will experience through the years in one's profession. A rise in status usually occurs when transiting Saturn is climbing upward on the right side of one's chart. This gives one a method to narrow down the choice of a person's birth time and his or her Ascendant.

Here, we'll show how one's career often hit a peak, when Saturn is at the top of his chart! This career height then diminishes as the ringed planet transits towards the bottom. At its ebb (the Nadir), Saturn turns around again, to began another 14 year uphill climb on the right side of the chart.

With that in mind, let's look at three peaks in Maggie Smith's career and then attempt to find a birth time that would place Saturn moving up the western side of her chart. A birth time of around 10:00 P.M. appears to work, at least in two major events in her career.

Significantly, with every major leap in her career, powerful aspects occurred between Maggie's natal and/or transiting Saturn, Uranus and Jupiter. This synchronicity is likely due to her natal Uranus being in Aries and its sextile to Saturn in Aquarius (the sign ruled by Uranus). Jupiter's transit fits into this pattern, as it also positions itself—to bring a fortuitous boost to her career!

In 1970, Maggie won an Academy Award for Best Actress in a Leading Role playing the determined teacher in *The Prime of Miss Jean Brodie*. With a 10 P.M. birth time, Saturn was climbing near Smith's 9th House cusp, while it opposed Jupiter and trined her Uranus. (These 1970 planets are shown in the BLACK CIRCLES).

In 2001, one full Saturn cycle after her first Oscar win, Saturn was at the top of her chart. (See GRAY CIRCLES). Lucky Jupiter was also perched on her Midheaven while transiting Uranus was conjoining her natal Saturn—a reversal of the 1970's transit of Saturn on her natal Uranus! It was in this year that Smith gained a new generation of young fans playing the head mistress of the Hogwarts School in the *Harry Potter* films. There, her lessons were not the reality lessons of Jean Brodie, instead she instructed the kids on the wizardry of Uranus transfigurations.

In 2012, Smith reached another peak in her career playing the sharp-tongued Countess in the highly popular TV series *Downton Abbey*.

Here, our described paradigm does not work since Saturn is descending in her chart, but it is significant that Saturn was then opposing her natal Uranus. This set of WHITE CIRCLES shows that Uranus was moving up the western side of her chart, closely opposing the position it held in Smith's chart in 1970. Since Saturn is the ancient ruler of Capricorn and Aquarius, this implies that Saturn's energy was rising at this time.

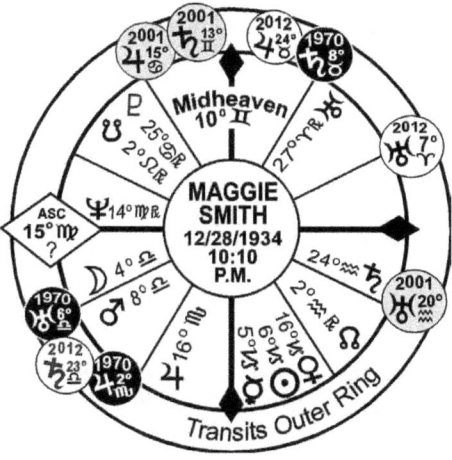

Without rectifying other events in her life, a birth time of 10:10 P.M. was chosen. This gives Smith the following components:

Virgo Ascendant?

Smith appears to have Virgo Rising. This fits the analytical mask she presents to the world. Notably, this time also places Neptune (Pisces' ruling planet) on her Ascendant. This factor explains her fluid eyes with their large pupils and the heavy eyelids that droop at the sides. Neptune adds an aura of compassion to what appears to be a very analytical persona.

When the luminaries are on hold, the mutable lines of Smith's underlying skeletal structure lift one side of the face above the other. Smith also has a noticeable gap in her upper front teeth, a trait common for most Virgo Risings. These mutable lines disappear when her cardinal luminaries light up.

Capricorn Sun

With her Capricorn Sun, Maggie had the stoic demeanor to play the aging Monarch of Grantham. With her broad high-set cheekbones, Maggies also had the look of authority that allowed her to keep the young Hogwarts under control.

Libra Moon?

After watching her 2013 interview on CBS's *60 Minutes*, this author concluded that Smith has a Libra Moon.

Every time the interviewer tossed her a provocative question, she would immediately disarm him with a non-answer, throw a look of marked indifference, or take the question in a counter direction. She rarely analyzed the questions and displayed few of the mercuric finger gestures of a possible Virgo Moon. Rather, what was seen was her light and expansive emotional reactions, as well as her charming and pleasant demeanor. This Moon choice also narrowed the time frame that was used to pick her Ascendant.

Progressions Change the World

With this portrait of Katie Couric (another triple Cardinal Sign), we look at how Couric's career (and the broadcast industry) were changed by progressions.

Katie Couric
1/7/1957, 11:55 P.M.
Arlington, VA

Earlier, we looked at progressions and how they capture the evolution of time in the giant wheel by registering the smaller cogs (COGnitives) in the hourly, daily and monthly units At all times, these shifting "units of time" affect all of the components in a chart, as they are "progressed" one day or one degree for every year of their existence. For individuals, changes are seen when a component progresses into a new sign or house. For countries, these progressions often indicate changes in social attitudes.

In the 2005 secondary progressions of the USA's Scorpio rising chart (based on the advancement of one day per year), this country's 3rd House of Communications progressed from Leo into Virgo. Notably, it changed the nature of this nation's news and journalism.

For thirty years, the USA's progressed 3rd House was ruled by masculine Leo. In this period, the news anchors were all male *and fixed signs!* Scorpios Walter Cronkite and Dan Rather, Aquariuses Tom Brokaw and Ted Koppel, Tauruses Jim Lehrer and Brian Williams and Leo Peter Jennings were good examples.

With the USA's 3rd House progression into Virgo, many mutable signs suddenly filled these network anchor seats: Pisces Charles Gibson and Bob Schieffer, Virgo Elizabeth Vargas. On cable, we saw CNN's Anderson Cooper (Gemini) and Fox's Bill O'Reilly (Virgo).

Capricorns Diane Sawyer and Katie Couric are not mutable, but they show the shift in polarity (from Leo to Virgo) that brought women into this male dominated profession.

With this progression into Virgo, the nature of the communication business changed, as newspapers and TV networks lost much of their audience to a new source of data—the internet. This "mutated" the news by fracturing the audiences. What we got was an abundance of reality TV (earth), lots of fake news and an array of overly critical opinions (Virgo). With cable news, there was also more time to thoroughly analyze the news. If there wasn't anything to worry about—there now was plenty! This became apparent in the Virgo-ruled field of health. We seemed to worry too much about Bird Flu, Mad Cow diseases, and the Ebola scare. Alas, news will never be the same.

According to Michael O'Reilly's article in the September 2005 issue of DELL HOROSCOPE, the secondary progression of the USA's natal Mars into retrograde suggested that women would emerge into higher positions of power. Notably, when Mars progressed into retrograde in that year, Katie Couric began her role as the first solo female network anchor.

As for Katie's personal progressions, her Sun progressed into Pisces and her Moon into Capricorn in 2004. This infusion of Pisces encouraged Katie to take a leap of faith. Her progressed Capricorn Moon made her emotionally determined to step up and break thru the glass ceiling in prime time news.

Amazingly, on that day of Katie's new anchor role, transiting Saturn was on her Midheaven! Also, Katie's progressed Sun (in Pisces) was also in her 10th House (conjoined TV's ruler Uranus)—and her progressed Moon was conjoining Mercury, while her progressed Ascendant was conjoining her North Node in the 2nd House. This was her day of destiny in the field of communications.

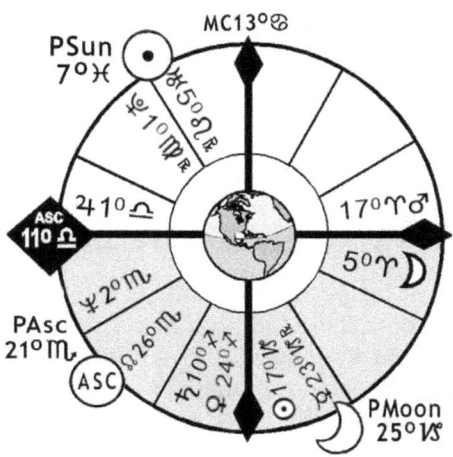

Sun: Capricorn

Couric's Capricorn Sun shows in her bookish looks, in her conservative attire and in her presentation of information. The upper photos show many goat features. The most obvious is Couric's wide, highly placed cheek bones.

These photos also show how these cardinal feminine energies drop the lower part of the face downward, as the upper half appears to be climbing upward. This down-to-up push is also seen in a goat's body language.

Ascendant: Libra

Katie's Libra Ascendant places her natal Saturn and Venus in her 3rd House of communication. The ringed planet also trines her natal Uranus in her 10th House. This combination gives her a gift for presenting information, as well as an ability to appear calm and controlled, even in the most trying of events.

Physically, we see the pleasant features of Libra—the wide smile and sparkling almond eyes. These Venusian features round the rugged edges of her Sun.

Moon: Aries

Even with a rambunctious Aries Moon, Katie rarely appears to get angry or emotional in front of the camera. This may be due to her Moon's trine to Saturn. It restrains Aries' temper tantrums, as it reinforces the discipline of her Sun. All the while, her Libra Ascendant lies in opposition at the midpoint between her Moon and its ruling planet Mars. This keeps the calming forces of her Rising Sign up front, some distance from the fiery Aries energies.

In 2006, when Couric's *Snapshot* was printed in *Dell Horoscope*, no birth time was available. On her birthday, the Moon changed from Pisces to Aries around 2:00 P.M., so, judging from the fact that she had five fires signs but little water in her chart, Katie's empathetic nature lead this author to state that her Moon was in Pisces. Oops! As you see here, it's in Aries!

Hindsight tells us the whole point of this discussion: Nature's cycles occur at many intervals. What this author saw was the physical transformations that were brought about by her Sun's progression into Pisces!

Now, let's see what a Fixed Moon does to the Cardinal Components

Denzel Washington
12/28/1954, 12:09 A.M.
Mt. Vermont, NY

♑ Capricorn Sun

In his persistent, cautious climb to stardom, Denzel has portrayed characters who have struggled against institutions, prejudices and established powers, as he built a path for "new social direction".

Denzel gained national attention playing a hard working intern on TV's *St. Elsewhere*. In his first film *Cry Freedom*, he portrayed the South African activist Steve Bilko. Shortly after, he was one of the brave members of an all-black civil war battalion in *Glory*. (It won him an Oscar for best supporting actor). This was followed by his powerful roles in *Malcolm X* and *Philadelphia*. In all these roles, Denzel demonstrated the cool and tenacious qualities of a Capricorn goat.

All of the photos show us something interesting about this Seagoat. The upper left one is noticeably stern and tense. In the photo to the right, he appears more happy and filled with life, even though the photo was taken years later. The photo with the gray hair supports the adage that Capricorns appear to get younger as they age. Perhaps this is true, since, with success, they are not so heavily driven.

Ascendant: Libra

The next time you catch Denzel in one of his free-form television interviews, watch for the "airy side" in his personality—that part expressed by his Ascendant and Moon. The first thing you might notice is the Libra mask that gives him a light, cheery, relaxed persona. Libra's sparkling eyes, the wide grin with the V-shaped smile-lines and the cherub dimples enhance this pleasant, easy going exterior. These cardinal breezes also erode and loosen his Sun's stony features. This air element was highly noticeable in Denzel's buoyant role in *Much Ado About Nothing*.

The rulers of Denzel's Sun and Ascendant (Saturn and Venus) are conjunct in Scorpio. This merges his normally conflicting Sun and Rising lights, as it adds a moody intensity to his personality. This was seen in his role in *Mississippi Masala*.

Moon: Aquarius

Even though pleasant and well anchored, Washington still provides surprising moments, notably when he attempts to express his feelings.

Watch how his eyes fold inward at the outer edges, as he appears to lock onto some distant train of thought. Very quickly, he'll return, excited and statically charged with a unexpected description of his feelings. Many of these out-of-the-blue concepts seem to be as surprising to Denzel, as they were to us.

These lunar urges contrast with Denzel's organized solar expressions. Positively, they give us a Seagoat who's optimistic, inventive and fun!

Here is another Air Moon, but the Ascendant is now a mutable Fire sign. There's also a look at progressions.

Nicolas Cage
1/7/1964, 5:30 A.M..Long Beach, CA

♑ Capricorn Sun

Against the odds, this thin haired, wispy voiced goat was determined to make it on his own! He even changed his name from Nicolas Coppola to avoid coasting on his uncle Francis Ford Coppola's famous name. Furthermore, in the 1989 film *Vampire's Kiss*, he even ate a live cockroach on camera for his art. It proves the adage that these goats will eat a tin can to prove a point!

Nicolas shows us how progressions can alter ones' creative urges—and well as their careers. At the start of his film career, (around 1987), Cage's Sun was progressing into Aquarius and Uranus was transiting his Rising Sign. In this "Uranian period", Cage pursued his offbeat and eccentric roles as the hapless bandit in *Raising Arizona* and as Cher's reluctant beau in *Moonstruck*. Cage's career was on a role!

In 1995, as Cage's progressed Aquarius Sun conjoined his natal Venus and Saturn in his 2nd House, Cage reaped Saturn's rewards with his Oscar winning role as a suicidal cynic in *Leaving Las Vegas*. Later, in 1997, when Cage's progressed Mars was conjoining his progressed Sun on his natal Saturn, Cage began the process of bulking up to play his action roles in *The Rock* and *Con-Air*. In 1999, this solid image became lighter and more etherial when Cage's Moon progressed into Aquarius. This was when he begin his delightful series of *National Treasure* adventures.

Moon: Libra

Nicolas' hangdog nature made him one of the 1980's least likely stars. Who'd expect someone with such a "sleepy" appearance to succeed in movies, much less in action films. These soft and seeming listless qualities are a product of Venus' conjunction to his Sun's ruling planet Saturn, and their trine to his Venus ruled Moon.

With Cage, the smiling face of Libra is not always out front (as we saw with Katie Couric). Rather, these Venusian forces only appear when Cage reacts to others. It explains why his responses often lack any sense of aggression.

Ascendant: Sagittarius

When Cage trots onto the stage, what we see is his jubilant, animated and restless Centaur Ascendant. Note how the fiery sparkle in his eyes dims, as he begins to express the practical opinions of his earthy Sun. The change is obvious.

Since one's physical container (i.e., the bone structure) is defined by the Ascendant, Nicolas shows us a facial shape not seen in any of our previous subjects. Note the long face and jaw, the neck that stretches out far beyond the shoulders and the lengthy thighs and arms. They all suggest the features of a horse. This is the look we see, when a person has a Sagittarius Ascendant.

A Look at How Decans Alter the Character of a Sign

The concept of decans was explained in this book's introduction material. Here, we will show how the decan changes in a person's key components can alter his or her physical appearance and/or mannerisms.

Jude Law
12/29/1972, 6:00 A.M.
London, UK

Bradley Cooper
1/5/1997, 5:09 P.M.
Philadelphia, PA

♑ Capricorn Suns

Here we look at two celebrities who have the same three key components. However, the big difference is that two of their three key components are in different decans. These differences alter their creative expressions and the manner in which they achieve their endeavors.

The early work of **Jude Law** includes *The Talented Mr. Ripley* and *Cold Mountain*, two films that won him Oscar nominations for Best Supporting Actor. Perhaps he is best recognized for his reoccurring role as John Watson in the *Sherlock Holmes* film franchise. His work often shows the calculating qualities of a tenacious and often overly serious goat.

Jude's 7 degree Sun makes him a pure, first decan goat. In solar expression, Jude's upper half of his face and cheekbones are pulled upward, as the mouth and jaw drop into the valley below. This pure cardinal force often gives him the demeanor and physical appearance of a pure bred goat.

Bradley Cooper gained initial recognition for his lead role in the popular TV show *Alias* (2001-2003). A decade later (2012), he garnered consecutive Oscar nominations for his work in *Silver Linings Playbook*, *American Hustle* and *American Sniper*. He won an Oscar for producing the latter film. Cooper's demeanor is one of strength, machismo and stubborn tenacity.

Bradley Cooper's 14 degree Sun takes us into the second decan, or the earth sign that follows Capricorn in the wheel: Taurus. When the light of his Sun is expressed, Bradley's nostrils widen, the jaw shortens and the eyes drop down on the outer edges. This gives his face the cubical features and the fixed bearing of a Taurus bull. This makes this goat appear far more contented than what we see in the mannerisms of Jude Law.

Libra Moons
(Both in Gemini Decan)

These upper photos show how the facial clay is reshaped when both of the men respond or emotionally react with their Libra Moons. Bradley's Moon is at 22 degrees and Jude's Moon is 27 degrees. Both of their Moons are in the third or Gemini decan of Libra.

The upper photos show the horizontally stretched lines and pleasant smile of a Libra Moon, but (with this decan) they also show the skewed features of Gemini. These dueling forces become more obvious, when these men are in a elevated emotional state. When the emotions are lowered, the face tends to reflect the calmer state of Libra.

This analytical emotion was seen in Law's role as Sherlock's confidant John Watson. The mercuric spark appeared in Cooper's wheel dealing character in *American Hustle*. Oddly, their Gemini-decan Moons appear to be a part of their public personas. This is likely due to the fact that their Sagittarius Ascendants are also mutable.

Ascendants: Sagittarius

Jude Law: Sagittarius Decan

Law's first decan 9 degree Rising Sign makes his mask that of a full bred stallion. Physically, it gives Law the domed forehead, ball tipped nose and the extended jaw of a horse.

Jude's films included dramas, fantasies, historical and futuristic works. Also, as we saw in his film *Spy*, he also has a gift for comedy. Still, most of his characters were professorial and philosophical in nature—their thoughts were more important than their actions.

Bradley Cooper: Aries Decan

When Bradley isn't expressing the sensual delights of his Sun or emoting the mental urges of his Moon, the long face of his Centaur Ascendant appears. Note how his forehead sweeps upward, rather than to the back (like we see in Jude). Also, his cheekbones give his face a convex appearance. He looks more like a ram, than a horse.

Cooper's 12 degree Ascendant is in the Aries decan. Mars placement on this Rising Sign enhances this Aries appearance and warrior persona.

Cooper earned his machismo image in the huge hit *The Sniper*. He also played a member of the *A-Team* and was an arm's supplier in the recent film *War Dogs*. These latter two action films were filled with the light levity of Sagittarius, a skill that Cooper mastered in his roles in *The Hangover, Parts I to III*. Even in his lighter roles, what we see is an aggressive goat who lacks the professorial image we see in Jude Law.

A Cancer Moon Changes the Appearance
Robert Duvall
1/5/1931, 5:10 A.M.
San Diego, CA

Capricorn Sun

Robert Duvall shows us the rock-solid stability we expect from a Capricorn Sun, as well as the chiselled features of a goat. More than what we've seen in the previous portraits, Duvall's appearance seems to match our Capricorn caricature. This is because Saturn sits on his Sun.

Saturn's placement also explains why Robert has consistently played ruthless and authoritarian characters. He was John Wayne's nemesis in *True Grit*, the hatchet man in *Network* and the blustery military man in *The Great Santini*. Also, who could forget his role in *Godfather I and II*.

Moon: Cancer

Since Robert's Cancer Moon is placed in its ruling sign, the surging waters are always present, to soften the rugged edges of Duvall's earthy Sun. Watch how his face rounds and swells when he beams his lunar reactions.

This Moon placement gives Robert a gift for expressing "the emotional side of his personality". He was the courtly, soft-spoken object of a woman's desires in *Rambling Rose*. In *Tender Mercies*, he won an Oscar for his portrayal of a sympathetic, faded country singer. Notably, his portrayal of Dr. Watson in *The Seven Percent Solution* was far more compassionate than the mercurial version we saw in Jude Law's version.

Ascendant: Sagittarius

Strangely, Robert's sensitive emotions are often masked by his fiery Centaur Ascendant. This Rising Sign also trines Uranus in Aries and Mars in Leo, and this gives Duvall an independent and confident demeanor—as well as a daring, and aggressive persona.

In his role as Lt. Colonel Bill Kilgor in *Apocalypse Now*, Duvall's Leo Mars was quite apparent as he boasted: "I love the smell of Napalm in the morning". This character displayed the Centaur's physical superiority and its reckless sense of invincibility.

In his film *The Natural*, Duvall's mutable fires appeared in his role as an enthusiastic sports writer. He loved the part, for Sagittarius' favorite subjects are sports and publishing.

Oddly, the younger lower-left photo of Duvall suggests hints of the Centaur, but the under-lying bone structure lacks the strongly skewed qualities we see in others. This likely is due to Duvall's Jupiter and Pluto conjunction in Cancer—and its opposition to his Sun, Mercury and Saturn. With these connections, Duvall appears to be a cross between a goat and a Crab. The horse was left out in the pasture.

The skewed patterns become obvious, when Mutable Signs dominate the chart.

Kevin Costner
1/7/1964, 5:30 A.M.
Long Beach, CA

♑ Capricorn Sun

Since his breakthrough role in the film *Bull Durham*, Costner has consistently displayed his Capricorn spirit, by working incessantly! At $12 million per movie (at 1993 prices), what true Capricorn could resist? However, this relentless toil took its toll. In 1994, Saturn was performing its work lessons while transiting Kevin's 6th House. There, the budget of *Waterworld* hit the stratosphere. Also, in that year, Saturn squared his natal Venus and entered his 7th House. His sixteen-year marriage broke up. His response was typical for a Capricorn: "There's a hungry world out there waiting for you to fall."

In his periphery of serious roles, Kevin projects the Saturnine qualities of his Sun, i.e., the steely eyes, and the face that seems to be cast in granite. In *JFK*, as Jim Garrison, Kevin gave us a solid impression of a dour goat. In TV's *The Untouchables*, fellow Capricorn Robert Stack set the tone, and in the 1987 film version, Costner also captured the essence of Eliot Ness. After many hits, Costner's career continues to endure. His 2015 hit: *McFarland, USA* premiered during the creation of this book.

Ascendant: Virgo

With his Virgo Ascendant, Kevin appears to be a perfectionist, who often becomes fussy and wrought with worry. As demonstrated in the movie *The Body Guard*, he appeared to be overly obsessed with the details in his surroundings. It's very different than the scattered fire that we saw in Nicolas Cage. Kevin's Rising Sign is in mutable Earth!

This Ascendant gives Kevin a long and lanky physical body, much like the frame we see in Cage's Centaur Rising. However, the main difference is that Kevin appears grounded in the midsection of his body, as he fiddles with the details that surround him. He lacks the impulsive and scattered persona of Cage's fiery mask.

Moon: Sagittarius

Kevin *Dances With Wolves* emotionally —as his Sagittarius Moon lifts his spirit, to pursue a giant array of enlightened challenges. This Archer Moon (and a Mars in Aries) gives Kevin the motor skills to perform in many athletic roles.

Kevin's films *Field of Dreams*, *Tin Cup* and *Bull Durham* are all classic homages to the world of sports. These lunar urges also account for his *Silverado* and *Robin Hood* adventures. Still, there is no mistake that Costner is a Capricorn. He is willing to take risks to build his dreams: *"If you build it, they will come."*

Here, the primary lights of our subjects are a mix of all three Modes.

Betty White
1/17/1922, 7:10 P.M.
Oak Park, IL

♑ Capricorn Sun

It is said that many Capricorns reach their peaks late in life. Betty White's career supports this adage.

Some of us recall her as a panelist on TV's early game shows. Others remember her on the classic '70's sitcom *The Mary Tyler Moore Show* where, in her role as "Sue Ann", she displayed the devious qualities we associate with grumpier goats. This hilarious character won her fame—and her first Emmy!

However, it was in 2010 (in her 7th decade as a performer) when Betty reached the top of her mountain! She won a Screen Actors Guild Award for *Hot in Cleveland* and an Emmy serving as a host on *Saturday Night Live*. The latter came from an massive internet campaign from the youth of this country who convinced producers to make Betty a guest MC on the show. Now, that's showing respect for your elders!

As for Betty's physical features, this author thinks the upper left photo is best "goat image" in this whole collection. Though it may not be complementary, it captures the traits outlined in our introduction.

Leo Ascendant

Betty began her career at 17, as her Leo Ascendant opened the doors to her long and distinguished theatrical career. You see this Rising Sign when Betty struts into the room. It shows in her aura of confidence and boastful persona. It gives the impression that royalty has just arrived!

This showy mask adds warmth and a fiery spirt to Betty's chilly solar light. Physically, it also infuses the attributes of a lion, notably the cubical forehead, thick mane and feline jowls.

Virgo Moon

Betty is also known for her role as "Rose" in *The Golden Girls*. In this seven year gig, she played an unfocused, delightfully ditsy and obsessively fussy character. This role truly reflected the mercuric lunacy of Betty's Virgo Moon.

Watch for the moments when Betty's stony solar gaze transforms into a quizzical expression—or how her fixed demeanor rearranges into distinctly skewed facial lines. When this appears, you know she is likely reacting with the mutable emotions of her Virgo Moon.

Betty and Ted's Moons and Ascendants are switched.

Ted Danson
12/29/1947, 10:58 P.M.
San Diego, CA

♑ Capricorn Sun

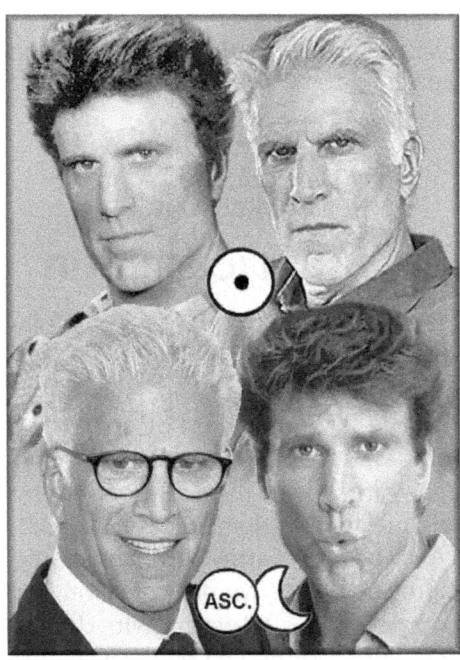

In the creation of TV characters, writers create dialog by embellishing on the unique gifts of expressions given by the actor or actress who plays the role. In the TV sitcom *Cheers*, Danson's character was a calculating wheeler-dealer, who boasted about his many "bedroom conquests".

When Capricorn Kirstie Alley showed up, both battled to be "king or queen of the mountain". Neither would concede position to the other. It was great comedy!

In his short lived TV show *Ink*, Ted's character was a close facsimile of the skirt-chasing *Cheers* role. However, Danson's serious side emerged in 2011, when he began his role in *CSI Las Vegas*. There, as chief of forensics, Danson begin every case by surveying the physical evidence. Next, he'd set out his plan, as he slowly directed his staff on a course of action. Once the case was solved, he proudly saluted his team, thanking them for "the good work". This methodology reflects the key components in Danson's chart.

Ascendant: Virgo

In his Sam Mallone role in *Cheers*, the moment that this goat stopped this urge "to conquer", he would immediately begin to worry about "where he was going and what he was doing". When Virgo Sun **Shelly Long** entered the scene, the questioning and criticism intensified, as Danson was surrounded by her constant need for perfection. It seemed to took forever to consummate their relationship.

Danson's appearance resembles that of Kevin Costner. Both have Virgo Rising and Danson's 2nd decan Leo Moon shows many of the qualities of Sagittarius.

Moon: Leo

Many show business celebrities have Leo Moons. Their reactions are quite dramatic and they love to attract attention! This was obvious in Danson's role in *Cheers* and in his loud and flashy role in the movie *Made in America*.

Positively, this injection of Lion blood not only instills confidence, it also warms up Ted's cool Capricorn/Virgo exterior, as it makes him delightfully playful and very generous.

With Jupiter in Sagittarius, trining Ted's 12° Centaur-decan Leo Moon, we see why Danson's is highly attracted to play sports and comedy roles. This Sagittarius decan makes his emotional reactions appear less self centered, animated and occasionally silly.

Here, we show how the placement of planets can out weight the force and power of the three luminaries.

Jim Carrey
1/17/1962, 2:30 A.M.
Newmarket, Ontario

♑ Capricorn Sun

Carrey has said that Joel, his painfully shy, lovelorn character in *Eternal Sunshine of the Spotless Mind,* is closer to what he's like when he's not "on". In that role (top/right photo) and in *The Truman Show,* Jim showed the rarely seen earthy and melancholy demeanor of the goat.

As a child, Jim Carrey was an incurable extrovert who performed constantly for anyone who would watch. With Uranus and Pluto near his Leo Midheaven, this goat was determined to achieve public attention and adulation.

This drive for success is a product of Jim's Capricorn Sun, Venus and Mars. Notably, Carrey won his fame with his outrageous physical humor. This physicality is a product of his Mars' and its aspects to Neptune, Pluto and his Ascendant.

Scorpio Rising

With a Scorpio Ascendant, one would expect Jim to a well controlled persona. No way! Carrey's Rising Sign conjoins Neptune, and both of them sextile his Capricorn Mars and Virgo Pluto. This gives Jim his highly distorted physical gestures, as well as his often disturbing persona.

This Ascendant also squares a Mercury/Jupiter conjunction in Aquarius. This electrifies and exaggerates the bizarre mask that Jim extends out to others.

Positively, Scorpio Rising gave Carrey a gift for portraying men whose lives were changed by supernatural and or unseen forces. His roles in *The Mask, Bruce Almighty* and *The Majestic* all contained the mysterious magic of Scorpio, as well as the make believe illusions of Neptune.

Gemini Moon

Uranus is Jim's only fire. Neptune and Ascendant are his only water. His Moon and three other components are in Air, and this equals his number of Earth signs. Oddly, Jim seems to have more fire. This may be due to Uranus' placement near his Midheaven.

Jim's Gemini Moon trines that Jupiter and Mercury conjunction in Aquarius, while it forms a snug square to Pluto. The first aspects "power up" the mental circuits of this mercuric Moon, but the square makes it difficult for Carrey to express the emotions of his Moon.

Furthermore, the secretive surface of Jim's Scorpio mask rarely allows these emotions to break free. When they do, they are often released in a giant whirlwind of words and chatter!

Look what happens, when fixed lights dominate the personality.

Muhammad Ali
1/17/1942. 6:30 P.M
Louisville, KY

"Champions aren't made in gyms. Champions are made from something they have deep inside them: a desire, a dream, a vision. They have to have the last-minute stamina. They have to have the skill and the will, but the will must be stronger than the skill."
—Muhammad Ali

Capricorn Sun

Capricorn goats know what it takes to reach the top, but their real status comes from what they do with their success. Ali became the World Heavyweight Boxing Champion at the age of twenty-two, but many say that his greatest achievements came later in life, as he traveled to raise the hopes of people around the world. Even hampered by Parkinson's disease, he pushed on, fighting against poverty, social inequities and racism.

At his career peak, Ali displayed the physical strength of a bull. This likely comes from his Midheaven Taurus Mars, which T-squares his Sun and Pluto. This fixed Earth (and his fixed Moon and Ascendant) gave him the focus to develop his boxing skills.

Physically, Ali shows many qualities of the goat mentioned previously.

Ascendant: Leo
"I am the greatest!"

Ali shouted this repeatedly when he won his first championship. As he strutted around the ring, the fires intensified and he became louder with each proclamation! It was one of boxing's most memorable moments and a true example of how a Leo Rising Sign can ignite a person's sense of pride. This fixed fire also gave him the will and desire to manifest the success that he envisioned.

Moon: Aquarius
"I float like a butterfly. Sting like a bee."

This famous reactive taunt to one of Ali's opponents introduced us to Ali's gift for poetic banter and the quirks of his rebellious Aquarius Moon.

In 1964, Ali's lunar emotions (as well as the forces of his Aquarius Mercury and Venus) were on a rebellious roll. He changed his name from Cassius Clay to Muhammad Ali, as he announced his new religion and status as a conscientious objector to the military draft. The riled establishment took away his title. In 1970, the ban is lifted and Ali regains his title in 1974.

Ali's humanitarian Moon carries his legend forward. In 2005, he opened the *Ali Center* in Louisville, KY. This center encourages others to *"Be Great; Do Great things."*

Orlando Bloom

1/13/1977, 9:15 A.M.
Canterbury, UK

"If life isn't about humanity, then tell me what it's about, because I'd love to know."
— Orlando Bloom

♑ Capricorn Sun

Orlando is a classically trained British actor who is very serious about his work. Think of the films *Kingdom of Heaven* and *Troy*, and you get a sense of just how seriously he views history and culture. Capricorns relish such studies!

When his Cardinal Earth lights shine, Orlando's face takes on the cool, gray shades of winter. Note how the wide, high-placed cheekbones drop rapidly to form the hardened cliffs in the face. The steely eyes of a mountain goat peer out from this craggy ridge.

With his Mars also in Capricorn, Bloom's physical motor runs at a steady pace, matching the persistent drive of his Sun. However, Mars' sextile to Venus in Pisces softens these martial qualities. In *Pirates of the Caribbean*, he was the most reluctant warrior of the bunch.

Scorpio Moon

Bloom's emotions lack the flare and showiness we saw in **Muhammad Ali**—and unlike **Jim Carrey**, they always seem to be under control. Orlando's Moon is in the fixed water of Scorpio.

This fixed presence is enhanced by Bloom's Saturn. It forms a T-square to Uranus (in Scorpio) and Jupiter (in Taurus). Jupiter squares his Ascendant. With all this fixity, he constantly appears to be "holding his space".

As "Legolas", the mysterious and emotionally intense elf in *Lord of the Rings*, Bloom found stardom. In this role, Bloom's hypnotic stare (and the fixed tides of his Scorpio Moon) would lock us into his dreamy magical spell.

Aquarius Rising

With **Ali**, we witnessed how the emotional reactions of an Aquarius Moon can make one a revolutionary figure. With Bloom, his Aquarius mask creates no activity—rather it is just a shield that deflects incoming light.

The LL photo shows Bloom's broad chin and highly optimistic mask, as well as Aquarius' down turned outer eyelids. Also, there's the expected rectangular jaw of an Aquarius Ascendant.

With his giant T-square of fixed planets and a fixed Ascendant and Moon, Bloom appears well anchored. The cardinal drive is less obvious.

~~~

Each of these collections concludes with a celebrity who displays some of the components that will be seen in the next Zodiac sign. Thusly, Bloom's strong fixity and Aquarius Moon ends this segment.

# Aquarius

	Page
Introduction to Aquarius	
Double & Triple Aquariuses	
Sarah Palin and Gene Hackman	43-45
Capricorn Ascendants:	
Tom Selleck and Alan Alda	46
Paul Newman	47
Elijah Wood	48
Capricorn Moons:	
Mia Farrow	49
Tom Brokaw	50
The force of Air runs strong	
Geena Davis	51
Carole King	52
James Spader	53
Garth Brooks	54
The force of Fire dominates	
Arsenio Hall	55
Jennifer Aniston	56
Oprah Winfrey	57
Justin Timberlake	58
Ellen Degeneres/Chris Rock	59
Joseph Gordon-Levitt	60
Water douses the Fire	
John Travolta	61
Nathan Lane	62

Aquarius — January 20 to February 18

Tune in to know, what needs to be known

Masculine Polarity, Fixed Air

In the crystal clear light of **Aquarius**, it is obvious that the days are getting longer. This increasing light (and a polar change to the positive and expansive force of Fixed Air) brings hope for a brighter future!

At every mid-seasonal point, the mode of fixity recycles once again—to counter the directional actions of the preceding cardinal sign. In Mid-Winter, it is time to focus on the New Year resolutions of **Capricorn**, so we can compose our wishful affirmations for the year ahead. This fixing-of-thought molds the revolutionary seeds that will bring new forms of life, in the Spring.

Ancient scholars believed that all past-and-present knowledge is stored in the Akashic Records—and these cognitive experiences are transmitted in the conduit of water. Yes, water is pouring out of Aquarius' vase, to feed revolutionary ideas out to the world—so that every individual entity can know "what needs to be known". That is why Aquarius is called *The Water Bearer*.

Our Aquarius friends have a gift for tuning into the thoughts of others. With help from the other air signs **Gemini** and **Libra**, they will find the right words to express their outrageous ideas, and make them more agreeable to others.

The more practical of these airy souls may be gathering funds to support humanitarian causes—and raise the hopes of the downtrodden. Those who are less practical, are flying off to attend Sci-Fi and UFO conferences.

Even with this intuitive knowing, it is difficult for these independent airheads to connect emotionally to others. It is **Pisces** (the next sign in the Zodiac) who has the gift to blend all of these desires, sensations, thoughts and feelings together—and merge them into newly imagined wholes!

Individuals with an Aquarius Sun, Moon, or Rising Sign (or a strongly aspected Uranus) often display the qualities described herewith. These Intuitive insights are activated when planets transit the 11th House, the natural home of Aquarius.

Ruling Planet ~ Uranus
(Also traditionally ruled by Saturn)

This gaseous planet was the first planet discovered beyond Saturn (the last planet viewable with our Nature given senses). Since the invention of the telescope made this discovery of Uranus possible, it's appropriate that all technological inventions and futuristic advancements in "knowledge and knowing" are said to be governed and regulated by the transits of this planet.

Uranus is associated with unexpected neurological changes, modern science and aeronautics, radio/TV (mass communication), space travel, science fiction or any concept that creates revolutionary changes in human consciousness.

Aquarius Physical Traits:

The first thing you will notice about Aquarius is their large cubical skull, the two knobs on the forehead and the broad delta between the brows. Note how this delta drops down onto the short bridged and square-tipped nose, as the upper cheekbones and wide based jaw create a cubical box on the lower half of the face. In the middle, you'll see how the fixed air forces are drawing the eyes close together, as they pull the eyelids down on the sides. This compaction also forms the dimples and the down-drawn, tight-lipped smile.

With most Aquariuses, their facial features are tightly compacted into the center, and they appear small in relation to the overall size of the head. That is why the front of any Aquarius' face is distinctly flat in appearance.

Gene Hackman is a triple Aquarius who clearly shows the compacted facial features, the delta between the brows and the water bearer's square-tipped nose. *Sarah Palin* (with her Sun and Moon in Fixed Air) displays the rectangular jaw as well as the distant look of "being somewhere else—other than here!"

Sarah Palin: February 11, 1964, 6:00 P.M., Sandpoint, ID
Gene Hackman: January 30, 1930, 7:45 A.M., San Bernardino, CA

Aquarius Body Language

The expansive forces of Aquarius rule the lower legs and calves. This rulership (in this part of the body) makes the body language of Aquarius far different than what was seen in Capricorn. There is little anchoring in the ground, for the calves of Aquarius are flapping to the front, and their feet are skipping freely above the Earth—like a hovercraft!

The resulting onslaught of frontal winds pushes the upper torso and arms to the back. Like a sail on a ship, everything is flattened, as it resists the prevailing winds.

These winds flattened the upper half of the body. From the hips on up, the body appears noticeably narrow in its front to back proportions. This can be seen in the hips, buttock, chest and face. In contrast, the calves appear lanky and voluminous.

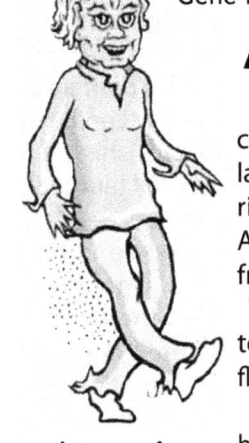

Aquarius rules the Calves

In the next three portraits, we show four Aquariuses with Capricorn Ascendants. This should help one recognize the changes that come, when any component moves from Cardinal Earth to Fixed Air.

Aquarius Suns:
Tom Selleck
1/29/1945, 8:22 A.M., Detroit, MI
Alan Alda
1/28/1936, 5:07 A.M., New York, NY

In the 70's and 80's, Alda and Selleck were the leads in the hit TV shows *Mash* and *Magnum PI*. Alan was the rebellious surgeon with the irreverent attitude. Tom was the beach party detective who played on his intuitive visions. With brisk chatter, light comedy and occassional departures from the norm, their shows became meaningful Aquarian social statements, from both ends of the political spectrum.

These two men display many common Aquarian traits. There's the sparkling eyes that seem to "blink from the sides", the high knobbed forehead, the highly recognized cheek dimples and the rectangular jaw and broad chin.

Ascendants: Capricorn

When the uplifting breezes of Aquarius subside, these men glide both back down to Earth. The airport for their landings is their Capricorn Ascendants.

On the ground, both men appear serious and business-like. This makes them more real as well as accessible to others.

When this ascending mask appears, you may notice the goat-like qualities discussed in the introduction. In these two men, we also see how Saturn's rulership of this sign gave these two men the determination to succeed. It also brought longevity to their careers. Their shows were among the longest running series in TV history.

Moons: Leo & Aries

Alan and Tom's reactive natures are similar in intensity since they both are fire signs. The difference can be seen in their responses.

Selleck's Moon is fixed fire. He holds the moment, adds dramatic flare and responds with his Leonine attempts at "one-ups-manship". In his show, he constantly taunted his cohort with put-downs.

Alda has an Aries Moon and his reactions are like a blowtorch— abrupt, fiery and "to-the-point". In the midst of a heated debate, Alda quickly becomes emotionally argumentative. But once done, that's it. It's over! These Aries lunar reactions are forgotten as quickly as they start.

Paul Newman
1/26/1925, 6:30 A.M.
Cleveland, Ohio

♒ SUN: Aquarius

The top right picture of Paul reveals a common trait with most Aquariuses—that distantly focused look in the eyes. At times, this look can be unsettling, particularly when you're talking with one of your Aquarian buddies and he or she leaves you feeling that "you're not even there". This quirk often gives the impression that they are aloof and indifferent.

Perhaps it's the inflated, angled eyelids that makes them seem that they're focusing on some point in outer space, rather than on what's in front of them. Or it might be that their brains are always tuning in to all the other ideas floating through the room. Still, it could be their habit of constantly checking the people who are entering the room—which means that they will abruptly end the conversation and skip away to greet another newly arrived friend. You'll be left there standing along, feeling lost in the crowd. To find more sympathy, seek out a water sign.

These Aquarian traits remind us of Paul's early roles. *Hud* and *Cool Hand Luke* were true misfits. In *Cat on A Hot Tin Roof*, he showed how these fixed air signs can lock themselves into their own separate world. Even Liz Taylor (with her intense Pisces and Scorpio energies) could not illicit an emotion from her alienated lover.

On the other side, Newman was a bearer of light, who showed Aquarius' friendly and social side. This was what we saw in his biggest box office movies, as he played Robert Redford's partner in the rambunctious adventures *Butch Cassidy and The Sundance Kid* and *The Sting*.

Ascendant: Capricorn

With prominent Capricorn (Ascendent, Mercury, Venus and Jupiter), Newman is incredibly grounded. This somber appearance is regularly displayed by his earthy mask, as those sky-blue eyes take on a wintery and chilly aura.

Paul had Capricorn's gift for endurance. He was highly successful in his later years, playing senior roles. In *Absence of Malice* and *The Verdict*, we saw Capricorn's tenacity and determination. In *Blaze*, he played the crafty and powerful Senator Huey Long. His 1961 role as Fast Eddie in *The Hustler* resurfaced in 1986's *The Color of Money*. It won him his first Oscar!

Moon: Pisces

Paul often undercut his insensitive and distant image by playing vulnerable and compassionate characters. This quality was a product of his Pisces Moon.

Paul fulfilled his lunar desires with his wonderful acts of compassion. Working with his Pisces wife Joanne Woodward, they built a camp for ill children, using the profits from "Newman's Own" food products. It continues after his passing.

Elijah Wood

1/28/1981, 6:46 A.M.
Cedar Rapids, Iowa

♒ SUN: Aquarius

"I think being different, being against the grain of society, is the greatest thing in the world."—Elijah Wood

When J.R.R. Tolkien wrote *Lord of the Rings*, Frodo must have been the Aquarius in his mix of characters. After all, Frodo Baggins was the optimistic Hobbit who constantly lifted the spirits of all of those around him. Anything was possible, even in the most hopeless of situations.

With the intuitive light of his Aquarius Sun, Elijah appears to project this eternal optimism and aura of good tidings. That's likely why he was selected to play the role of Frodo.

Wood displays many of the physical traits of Aquarius, but there is something here that makes him unique. With his Jupiter and Saturn conjoined in Libra and both of these planets trine Elijah's Sun, Wood also presented a sense of calm and balance—energies that supported his Frodo' character.

Elijah's eyes (with their big pupils) are larger than expected. Also, the beak is noticeably pointed. This could be due to the fact that his Sun's ruling planet Uranus and his Moon are in Scorpio.

Moon: Scorpio

"If I wasn't an actor, I'd be a secret agent."

Frodo was the Hobbit who had a gift for resisting the intrusion of "other powerful forces." What Moon sign would be the most likely to ward off such emotional assaults? Scorpio, of course! Scorpio Moons keep their emotions private and protected. These Moon signs also have an ability to feel the harmful intent of any "physic vampire". This enables them to shield themselves from the power plays of others.

When Elijah's Moon reacts to others, the fixed quality of his Sun remains, as the lunar tides draw in an ocean of water, to dampen the light of his airy Sun. This turns his sparkling gaze into a hypnotic and intense stare.

Capricorn Ascendant

Since Elijah's Ascendant sextiles his Sun's ruler Uranus, the features of Aquarius are stronger than Capricorn. Wood's goat features can be seen in his wide and high-placed cheek bones—which plant his eyes up high under the brows.

Also, his 25° Ascendant is in the decan of Virgo. It explains the wide gap in his frontal teeth and his skewed brows and offset eyes.

Mia Farrow
2/9/1945, 11:27 A.M.
Los Angeles, CA

The Capricorn mask on our four previous subjects is no longer present, for this lady has a Capricorn Moon. Here, the image of a goat appears in the moldings of her facial flesh (rather than in her bone structure). It can be seen when she reacts to others or becomes highly emotional!

♒ SUN: Aquarius

This rebellious lady has created quite a stir in this world: personally, politically and in her career! Mia's first major role was in the 1968 *Rosemary's Baby*, a true horror genre classic. Shortly after, Mia was to be cast as "Mattie" in the film *True Grit*. However, she heard that it's director had "a reputation for being rude to actresses." Farrow insisted that producer Hal Wallis replace the director. He refused and gave the role to Kim Darby. This bold action shows Farrow's rebellious Aquarius nature and her tendency to rebel against anything she considers unjust.

A decade later, in her professional and personal relation with director Woody Allen, Mia once again showed her flair for independence. She starred in nearly all of Allen's films in the 80's and 90's. The films were wonderful. The relationship was a disaster. (See Moon).

In 2000, Mia's showed the humanitarian side of Aquarius when she became a UNICEF Goodwill Ambassador and an advocate for human rights—raising funds for children in conflict-affected regions like Darfur. She also helped to draw attention to the fight that helped eradicate polio in Africa.

Capricorn Moon

Mia's Venus, Saturn, and Neptune are all joined in a powerful grand cross with her Capricorn Moon. Positively, this cross gave Mia the tenacious drive to pursue her social causes. However, Venus' placement in this arrangement accounts for the struggle in her personal life. Her marriage to Frank Sinatra was short and the one with Woody Allen brought headlines in the tabloids and elsewhere.

Mia's Mars is also in Capricorn. The stern force of the goat appears when her arguments are beamed at others.

Taurus Ascendant

In many of Woody Allen's scripts, the complex concepts of human relationships were skillfully presented to show the rebellious light of Mia's Sun.

However, in her youthful roles, Mia's public persona was that of a vulnerable and sensual being. What her audience saw was the doe-eyed beauty with the big eyes—her Taurus Ascendant!

Tom Brokaw
2/6/1940, 3:40 A.M.
Webster, SD

In **Kati Couric**'s portrait on page 26, we discussed how the network news anchors were all fixed signs as well as males (at least up to her reign). There, we noted how, since the days of Edward R. Murrow (a fixed Taurus), the networks has placed people in the anchor chair who "hold a steady, unflappable pace of presentation". Perhaps that is why they call these newscasters "anchors". Our subject here is also a fixed sign.

 SUN: Aquarius

With his Aquarius Sun, **Tom Brokaw** presented his "cool and collected" interpretation on the evening news. His Fixed Air gave him an ease with words, a calm and centered disposition and an ethereal sparkle to the eyes. He seemed above the fray and even slightly amused by his so called importance. As NBC News' Managing Editor, Brokaw shaped the content of his daily "Aquarian reports" which included many stories on human events, oddball activities and of course, new inventions and technology.

Peter Jennings (a fixed fire Leo Sun) set a different tone at ABC. With a rapid-fire clip and his self-assured authority, he dished out stories on entertainment, shows and celebrities.

Dan Rather, with his moody, intense Scorpio Sun (fixed water), kept the CBS eye focused on "what was wrong in the world".

Moon: Capricorn

In his book *The Greatest Generation*, Brokaw gave his emotional take on the hard social realities of that generation, as he saluted their individual sacrifices and contributions.

When Tom emotionally reacts to "what's happening", his responses are often serious and controlled. This kept this Aquarius anchored to the Earth, as it restrained his Centaur fires.

Ascendant: Sagittarius

When Tom is out of his anchor chair, the expansive fires of his Centaur Ascendant take reign, as he becomes philosophical and surprisingly whimsical. With this window to the world, Brokaw gains two needed temperaments for his craft: He loves to travel and he has an ability to see the "big picture". When he was not journeying around the world, this Centaur often escaped to his second home in Montana, and he constantly worked out in the gym.

The Upper Right photo shows how the features of one's Ascendant are more obvious in the years of adolescence.

50

Let's kick up the "Air Pressure"
Geena Davis
1/21/1956, 12:06 A.M.
Wareham Center, MA

♒ SUN: Aquarius

Geena's film career began with the offbeat *Tootsie* and her successes came rapidly with *The Fly*, *Beetlejuice* and *The Accidental Tourist*. (In the latter, she won an Oscar, playing the enthusiastic and batty dog trainer). Three years later, she gave us her stellar performance in *Thelma and Louise*. With her flair for comedic timing and her attraction to eccentric roles, Geena displays the quirkiness and the optimistic demeanor of Aquarius. Uranus, the ruling planet of Geena's Sun opposes her Sun as it squares her Moon and Neptune. Notably, these four components are placed in fixed signs, all near the main cross created by her late degree Libra Ascendant. These empowered fixed forces give Geena a very active Neptunian imagination, a "intuitively connected memory" and a very high IQ. She's a member of MENSA, the club for geniuses.

With seven components in fixed signs, these holding forces are apparent in her reactions, in her gestures and in her sparkling eyes, which seem to be focused on the Universe circling inside her head! Physically, the rectangular jaw assembly is her most apparent Aquarius feature.

Ascendant: Libra

Aquariuses often seem distant and remote, but with her Libra mask, Davis readily presents a broad V-lined Libra smile, and this gives her a charming and approachable presence, as it covers her Sun's impulsiveness with a layer of serenity. Her Venus-ruled Moon enhances these Venusian qualities.

Moon: Taurus

When Geena becomes emotional, there seems to be little elemental change in her reactive nature. Perhaps this is due to the fact that her Moon is the only Earth in her chart and it is diffused by its position in the previously mentioned cross of fixed components.

This Moon's earthy nature is also scattered by the expansive forces of Geena's natal Mars. It's in athletic Sagittarius, and it conjoins Saturn, sextiles her Sun and squares her Jupiter and Pluto. Saturn brings the discipline, while Pluto gave her the power to become an incredible athletic. We saw this in her baseball film *A League of Their Own* and in her efforts to become a semifinalist on the US Olympic Archery Team.

Carole King

2/9/1942, 11:42 P.M.
Brooklyn, NY

Carole King was the USA's most successful female songwriter in the latter half of the 20th Century. Her compositions became top hits for a variety of musicians—too numerous to list!

In 1971, her album *Tapestry* remained on the Billboard charts for over a record-setting six years. Today, her songs continue to be covered by artists of multiple generations around the world.

Naturally, this Aquarius rebel rouser is also heavily involved in many political and environmental causes.

 SUN: Aquarius

Carole has four Earth and four air components. Pluto and her Moon are her only Fire—and she has no Water. Thusly, King's music is often thoughtful and substantial, but rarely emotional.

With Saturn conjunct her Mars and her Sun's ruler Uranus in Taurus, King's voice is earthy and natural. Her Taurus Mars may be the origin of her lyric: *"I feel the Earth move, under my feet".*

King shows the physical traits of Aquarius, i.e., the dimpled cheeks, the wide square chin and the eyelids that tilt inward on the outer edges. When she interacts with friends, her face radiates an electrical aura of optimism. In private moments, her focused eyes appear to be starring into outer space. Fortunately, these fixed features of her Sun are loosened by the mutable and cardinal energies of her other key lights.

Ascendant: Libra

For most of us in the '70's, our first impression of Carole was that she was a Venusian "flower child". This can be attributed to Carole's Venus-ruled Libra Ascendant and her Sun's square to those three planets in Venus-ruled Taurus. Furthermore, Carole's fiery Moon sextiles Venus and this planet opposes Pluto on her Midheaven. Pluto's placement explains why King was so reluctant "to perform in public", in the early days of her career. (Her record company insisted it was necessary "to sell more records"). Also, this MC Pluto (and her Taurus planets) shows us why this lady displayed little of the expansive qualities of fire and air, when she was on stage.

Moon: Sagittarius

All of King's Venusian creativity is fired up by her Venus' sextile to her Moon. With this Centaur Moon opposing Jupiter, the fire of King's lunar arrows were constantly lighting up a giant array of thoughts and feelings—to use in her creation of music!

Watch how these ideas pour out and how her face lights up—when she interacts with her friends.

Mutable Forces Stir the Air

James Spader
2/7/1960, 8:02 P.M., Boston, MA

 SUN: Aquarius

As the revolutionary member of TV's *Boston Legal* team, James' TV character challenged all obstacles as he projected his enthusiastic optimism and the inherent disrespect for authority. It's an attitude commonly expressed by many Aquariuses. With Uranus opposing his Sun, this unorthodoxy often goes to the extreme, as we saw in his roles in *Sex, Lies and Video Tape* and the disturbing *Crash*.

The top photos show the two ways in which Fixed Air manifests in Spader's personality. The left-top photo conveys the expression that appears when he attempts to express his hope-filled ideas. The right photo shows how Aquariuses lock into the thoughts inside their heads, to avoid contact with others. In both cases, the tight lipped mouth and compacted facial features appear.

Moon: Gemini

Spader's fixed nature of Air is seen in Spader's solar projections, but when he gets emotionally excited, his airy Moon switches the mode to mutability.

The mercuric quality of Gemini was seen in Spader's analytical summaries in *Boston Legal*. In these emotional diatribes, Jim's eyes would rapidly blink, as his animated hands and arms flew outward and fluttered some distance from the body. The Mercury Messenger was there to present the facts. With the onslaught of words, his true emotions were hard to detect.

Ascendant: Virgo

In his moments of non-projection and non-reaction, the flighty energies of Spader's luminaries subside—as the mask of his Virgo Ascendant rises up, to ground his physical body in Earth.

When Spader enters the room, he immediately analyzes the details in his surroundings. In this moment, his arms and hands hover close to the torso to create a "center of gravity" in the pit of his protruding stomach. James is presenting the mask of his Virgo Ascendant. Once he begins to chat with others, the expansive force of his Gemini Moon appears.

As we saw in his role in *Black List*, James' persona came to resemble that of Taurus, rather than Virgo. His new character was bullheaded and always in control. There, James refined his public image to reflect another layer of his personality—the 27° of his Virgo Ascendant. Yep, it's in the Taurus decan!

Garth Brooks
2/7/1962, 1:07 P.M., Tulsa, OK

♒ SUN: Aquarius

On stage, this "King of Country Music" arrives with all of the thunderous energy of a tornado. His high energy performances are breezy, and cerebral—the electrical light show of Aquarius!

Garth's Sun, Mercury, Venus, Mars, Jupiter and Saturn all vibrate in the water-bearer's magnetic field. Also, his ruling planet Uranus is in Leo and Neptune is in Scorpio. This gives Garth eight fixed planets! It's no wonder he's so inflexible and controlling.

In the mid-90's, Uranus transited thru Aquarius—hitting all five of Garth's Aquarius components. When his Sun's ruling planet transited near the top of his chart, there were big changes in his career. As first it brought huge success as his music crossed from country to "pop tune" status. However, in 2000, when Uranus approached his Venus, his long time marriage ended in divorce. Deeply troubled, Garth quit recording and performing through 2009. In this period, he made a deal to distribute his recordings exclusively at Walmart. This alienated many of his fans, as well as many in the music field.

Ascendant: Gemini

On stage and in TV interviews, fans often saw the mercuric veneer of a highly animated performer—with a gift for dispensing words and chatter.

With his Gemini Ascendant, Garth had the mutable mask that enabled him to interact freely with his audience.

This Mercury-ruled Ascendant also gave Garth his gift for analyzing and assembling a wide range of words and ideas, many of which became lyrics for his compositions.

Moon: Pisces

When the cerebral forces of air cool in the lunar night, Garth withdraws into the dreamy world of his Pisces Moon. Here, in these delicate moments of emotion, Garth transforms into a very private person. He doesn't want to be out there, in front of all those people.

In these cooler temperatures, the moisturized clouds of air precipitate into liquid droplets—to fill Garth's deep pooled eyes and saturate his facial flesh. His Pisces Moon has taken over the sky.

On Pisces' watery lunarscape, Garth does "The Dance", playing with his changing feelings and emotions. The rhythms flow smoothly, connecting his ideas and feelings together, to create the poetic ballads and romantic songs that became his biggest hits.

Watch the Air feed the Fire!

Arsenio Hall
2/12/1956, 3:18 A.M.
Cleveland, OH

Arsenio's first talk program premiered in 1989 in an era before cable TV. There, Hall gave us the first network presentations of many hip hop and grunge musicians, as well as looks at other fringes of culture. This made his show special and unique.

In 2013, after a 19 year hiatus, Hall returned to begin his new late night talk show on "a cable network". Unique fringe talents were now seen everywhere. Arsenio had also changed.

In the '90s, Uranus (the ruling planet of Arsenio's Sun) was in Capricorn and this gave his Capricorn Mercury the mental discipline to manifest the inventive insights that made his first show so special. However, in 2013, Uranus was in fiery Aries. This author maintained it could be problematic, since Arsenio has six fire components in his chart. This author wondered if he would come off as being too aggressive or would he continue to deliver the surprising revelations of his Aquarius luminaries? The show was cancelled less than one year later.

Aquarius Sun and Moon

Watch how Arsenio lights up when he projects the enthusiastic optimism of his Sun. Then look at what happens when he reacts to his guests. The fixed air patterns are the same, since both of his luminaries are in Aquarius.

When these luminaries light up, these Aquarian "radio waves" seem to have their own internal power, as they broadcast into great distances in space. Both of Arsenio's luminaries oppose a Jupiter and Pluto conjunction in his 8th House.

Sagittarius Rising

Arsenio's Sagittarius Ascendant is conjoined by Mars. This red planet trines the previously mentioned Jupiter and Pluto conjunction as it sextiles Hall's Sun and Moon. This martial force was seen in Hall's pumping fists as he fired up his audiences with his aggressive "roo roo roo" chant.

The lower photos shows how the physical features of a horse dominate over the compacted and cubical facial features we'd expect from Aquarius. The LR photo is the best example yet, of someone who has the horsey mask of a Sagittarius Ascendant.

Hall's luminaries aspect his Mars and Jupiter. Our next subject is very different. Her Sun and Moon are sextiled by rigid Saturn, and her Mars is in water, rather than a fire sign.

Jennifer Aniston
2/11/1969, 10:22 P.M.
Los Angeles, CA

Jennifer played a charming, free-spirited and ditsy character in TV's *Friends*—a role made to order from her chart. (See Lisa Kudow's portrait on page 176)

♒ SUN: Aquarius

First of all, "friends" is a key word for Aquariuses. They always seem to have a multitude of such acquaintances. So it was with Aniston's TV character. She was a social gadfly, who was friendly to everybody!

The UL photo captures the electric expression of surprise that Aquariuses regularly display. The UR photo shows "the connection that you sense" when they greet you as a friend. Beware, for just when you think that you're on "the same wavelength together", they will bounce away to greet another friend—and leave you there, standing alone and confused.

Jenny's Aquarius Sun squares Mars and Neptune which are conjoined in Scorpio. These are her only water planets, but they give her the sultry illusion, and the magnetic physicality that made her a star.

Moon: Sagittarius

With a Moon in mutable Sagittarius, Jenny's emotional reactions heat up and scatter her airy solar energies. This lunar placement gives us a free spirited lady—but not totally—for her Saturn sextiles her Sun and trines her Moon. This gives her a dry sense of humor, as well as the discipline to orchestrate a very successful career.

After the *Friends* gig, she moved on to the silver screen and became a media producer. In 2014, she produced and starred in the highly acclaimed film *Cake*.

Ascendant: Libra

When her Aquarius is not rebelling and her Centurion Moon isn't kicking up its heels, Jennifer presents her pleasant and charming persona. When the cardinal air of her Libra Ascendant moves to the front, it balances the winds of her impulsive Sun—as it calms her emotional fires!

Libra's wide smile and sparkling eyes were always there in *Friends* and this charming persona was also seen in *Picture Perfect*, a film where Jenny played a public relations consultant, who manipulated the exterior image of people. She found that these images can be altered, but they will never mask the true nature of the real person—the appearance that people see in the Ascendant.

A Questionable Ascendant?

Oprah Winfrey

1/29/1954, 4:30 A.M. (?)
Kosciusko, MS

At Oprah's birth, the heavens provided an opportunity for "fixed air" to find new levels of expression. Not only was the Sun in Aquarius, four planets were in Air signs and five planets were in fixed signs. Notably, many people were born at this time, but it was Oprah who used these gifts to become the most successful communicator of her time!

 SUN: Aquarius

Watch as the antenna fingers of Aquarius search for distant radio waves. When incoming data is received, the breath seizes with a deep gasp, as the whole body shivers, then freezes. This draws the mouth tightly down to expose the lower gum. The resulting expression reflects a look of awe and surprise.

Moon: Sagittarius

When Oprah becomes emotional, watch her exuberant reactions: "Wow!" "Amazing!" Oprah's archer arrows are shooting at the Moon— to light the path, to explore a huge array of grand ideas. The radiant light of these luminaries gives us a personality who appears to be friendly, as well as open to everyone.

Ascendant: Sagittarius?

In 1999, the recorded birth time gave Oprah a Virgo Ascendant. The new time is the rounded figure above. This gives Oprah 29°+ of Sagittarius Rising. With this time, she has no Earth in her chart, and just a few minutes later gives her a Capricorn Ascendant. Would not this Cardinal Earth give her the substance she needed to build her giant business empire?

The LR photo shows what happens, when Oprah's luminaries are in repose. Note how the inactive flesh sets on the underlying bone structure. You will also notice that the long face of the horse is missing. This may be due to her Moon being in the Leo Decan and her fixed Sun, or it may be her Sun's square to Capricorn's ruler Saturn. Whatever, the high cheek bones still suggest that Capricorn is rising.

Earthy Capricorn would explain this lady's conventional attire. A double Centaur would likely be wearing fiery colored and free-flowing clothing. Furthermore, there's Oprah's dedicated sense of duty, that she displays in her work and Aquarian crusades. This author sticks with her having a Capricorn Ascendant.

This shows why it is hard to guess a questionable Ascendant.

Set the stage on fire!
Justin Timberlake
1/31/1981, 6:30 P.M.
Millington, TN

 SUN: Aquarius

As a member of *The New Mickey Mouse Club*, Justin showed the enthusiasm of a typical "Disney performer", presenting the cheery optimism of his Aquarius Sun. But, with Uranus (the ruler of his Sun) in Scorpio, this sugary image wouldn't last. As Justin grew more independent, he mocked many social taboos, as his solar expressions took on explicit sexual overtones.

Be it with the group 'N Synch or in his work with other recording artists, Justin often collaborates with others. This is inspired by his Sun's trine to Saturn and Jupiter—in partner friendly Libra.

Justin shows many of the traits of Aquarius. The square forehead and jaw are more pronounced, since he also has a fixed Ascendant.

Leo Ascendant

Justin's Leo Rising spotlights the stage upon which he stands, as it lights the path of his theatrical pursuits. This fiery mask gives him the thick mane and wide chin, often seen in a lion.

Sagittarius Moon

With Neptune dancing on his Centaur Moon, Timberlake's emotions can be wildly reactive or sublimely imaginative. His Moon's sextile to Mars in Aquarius makes him emotionally more playful and wary of permanent attachments. There were many abrupt changes in his early relationships.

The Infamous Wardrobe Malfunction

At Super Bowl XXXVIII (Feb. 1, 2004, about 7:30 p.m., Houston, TX), Justin and Janet Jackson shocked the world with the legendary "Nipplegate". At this revealing moment, the transiting Moon had just finished a grand square in the sky with Venus, Jupiter and Pluto.

Notably, this Pluto was also sitting on Justin's natal Moon and Neptune, while the transiting Moon was in opposition in his *10th House*! In addition, there were many other intriguing aspects, too numerous to list here. It was a strange moment in the heavens, and also one for the Super Bowl.

Just for fun, you may want to study these transits, and compare them with Timberlake's chart. Was it a defiant act? Or was it *an act of destiny?* You may be fascinated by what the stars can reveal!

Ellen DeGeneres
1/26/1958, 3:30 A.M.
Metairie, LA

Chris Rock
2/7/1965, 10:00 A.M.
Andrews, SC

♒ Suns: Aquarius

With the fixed mental energy of Air, these "bearers of light" pour out their wordy diatribes and outrageous streams of thought.

These folks have similar Neptune and Jupiter aspects. The big difference is Uranus (Aquarius' ruling planet).

This electric generator opposes Ellen's Sun, while it trines her Moon. In contrast, Chris' Uranus conjoins Pluto while it lies in opposition to Saturn. Ellen's electrical lights are well lit, while Chris' appear much darker. His comedy has a harder edge, and it is far more disturbing than that of Ellen's.

The upper photos shows optimistic zeal of Aquarius, as well as the whimsical expressions of Fixed Air.

Moons: Aries

With Aries Moons, both of these comedians are driven to express their feelings, in a direct and pointed manner. Watch how their airy Suns heat up, when their fiery lunar emotions charge to the front.

Ellen's Aries Moon trines a Mars and Saturn conjunction in Sagittarius. The ringed planet's placement on her Mars (the ruler of Aries) restrains her lunar emotions. This gives her a remarkable comedic gift for "understatement".

Rock's Moon and Ascendant are both in Aries. This explains why his comedy is one of "overstatement". With his Mars in Virgo, it also is never simplistic. Mars accounts for Chris' nervous physical energy, as well as his tendency to be obsessed with small details.

Fiery Ascendants

Rock's Aries Ascendant places his Moon and Jupiter in his 1st House. His Jupiter trines Uranus and squares his Sun. This makes Chris' comedy more exaggerative and aggressive than Ellen's.

Ellen's Sagittarius Ascendant sextiles her Venus and Sun (and these two components square Neptune). Ideas are rarely held back by this blunt and truthful Ascendant. Fortunately, with these Venus/Neptune aspects, Ellen is always considerate of others.

With their Moons in the same element as their Ascendants, the lower photos capture the essence of both components. Ellen's photo shows the skewed lines and protruding jaw of the horse. In Chris' Moon photo, we see the vertically stretched features of a Ram.

Joseph Gordon-Levitt
2/27/1981, 8:08 A.M.
Los Angeles, CA

Joseph Gordon-Levitt's career debut was in Robert Redford's *A River Runs Through It* (1992). After a string of film roles, he found his claim to fame in the hit television series *3rd Rock from the Sun* (1996-2001). In this series, he played a highly intelligent and boastful character in a family of space aliens. It was a perfect role for someone with an Aquarius Sun and a Leo Moon.

Sun in Aquarius Moon in Leo

Even though he had won several awards on *3rd Rock*, Joseph was anxious to move beyond his secure position in TV comedy and begin his work in small independent films. This attitude can be attributed to his Sun, Mercury and Venus. All are in the highly independent sign of Aquarius! This move was also assisted by the emotional confidence he felt with his Leo Moon.

In Gorden-Levitt's luminaries, we see the fixed force that gives his features a square and cubical shape. There's also the masculine polarity that activates the expansive urge to attach to external sources and forces—that exist outside the light of his luminaries.

In the cool atmosphere of his Fixed Air Sun, Joseph seems to be connecting with concepts far beyond his personal thoughts. As he intuitively focuses on these distant ideas, his tilted eyelids appear to "flap inward from the sides". This action compacts the facial elements into the center of the face.

In contrast, when Joseph emotionally responds, the warm and magnetic glow of Leo radiates outward—to attract the attention of others! This fiery force reshapes the flesh to mold the feline eyes, flat cheekbones and puffy jowls of a prideful lion.

Ascendant: Aries

Joseph's underlying bone structure mimics the concave features and large snout of Aries. However, his persona shows little of the frontal charging force of the Ram. This could be due to the fact that Joseph's Mars (the ruling planet of Aries) is in Pisces! With this Mars, Joseph's physical metabolism runs in a meandering and liquid manner. This is what we saw in his youthful character in *Third Rock*. Another factor is Neptune's placement near his Midheaven in joyful Sagittarius. Sag gives him a gift for comedy. Neptune explains why his public sees him as being soft and sensitive, rather than aggressive like a Ram.

Add a splash of Water

John Travolta
2/18/1954, 2:53 P.M.
Englewood, NJ

John Travolta danced to a different drum when he portrayed eccentric and free-spirited characters on TV and film. He often played the latest social conception of "what was cool." In *Welcome Back Kotter*, he was the hippest kid in the class. After *Saturday Night Fever*, white suits became plentiful at discos. Nearly twenty years later, in the movie *Phenomenon*—he communicated new age ideas in a '90s way!

In *Pulp Fiction*, Travolta's dimpled grin returned to prominence, as he (once again) showed his ability to remain nonchalant and collected, even in the most grisly of situations. This was followed by *Face Off*—a movie that showed us John's Aquarian gift for "total mental control". In the 1997 film on "switched identities", Travolta's cold blue eyes would reveal little about "the person within". Oddly, that is the way you feel, when you meet a new Aquarius friend for the first time.

Ascendant: Cancer

When the luminaries recede, the cardinal tides wash the crab onto the shore. Quickly, this creature checks out its new surroundings. If all is well, we see the crab's beaming face, with its rounded lunar temples and the large pupillage in the eyes. If things appear insecure, the crab raises its claws for protection, steps backwards—and then returns to the comfort of the sea below.

Since his Cancer Ascendant is ruled by the Moon, John's appearance also takes on the attributes of the sign in which his Moon is placed.

Moon: Virgo

When John steps outside the door of his Cancer Ascendant, he is forced to interact with his surroundings.

With his Moon in Virgo, John's first emotional instinct is to "digest the input from his senses". In the process, he becomes highly mercuric and talkative. Often there is also the noted presence of worry.

With Saturn in Scorpio sextile his Moon, these mercuric feelings are markedly restrained and controlled. Also, Virgo's ruling planet Mercury is in dreamy Pisces, and it trines Uranus.

This rebellious is the closest planet to John's Rising Sign, and it makes him appear emotionally distant. Mercury in Pisces makes it difficult for him to express his emotions. Thusly, it is difficult for Travolta to display any of his more sensitive feelings.

Nathan Lane
2/3/1956, 2:29 P.M.
Jersey City, NJ

Nathan Lane is an acclaimed film, TV and Broadway star. Who can forget his performance in the film *The Bird Cage* (which won him the American Comedy Award for funniest actor in a motion picture). On Broadway, he brought the house down with *A Funny Thing Happened On The Way To The Forum* and *The Producers*. He also played reoccurring comedic roles in TV's *Fraiser, Modern Family* and *Mad about You*.

Nathan's work is outrageously broad and also markedly emotional and controlled. His chart shows us why.

Sun in Aquarius
Moon in Scorpio

Nathan's Sun and Moon are both in fixed signs with opposing polarities.

In his Aquarius Sun, we see the fixed force in its expansive mode, constantly reaching out to connect to outer sources for ideas. This data is stored in the mind, until the surprising moment—when the "water bearer" decides to empty the precious vase. Watch how the compacted face of Aquarius appears, as Lane's dishes out the information.

Oddly, the traits of Aquarius are rarely seen in this timid soul. This is due to Lane's Sun being the only air in his chart—and it's ruling planet Uranus is in Cancer. Also, Lane's Ascendant and Moon are in feminine water signs, and Venus sits in Pisces on his Midheaven.

This switch to feminine energy can be seen when Nathan's Scorpio Moon is activated. In these reactive moments, the pupils become noticeably larger, as they draw us into the inner sanctum behind his eyes. The two right photos show how his luminary expressions change from one of "openness" to one of "veiled secrecy".

Ascendant: Cancer

In talk show interviews, Lane readily presents his friendly, effervescent and chatty solar personality. However, what we see physically is quite different. The long legs and flat chest of Aquarius are nowhere to be seen. Rather, we see the large shell of Lane's upper torso—with its stubby arms and legs. This body shape is associated with the Cancer Crab—the sign of Nathan's Ascendant.

When Nathan enters the room, we often see the dumpling-shaped flesh of a shy Cancer. This image is reinforced when the tides come to an abrupt halt, when Lane's reactive Scorpio Moon sends him into "protective mode". With this Aquarius Sun, you will never know which way it will go.

~ ~
Lost in these swirling waters, we now enter the next sign in the Zodiac: Pisces

 Pisces

	Page
Introduction to Pisces Traits	63-65
Johnny Cash & Vanessa Redgrave	
Albert Einstein/Edgar Cayce	66
Emily Blunt	67

The Passages of Life
Drew Barrymore	68
Dakota Fanning	69

The waters run deep
Alan Rickman	70
George Harrison	71

Shades of Aquarius
Bruce Willis	72
Glenn Close	73
Steve Irwin	74-75

Contain the Water with Earth
Bon Jovi	76
Gary Sinise/William H. Macy	77
Billy Crystal	78
Queen Latifah	79

Fire spreads across the land
Elizabeth Taylor	80
Alan Greenspan/Rupert Murdoch	81
Ron Howard	82
Steve Jobs	83
Daniel Craig	84

Pisces  February 19 to March 20
Feminine Polarity, Mutable Water
Dream the impossible dream; Imagine the possibilities

When the New Year began, the cardinal Earth of **Capricorn** drove many to pursue their future goals. A month later, intuitive **Aquarius** brought new ideas and resolutions into focus—to spark the hopes and wishes of everyone!

Now, when the Sun enters **Pisces**, the warming light is melting Winter's snow and the universal solvent of water is flowing freely again! It is now time to release ourself from all of our previous pursuits, and accept that our creative efforts are complete. With this "letting go", all of those previous endeavors are made available to serve everyone. Imagine the possibilities, when they ignite the creative spark in thousands of individuals around the world.

In the interweaving currents of **Pisces**, the feelings of all individuals are magically connected. This gives our Pisces friends an uncanny ability to feel and anticipate the actions of others. With this, they can dance in synchronicity with the movements of others—just like we see in a school of fish! These souls know that every misguided action by one, inevitably affects all of the others—and *"What you give, will determine what you will receive in return".*

Many of these water creatures believe that there is a divine power in operation on this Earth. Perhaps that is why they are so willing to "take a leap in faith"—and bite on every twinkling lure that shines before their eyes! It is this selfless empathy that also enables them to "walk in the shoes of others".

With this compassion for others, it is often difficult for Pisces to fulfill their desires or complete their own creative goals. Fortunately, with the nurturing support and unwavering determination of their **Cancer** and **Scorpio** friends, they can find the emotional balance, to dance in step with the rhythms of Nature—and made their imagined dreams a reality!

It is the intuitive emotions of Pisces, that allows others to "swim in the flow of Nature's currents". In this stream, the path ahead is clearly seen—and this inspires many individuals to begin their own creative adventure! This journey of self discovery begins at the Spring Equinox, when the Sun enters **Aries**.

♆ Ruling Planet~Neptune (Traditionally, also Jupiter)

Neptune is the ruling planet of Pisces and Lord of the Ocean. She reigns over liquids, oil, perfume, fishing, and all things nautical. This planet represents the higher octave of Venus and all of the illusions created in the imagination— i.e., the arts of dance, music and poetry—or the healing found in hospitals or religious inspiration. This planet also represents the altered states of mind induced by drugs, anaesthetics, the thalamus, and all things that distort perception. The darker manifestations are seen in Neptune's rulership of poisons, insanity and prisons.

The "feeling of universal connection" runs strong in individuals with a Pisces Sun, Moon, Rising Sign, or a strongly aspected Neptune. This sensitivity becomes more apparent when planets transit Pisces' home in the 12th House.

Pisces Physical Traits:

With the presence of Water, the facial flesh appears round and bubbly. However, when Nature's mutable forces are activated, the water pressure constantly changes in different areas of the face. With this, the facial features bob up and down as they drift from side to side—like flotsam on the ocean's surface!

In more excited moments, Pisces' undulating facial features become more pronounced. This often floats one eye upward, as the other sinks to the ocean floor. In moments of luminary inaction, the facial flesh tends to droop and sag, since water always runs down hill.

The wide, inflated cheek bones are the inflated buoys, that keep the eyes and brows above the wavy surface. These cheek bones and the ballooning skull appear to be the only solid structure in this liquid face.

Johnny Cash
2/26/1932, 7:30 A.M.
Kingsland, AR

Lynn Redgrave
3/8/1943, 8:15 A.M.
London, UK

The Pisces Suns of these two celebrities show the oblique bone structure as well as the skewed molding of the flesh. Johnny shows how the eyes can be large and full; Lynn shows us how the eyes and brow align to form the shape of a rolling wave. Both eyes seemingly sit on the side of the face, as they offer port and starboard views of the worlds.

Pisces Body Language

As the body rulership slides into the feet, the feet of the fish paddle "to the front". Consequently, these Fish seem incapable of pursuing a forward assault. After all, the body is weighted to the back by the ballooning head, shoulders and upper back. This bulging mass becomes the "life preserver" that keeps Pisces' from sinking into the depths below.

Miraculously, the meridians in the feet connect to all parts of the body. With each step, these connective circuits send out their liquid biorhythmic pulses—to stimulate the body's desires, thoughts and feelings. Naturally, this keeps the physical body whole and healthy.

With the changing ocean currents, the fish is often redirected by forces greater than their own. It is the alternating flap of their paddling feet that keeps them on course—to follow their paths of destiny!

Pisces rules the Feet

Above and Below, Everything is Guided by the Ticking Clock of Time

♓ Albert Einstein Edgar Cayce
& the 2013 Pluto/Uranus Square

These two men showed the world how "everything is connected" as they saw the past and future manifestations of Time on a universal scale. Appropriately, they are our opening subjects for Pisces.

Both men were born in a rare multi-generational square of Uranus to Pluto in an Earth Sign! When Pluto transits an Earth sign, the *mysteries of the physical universe* are exposed. When Uranus squares this outer planet—*individual intuitions are activated* to recognize new directions (and dimensions) in physical reality and social consciousness.

In 1762, the last time Pluto entered Capricorn (while also squaring Uranus in Aries), the seeds of revolution were planted in the minds of American colonists (including a 30 year old George Washington). This gave the world a new nation—and a new form of governance.

In the 1870's, this powerful aspect appeared again, giving the world a generation of intuitive minds. The most notable were physicist **Albert Einstein** (born 3/14/1879, 11:30 A.M., Ulm, Germany) and psychic **Edgar Cayce** (3/18/1877, 3:20 P.M., Hopkinsville, KY). This brought the world an era of incredible scientific and spiritual advances.

In 2013, Uranus began another square to Pluto in the Earth sign of Capricorn and another era of massive "physical and spiritual discoveries". To give us hints on what this aspect may bring to those born in this period, we will look at it's effect on our two subjects.

Pisces Suns

Albert's Jupiter opposed his natal Uranus as it formed a T-square with Pluto. This giant planet (in the sign of Aquarius), gave him his intuitive gift for "seeing the bigger picture".

In contrast, Edgar's Pluto was near his midheaven, sextiling his Sun in the Scorpio-ruled 8th House. Cayce found a way to use the universal power of Pluto, to heal the physical bodies of his clients.

Moons: Sagittarius & Taurus

With different Moon Sign aspects, these men had contrasting lunar reactions.

Einstein's Sagittarius Moon trined this Aries Venus. Instantly, he sensed Time on a grand scale—i.e., his *Theory of Relativity*!

In contrast, Cayce's Taurus Moon sextiled Saturn. Emotionally, he could feel the cogs in Saturn's clock. This enabled him to make his remarkable predictions.

Ascendants: Cancer & Leo

Einstein's Cancer Ascendant placed all of his components on the left side. He was a self driven person.

Cayce's Leo Ascendant weights the right side of his chart with components. He was guided by other forces beyond his control.

The Zodiac Wheel Turns, as Time Progresses On
Emily Blunt
2/23/1983, no time
London, UK

Einstein and Cayce showed how outer planet transits define the changes in an Era. Here, we show how progressions bring recognizable alterations in one's personality. (See intro on page 3).

Sun: Pisces Moon in Cancer

In 2004, Emily caught the public's eye, winning a Golden Globe for "Best Supporting Actress" for her role in the TV miniseries *Gideon's Daughter* and a BAFTA nod for her role in *The Devil Wears Prada*. The fantasy side of her Pisces Sun was seen in the wonderfully serendipitous *Salmon Fishing in the Yemen* and the film *Into the Woods*, a extravagant retelling of *Little Red Riding Hood*.

In these fantasy roles, Emily's face would project the skewed lines of mutability, as well as the oblique and bubbly features of water. Note how one eye floats some distance above the other—and how the eye sockets appear to drift off to the sides—to give this fish a portal view of her surroundings.

Emily's Sun forms a grand trine with her Cancer Moon and a Saturn/Pluto conjunction in Scorpio. Saturn stabilizes the fluidity of her luminaries as it gives her a remarkable ability to control the image she projects to others.

Emily's Sun also sextiles its ruling planet Neptune, and this dreamy planet also forms a square with her Pisces Mars and Aries Venus. Furthermore, a conjoined Jupiter and Uranus in Sagittarius squares her Sun. This makes her Sun the most aspected component in her chart. With those Centaur fires, her Pisces and Neptune energies run strong! These aspects give Emily a gift for performing a wide range of dramatic/comedic and fantasy roles. This all changed when her Sun progressed into Aries.

Sun progresses into Aries

By 2010, Emily's Mercury, Sun and Mars had all progressed into Aries. Around that period, Emily finished her work on the fantasy *Gulliver's Travels* and the animated movie *Gnomeo and Juliet*. Soon after, she began her regimented physical and martial arts training to "buff herself up" for the action films *Edge of Tomorrow* and the 2015 film *Sicario*. This fish had turned herself into a warrior!

This progression from Pisces to Aries can also be seen in Blunt's physical appearance. The LR photo (circa 2014) shows a leaner and longer face that suggests the features of a Ram.

Previously, we explained how the cycles of time change the course of events, as well as the nature of one's making. Now, we'll show how the Earth's 3 major "light cycles" represent the passages in human growth, and how all of Nature's light creations are connected to a common source. That is what our Pisces friends feel—all of the time!

Drew Barrymore
2/22/1975, 11:51 A.M.
Culver City, CA

Moon: Childhood

From birth to 8 years or so, children have few shields and little self identity. Their initial response is to "react emotionally" to their worlds—"Ouch, stove hot!" They are expressing the qualities of their Moon. *(Check this out with your little rascals!)*

At six years old, Drew won world fame with her "beaming" performance in *E.T.* This child had a gift for "moving our emotions". She was the one who had the mothering persistence—to keep the little alien out of harm's way.

With her **Cancer Moon**, this sensitive child needed the comforts of a loving home. However, Drew has her natal Saturn joining her Moon (and Mars in opposition). She faced an abusive father and emotional suffering. At age 9, Drew was doing drugs and at the age of 13, she was placed in rehabilitation. With these experiences, she all too quickly rushed through her Ascendant's door—to face the demands of adolescence.

Ascendant: Adolescence

Relying on their lunar memories and instincts, Drew entered the next phase as she began to "find her place in the world". What she saw through the door of her **Gemini Ascendant** was a world of conflicting dualities! Drew grew up all too quickly—shocking others with her constantly changing public persona. She became known as the "Wild Child of Hollywood"! This mutable air also gave her the flexibility to change and adapt and star in different genres of film. In true Gemini style, she wrote a book about her early fame and tragedies.

Sun: Adulthood

In adulthood, Drew's **Pisces Sun** finally found "the peace within". In the Cinderella fable, *Ever After*, Drew seemed like a totally different person. Emotionally, she appeared happy and connected. Soon, she began to portray characters who suffered greatly, but still found goodness in other people. Notably, her friends insisted that she is just as compassionate in her real life: "She easily connects with the feelings of others". "She has a sincere desire to give energy back to others".

In adulthood, Drew finally learned to use the *totality* of her chart's potential as she found ways to express her soul's purpose to the world.

A change of signs makes a difference!

Dakota Fanning
2/23/1994, 10:00 A.M.
Conyers, GA

At the age of 6, Dakota made her breakthrough in the acclaimed *I am Sam*. This film won her Critics Choice's *Best Young Actress* award. She became the most recognized child star at the start of the millennium.

Moon in Leo

As noted with **Drew Barrymore**, children begin life by "reacting to their worlds" with their Moons, rather than their Suns or Ascendants.

With a Leo Moon, Fanning showed the self-assured pose of the Lion in many of her earlier roles. (See lower left photo). This precocious child instinctively expressed her theatrical qualities, often upstaging her adult co-stars with her fiery lunar reactions. (She was not the moody child that we saw in the early years of Drew Barrymore's career).

Ascendant: Taurus

Continuing with this approach, let's look at the next passage in life, when youngsters grow beyond their childhood reactions and proceed to become obsessed with their appearance. This image (or how one thinks he or she should be seen by others) is often shaped by the sign of a person's Ascendant.

At "sweet 16", Dakota's image changed as her feline eyes took on a bovine appearance—as she proudly displayed the sensuality of her Taurus Ascendant.

With her role in the *Twilight Sagas: New Moon* and *Eclipse*, Dakota created her new "public image". Playing a controlling and evil vampire, Dakota showed us a dark intensity not seen previously in her work. However, with her Ascendant's sextile to her Sun, this focus on "heaviness" was short lived, for soon, Dakota's work began to express the light of her Pisces Sun.

 Sun: Pisces

When Dakota entered adulthood, the fixed assurance and determination of her younger years became less obvious, as hints of Dakota's soft solar expressions became more apparent. (This was seen in her large dreamy eyes and in her liquid facial expressions).

However, Fanning's vulnerable Sun conjoins her Saturn. As she aged, this dreamy Pisces' work would became more substantive and serious.

In 2013 and 2014, she starred as a young bride in *Effie Gray* and *The Last of Robin Hood* (a depiction of Errol Flynn's career destroying marriage). Three years later, she began production on a remake of the physiological drama *The Bell Jar*. With her fixed components, she was determined to endure in her career.

The Fish Swims In The Sea
Alan Rickman 2/21/1946, no time / London, UK

Alan Rickman was a member of the Royal Shakespeare Company, but most of us recognize him for the unsympathetic characters he played in many films. His role as Hans Gruber in *Die Hard* earned him the 46th spot on the list of AFI's *Top 100 Villains*. His role as the Sheriff of Nottingham in 1991's *Robin Hood: Prince of Thieves* was also delightfully villainous. Shortly after, he branched out into fantasy and comedic roles, like we saw in *Dogma, Galaxy Quest* and *The Hitchhiker's Guide to the Galaxy*. He is best known for his role as Professor Severus Snape in the *Harry Potter* films.

Sun in Pisces

Amazingly, Rickman's chart is totally connected. First, his Sun conjoins his Mercury and Venus; All three trine his Scorpio Moon. ALL of his components form a trine with at least one of the others. Wow! The aspects are too numerous to list, so you have to check out his chart.

These interlinked water signs gave Alan a gift for displaying a wide range of emotions. The aspects explain why he was "totally submerged in his characters" and why this fish had a powerful imagination, a delightful sense of fantasy and an outrageous touch of lunacy!

Alan's face often appeared bubbly and saturated. When it became activated by the undulating waves of mutable water, it gave us the amazed, bewildered and joyful expressions of his Pisces Sun. They were a delight to watch!

Moon in Scorpio

In his role in the *Harry Potter Franchise*, Alan garnered a new generation of fans, as well as critical acclaim. In his review of the final Harry Potter film: *The Deathly Hallows: Part 2*, Peter Travers of *Rolling Stone* noted that Rickman was "sublime at giving us a glimpse at last into the secret nurturing heart that...Snape masks with a sneer." The nurturing heart may be a product of his Cancer Mars and its trine to his Pisces Venus. Meanwhile, Alan's sardonic sneer can be attributed to Saturn's conjunction to his Mars, and his Moon's square to Scorpio's ruling planet Pluto.

With these many lunar aspects, Alan's Scorpio emotions are powerfully presented, so much that it changes his appearance and body language.

The sharply focused and piercing eyes in the LR photo reveal the mysterious intensity of Alan's lunar reactions. The UR profile photo shows how these fixed emotions curve the upper back to the front, as they tilt the head sharply to the front. This profile image resembles what we see in an Eagle.

The profile pic suggests qualities of a fixed Ascendant, but the long face suggest some thing else. What is your guess?

George Harrison
2/24/1943, 11:42 P.M.
Liverpool, England

The Beatles were a combination of Air and Water personalities. Libra *John* and Gemini *Paul* provided the words and "mind music". Cancer *Ringo* and Pisces *George* were the water signs who provided the "rhythm and flow"—as they added dimensional layers to the sound of the band. *(Paul's portrait is on page 148. John's is on page 225).*

 Sun: Pisces

With a Pisces Sun and a Scorpio Moon, George became the group's mystic, as he introduced the sitar and India's spiritualism to the band. His compositions (*Here Comes The Sun, My Sweet Lord*) often had a spiritual tone. *All Those Years Ago*, his loving tribute to John Lennon, was incredibly emotional.

George's creative nature was enhanced by his Venus' opposition to Neptune, and its trine to Pluto and sextile to Uranus. This explains his involvement in many humanitarian projects. He organized the *Concert for Bangladesh*, the 1971 precursor for all of the benefit concerts that followed. He also started his own music and film production company. Their comedy *Time Bandits* was a big hit. These talents can also be attributed to George's Sun and its square to a conjoined Saturn and Uranus. Saturn's discipline helped him to achieve his goals.

Scorpio Moon

With his Moon in the 1st House and its square to Pluto (on the Midheaven), George's Scorpion energies run strong. This Moon also trines his Pisces Sun. This explains the heavy stream of Pluto and Neptune imagery in his work.

Of all of the Beatles, Harrison's private life seems to be the most secretive. He was the one who went into the longest period of hiding after the group's breakup. As the press became more aggressive, he'd became more reclusive. (Note: In contrast, Lennon's Air and Fire sent him on a wild binge).

Libra Ascendant

On stage, George was the most serene and quiet of the bunch, for he rarely pushed his way into the spot-light. Save for the cheery "yeah, yeah, yeah songs", George exhibited little of the airy energies of Libra. What we saw was a relaxed persona, but the eagle-beaked mask of Scorpio. His Scorpio Moon sits just two degrees from his Libra Ascendant!

This force was seen in George's compositions: *Taxman* and *Piggies*. Both were stinging indictments of social injustices.

Bruce Willis
3/19/1955, 6:33 P.M.
Idar-Oberstein, Germany

 Sun: Pisces

With *Hudson Hawk* and *North*, Bruce took us to worlds few of us could comprehend. With the *Diehard* films, he gave us a reluctant hero, who runs on his feelings, predicting the mind-boggling destruction that always followed. Through it all, he softly mutters his streaming dialog on "how things could be better—if only?" And he wonders aloud, "What am I doing here?" No matter how hard the reality, this Pisces still finds time to fantasize.

In those moments of doubt, Bruce expresses the mannerisms of a true Pisces! Watch his heavy eyelids tilt sideways and how his eyes point in two directions. They make him look like he's in some other world. He is!

Ascendant: Virgo

This fish often appears grounded, like a ship on the reef, anchored to Earth but still teetering. With a mutable Sun and Ascendant, the sands and currents are always shifting. With Virgo Rising, he protects himself with a constant surface of analytical chatter, but unlike most Virgo Ascendants, he often seems to have a ruffled and disorderly appearance. This lackadaisical nature is likely due to his 7th House Sun. It's distance from his Rising Sign disarms any concern on how he may appear to others.

The presence of Earth in Bruce's character becomes more apparent, when he goes into action! Bruce's natal Mars is in Taurus (opposed by Saturn). His movements are slow and rigid.

Moon: Aquarius

In the TV show *Moonlighting*, Willis was called "the fastest mouth in prime time." He played a finger-popping wise-guy whose dialog included: "Does a picket fence?" Does butter fly?" and the strange "Great Googlymoogly!" In this show Bruce won fame for the outrageous reactions of his Aquarius Moon!

When Bruce reacts to others, his eyes lock on hold, seemingly looking inward. His face appears momentarily fixed as he receives his "reactive material." Then impulsively, he pours it back out, surprising everyone with his inspired lunacy.

Bruce's co-star in this series was **Cybill Shepherd**. His Moon was in the same sign as her Sun and her Moon conjoined his Pisces Sun. Each one's Solar expression would light up the other's Moon, as it prompted a complementary response. Their psyches were in perfect sync! Perhaps that's how *Moonlighting* got its name?

Glenn Close
3/19/1947, 2:12 PM
(EST) Greenwich, CT

♓ Sun: Pisces

When Glenn Close performs in her theatrical roles, she totally submerges herself into her characters. In her own words, she describes the essence of her Pisces Sun: *"I really think that effective acting has to do literally with the movement of molecules."* It's no wonder she does for acting what her fellow Pisces Albert Einstein did for physics. Everything becomes part of a unified creative act.

The upper photos capture the two expressions of Pisces. One presents the "look of puzzlement and confusion". The other: a beguiling look of "total contentment". For Pisces, everything is connected—or it's not.

Ascendant: Leo

When Close enters a room, she instantly attracts attention, as she presents the aristocratic mask of her Leo Ascendant. Oddly, Close's sense of majesty is not always out front. This may be due to her Rising Sign's sextile to her Sun's ruling planet Neptune in serene Libra. On first impression, as we saw in Glenn's role as the reincarnated 1920's flapper *Maxie*, she appears confident and pleasant. But wait, that pleasantry is just a momentary Neptunian illusion. Who can forget Glenn's intensely disturbing and powerful performance in *Fatal Attraction*—or the hints of evil that were seen in *Dangerous Liaison* and *Reversal of Fortune*. Yes, the planet Pluto conjoins Glenn's Ascendant!

Moon: Aquarius

In emotional moments, this Pisces' concern for individuals quickly chills, as Glenn's Moon locks on to the far greater humanitarian concepts, that she is feeling in her head. With Uranus (Aquarius' ruling planet) forming a grand trine with her Moon and Neptune in Air Signs, Glenn often appears "emotionally distant".

Positively, these aspects gives her a very inventive imagination. It was all there in her wacky role as Cruela De Vil in the film *101 Dalmatians*. This hammy and wicked performance had all the appearances of Leo/Pluto and the bizarreness of Aquarius! Ditto with her role in Tim Burton's hilarious film *Mars Attack*.

Off-camera, Glenn is said to be rowdy and playful. Why not? Leo and Aquarius always want to have fun. All the while, Pisces' imaginary images are swirling in her head—and soon, she will joyfully present them to the world.

Steve Irwin
"The Crocodile Hunter"
2/22/1962, 4:18 A.M.
Essendon, Australia

At certain times, the energies apparent at a moment of birth are very unusual, and they suggest that a special creative potential awaits. There will be many people who share similar chart characteristics, but only a few will have the circumstances and determined will to fulfill the potential. Steve Irwin, the famed *Crocodile Hunter* stands out as such a person.

♓ Sun: Pisces

Raised on his parent's Australian zoo, Irwin nurtured his dream—to protect wild life, animals and the environment. Guided by his Pisces Sun, Irwin soon found the creative voice of his Venus (also in Pisces). Consumed by his passion, Steve's Aquarius Mars (and its square to his Sun's ruler Neptune) drove him to manifest the intuitive concepts that would make his dream a reality. With these inventive ideas, Irwin won the hearts of millions, as he made his family Zoo known all around the world.

Irwin strongly showed the physical traits of the Pisces fish. Notably, he had the oblique skull which seemed to be coated in bubbly layers of ever-changing, liquid flesh. The heavy-lidded and deep-pooled eyes drifted up and down and sideways, shifting with the twisting facial currents as they reflected his innermost emotions and feelings.

Moon: Virgo

Irwin's Moon was in the late degrees of Virgo. These mercuric lunar forces added an analytical precision to Irwin's dreamy Sun. In his reactions, you may recall how he was so gifted at verbalizing the details of "what he was seeing". In contrast, his Neptunian solar expressions were often lost for words, but full of heartfelt feelings.

This lunar placement makes some people sensitive to personal criticism— but it also gives them an ability to defend their ideas and actions in precise detail. We saw this in Irwin's response to the "dangling of his son before an alligator" incident. Rarely did we see him so emotionally concise.

When Irwin reacts, his watery solar expressions solidify into crystalline form. The facial components are still skewed by the mutable forces, but they are more obvious, since the flesh is contained in the element of Earth. Note how the flesh is less inflated and how it makes the face appear longer and leaner.

Ascendant: Aquarius

When Steve was a subject in *Dell Horoscope's Celebrity Snapshots* (2007), dirty data sources gave him Capricorn and Aquarius Rising. This author wrote:

"Pictures of Irwin presenting this reserved mask were hard to find. In front of a camera, Steve never seemed to show the serious persona of a goat." This article also stated that Steve had a *"weak goat mask but this could be due to the four Aquarius planets and the powerful aspects in his chart."* The article also noted that Irwin had no cardinal planets in his chart—and *"his drive to build an empire supported the possibility of him having Capricorn Rising".* This shows the frustration that one faces, when one attempts to justify incorrect data.

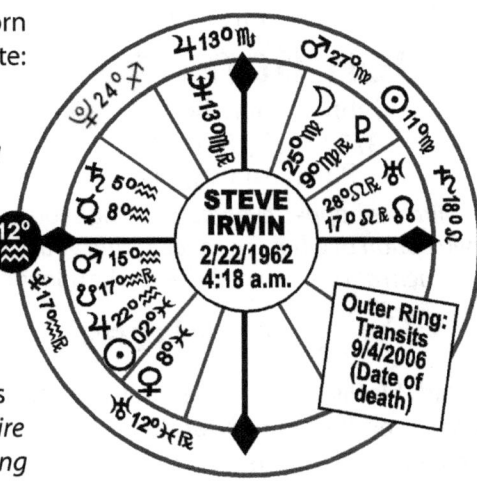

Notably, the new data supports the comments in the article—since it places Mars on Steve's Aquarius Rising Sign (a possibility this writer did not consider at the time). Yep, that Mars would give him the "drive" that he needed to make his family zoo a top tourist attraction.

Still, Irwin's physical bone structure appears to be a mix of Capricorn and that of Aquarius. The high and wide cheek bones suggest the goat; The delta between the brows and the large, square skull are traits of Aquarius. The constant presence of static electricity, and the eternally optimist persona tilts the scale to Aquarius Rising.

Lots of Aquarian Spark

In Irwin's birth chart, natal Uranus opposes Jupiter. Saturn, Mercury, Mars, the South Node, and Jupiter lie in Aquarius. Mars tells us why he had such an impulsive and exuberant physical drive. The Mercury/Saturn conjunction shows why he was so inventive in explaining the processes of Nature in his wildlife documentaries. The First House Jupiter in Aquarius implies that he would become recognized through his work in broadcast media. (Aquarius is the ruler of TV and mass communication.)

Irwin's success was likely a product of the abundant Aquarius energies in his First House. To the world, he always appeared eternally optimist, and this encouraged thousands of Irwin's fans to support his hopes for purchasing land sites around the world—to preserve them forever, as wildlife habitats!

...and Ominous Aspects

At the time of his unexpected death, (9/4/2006), the Virgo Sun was transiting over Irwin's Pluto in his 8th House (of death). Also, this natal Pluto was being opposed by transiting Uranus, while Mars was transiting his eight House Moon while squaring transiting Pluto in Sagittarius.

To add to all this, Steve's Mars, Rising Sign, and Neptune were all forming hard aspects to transiting Saturn. These ominous signs suggested the possibility of a fatal accident.

Contain the Water with Earth!
Jon Bon Jovi
(John Francis Bongiovi)
3/2/1962, 8:45 P.M.
Perth Amboy, NJ

"Miracles happen everyday. Change your perception of what is a miracle, and you'll see them all around you." —Jon Bon Jovi

♓ Sun: Pisces

With his Pisces Sun trine Neptune, Jon has an endless supply of dreams. The cardinality in his personality give him the drive to make these dreams come true!

Jon's initial success faded with the advent of the grunge fad, but this hard-working lad wouldn't quit and his mutable Pisces was willing to try anything. In 1992, Jon created the score for *Young Guns II* and his *Blaze of Glory* tune became his first number one hit.

Later, Jovi continued to adapt, as his soul grew to express his softer solar nature. This was apparent in his emotionally uplifting anthem which encourages "all to live life to the fullest"—i.e., his recording of *It's My Life*. This altruistic song reflects his faith in human potential, a quality given to him by his Mercury, Mars, Jupiter and Saturn in Aquarius. (These are the same planets as **Steve Irwin**).

Jon shows the physical traits associated with the sign of Pisces. Most noticeable are the thick-lidded eyes and the fact that his facial lines are noticeably skewed. Features are similar to what we have seen in our previous portraits.

Ascendant: Libra

With Libra rising, Bon Jovi presents a pleasant and charming mask, which clearly depicts his public persona. Jovi isn't the typical "in your face" rock star. He's likeable! Perhaps that's why, in 1996, *People Magazine* named him one of the world's 50 most beautiful people.

Physically, Jon's Libra traits include the wide V-shaped smile with the cherub dimples. When this sign rises, the round, deep pooled Pisces eyes turn into narrow slits of sparkling light, as the cardinal energy straightens the skewed solar features into balanced horizontal lines.

Moon: Capricorn

With his Moon in Capricorn, Jon is emotionally driven to excel and work hard to make his mark on society. He found his first title role in *"National Lampoon's The Trouble With Frank"*. In 2004, he campaigned for John Kerry, purchased co-ownership in an AFL Football franchise and finished a new album. Furthermore, in 2015, he celebrated his 25 year marriage with his wife. Jon shows this love (and the material nature of this earthy Moon) in his quote: *"The only thing I like more than my wife is my money."*

Sinise and Macy share a Capricorn Moon with **Jovi**. However, (unlike Jovi), these men have Saturn (rather than Neptune) aspecting their Suns. Their mannerisms are far more rigid.

Gary's Sun is part of a grand water trine that includes his Saturn in Scorpio. (He appears to be always in control). Macy's Sun opposes Saturn in fussy Virgo. He appears extremely malleable.

Both of these men lack the fluid nature of Jovi. Here, we will show how this is due to the placement of Mars in their charts.

♓ Sun: Pisces

Gary Sinise
3/17/1955, Blue Island, IL

Gary Sinise is known for his roles as Lieutenant Dan in *Forrest Gump* and as the caring but highly professional leader in the TV series *CSI, New York* and *Criminal Minds, Beyond Borders*. The latter "globe-trotting show" was likely inspired by Gary's Sun's trine to Jupiter.

Watch how Sinise appears to be fixed and focused as he moves at a steady, measured pace to perform his duties. His Mars is in the Fixed Earth of Taurus, and since it is in harmonious trine to his tenacious Moon, Gary's emotions are markedly contained and controlled, a trait usually not seen in a Pisces Sun.

William H. Macy
3/13/1950, Miami Beach, FL

William H. Macy is known best for his roles as the quixotic car salesman in *Fargo* and as the substance abusing anti-hero in Showtime's *Shameless*. His impulsive and nervous energy likely comes from Pisces' ruling planet Neptune and its trine to expansive Jupiter in Aquarius. These impulses are exacerbated by William's Libra Mars, which forms a hard square to Uranus. Macy's physical metabolism initially strikes us as breezy and calm—until (like a bolt of lightning), it explodes in a electrified burst of impulsive actions.

Moons in Capricorn

When these two men react to others or become emotional, their liquid faces transform into stone, as their eyes take on a steely and distance glaze.

Sinise's Moon trines his Taurus Mars. This makes his emotional nature turgid and tightly controlled. The only aspect of Macy's Moon is its sextile to his Sun. He is more fluid than Sinise, but he still has a Goat Moon. He is more emotionally grounded than he appears. He has fooled us with the roles that he has chosen to play.

Fixity takes its hold!
Billy Crystal
3/14/1948, 7:48 A.M.
Manhattan, NY

 Sun: Pisces

Over the years, Billy has entertained us with his humorous imitations of the voices and gestures of celebrities. Whether it's his Fernando Lamas' "You look mahhvelous!" or his Sammy Davis Jr. impression, Billy totally captured the nuances in their personalities. This gift for "seeing and feeling patterns" is common in people with a Pisces Sun.

Crystal has more than an ability to imitate others. In *City Slickers*, Billy played a mid-life crisis sufferer, who was rediscovering his lost feelings from childhood. You may recall the touching scene where he marveled at the joy of life, as he bonded with a tiny newborn calf. There, we saw how the undulating waves of water ballooned and twisted his mesh of facial flesh—to present to us, the ecstasy of Pisces!

Billy's eyes are rather small for a Pisces fish, but the waves of water still have their effect. The eyes appear to form the lines of a sine-wave curve, as one eye looks up in one direction, and the other drifts down into its own separate world, on the other side of his face.

Billy's outrageous sense of humor likely comes from his Sun's T-square to Jupiter and Uranus. Jupiter's trine to his earthy Moon and Ascendant makes his characters funny, but also real.

Ascendant & Moon: Taurus

With Venus (Taurus' ruling planet) conjoined his Sun and Rising Sign, Billy is firmly anchored in his space. Since the Taurus throat is the home of the voice (and Pisces provides a wonderful sense of rhythm), Bill has a gift not only to feel, but also sense the pitch, tone and pace of everything that surrounds him. His Taurus allows him to keep it all in control and make it real.

However, Billy shows few moments of bovine contentment, for his Venus and Moon are squared by his Mars/Saturn/Pluto conjunction in Leo. Since these three planets also sextile his Sun's ruler Neptune, Crystal is driven to create the theatrical alter-egos of many characters, other than his own.

Billy's words describe it well: "I am completely obsessive. I haven't slept since 1948, worrying about whether my shtick is going to be funny or not".

He shouldn't have to worry. His act is "mahhvelous".

Fire heats the Water
Queen Latifah
3/18/1970, 8:07 A.M.
Newark, NJ

♓ Sun: Pisces

This lady's Universe is filled with conflicting energies. All of her Planets (except Neptune) form tight squares or oppositions. These hard aspects make Latifah intensely energetic.

As we saw in her musical responses to misogynistic male rappers and in her powerful role in *Chicago*, these forces rein over the softer energies of her Sun.

With Pluto and Uranus opposing her Sun (and five components in fixed signs), this lady's mutable and watery light is difficult to see. When it does appear, we'll see the offset, heavy-lidded and deep pooled eyes of the Fish, as well as the sensitivity of her kinder nature. Notably, this soft side is rarely seen, since these waters have to find the power to break loose from those fixed components in her chart, and also find a way to moisturize the encrusted mask of her Ascendant.

Ascendant: Taurus

With her massive physical presence, square features, broad shoulders and her sensual earthy persona, Latifah displays the physical container of a Taurus Bull. This presence is enhanced by Saturn's conjunction to Mars—both of which sit near her Ascendant.

Latifa's Mars brings a fixed steadiness to her physical movements. Put this lady in a shop of delicate china, and you'd think there is little to fear. That Taurus Mars and Saturn makes her seem totally controlled and stable. However, expansive Jupiter opposes these two planets, and her flamboyant Leo Moon squares all three components. Quick, take the china off the shelves!

Moon: Leo

Latifah's heavily aspected Leo Moon certainly can trigger a lot of excitement. As we saw in her loud and fiery role in *Beauty Shop*, this Moon gives her the boisterous reactions—those that constantly attempt to outshine the expressive attempts of everyone else in the room.

Also, this Queen's Venus in Aries trines this Moon, while her Sun's ruling planet Neptune completes a loose grand Fire trine. This enforces her image of fiery self confidence. On a grand overview, she truly feels she's royalty. Oddly, so does everyone else!

Fire spreads across the land
Elizabeth Taylor
2/27/1932, 2:30 A.M.
Hampstead, London (UK)

Sun: Pisces

The "roller coaster ride of fame" came early for this sensitive soul. After the debacles of *Cleopatra*, seven marriages and the latest "tell-all book", you wonder how she managed to keep it all together.

With her Moon trine her Pisces Sun, and the latter opposing Neptune, Liz had a special gift of creating beautiful illusions. None were as remarkable as her ability to resurrect her own beauty—again and again! It seemed to happen every time she found "a new true love" in her life. This transformational magic was likely due to her Venus' conjunction with Uranus, trine to Jupiter and its square to rejuvenating Pluto. (Sadly, Uranus also accounts for the many dissolutions in her love life).

When Liz expressed her Pisces Sun, her deep purple eyes would widen as her face bloomed and rounded. Her expressions would change fluidity and shade, when she interacted with the other people around her.

Moon: Scorpio

Recall Liz's performance in *Cat on A Hot Tin Roof* and *Who's Afraid of Virginia Woolf* when her lunar emotions were riled. In those roles, Liz's temper was often sharp and venomous, especially when her desires weren't fulfilled. This gives you an idea on how a Scorpio Moon reaction can really sting!

Fortunately, this Moon placement also gave her compassionate Pisces Sun the determination to battle for her convictions. Many believe that she may be best remembered not for acting, but for her valiant fight to cure AIDS.

Ascendant: Sagittarius

For many years, astro-data gave Taylor Libra Rising, perhaps because she was known for her exceptional beauty. However, just look at what happens when the waters of her two luminaries recede. This reveals the underlying bone structure with its domed skull and the long jaw and neck of a horse.

These Centaur energies ran strong in Liz's adolescent years, when she galloped across the screen in the legendary *Black Beauty* films.

Oddly, (even with Jupiter's trine to her fiery Ascendant), Liz showed little of the humor that we'd expect from Sagittarius. Furthermore, the joyful persona of the Centaur was rarely seen. This may have been due to Jupiter's exact square to her highly controlled Scorpio Moon.

Dream the impossible dream!

These two business kingpins proved that Pisces Suns are not ineffectual, for each of them had Pisces' gift to understand that every nation and all individuals face a world of constantly changing forces. This enabled the two men to achieve their incredible positions of power.

♓ Suns in Pisces
Alan Greenspan
3/6/1926, No time, New York, NY

Alan Greenspan was the longest running chairman of the Federal Reserve. Through the years, he dispersed his Neptunian view of the economy, as he danced around the financial numbers to create a euphoria that give the USA one of its longest economic booms. His Piscean ability to quell fears (and induce a sense of optimism and confidence in human endeavors) was likely a product of the conjunctions of Uranus on his Sun and Jupiter on his Venus.

Sadly, as astrologers know, the cycles of Nature affect all things, including the financial cycles. With the 2007 crash, Alan's theories proved to be delusional, perhaps because he refused to believe that the human foible of greed could wreck the economy. His belief that "anything was doable" was likely supported by his Saturn's conjunction and Uranus' trine to his expansive Centaur Moon.

Rupert Murdoch
3/11/1931, 1:59 A.M., Melbourne, Australia

In contrast to Greenspan, Rupert Murdoch has Uranus T-squaring Saturn and his Pluto/Jupiter conjunction in Cancer. Furthermore, his Neptune's only aspect is its inconjunction to Venus. Rupert shows little of the passion of Pisces or the altruism of Uranus. With Capricorn rising and Saturn sextiling his Sun, the ringed planet rules his chart. Murdock was driven to pursue power!

With his Pluto and Jupiter in the 7th House, Rupert is acutely aware of the fears of the general public. This helped him to build a worldwide media empire. With Mars conjoined Pluto, Rupert built it by playing on people's morbid curiosity.

~~~

Both men show the heavy-lidded eyes, and the drooping facial flesh, that forms the baggy cheeks and jowls.

Moons: Sagittarius

With their Centaur Moons, both of these men' responsive reactions are unbridled. Watch how they rear back, throw their heads up into the air, and then exuberantly respond—often with an infectious whinny! This expansive lunar emotion gives them an ability to feel and sense the bigger picture.

Alan's Moon sextiles Jupiter, and this made him an eternal optimist. Rupert's Jupiter conjoins Pluto. Emotionally, he aspired to build and control a Journalism empire.

Ron Howard
3/1/1954, 9:03 A.M.
Duncan, OK

Sun: Pisces

Ron Howard's cinematic works are larger than life and most of them leave us feeling optimistic about the human condition. He has truly mastered the gifts of his Pisces Sun.

In *Splash, Cocoon* and *Willow*, Ron showed us Pisces' fascination with fantasy. In *Parenthood*, he celebrated the continuance of life as an ensemble of actors (of all ages) reacted to the newborn beings entering their lives. In *Apollo 13*, he marveled at mankind's technical achievements in the conquering of outer space. True to his Sun, Ron took common themes and built them into a grander overview.

With his Pisces Sun, Mercury and Venus T-squaring his Jupiter and Centaur Mars, Ron was driven to search for the imaginary worlds beyond his reach.

Moon: Capricorn

Ron began his career early in life, playing Opie on *The Andy Griffith Show*. Here, we saw an incredibly mature and serious child, who seemed very old for his age. This is quite common in children with Capricorn Moons.

At noted earlier, children tend to react to their worlds with their lunar emotions. Ron's Moon is near his Midheaven in the 10th House, squaring Neptune and opposing Uranus. This young actor was emotionally comfortable, producing the imaginary illusions, that he saw in the window of his Aries Ascendant. This sign gave him the clarity and sense of independence to build his own dream machine. Appropriately, his production company was named *Imagine Films*.

Ascendant: Aries

Ron's teenaged character in *"Happy Days"* rarely showed the anxiety of a youthful Pisces Sun. Rather, he was decisive and assertive, as he projected the image of his Aries Ascendant!

In the simplified world of TV sitcoms, all problems get solved in less than 30 minutes. Real life isn't that instant—unless you have lots of cardinal signs in your chart. Ron has just four, but they are on the Cardinal Cross in his chart.

This "let me be in charge urge" fed Ron's desire to become a film director and producer. In his early 20's, Ron was creating, as well as starring in his own movies. His first films *Grand Theft Auto* and *Eat My Dust* reflected the brashness of his Aries Ascendant. These drive-in crash derbies were filled with adolescent struggles and hot rod action. Fortunately, in time, these youthful adventures matured, as the spiritual insight of Ron's Sun found its true expression.

Steve Jobs
2/24/1955, 7:15 P.M.
San Francisco, CA

♓ Sun: Pisces

In his youth, Jobs was a wanderlust hippy who dropped out of school and went to India to *"develop his intuition"*. This helped him establish his philosophy: *"Simplicity is the ultimate sophistication."* This reality gave him the magical thinking, will power and intuition to create a simpler way to use computers. He was the genius behind the company *Apple*.

Physically, Jobs showed the oblique facial structure and many of the features of the fish. But, in his personal expression, he was very forceful and driven—not a typical Pisces. This is due to the dynamic aspects in his chart.

Steve's Sun trines its ruler Neptune. This planet forms a powerful grand square with his Venus, Mars and a Jupiter/Uranus conjunction in cardinal signs. These two latter planets also trine Saturn (in Scorpio).

These aspects gave Jobs a hugely inventive Neptunian imagination; Saturn gave him the ability to focus and construct his creative dreams. Significantly, his Neptune (as the ruler of his Sun) allowed him to believe that anything that he imagined could be created. His Aries Moon and Mars give this "Type A Personality" the will and the drive to create his own destiny. Saturn gave him the tenacity to get it done.

Moon in Aries

Aries loves to clear away the clutter. With his Moon and Mars in Aries, we see why Jobs was so driven to keep things simple. Oddly, Job's Moon had no aspects, but he loved to argue, for when he became emotional, his nearby "highly-aspected" Aries Mars would take control. That is why, in his interaction with others, he often became fiery, direct and forceful.

Ascendant: Virgo

Steve's Virgo Ascendant places Aquarius on his 6th House of work and health. With this Virgo window we see why Jobs' desired to work *"with people who demand perfection."*

This Rising Sign places Uranus and supercharging Jupiter in Job's 10th House of Career. This portends success in electronics and communication, i.e., the multi-media world of computers and movies. Steve purchased George Lucas' animation company, which later became Pixar Studios. It went on to produce wildly popular animation films such as *Toy Story* and *Finding Nemo*.

With Aquarius on the cusp of his 6th House, and a Sixth House Sun trine Neptune, Jobs often had an unrealistic approach to his work and health. This idealistic view of his physical body may have been what led him to delay the cancer treatments that could have saved his life.

Aries planets bring action

In the two previous portraits, we showed how Cardinal Fire changes the nature of a Pisces Sun. Here, we conclude this section by looking at another person with strong Aries and Mars in his chart.

Daniel Craig
3/02/1968, No Time
Chester, England

When Craig became the new James Bond (*Casino Royale*, 2006), there was a backlash to his portrayal of Bond being a questionably immoral super agent. However, by the time of his fourth film (*Spectre, 2015*), it was clear that his aggressively driven character had brought the franchise back to life.

When asked on how he approached his work as an actor, Craig commented: *"I've got to step up to the plate and deal with it. I have a confidence about it but then that's because of the people around me who made me feel good about it."* The first comment is his Aries Moon. The "good feeling" is a product of Craig's Pisces Sun.

Sun: Pisces

Craig's Sun and its ruler Neptune are the only water in his chart. Also his Neptune sextiles Uranus and Pluto in earthy Virgo. This gives him only four feminine signs in his chart. With Pluto opposing his Sun, it is very difficult for the light of Pisces to shine.

However, in Craig's roles in *Golden Compass* and *Cowboys and Aliens,* his Piscean gift for fantasy was apparent. It also was obvious in 2012, when Craig served as the host on *Saturday Night Live*. The UR photo was taken during that performance. In this moment, we saw the bubbly, rounded and skewed

features of Daniel's Sun. However, most of his work showed the Aries components in his chart.

Moon, Mars & Saturn in Aries

Daniel's Moon conjoins Saturn and Mars in Aries. These three components also sextile Daniel's Mercury and Venus in electrical Aquarius. Furthermore, his Neptune squares Jupiter in fiery Leo. With these fiery aspects, the temperature of Craig's watery Sun raises significantly.

With his Aries Mars, Craig runs on overdrive—as he charges headfirst into action. However, with Saturn's snug contact to his Mars, every movement appears to be deliberate and calculated. Watch Craig, when he performs his James Bond stunts. You will notice that his movements are abrupt, but at the same time, they also appear to be cautiously planned.

~~~

After Pisces, the next sign in the Zodiac is Aries.

♈ Aries

	Page
Introduction to Aries Traits	85-87
Marlon Brando & Lucy Lawless	

May the force be with you
Alec Guinness, Evan McGregor	87
William Shatner, Leonard Nimoy	89
Celine Dione	90

Throw water on the Fire
James Woods	91
Rachel Maddow	92
Gloria Steinem, Hugh Hefner	93
James Franco	94
Lady Gaga	95

The force of Air stokes the Fire
Alec Baldwin	96
Russell Crowe	97
Reba McEntire	98
Sarah Jessica Parker	99

Mutable Forces break the Cardinal Spell
Emma Watson	100-101

Earth smothers the fire
David Letterman	102-103
Al Gore	104
Elton John	105
Robert Downey, Jr.	106

Aries ♈ March 21 to April 19
Masculine Polarity, Cardinal Fire
In the light, the path ahead is Seen

At the end of Winter, the **Pisces** Sun presented its newly imagined arrangements. Now, as the Sun crosses the equator at the Spring Equinox, the solar light begins its rise into the upper hemisphere, for the first time in the year. This crossing into a new season (and quadrant) ignites the Cardinal Fire of Aries. In this morning of the year, new born life awakens—to begin its individual path of self expression!

In the light of Aries, life bursts out everywhere, as sprouts pop out of the ground and leafs emerge from their cocoons. Here, all individuals are driven by this Cardinal light—to pursue their three month journey of identifying (**Aries**), relishing (**Taurus**) and understanding (**Gemini**) the nature of their being.

These Aries pioneers see few barriers, and the path ahead is always open. When these rams charge headfirst in their pursuits—they are usually the first in line, and the ones to lead the way! In the process, they will espouse the opinions and make the points that will empower their view of what "they see through their eyes". In these moments, some of these Rams can become selfish, arrogant and pushy. Diplomats, they are not!

Give your Aries friends unrestricted tasks and let them be in charge! They will *"plow away the clutter"* as they initiate the actions that will get any stalled endeavor on the move again. Also, be aware that once a project is started, many Rams will quickly lose their interest and then charge off to chase other pursuits. You may have to find someone else to finish the job.

This light of Aries is colored by the visions of **Leo** and expanded into multiple dimensions by the mutable spirit of **Sagittarius**. The fiery drive of **Aries** is countered by the fixed Earth of **Taurus**, the next sign in the Zodiac.

Individuals with an Aries Sun, Moon, or Rising Sign (or a strongly aspected Mars in a masculine sign) often express the aggressive, head-butting mannerisms of a Ram.

Rulerships and Associations for Aries

Mars is the ruling planet of Aries. This planet governs an individual's physical metabolism as well as the conquering actions of warrior Rams. Traditionally, Mars also co-rules the feminine sign of Scorpio.

Mars governs the sympathetic nervous system—the body's fight-or-flight response that activates the muscular and urogenital systems and the adrenal glands.

Aries' associations include the color "red", iron and diamonds, all thorn-bearing trees and shrubs, the military, courage and pursuits of self discovery. Mars is also associated with C.G. Jung's Animus, the masculine influence which operates in both sexes. It is "the force that we project" to attract others.

Aries' natural home is the First House, the point in the wheel that is created at an individual's time of birth, i.e., the Ascendant. This point in the wheel starts the quadrant where "the act of self-discovery" begins.

Aries Physical Traits:

Aries' vertically stretched head resembles that of a Ram. Note how the arched brows push forward, as the forehead sweeps to the back. Below lies the large, prominent snout, which protrudes sharply out from the recessed chin. In any profile view, the convex face becomes obvious. Watch how those fiery eyes lift up on the sides—as they aim the eyes straight to the front! Note the indented membranes at the bottom edges of the snout, and how the long muscular lines that run down from the nose.

Below, we see the wide upper lip plate and the thin lipped mouth. These features also mock those of a Ram.

Marlon Brandro
4/3/1924, 11:00 P.M.
Omaha, Nebraska

Lucy Lawless
4/29/1968, 6:25 A.M.
Auckland, New Zealand

Marlon Brando had an Aries Sun and Moon and an Ascendant in Sagittarius. There's lots of fire, but his Mars (the ruling planet of Aries) was in earthy Capricorn. This kept his physical movements cool and grounded. **Lucy Lawless** is a triple Aries. Her Mars is also in Earth, but in fixed Taurus. Rather than flash, her actions contained the strength of Taurus—what she needed to play the Warrior Princess Xena.

Aries Body Language

As noted in the introduction on body language, everything starts on the left side of the chart, where the Sun is rising on the eastern horizon).

At this point on the Zodiac Wheel, the Head and Eyes are awakening in the morning light on the eastern horizon. Therefore, these body parts were assigned to be the ruler of the sign Aries.

With the driving force of cardinal fire emanating from the head, the battering horns of the Ram lead the way, as Aries charges forward down the path—to pursue a new adventure of discovery.

Watch how the whole upper torso of Aries tilts forward. This swoops the upper back, shoulders, neck, and head to the front—as the rest of the body follows behind. With this body language, these creatures seem unstoppable.

Aries rules the Head & the Eyes

May The Force Be With You!

Let's begin Aries with a look at four celebrity warriors and pioneers.

Ewan McGregor  Alec Guinness
3/31/1971, 8:10 P.M.   4/2/1914, 5:45 A.M.
Perth, Scotland   London, UK

These two actors played the youthful and elder roles of Obi-Wan Kenobe in the original *Star Wars* trilogy and two prequels. Amazingly, though born over 50 years apart, both of these men have Mars, Jupiter and Uranus in aspect to their Suns and Ascendants. Assuredly, *The Force* was running with both of these stars!

Furthermore, both of these gentlemen's aspects to Jupiter suggest that Alec and Ewan would be seen as "professorial teachers". The Uranus aspects portend that they would be in a futuristic time, in the Uranus' ruled arena of outer space. Also, both men would perform as Jedi Warriors—since both of their Mars square their Suns and Ascendants. (Ewan's Mars is in Capricorn; Alec's is in Cancer).

Both men display Aries' convex facial lines and large snout. Note how the forehead sweeps to the back and how the eyes set high on the face.

Moons in Gemini

Amazingly, both men have their Moons in the mercuric sign of Gemini. This makes the reactions of both men similar. When these men become emotional, their facial lines skew, as their eyes blink rapidly and spark with electricity. With this Moon, their interactions often become chatty.

The incredible similarities in the charts suggest that perhaps the producers hired an astrologer to find an individual to play the younger Obi in the later prequel film.

Ascendants: Aries & Libra

Ewan McGregor's Sun opposes his Libra Ascendant. Uranus conjoins his Rising Sign—and this gives Ewan a light, breezy and noticeably sparkling persona. As this cardinal air counters the vertical thrust of Aries, it quells the aggressive nature of his Sun. Physically, it also makes his facial features appear more calm and balanced.

Alec Guinness' Sun and Ascendant conjoins his Venus. Even with Aries Rising, he appears calmer than Ewan. Alec also has the sleepy eyes that we saw in Libra Moon **Nicolas Cage** (page 33). This shows what a planet on the Ascendant can do.

William Shatner
3/22/1931, 4:00 A.M.
Montreal, Quebec

Leonard Nimoy
3/26/1931, 8:30 P.M.
Boston, MA

While we are still in outer space, let's look at these two Aries pioneers who—*Boldly Go Where No Man Has Gone Before!*

Suns in Aries

Both men display the directness of cardinal fire and the physical traits of the Ram. Note the high arched eyebrows that sweep down into the long, wide-bridged nose, and how the mouth is placed low on the chin, which heightens the upper lip plate. This makes the upper lip thinner than the bottom one.

Born four days apart, these two have similar planets and many other common personality traits. However, the different dates and times change their Ascendants and Moons.

Ascendants: Aquarius & Scorpio

The Ascendant is the window that frames the way one is seen by others. This mask is also a two way portal. From the inside, it dictates how we see the world before our eyes.

With Aquarius rising, William fits right into the futuristic and high tech world of *Star Trek*. There, he was attracted to the inventive ideas and this gave him the images he needed to lead his crew of space cadets.

Physically, Shanter shows the cubical structure of his fixed Aquarius Ascendant, rather than the vertically stretched face of a Ram.

Nimoy's birth time gives him a fixed Scorpio Ascendant. This explains his fascination on the deeper mysteries of life, as well as his highly controlled and shielded emotions. Physically, we saw the square skull, flat cheek bones, large beak and focused eyes of the eagle.

Moons: Taurus & Cancer

When Shatner becomes emotional, the fires of his cardinal Sun are often smothered and contained by the Earth of his Taurus Moon.

Note how Bill's facial expressions take on a contented and bovinely pose, as this Moon

quells the expansive forces of his Sun and Ascendant.

In Nimoy's portrayal of *Spock*, we never saw any emotions, for that was a role to play. In real life (with a water Ascendant and Moon), friends found him be quiet and markedly caring of others. This caring nature came from his Moon and Mars in Cancer. The quietness from his Scorpio Ascendant.

Earlier data gave Leonard a Gemini Moon and Ascendant. This data was likely wishful thinking from those who were fooled by his totally logical and emotionless role as Spock.

Celine Dion

3/30/1968, 12:15 P.M.
Charlemagne, Québec

In our first two portraits, we saw the force of Aries in combination with assorted other components. Here, we have a triple fire, with her luminaries in Aries and a Leo Ascendant. Celine Dion gives us a portrait that displays the traits and mannerisms of a Ram as well as those of a Lion.

Aries Sun & Moon

Aries is the first sign of the Zodiac, and therefore they want to be first in line—and Number ONE in everything that they purse. Amazingly, Celine has achieved the #1 spot on many lists. Her 1995 album *D'eux* was the best selling French recording of all time. Her #1 hits are too many to list and she was the top earning artist for the 2010 decade. Last and not least, her decade-long run (2007-2017) of many sold out shows (in Las Vegas' 4,000 seat Coliseum) will likely be the most successful residency show of all time! With Saturn conjoined her Midheaven Sun and her Taurus Mars conjoined her Aries Moon (in the 10th House), we see why this lady had the drive and determination to conquer the world!

Dion's Venus and Mercury are in Pisces and opposed by Pluto and Uranus. Her personal planets trine melodic Neptune, while the outer planets are in sextile. This ruler of Pisces contributes to Dion's amazing sense of rhythm and musical talents, as it does to many successful musicians.**

Dion's Mercury and Venus are in her 9th House. This enables her to sense the tonal differences in multi-cultural languages. Celine songs are performed in French and English, and in six other languages.

Celine displays many of the features of Aries. The upper photos show how the convex face with its upward sweeping brows pull the eyes high on the face. It all changes, when the cardinal fires of both of her luminaries cease—and her cubical Leo mask rises to the surface.

Ascendant: Leo

Earlier, we noted that Dion's Mars is placed in the fixed sign of Taurus. In addition, Dion's Sun and Saturn are placed in the Leo decan of Aries—and she has Leo Rising! As the lower photos show, when her luminaries are in repose, she appears markedly fixed. What we see are the features of a lion.

The first thing you'll notice is Celine's reddish mane and fiery aura. The second item that stands out is her regal sense of showmanship. The light of Aries runs strong, but Leo is there, to capture the glow!

***See Neptune's influences on **Adele** on page 110 and with **Pink** on page 206.*

Throw Water on the Fire
James Woods
4/8/947, 10:30 A.M.
Vernal, Utah

Sun: Aries

In his TV role as the prosecutor *Shark*, James Woods showed the in-your-face aggressiveness of a ram. In this show, the highly driven cardinal fire of his Sun would dominate as he lead the charge—ordering his staff to "Go" or "Find it now"! Like most Aries, he was always in a hurry.

James also shows the physical traits of a Ram. Note how the energy seems to sweep forward and upward from the narrow chin to the cheek bones. From there, the energies rush up and back, to form the arched eyebrows, the muscular plates on the forehead and the hornlike tuffs at the top, that suggest a double crown of hair.

The upper right profile photo not only shows the convex, sheep-like structure of the Ram's face, it also shows how every Aries expression brings a "forward thrust of the head", the body part ruled by Aries.

With his Sun's ruling planet Mars also in Aries (conjoined his Mercury), Woods' physical actions are turbo-driven. His mind works at a rapid speed, and he has a very high I.Q.

Ascendant: Leo

The proud strut of the lion often appears when Woods enters a scene. In these introductory moments, this Leo facade gives Woods an aura of confidence and a dramatic flair. This holding-of-fire also gives Wood a needed sense of warmth. At times, this combination can also create an exaggerated sense of self importance.

Saturn sits near James' Ascendant and Pluto is in his 1st House. Saturn subdues the fire as it makes him appear more rigid. Pluto gives Woods a hard-edged and sometimes disturbing persona. It is what we saw in *The Onion Field, Killer: A Journal of Murder* and the Emmy award winning *My Name is Bill W,* a tale of AA's founder.

Moon in Pisces

With his Moon in Pisces, conjoined his Venus, James' martial qualities become noticeably subdued—when he emotionally reacts to others. This sensitive Moon helped him to connect with his audience.

When James' mutable waters quench the fire, the liquid infusion fills his eyes and swells the face. This gives him a momentary appearance of vulnerability—but not for long—for all too quickly, he would jump back into the fire, to make sure his opinion is heard by others.

Rachel Maddow

4/1/1973, 12:23 P.M.
Hayward, CA

 SUN: Aries

With a rapid fire delivery, the cardinal fire of Rachel's Sun delivers data to her fans at the MSNBC Cable News Network. With her Sun, Venus, Moon and Mercury residing in her philosophical 9th House —and her Sun's trine to Neptune in Sagittarius sextiling her Mars and Jupiter in altruistic Aquarius— Maddow has a gift for developing very complex ideas and delivering a grander overview. Oddly, in the process, many of her fans rarely see her as being "authoritarian or opinionated"—a rare feat for an Aries!

Moon in Pisces

Maddow's Moon and Mercury are in Pisces. This gives her an ability to walk in the shoes of others and sense the nature of their feelings. Notably, these two components square Saturn, while the ringed planet trines Uranus in Libra. This installs a sense of fairness, while Saturn's aspect makes Maddow's faith in humanity all the more enduring. Furthermore, Saturn is in Gemini and it sextiles her Sun. This gives her the sense of authority and substance that she needs, since she has no Earth in her chart.

In her more emotional moments, Rachel's lunar forces take control. Note how the fiery eyes are doused by the water, as her hard-edged Ram features are hidden by the rounded, saturated flesh. The patterns of mutability are also apparent as they skew and twist the vertical lines of Maddow's Ram-like face. The resulting expressions resemble the solar features we saw in the previous sign of Pisces.

In her show, these undulating emotions of Pisces became obvious, when Rachel does her weekend "cocktail party". Watch how she escapes into her fantasy land, mixing a drink while imagining she's sharing it with a friend.

Cancer Ascendant

When Rachel's luminary lights recede, the cardinal forces return once again, but instead of the headstrong outward charge of Aries, the forces are drawing her downward—into the watery base of the ocean below.

This reverse in polarity is seen in the rare moments when this Ram is "lost for words". Physically, this Rising Sign gives Rachel the round, full moon temples of the Cancer crab. It also explains why her eyes often appear as deep pools of water.

Gloria Steinem
3/25/1934, 10:00 P.M.
Toledo, OH

Hugh Hefner
4/9/1926, 4:20 P.M.
Chicago IL

Here, we look at two pioneers in publishing, who led the way to define new frontiers of independence for both genders. Their different philosophies are reflected in their charts.

Suns: Aries

Steinem's Sun is conjunct Mars. This double whammy of martial energy gave Gloria the drive to create *Ms. Magazine* and lead the charge to empower the feminist movement.

Hefner's Sun trines Neptune, sextiles Jupiter (in Aquarius) and squares Pluto on his Midheaven. This impelled him to create *Playboy Magazine*—a publication filled with articles on politics and personal satisfaction. It started a sexual revolution for men in America.

Ascendants: Scorpio & Virgo

With Steinem, we see the intense and power-controlling persona of a Scorpio Ascendant—the same Rising Sign as **Leonard Nimoy**! This explains why she has won public recognition projecting her Sun's self confidence, while giving an appearance of power and control.

With Virgo Rising, Hefner steadily presented his analytical mask to the world. Did his readers read his magazine for its "thoughtful articles", or were they viewing the picture-perfect photos of his chosen objects of desire? This clinical approach to sexuality was rationally accepted by his readers.

Moons: Leo & Pisces

Gloria's dramatic Leo Moon gave her the emotional confidence to inspire other women to find their own place in a male dominated world. With this Moon trine her Sun, Gloria had a special gift for showing others how to discover their own sense of Aries independence and feelings of personal worth (Leo).

Hefner's emotional interactions with others are cool and clinical. His Pisces Moon is in his 6th House, Uranus is on his Descendant and his Moon's only aspect is its trine to Pluto (in his 10th House). Hefner won his fame examining and redefining the sexual morals of his generation.

James Franco

4/19/1978, 7:04 P.M.
Stanford, CA

On these two pages, we will show two Aries with reversed fixed and mutable secondary components. We'll also show how the House placements impact the nature of their components.

SUN: Aries

Franco displays the long and convex facial structure of the Ram. Like we saw with **James Woods**, the UR photo shows how the forehead of this Ram "trusts to the front", when he presents his opinions to the world.

Born near sunset, Franco's 6th House Sun is near his Descendent. Thusly, his solar sense of self is oriented to "other things and people". Perhaps that's why he believes that "....aiding others is the key to happiness". With his Sun in Virgo's House (and his Sun's trine to Jupiter), James' assertive Sun has a cheery and expansive nature. It also accounts for his urge to pursue, gather and analyze a huge range of data. This giant planet also explains why he once took 62 course credits at UCLA in one quarter. The normal course load is around 19. He still got a 4.0 GPA.

Ascendant: Scorpio

The underlying structure of Franco's Scorpio Ascendant sinks his eyes inward from the wide, flat cheekbones, while the fixed force gives him a cubical forehead and square chin. (This shape is very similar to what we saw in **Gloria Steinum**, who also has Scorpio Rising).

However, Franco's mask appears more reserved, likely since his fixed Leo Mars forms a T-square to his Sun and this fixed Ascendant. Mars also resets his martial forces into a holding pattern. This helps to keep his aggressive Sun and analytical emotions in control.

Moon in Virgo

James' Moon trines his Venus, that rests in his 7th House in the sign of Taurus. This creative planet keeps him emotionally grounded, but it also opposes Uranus, as it squares Saturn in his 10th House. This gives James an inventive array of creative abilities. Besides his film work, he's a writer, an artist and he plays music in a band.

With his Moon's placement in Virgo (in the 11th House of Aquarius), Franco is emotionally altruistic, but also likely to "question every detail in what he feels". With Mars on the MC, he has become a warrior for many health and education causes.

Theses components helped Franco to master his Golden Globe winning role in the biographical film of *James Dean.**

*James Dean was an Aquarius Sun with Aries Rising and a Scorpio Moon.

Lady Gaga
(Stefani Germanotta)
3/28/1986, 5:07 P.M. or 9:53 A.M. Yonkers, NY

 SUN: Aries

Early on, Stephani Germanotta was insecure and terrified of performing in front of others—a likely consequence of her Sun's square (or distancing) from its ruling planet Mars.

Fortunately, Stefani's Sun is at the top of her chart. This (and a giant array of lunar and Neptune aspects) likely inspired her to redirect the once obstructed light of her Sun—and blow the world away with the illusions of her alter ego: "Lady Gaga".

More than most of the others portraits, this lady displays the physical traits of Aries—notably the arched eyebrows and the convex shaped face.

Ascendant: Gemini

Stefani's original birth time gave her a Virgo Ascendant. A newer birth time gives her Gemini rising. Her "non-virgin" persona suggests that her Ascendant is the latter mutable sign.

In the LR photo, we see Gaga in a non-performing state. There, her bone structure displays the twin frontal rabbit teeth, the offset brows and eyes, and the rectangular jaw that juts out from the upper half of the face. These are features common with Gemini.

This Ascendant is opposed by Mars and Uranus. These two planets are trined by Gaga's Venus in Aries. This gives Gaga the drive and the inventive creative skills to build her outrageous and ever-changing personas. They run the gamut from "beautiful glam" to techno-metallic, and all the way down to disturbingly bizarre. Who can forget seeing her accept an award, while being wrapped in red gauze, or that time when she wore a dress made up of raw meat? These grotesque images were likely inspired by her Moon.

Moon in Scorpio

Gaga's Pluto conjoins her Moon in Scorpio. These two components also sextile Neptune. This gives Gaga a powerful sense of fantasy, as well as the emotional strength to conquer the world with her daring imagery.

The LL photo shows the power of Pluto and how it can appear in Gaga's emotions. At times, it is intense and gross, but this Pluto and Moon are activated in her theatrical 5th House of creativity. Since these components also trine Jupiter on her MC, many people find her work to be disturbing—but also outrageously hilarious!

Air feeds the Fire!
Alec Baldwin
4/3/1958, 12:45 P.M. (?)
Massapequa, NY

Alec Baldwin's first major role was as Jack Ryan, the Tom Clancy character in *Hunt for Red October,* (1990). Even though it was a huge hit, perhaps foolishly, Alec gave up this lucrative role to perform on Broadway. He was replaced by Harrison Ford and the studios refused to give him another leading role. Such independence runs strong in Aries Suns.

SUN: Aries

In time, Alec re-established his career performing in smaller, supporting roles. His role as the sales manager in *Glengarry Glen Ross,* and later as the casino boss in *The Cooler* showed that he had an exceptional gift for creating characters of incredible intensity and edginess. It also shows in his chart.

Alec has his Sun and two planets in fire signs—and the fire is fed by his four air sign components! With his cardinal luminaries trine and sextile his Aquarius Mars and Leo Uranus, we see why charges head-first into his diatribes—espousing his Aquarian causes, with his shotgun "gift of gab".

Moon: Libra

Fortunately, Baldwin has the calm and balancing reactions of his Venus-ruled Libra Moon to disarm the self-centered aggressive nature of his Sun. This Venusian force dissipates Baldwin's charging martial force, by directing it off to the side.

Alec's Venus is in Aquarius (and opposed by Pluto). This explains his intense and erratic relationships. This was seen in his very public conflict with his ex-wife Kim Bassinger.

In his lunar reactions, the V-shaped smile and squinted eyes of Libra gives Alec a relaxed and pleasant demeanor. This likeable nature earned him many runs as a host for *Saturday Night Live.*

Ascendant: Leo?

With his cubical skull, his mane of hair, his large barreled chest and his loud and pompous persona in *30 Rock,* it is possible that Alec has a Leo Ascendant. (Or we may be fooled, since his Sun is in the Leo decan?)

If born around 12:45 P.M., this birth time would place his natal Uranus on his Ascendant. (This would support his impulsive nature). Notably, this time also placed transiting Uranus (the destroyer) in his 7th House of marriage during his 2002 divorce.

When these 20 Aries snapshots were gathered, it was surprising to find that none of them were "All Cardinal Signs". (In Capricorn, there were three). Aries apparently needs another mode, to counter the incredible drive of their fiery cardinal Suns.

Russell Crowe
4/7/1964 2:00 A.M.
Wellington, New Zealand

Sun: Aries

With his roles in *LA Confidential* and *The Insider*, Russell Crowe gained international recognition. (The latter film brought him his first Oscar nod). With *Gladiator*, he became a major star, winning his first Oscar.

With his innate animal magnetism and mental acumen, Crowe was able to skillfully apply his talents in an amazing array of film genres.

Like many Aries before, when Russell projects his "true self and beliefs", the cardinal fires propel his head to the front. With his natal Mars also in Aries, Russell seems to be fully consumed by his actions. Consequently, the physical intensity is often overwhelming.

This planet's placement also accounts for his short fused temper, which early in his career, resulted in many well publicized brawls. Fortunately, with his maturity, these aggressive tendencies became less prevalent.

Ascendant & Moon: Aquarius

Russell doesn't display the physical traits of a typical Ram, for his face appears to have a cubical appearance. This could be due to his two Fixed Air Aquarius lights—and the fact that his Sun is in the Leo decan.

Unlike most Rams, Russell's brows are not arched and his eyelids balloon downward on the outer side. This gives the impression that his eyes are focusing inward, and that he is locked into another world—inside his head!

In his Oscar nominated role in the film *A Beautiful Mind*, Russell played a mathematical wizard who walked the thin line between madness and genius. With his Venus in Gemini trine his Sun and sextile his Mars, Russell has the gift for dealing with the data, numbers and words that were needed for this role. Also, with his Aquarius components, Russell was able to portray the mental eccentricities of this character.

As we saw in his role in *Master and Commander*, Crowe's Gemini Venus also gives him a gift for socializing and telling stories. And when he talks, his speech sounds rich and grounded. This is likely due to his Mercury in Taurus and it sextile to Saturn!

Reba McEntire
3/28/1955, 10:00 A.M.
McAlester, OK

SUN: Aries

Reba's first album was in 1977, and soon she became known as the Queen of Country Music. Reba is also known for her other talents. She was in the cult horror film *Tremors*, played the rambunctious Annie Oakley in *Buffalo Girls* and starred in her six-season hit TV show *Reba*. In 2012, she began her second ABC TV series: *Malibu Country*. Nothing stops this Ram!

Reba displays many the standard features of the Ram, but what makes her unique is the "redness in her aura". Some would say that it's just a reflection of her vivid red hair. Astrologers know that it's the glow of the red planet Mars.

Mars is the ruling planet of her fiery Sun and it is the most aspected planet in her chart. Reba's Taurus Mars forms a grand fixed square with Venus, Saturn and Pluto. This red planet also sextiles Mercury, Jupiter and Uranus in water signs! Perhaps that's why she became the most recognized redhead in the first decade of the new millennium?

These multiple aspects of Mars gave Reba the athletic focus to become a barrel-racing rodeo star. The water components and four Neptune aspects brought her gift for music. The Mars in Taurus (like with **Celine Dion**) brought a earthy resonance to her voice.

Moon & Ascendant in Gemini

In her book, Reba said she was born around 10 A.M. The original *Celebrity Snapshot* had a birth time of 10:50 and this gave her Cancer Rising. This new source gives her Gemini Rising.

In the original article, we caught the essence of her Moon, noting: *"When Reba becomes highly emotional, these cardinal fires quickly dissipate into vaporous whiffs of mutable air. When she interacts with others, her eyes sparkle, as her hands fly about. This interaction often includes an aerated barrage of mercurial chatter."*

However, as for that assumed Cancer Rising, we noted that on TV, she played a strong-willed mother caring for her brood and... *"even with her vibrant energy, she displays a down home and caring persona....and the round, lunar temples of the Cancer Crab."*

The original "cancer crab" picture is still in the collage above. The reason for this, is that the new time reveals that Reba's 12th House Moon (the ruler of Cancer) is the closest component to her Ascendant. Also, Mercury (the ruler of Gemini) is in Pisces and it forms a snug square to her Ascendant. It is believed that these factors are the reason that the Cancer traits were apparent in her appearance.

Earth smothers the Fire
Sarah Jessica Parker
3/25/1965, 9:00 A.M.
Nelsonville, Ohio

 **SUN: Aries**

On Broadway, TV and in the movies, Sarah is everybody's favorite fireball. With her unquenchable spirit, she keeps her fans enthused and excited. These fiery qualities are what we'd expect from an Aries Sun.

Oddly, the Aries physical traits of Sarah appear much stronger than what we saw in Reba. Sarah's face is longer and it hints of the Centaur. This may be due to Jupiter's placement near her Ascendant.

Ascendant: Gemini
(and Mars in Virgo)

Sarah is known best for her role in *Sex in the City*, where she played a sex columnist who constantly analyzed her own sexual drive, as she critically observed the peccadillos of others. This mercuric role as a journalist certainly fits her Gemini Ascendant. It also exhibits qualities of someone who has a Mars in Virgo.

As the ruler of Sarah's Sun, her Virgo Mars has a strong impact on her personality. The red planet also defines her physical energy and the nature of her movements and actions.

When Sarah is physically working, or just performing a routine activity, she operates at the pace of her Virgo Mars. Uranus and Pluto conjoin this planet and both also trine her Moon. Sarah's mercuric energies are also seductive.

With her Gemini Ascendant and Virgo Mars, Sarah's energies are not always centered in her Aries head—rather they seem to activate her fingers and hands. When discussing large concepts, her hands fly some distance from the torso. When intertwined in details, the hands hover close to the body, around the stomach—the body part ruled by Virgo.

Moon: Capricorn

With her luminaries in cardinal signs, Sarah is highly driven. With her Moon in Capricorn (trine her Mars and sextile Saturn), she is emotionally determined to climb many mountains. After her TV gig, Sarah went on to produce several films and perform on Broadway.

When Capricorn Moons interact with others, they often appear to be orchestrating the tasks of others. Such was her nature in her *Sex in the City* series. In the process, Sarah's flesh would form rocky ridges on the downfallen cheek bones. This would give Sarah a very serious appearance.

Stir the Fire with Mutability
Emma Watson
4/15/1990, 6:00 P.M.
Paris, France

Who can imagine becoming one of the world's greatest box office stars at the age of 11? So it was with Emma Watson, who had the fortune to be selected to play the role of Hermione Granger in the *Harry Potter* movies. You could say: "Such luck would happen to someone who has Jupiter on her Midheaven in the 10th House." Others would say: "She had just the right personality to win the role." Both ideas are supported by her chart!

J.K. Rowling, the creator and author of *Harry Potter*, participated in the audition and selection of the lead stars in the movie franchise. Since Rowling was a student of astrology, it was likely she drew charts on the main characters.

With Emma, what the producers and Rowling likely saw was a joyful child, beaming the optimism of a Sagittarius Moon as well as the emerging mask of her Virgo Ascendant. Rowling may have sensed that (in the years to come), Emma would display the warrior force of her Aries Sun—so that she could lead the others on their paths to self-discovery!

SUN: Aries

The top photo shows Emma at the premiere of the first Harry Potter film: *The Philosopher's Stone* (2001). The facial lines show the mutable features of Emma's Ascendant and Moon, rather than those of her Sun. (Her warrior nature had not yet developed, since the force of one's Sun usually does not appear until a person develops his or her true solar identity in adulthood).

In the lower left photo, Emma is 14 and the cardinal drive of her Sun is becoming more apparent. This martial energy is just what she needed to portray the increasing assertive nature of her Hermione character.

Some critics claimed that J.K. Rowling's novels were witchcraft, but youngsters loved these magical tales because the book helped kids to find their identity and discover ways to empower their creativity.

The first step in this "discovery of self" is the prime task of Aries. The next step in spiritual growth was seen in the confidence and visionary zeal of the title character *Harry Potter*.

In the book, this title character was given the same birthday as the Leo author. It is interesting that the star who played Harry (Daniel Radcliffe) also happens to be a Leo!

In the 10 years it took to produce these 8 films, we watched these students of wizardry learn their spiritual lessons, as they grew up before our eyes!

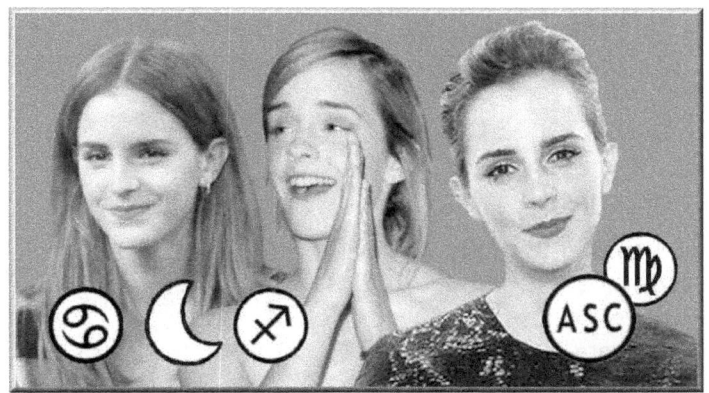

Moon: Sagittarius   Ascendant: Virgo

In the character of *Hermione*, Rowling created the "teacher in the group", to disperse lessons out to others. Emma's Sagittarius Moon fits this "purpose".

With the fire of her cardinal Aries Sun, Watson supplied the missing modes of fire, that were needed—to complete the fixed visions of the book's Leo character (Harry Potter).

Interestingly, since Jupiter (the ruler of Emma's Moon) is positioned in Cancer (the sign ruled by the Moon), Emma appears to have two uniquely different emotional reactions:

At certain times (as the upper left photo shows), the tidal waters of Cancer will swell and round the facial flesh. The center photo (likely taken in one of Watson's highly spirited moments), shows the animated and fiery gestures of a rambunctious filly.

Notably, Watson's Ascendant forms a T-Square to her Moon and Jupiter. This giant planet is at the farthest point from her Moon, and this implies that Emma must reach beyond her emotions—to realize "higher states of understanding". All of the details of his information enter through the door of Emma's mercuric Ascendant. Furthermore, Saturn's trine to this Rising Sign makes them real.

J.K. Rowling has a Virgo Moon and Gemini Rising. Mercury runs strong in her magical tales, as well as in the lead female character in her books.

Interestingly, J.K. gave Hermione the birthday of a Virgo Sun. Why not? This child was the "know-it-all" bookworm of the group, who would search through the ancient texts to find solutions for her friends. With her Virgo Ascendant and her Mercury trine to Venus, Emma had a gift for presenting these mercuric details to others.

Rowling and Emma both have Uranus in the 4th House. J.K.'s Uranus conjoins Pluto, and this enabled her to invent a powerful tool to teach kids valuable lessons. In contrast, Emma's Uranus conjoins Neptune. Her interpretation of this intuitive child sparked the imaginations of youngsters around the world!

Besides the fortune of her Jupiter on her Midheaven, Emma was given special gifts at birth and this allowed her to be chosen to play one of the most important child roles in film history.

In adulthood, Emma must now express the light of her Aries Sun. Like with most of us, her success will take a lot of work, and it will not be just due to luck.

See J. K. Rowling's portrait on page 194

Here, the Ground of Earth smothers the Fire
(as the Saturn Cycle manifests its rewards)

David Letterman
4/12/1947, 6:05 A.M.
Indianapolis, IN

In 2015, David Letterman stepped out of the lime light to end his 32 year run as the longest running late-night talk show host in TV history. (It was two years longer than Johnny Carson's record run).

Here, we will examine how his chart components contributed to his success, as we also examine how the transits of Saturn influenced his career. Notably, this ringed planet is the most aspected planet in his chart and the ruler of Capricorn, the sign of his Moon.

The Force of Fire
Sun and Mars in Aries

It is the combination of the daily, monthly and yearly lights at birth, that indicate the nature of one's personality. However, it is the long-range cycles and aspects between the Sun and planets, that define the creative course that each and every individual pursues in life.

Letterman's Aries Sun sextiles his Uranus in the mercuric sign of Gemini. Since Uranus is the ruler of television, we see why he succeeded at being a popular and unconventional TV talk show host.

While hosting CBS's *The Late Show*, Dave also created his own production company *Worldwide Pants*, a winning race team and several charity foundations.

Interestingly, David's key lights are all in "animal signs": The Aries Ram, The Taurus Bull and the Capricorn Goat. Therefore, the physical features of the Ram are not obvious. What we do see is the prominent nose, the large upper lip plate and the long jaw.

With six components in fire and air (and a grand trine between Jupiter, Saturn and his Aries Mars) Dave's physical energy can be intense, forceful and highly driven. Oddly, to his audience he often appeared relaxed, easygoing and also tenaciously serious at times. This can be attributed to his other two key components. They are both in Earth signs.

The Solidity of Earth
Moon in Capricorn

In his interviews with guests, this Ram often butted in—with his wise crack observations. But when the conversation becomes emotional, he would always redirect the conversation in a more serious direction. David has a Capricorn Moon.

Watch how Dave made these goatlike moves—as he injected his snarky and poignant observations into the discussion. This is the stuff that made Dave different from the other TV hosts. It was not all fun and games!

Ascendant: Taurus

When the cardinal lights of Dave's solar and lunar energies dim, the Taurus Bull anchors himself in his chair—to relish the content of its surroundings! Here, David casually presented his fixed and lackadaisical bovine persona as he welcomed his guests into his earthy comfort zone.

With his Ascendant trine his Moon and sextile its ruling planet Venus (in Pisces), Dave's personal feelings were openly presented to his audience. When he had his heart surgery, he brought his medical team onto the stage. When threatened by a blackmailer, he laid it out for all to see. And who could forget his post 9-11 comments. No one else was more moving! What we saw was raw and real.

Note: Data claims a 6:00 A.M. birth time, but that appears to be a rounded set of time. We set it for 5 minutes later to place his bone-shaping Ascendant in the mutable Virgo decant. This would account for the wide gap in his frontal teeth.

Saturn Brings Its Rewards

With his grand trine of Saturn, Mars and Jupiter, David manifested an exceptional career in comedy. Saturn's cycles indicated the timing of its unfolding!

For years, Dave struggled as a standup comic, but by the time of his first Saturn return (1977), he became so popular he was selected to became a regular guest host on Johnny Carson's *Tonight Show*.

In 1982, when transiting Saturn was in Dave's 6th House of work sextiling his empowering Pluto, David became host of the post-Carson show: *Late Night*.

In 1992, Johnny Carson retired. Everyone expected Dave to replace him. Surprisingly, it went to Jay Leno. At this time, transiting Saturn was in Dave's 10th House; portending short term restrictions in his career. Also, Saturn was opposing Dave's natal Pluto and squaring Pluto's transit in Scorpio. When Dave begin *The Late Show* on CBS. the "night show wars" got nasty, but in time, it proved to be a very positive move.

By the time of Saturn's second return (2006), Dave had 15 wins and 47 Emmy nods—the second highest total of all time!

In 2012, Saturn transited his 6th House of work again when he received his *Kennedy Center Honor* for being...."One of the most influential personalities in the history of TV." Shortly after, he became the U.S.A.'s longest serving late-night host.

Albert Gore, Jr.
3/31/1948, 12:53 P.M.
Washington, DC

SUN: Aries

Al Gore was one of our nation's most active Vice Presidents and the first to be totally involved in creating executive branch policies on ecology and the internet. He has shown his Aries gift for clearing away the clutter, by attempting to make government more simple.

Gore shows many of the physical traits of the Ram, notably the convex facial features and the eyebrows that sweep back from the protruding muzzle. The double-crowned horns on his hairline also suggest the presence of Aries.

Missing in this equation is the raw, gusto force of cardinal fire—for Gore's fires would never seem to ignite! Some have even said he has "the wooden expression of a tree".

Once, Gore made fun of his stolid image by dancing "The Macarena". He just stood there like a stone, moved nary a limb and responded—"Want to see it again?" Why so much substance and so little flash? Check out the rest of his chart!

Ascendant: Leo

This Aries has Leo rising and a Leo grouping of Pluto, Mars and Saturn conjoined in his 1st House. Saturn is in the center, locking them together in a tightly fixed position. This stony stellium also trines his Sun.

Mars is the planet that rules Al's Sun. It also indicates the manner in which he physically moves. Saturn's conjunction with Mars would make his actions "wooden". Pluto's conjunction with Saturn intensifies this fixed and rigid demeanor.

Surprisingly, Gore reflects little of the self importance of Aries and Leo. He rarely uses the word "I". The plural "We" is more often spoken. Gore's Uranus sextiles his 1st House stellium. Also, with Mercury in Pisces and his Venus in Taurus, we see why this Aries identifies with the conditions in his environment.

Moon: Capricorn

If you try to ignite Al's fires, or arouse his emotions, you will often notice how he becomes ever more cautious and rigid. Such is the nature of most folks who have a Capricorn Moon. Surprisingly, Al's Moon is conjoined by Jupiter (in Sagittarius). This sends Gore off on his famous, enthusiastic excursions, but it does little to loosen the rigidity of his emotions.

Jupiter enabled Al to take the daring leap with his book *Earth In The Balance*. With this work, Gore became the Aries Pioneer, who helped to awaken the world to the dangers of climate change. This Moon give him the tenacity to get it done.

Elton John
3/25/1947, 2:00 A.M.
Pinner-Middlesex, England

SUN: Aries

Elton John displays the creative drive and originality that one would expect from an Aries Sun. However, Elton doesn't look or act like a typical Aries. This may be due to his Midheaven Neptune. It opposes his Sun and sextiles his Ascendant and Pluto. Also, his Mars (Aries' ruler) and Mercury are in Pisces. These Neptunian forces dampen the fire, as they soften and round Aries' normally angular physical features.

On talk shows, Elton seems surprisingly timid—until he starts pushing an opinion or a cause, or goes into one of his charged up performances. Once the fires start, these Neptunian forces quickly evaporate.

In 1979, transiting Neptune was opposing Elton's Saturn and squaring his Moon. This transit (and these heavy Neptune aspects) may have contributed to Elton's acknowledged drug problem and career downturn. Soon after this transit, Elton resurrected his creative path, as his music became less hard rock and more lyrical and compassionate. From then on, it was one hit after another.

Ascendant: Sagittarius

With his Sun trine Jupiter, (the ruler of his Ascendant), you can expect someone who's capable of putting on an fiery show. With an Aquarius Venus trine Uranus—and his Mars forming a T-square to his Ascendant and Uranus—you can expect this show to be absolutely outrageous! Who can forget the 12 inch high-heeled shoes, the giant glittering glasses and fur coats? These props were often strange and seemingly from another world.

Outrageous costumes are also part of **Lady Gaga**'s act. Her Uranus also trines Venus and aspects her Ascendant. (See page 91).

Elton has a huge and high forehead that slopes rapidly to the rear. This pushes the skull to the back, and it suggests the head of a horse. However, the long nose of the Centaur is missing and Elton has a stubby nose with wide nostrils. This may be due to the fact that both of his luminaries form aspects to Saturn and Pluto in the fixed sign of Leo—or it may be a product of his Moon.

Moon: Taurus

Elton's solar and rising fires may burn brightly on stage, but emotionally, Elton desires to escape to pastures. His Moon is in the Fixed Earth sign of Taurus.

Elton's earthy Moon sextiles Mercury in watery Pisces. This gives him highly acute sensations, as well as a gift for feeling (and voicing) the rhythmic and melodic patterns experienced by his senses.

This Taurus Moon also gives him the focus to produce his prolific output of music. Without this practical, earthy element in his personality, the candle may have burned out a long time ago.

Robert Downey, Jr.
4/4/1965, 1:10 P.M.
Manhattan, NY

SUN: Aries

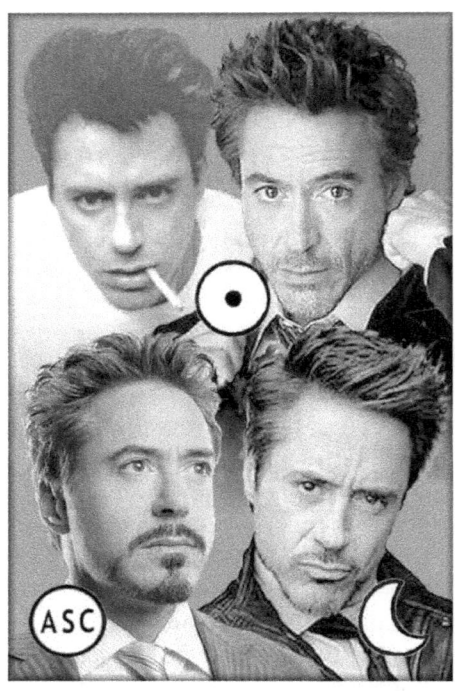

Born into Hollywood's fast lane, Robert Downey Jr. began his excesses early—just what you would expect from someone with Sun, Mercury and Venus in Aries. Here is a person who lives in the moment, leaps before thinking, and sees himself as his own authority. Also, his Sun's ruling planet Mars conjoins Pluto and Uranus, and the latter two trine his Moon. This takes this Ram to impulsive and emotional extremes. As he says: "The higher the stakes, the happier I am".

In 1992, Robert receiving a BAFTA Award as Best Actor for his role as *Charlie Chaplin*. However, by 1999 (when Saturn was at the top of his chart), Robert's career was at rock bottom. That year, he began his three year sentence in a drug abuse center.

This contradicts the norm for having a career boost when Saturn is at the top of a chart, but it shows how one receives the rewards they've earned. However, Robert's resulting sobriety brought him his later rewards: his roles in the hugely popular film franchises of *Sherlock Holmes* and *Iron Man*.

Robert displays the Ram's vertically enhanced face, but his Aries snout is smaller than expected. Like with Elton John, this is likely due to the fixed components in his chart.

Ascendant: Leo

Downey's Leo Ascendant enhances the fires as it contains the heat in a fixed and holding pattern. This changes the nature of his expression, as it makes him appear cocky and proud—and a bit of a ham. Since Robert's Sun and Moon aspect his Ascendant, he appears to be a mix of a Ram and a Lion.

Moon: Taurus

Like **Elton John**, Robert also has a Taurus Moon. His fires also subside, when he reflects on life's pleasures. The big difference is that Elton's Moon aspects a Saturn/Pluto conjunction; Robert's Moon conjoins Jupiter as it trines a grouping of Mars, Saturn and Uranus. Guess which one had the most trouble controlling his temper?

Positively, Robert's Mars, Saturn and Uranus are all in Virgo. This earthy energy supports his Taurus emotions, and this allows him to control the moment and master his acting craft.

Robert's Virgo Uranus gives him the ability to display the technical genius of *Iron Man*. Pluto and Mars gave him the control to capture the essence of *Chaplin* (who was another Aries with strong fixed elements in his chart).

Taurus

	Page
Introduction to Taurus Traits Kate Hepburn & George Lucas	107-109

Transition from Aries to Taurus

Cate Blanchett	110
Daniel Day-Lewis	111

Lots of Earth, but add some Water

Candice Bergan	112
Mark Zuckerberg	113
Adele (Adele Laurie Blue Adkins)	114-115
George Clooney	116
Cher	117

Heat the Earth with Fire

Michael Moore	118
Renee Zellweger	119
Jack Nicholson	120
Al Pacino	121
Kirsten Dunst	122
Barbra Streisand	123

Add the Element of Air

Tina Fey, Stephen Colbert	124
Jay Leno	125
Jessica Lange	126
Craig Ferguson	127
Michelle Pfieffer	128

Taurus ♉ April 20 to May 20
Feminine Polarity, Fixed Earth
Arouse your senses with a TAURUS friend!

When the Sun enters the middle month of Spring, the expansive fire of **Aries** is countered and contained—as the femininely polarized and fixed force of **Taurus** takes control. Here, the roots of Nature sink deeply into the Earth, as the showers of April bring the flowers of May. The resulting plethora of beautiful delights provides the planet with its most productive month of physical growth! These earthy treats are refined and made ever more useful by the input from the other Earth signs: **Virgo** and **Capricorn**.

Look in shady and quiet places—or in lush settings where green, brown, and earthy tones dominate. There you will find these mellow bovine souls, grazing on delicious treats and exotic liquids. Their firm smiles and glazed eyes tell us of the condition of their sensual state. Few words are needed to explain the pleasures they are feeling.

These powerful creatures are the builders of the Zodiac. Physical work is rarely shunned. So put them to work—to prepare and plant your garden. Better yet, have them build your home or any other physical structures you may need.

Negatively, these creatures can become self-indulgent, lazy and obsessed with accumulating wealth and massive possessions. They also can be extremely stubborn! So, don't wave a red flag in their face by disagreeing with one of their firmly fixed opinions. This will likely arouse their anger!

Individuals with a Taurus Sun, Moon, or Rising Sign (or a strongly aspected Venus in a feminine sign) often express the passive, immovable qualities of Fixed Earth. These natures are intensified, when planets transit the 2nd House.

These inflexible tendencies are loosened, altered and expanded with the Sun's progression into the next sign in the Zodiac: the Mutable Air sign of **Gemini**.

Rulerships & Associations for Taurus

Venus' association with personal enjoyment (on a raw, physical level) is manifested in its rulership of the feminine sign of Taurus. Everything is kept simple, not arty or complex, as seen in the highly mental creations of Venus' co-ruled masculine sign of Libra.

The feminine nature of the Goddess Venus is captured in C.G. Jung's Anima. This is the passive "magnetic force" of attraction, that makes one individual appealing to another. This attraction operates in both sexes.

Taurus is anchored in the acreage in the 2nd House in the chart. There, we find our worthy physical possessions, i.e., buildings, land, and real estate. The value of these owned objects are determined by our neighborhood Taurus bankers.

Taurus rules the metal copper, the sapphire stone, the fragrant and aromatic rose, and all things that arouse our senses.

Taurus Physical Traits:

The large bovine eyes of Taurus are their most obvious features. Note how the large pupilage (and earthy colored corneas) sit high under their heavy eyelids. This lifts the outer edges of the eyes upward—as it drops the lower portion of each eye and pulls it into the center.

These bovine eyes are firmly placed under the wide-set eyebrows, that dip sharply downward in the center. These upper features are anchored on the wide nostrilled nose, the square, short jaw and the dimpled chin.

Watch what happens when these bovine eyes focus on a colorful butterfly—when their ears hear the music of buzzing bees—or when the nostrils spread to capture the delightful aroma of a nearby flower. In these moments of divine contentment, these bovine creatures have little reason to move. Well, at least until their senses are attracted to the greener pasture just down the road.

Katharine Hepburn and *George Lucas* are both triple fixed signs! Along with their Taurus Suns, Kate has a Taurus Moon and Scorpio Ascendant. George has Taurus Rising and an Aquarius Moon. Thusly, the cubical features of fixity appear in their bone structure, as well as in the moldings in their facial expressions.

Taurus Body Language

When the center of body energy shifts down from the head of Aries, it is concentrated in the throat, neck and shoulder region—the area of the body ruled by Taurus.

With the forward-trust of Aries' head, the Ram charges forward, uninhibited. However, when the internalized and feminine energies of Taurus are placed in this region, the mechanics bring the "forward movement" to a halt.

Note how the forward lean of the shoulders pushes the lower torso and butt to the back. This distribution of weight bows the legs, as it plants the feet firmly in the ground. Tauruses have to lift all of this heavy weight—to begin their forward trudge.

This body rulership and the fixed earth energies also define this creature's body features. Most notable are the heavy shoulders, the massive bones and torso, and the stocky arms and legs.

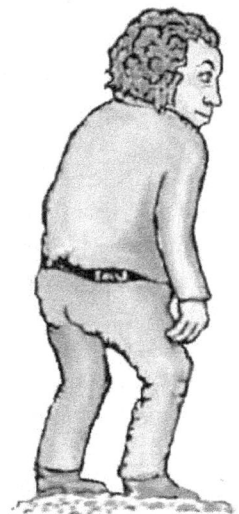

Taurus rules the throat, neck and shoulders

This portrait is a double Taurus but she shows little of the physical traits of fixed Earth. The decans of her Sun and Ascendant are not in Taurus.

Cate Blancett
5/14/1969, 6:40 A.M.
Melbourne, Australia

Taurus: Sun & Rising

Sun in Capricorn Decan

In this book's *introduction to decans* on page 10, it was noted that Blancett's 22° Taurus Sun was placed in the Capricorn decan. We illustrated the physical impact of this decan by stating: "The sensuality of Taurus seems cooler and paler, as Cate's steely eyes and high-set cheek bones suggest the qualities of a cardinal driven goat." Here, we have room to add more to the discussion.

The calculating qualities of Capricorn were seen in Cate's Oscar winning role in *Blue Jasmine*. And who can forget her portrayal of the nuances of movie star Kate Hepburn in the film *The Aviator*? Was it because Hepburn's Taurus Sun was also in the decan of Capricorn?

Still, there's something else here besides the decan effects on Blancett's Sun. She seems far too etherial for an Earth sign. This may be due to her Sun's trine to Jupiter, Uranus, and Pluto (in Virgo), and their sextile to Neptune. These aspects pull her away from the pleasures of Earth, into distant space. This cools her mid-Spring light as it makes her appear that she is living on another world.

Ascendant in Virgo Decan

This "untouchability" is also a product of Cate's 15° Taurus Ascendant. This degree places her Rising Sign in the decan of Virgo. This explains the delicate virginal persona we saw n her role as the Elf Queen in *Lord of the Rings*. It also explains why she loathes the idea of being "a silver screen sex siren."

With this decan, Cate's bone structure lacks the square shape we'd expect from a Taurus Ascendant. What we see is the long face, thin neck and lanky body of Virgo. These long facial features are enhanced by her Aries Moon.

Moon: Aries
in Sagittarius Decan

As the warrior queen *Elizabeth* and the Russian agent in Indiana Jones' *Kingdom of the Chrystal Skull*, Cate showed the martial qualities of her Aries Moon. With this Moon in the Sagittarius decan (and her Mars is in Sagittarius), this lady is always ready to jump into action!

This Centaur force makes Cate athletic and adventurous. With her Mars trine her Venus in Aries, she rarely hesitates, as she gallops away to conquer new creative adventures. Few Tauruses would make the jump to establish their own live theater company, like she did in her homeland of Australia.

The Voice comes from the throat

The quality of anyone's voice is often defined by the signs of one's Sun, Moon, Venus or Mercury, or the ruling sign of the 3rd House. The voice often mimics the tone of the element of the signs involved. With his Sun, Mercury and Venus in Taurus, Daniel's voice resonates with the deep tones of Earth. Water signs are liquid and melodic. The Air signs are usually high pitched and breathy. Fire voices are sharp and intense.

Oddly, Daniel's only Air is his Mars in Gemini. So, how was he able to re-create the historically correct, but surprisingly "high pitched and breathy voice" of President Abraham Lincoln in the 2012 movie *Lincoln*? Let's look at some possibilities.

Daniel Day Lewis
4/29/1957, 12:47 A.M.
London, England

Sun in Taurus

Lewis' deep baritone "Taurus voice" was heard in *There Will Be Blood* and *Gangs of New York*, as well as in many other films. In Lincoln, it was something else! This may be due to Daniel's 3rd House cusp being Aries. Aries' ruler is Mars and Lewis' Mars is in the Air Sign of Gemini—in the Aquarius decan, the sign of Lincoln's Ascendant and Sun! Notably, Lincoln's Mars was also in an Air Sign, but in Libra. This likely helped Daniel to replicate the tone of Lincoln's voice.

Daniel's Neptune rules his chart; it sextiles his Pluto, trines Mars, squares Uranus and opposes his Sun and Moon. This gives Daniel a powerful, yet melodic voice, capable of creating a high range of tones and rhythms.

Ascendant: Capricorn
Moon in Aries

With his earthy Sun and Capricorn Rising, Daniel easily projected the tone of Lincoln's Capricorn Moon. With his fiery Aries Moon, Daniel also was able to bring the strident intensity (or force) of Lincoln's Venus-in-Aries voice to the front. Notably, Lewis' Moon forms a sextile to Lincoln's Aquarius Sun and Ascendant. This likely contributed to Lewis' intuitive performance of Lincoln's voice and personality.

Karmic Connections

Oddly, both men have Neptune on their Midheavens. Also, Lewis' Neptune is conjoined by Abraham's Uranus. Another karmic link is Daniel's Pluto and its opposition to Abe's Aquarius Sun and Ascendant. With this view, Daniel was able to see the world "through the eyes of Lincoln". This is just what Daniel needed, to win himself another Oscar.

A Triple Earth Sign!
Candice Bergen
5/9/1946, 9:52 P.M.
Los Angeles, CA

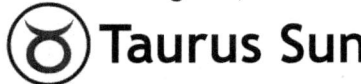 **Taurus Sun**

Candice exhibits all three of Earth's modes of expression—cardinal, fixed, and mutable. The fixed mode appears when her Taurus Sun attempts to project its light. Watch how her eyebrows turn down, her nostrils widen, and how those large bovine eyes lock in place, when she attempts to maintain control.

This strength was seen in her role as a journalist in the film *Gandhi*. Taurus' sensual side was exposed in her role in *Carnal Knowledge*.

Bergen's Mars conjoins Pluto (in Leo and her 8th House). This makes her physical actions flamboyant as well as mysteriously powerful. It really shows when she gets angry! This powerful fixed sign conjunction adds an undercurrent of intensity to her easy going Sun-Sign. It also enhances the thick hair and the square forehead and jaw that is often seen in Taurus.

Moon: Virgo

When Candice's Virgo Moon reacts to others, her energies go into mutable mode. Watch how her fingers point and count, as she twists words and nitpicks over an endless string of details. This distorts the fixed lines in her face.

Emotionally, Bergen wants to arrange these details into a more perfect order. However, with these mutable emotions, she often ends up changing her mind. That is a rare feat for a Taurus!

This lunar light squares a Venus/Uranus conjunction in Candice's 6th House. Thusly, Candice is able to work well with quirky Virgos like Pee Wee Herman (Paul Reubens) and Lily Tomlin.

With this triad of earth, Candice keeps closely attached to the physical plane. Her work rarely sizzles or soars, and her matter-of-fact demeanor and emotional expressions eliminate all flights of fantasy. Her comedy is made from real stuff. That is what makes it work.

Ascendant: Capricorn

When her Sun and Moon are in the background, Candice's fixed nature shifts into cardinal mode, when her Capricorn Ascendant rises to the surface.

In this state of repose, the flesh is layered on the underlying bone structure. This revealing of the highly placed cheek bones gives Bergen the solemn appearance of a tenacious goat. Note how her eyes look upward, as if they were seeking higher peaks to pursue. This sardonic mask helped her to create the grumbling character in her hit TV show: *Murphy Brown*.

Add some Water to the Fire
Mark Zuckerberg
5/14/1984, 2:39 P.M.
Dobbs Ferry, NY

Sun in Taurus, Moon & Mars in Scorpio

Mark's Sun and Venus are in Taurus. His Moon, Mars, Saturn, and Pluto cluster together in fixed Scorpio. This gives a powerful ability to focus his energies. (Many programers share these traits). With these fixed forces, Mark built his very profitable social site *Facebook*. They also show why he totally controlled and refused to let go of any his creations.

In more contented moments, Mark reveals hints of the bovine eyes of the Taurus Bull, but when he emotionally reacts to others, his Scorpio eyes take on a laser-like focus, suggesting that he's ready to pounce on unsuspecting prey.

With all of this fixity, we'd expect Mark's physical features to show more square and cubical shapes, but what we see is a rather long and skewed face. This may be due to heredity, or it could be a product of his mutable Ascendant.

Ascendant: Virgo

Looking at Mark's facial structure, we see the features of mutability, and the thin-bridged nose of his Virgo Ascendant. This Rising Sign sextiles his Moon and Mars; it also trines his Venus and Jupiter. Mars explains his ability to work with the insufferable details of computer programming. Jupiter's aspects account for his hyperactive demeanor.

The Saturn Cycle

In previous discussions on Saturn, we demonstrated how the ringed planet's transits indicate the arch in one's career. When Mark launched *Facebook* on February 4, 2004 transiting Saturn was in his 10th House of Career. This created the world's youngest billionaire, but it was not all sunshine. In late 2007, as Saturn entered Mark's 12th House (the home of hidden enemies), Mark faced lawsuits from his fellow Harvard students. Later, he launched the failed file-sharing *Facebook Beacon,* just as transiting Saturn passed over his Ascendant. Shortly after, the film *The Social Network* was released—to cast Mark's public persona in a very negative light.

In 2011, Saturn began its transit through Mark's first quadrant. This was his time to shift from his outer world responsibilities and focus on his own personal development. With his marriage and a child, he learned valuable lessons, as his Virgo Ascendant showed him that it was time to serve others.

In April of 2018, ALL of Mark's planets (save for Jupiter) were transiting the right half of his chart. In that period, powers beyond his control took over, as he was called before congress to discuss his company's release of the personal data of his company's users.

How Aspects (and Neptune) Change the Tone of the "Taurus-Ruled" Voice
ADELE
(Adele Laurie Blue Adkins)
5/5/1988, 8:19 A.M.
Tottenham, England

Adele Laurie Blue Adkin's music has been described as being "a perfect backdrop to a lazy afternoon in the coffee shop." It's just what we'd expect from a Taurus with four of her other components in Earth signs. However, there is something else about Adele's music. It is also thought-provoking and emotionally inspiring! These gifts can be attributed to her four Air Signs, her Moon and Neptune—the planet that brings heavenly music to the Earth.

Taurus Sun

Adele's five Earth planets and four fixed components gives her an abundance of "Earth and Fixity". This reinforces the stocky features of her Taurus Sun. It shows in her broad shoulders and rectangular bone structure. In the face, we see the fixed brows, the large bovine eyes and lips, and the square chin.

Taurus rules "the throat" and Venus is the ruler of Taurus. As one would expect, these components in Adele's chart are empowered by several aspects.

Adeles' Sun conjoins Jupiter, opposes Pluto and also trines Neptune. These aspects to her Taurus Sun may be why she became "obsessed with her voice" and begin singing at the age of four.

Adele is known for her music's emotional effect on others. This emotional gift comes from her Sun's trine to Neptune and the five other Neptune aspects in her chart. This lady also has a remarkable gift for finding the right words for her music. This is likely a product of her Gemini Venus. It conjoins her Ascendant, opposes her Moon, Uranus, and Saturn—and trines her Mars.

Adele's 9th House Aquarius Mars is the nearest planet to her MC. This intuitive planet's trine to Venus drove her to compose her thoughtful lyrics, many of which are filled with hope and the altruistic messages of Aquarius.

Moon: Sagittarius

Adele's Moon, Uranus and Saturn form a string of conjoined planets in her 6th House. The two planets are in orb to Neptune (which sits in her 7th House). These three Capricorn planets are driven upward (from below) by the fling of fiery arrows—that fly from the bow of Adele's Archer Moon. With boundless enthusiasm, this lady presents her thoughtful emotions to the world.

This Moon also accounts for Adele's admittedly "blunt and mouthy nature". You'll see the fire in Adele's talk show interviews, when her hands fling arrows in all directions, as she attempts to light up new avenues of conversation.

Cancer Ascendant

Adele's Venus lies near Adele's Cancer Ascendant and all of those Capricorn planets lie in opposition. The gray of Winter is far away and the morning light of Cancer constantly appears before her eyes.

With this watery and misty shield, the range of view is contained, to reveal only things that are near and dear—i.e., those that reside in the comfort of her home. This is why Adele *loves her home* and she finds her Sun finds its anchor there.

In this private base, she creates her inspiring music. On the other side, the world is viewing this sensitive mask and the emotional comfort that it provides!

Since Cancer is ruled by the Moon, The round Moon-beam features of the Crab can be seen in Adele's facial bone structure. This also accounts for her round and full body—and her large upper torso.

Adele's voice finds its full expression

Here is an imagined scenario on how Adele's "musical voice comes into the light". The sound originates in the languid fields of Taurus, but its outward projection (to others) begins in the cluster of planets around Adele's Descendant.

The fervor is ignited by the fiery arrows, that sling outward and upward from the bow of Adele's Archer Moon. In the path lie the stepping stones of her three Capricorn planets. Listen to how the pitch rises, when it vibrates in the electrical fields of Uranus. Then, note how the tone lowers, when Saturn edges in, to give her voice substance. In finale, the weaving waves of Neptune pour out thru the portal of her watery Ascendant. It brings many of her fans to tears!

Saturn and Uranus

Adele's first album was entitled *"19"*. (It was her age when she composed many of its songs). The next albums *"21"* and *"25"* covered the years and ages of her transformation into becoming an adult. These passages of time are the stuff of Saturn.

This ringed planet's conjunction to Uranus is what makes her music so different. It also explains why she intuitively connects with her fans. One music critic beautifully stated the impact of Adele's Uranus: "Her music perfectly translates individual experiences into collective feelings."

*See Neptune's influence on **Celine Dion** (page 90 and **Pink** (on page 210)*

George Clooney

5/6/1961 / 2:54 A.M.
Lexington, KY

 Taurus Sun

In his work, Clooney often expresses the steady and deliberate pace of Fixed Earth. This easy going demeanor (with its calm, polite and well mannered qualities) was part of the persona of legendary Taurians Jimmy Stewart and Gary Cooper. Clooney is the "Taurus Rock" in his generation of movie stars.

Taurus is the worker of the zodiac, perhaps that is why George played the hardest working doctor in the TV series E.R. This doctor was always on task (see Moon) and he rarely became emotionally or mentally riled—even in major emergencies. He was "the island" in a sea of chaos. His earthy nature also gave him the sensual attractiveness, that won him a huge base of adoring fans.

George displays many of the Taurus traits mentioned previously. The most obvious is the bovine eyes, clearly demonstrated in the upper photos.

Moon: Capricorn

Like all of us, when George becomes emotional, he can only react. This kicks in his Capricorn Moon. This makes his emotions chilly—and noticeably more orchestrated and tenacious.

As we saw in *Ocean's Eleven* and *Three Kings*, Clooney has a knack for playing rogues and con artists. The cool and steely emotions of his Capricorn Moon give him the temperament of a true wheeler-dealer. This granite exterior was visually seen in his role in *The Perfect Storm*. As the situation became more intense, George's became more serious—and all the more determined to ride out the storm.

With an independent Aries Venus and a Mars in Leo, George held the title as Hollywood's Most Eligible Bachelor. However, in 2014, he married Amal. This human rights lawyer became the emotional anchor who lit up the light of his compassionate Rising Sign. They are working together to fix the problems in the world. Such work inspires most Capricorn Moons.

Ascendant: Pisces

With Pisces Rising, George sees the suffering in the world. This empathy washes away the hard granite edges of his luminaries, as it rounds the flesh and softens his facial lines. The lower left photo shows how shape of the face is also noticeably skewed by the mutable Mobius pattern.

In full saturation, George's eyes become full and deep, as they dream of a more perfect and loving world. With his earthy luminaries, he has the right stuff to make it work.

Cher
(Cheryl Sarkisian LaPiere)
5/20/1946, 7:25 A.M.
El Centro, CA

 Taurus Sun

Cher shows us what's so special about Taurus' fixed earthy voice. First of all, the cadence is steady and controlled. Secondly, it seems to track at a slightly slower speed. Vinyl collectors would say that she's running on 33 1/3 instead of 45 revolutions per minute. The slower speed lowers the pitch. The voice sounds full and massive, as it echoes from the hallows of the Earth.

When not on stage, Cher appears markedly content, as she plants herself firmly on the ground. However, put her in front of a thousand lustful sailors—and it's a different story!

Watch how her fires ignite, as she struts about on the ship's deck! This heat is generated by her Leo Mars and its sextile to Uranus and Jupiter (the most aspected planet in her chart).

This lady knows how to put on a spectacular and outrageous show.

Moon: Capricorn

On *The Sonny and Cher Show*, Cher would patiently listen to he husband's Aquarius chatter. In little time, her face would take on that cold and steely stare—and then respond with the dry and sarcastic wit. We all knew that she was the real ruler in the house.

This TV show was followed by work that was less child's play and ever more serious. Her first major film *Mask* was a powerful comment on overcoming obstacles. Shortly after, in film *Moonstruck*, it was clear that she had mastered another medium. This won her an Oscar for Best Actress!

Cher was emotionally driven to succeed in fields beyond her music. This tenacious Moon gave her the drive to create her enduring career.

Ascendant: Cancer

When her luminary lights recede, the watery tides wash over and coat Cher's facial plane. This softens her rugged Earth, as it brings her feelings to the surface. Note how the rounded, lunar temples of the Crab are set low on the face. This places the eyes very high above the cheek bones, a factor enhanced by her Capricorn Moon.

Cher has the wide shoulders and large head of Taurus, but she does not have the typical body type of Cancer Rising. This may be due to Jupiter's T-square to her 1st House Saturn and her Moon (the ruler of Cancer). Thusly, Jupiter blows Saturn's skeletal structure out of proportion! Cher's tall, lanky body and narrow hips do not suggest those of a Crab.

Heat the Earth with Fire
Michael Moore
4/23/1954, 12:45 P.M.
Flint, MI

 Taurus Sun

Michael certainly fits the image of a Taurus Bull. There's the large bovine eyes, which appear either contentedly relaxed or enraged. These eyes are set high under the broad, flat eyebrows. There's also the usual physical traits of Taurus, but the most obvious is the broad shoulders and massive carriage, which may have been enlarged by overgrazing. Let's be kind and blame it on the stars.

Michael shows the stubbornness and deliberateness of Fixed Earth. Like him or not, he has an ability to assemble the images and sensations into hard hitting observations on the moneyed elements (i.e. Taurean powers) in our society. In addition, he appears to be a tenaciously driven bull, capable of exposing and busting up powers that some of us see as being unbreakable. This can be contributed to the Saturn and Capricorn connections in his chart.

Moon: Capricorn

With his cardinal Earth Moon, Moore has a gift for sensing and understanding the corruption and power plays in our institutions and government.

With Mars sitting snugly on his Moon, (in trine to his Taurus Sun and Saturn in the sign of Scorpio), Moore seems to be obsessively driven to "make a point".

In *Roger & Me, Bowling for Columbine* and the infamous *Fahrenheit 911*, this film maker did his Taurean task, building what he saw to be "the real truth". All of this Saturn and Capricorn put the wily grumblings of his goat Moon into overdrive. With Jupiter in opposition to his Moon, there seems to be little reprieve from the heavy handed pushiness of his Moon.

Ascendant: Leo

Michael's Leo Rising likely added to his large-chested frame. It also lights up his earthy luminaries—as it gives him the aura of confidence that enables him to succeed in show business.

With Pluto conjoined to Moore's Ascendant, he has the ability to see through and expose the power trips of others. On the other hand, it is hard for him to transcend the "heaviness".

Luckily, his Ascendant is in the second decan of Sagittarius and that nasty Pluto sextiles joyful Jupiter. This gives Michael the gift for humor that made his work so successful.

Renee Zellweger

4/25/1969, 2:41 P.M.
Katy, Texas

♉ Taurus Sun

On screen, Renee is known for her down to Earth roles. In *Cinderella Man*, she played a downtrodden depression era wife. In *Cold Mountain*, she showed the bullheaded stubbornness of a backwoods girl, determined to "make something of herself". This role won her an Oscar! This stable and grounded side of Renee's personality can be attributed to her Taurus Sun's conjunction to Saturn, and its trine to her earthy Ascendant.

When Zellweger's solar lights turn on, she displays several physical traits of Taurus: the fixed eyebrows, the stubby nose, the firmly set bovine eyes, etc. What stands out is the full lips of her sensuous mouth.

Moon: Leo

After seeing Zellweger's showy performance in the dazzling *Chicago* and the boisterous reactions of her earthy character in *Cold Mountain*, one can suspect she has Leo in her chart. Yep. It's her Moon!

Leo Moons often try to "one-up" the expressive attempts of others. In the process, their fixed Fire responses become ever more dramatic, as they react to the "projected light" of others. Positively, this lunar position gives them great theatrical instincts and an almost unbreakable sense of confidence.

These "flames of fire" burn brightly in Renee's personality. This may be due to her Moon's grand trine to two of her personal planets: Venus in cardinal Aries and her Mars in mutable Sagittarius. This makes her emotional, creative and physical energies very intense. Since her feminine and masculine components are "about even", both sides appear, depending on the situation.

Ascendant: Virgo

In any "situation", when Renee is not expressing, reacting or doing physical activities, the earthy mask of her Virgo Ascendant rises up, to solidify the consistency of her flesh and twist the facial lines into mutable form.

Though she is "doing nothing", her mercuric eyes flitter, as the hands and fingers gyrate close to the body.

Renee's Taurus Mercury trines her 1st House stellium of Jupiter, Uranus and Pluto. Thusly, the mercuric force of Virgo permeates every thought in Renee's sensation oriented brain.

This explains her mercuric persona, and her gift for language. We saw this gift in Renee's roles as *Bridget Jones* and *Miss Potter*, where she mastered the language and accents of two English ladies from two eras of history.

Jack Nicholson
4/22/1937, 11:00 A.M.
Neptune N.J.

Taurus Sun

Jack Nicholson has five planets in Earth signs and a Taurus Sun. He has won fame showing us how one's "sensual fixations" define reality. Physically, you can see the bull's features in the bovine eyes. Also, note how the cowlicks on the sides of the mane mock the ears of a steer.

The looks are there, but as we know, this is not a contented beast, calmly grazing in a field. He smells the smoke in the air and red flags of fire are waving in his face.

Like Zellweger, Jack has his Venus in Aries and his Mars in Sagittarius. Since Venus is the ruler of his Sun, this bovine charges ahead—and when he does, Mars brings the fiery metabolism and the resulting clumsiness that warns us of the dangers of putting a bull in a china shop.

Unlike Renee, Uranus conjoins Jack's Sun in his 10th House. Venus (his Sun's ruler) is even closer to his MC—forming a T-square to Jupiter and Pluto! This makes his Fixed-Earth solar expressions quirky and also more intense and exaggerated.

Ascendant: Leo

The big difference between Jack and Renee is that Pluto is in Jack's 12th House, hovering close to his Ascendant and sextiling his Sun and Moon. (Zellweger's Pluto is out of orb to her Rising Sign). Also, Jupiter, Uranus, and Pluto aspect all three of Jack's key lights. Pluto is there on the Ascendant, ready to do its "show-and-tell"—to unveil an unsettling view of Pluto's deeper mysteries.

In *The Last Detail*, the Leo mask was out front—roaring to get attention! In his Oscar winning role in *One Flew Over The Cuckoo's Nest,* he showed us a proud individual, who made us wonder who was really insane. In *The Shining*, Pluto took over and left no question.

When Leo rises, the eyes turn from bovine to feline and the jaw juts out to reveal his once hidden lion jowls. In the moment, Jack holds the fire to purr and preen—and assure himself that everything is in control. With Pluto just below the surface, you feel that you'd better not mess with this kitty.

Moon: Virgo

When emotionally riled, Virgo Moons become nervous, obsessed with frivolous details and often critical of others. Jack's late degree Virgo Moon sextiles his Ascendant, Mars, Uranus and Pluto, so expect all courtesy to fly out the window! Recall the restaurant scene in *Five Easy Pieces,* where Jack reorders his breakfast. Or watch his questioning responses in *Chinatown*. Better yet, view the 1997 movie where Jack plays a hypochondriac, consumed by life's imperfections. For a Virgo Moon, that is *As Good As It Gets!*

Let's stoke the Fire!
Al Pacino
4/25/1940, 11:02 P.M.
New York, NY

⊙ Taurus Sun

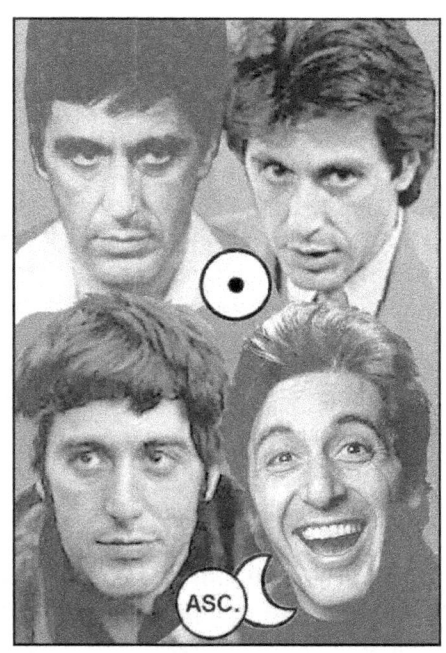

In many of his roles, Pacino played characters who stubbornly controlled all of those around him. The best example was his roles in *Godfather I* and *II*, where he played the mafia boss who found that he would be in danger "if he let go of any of his power".

In *Scent of a Woman*, Pacino played a blind man who compensated for his lack of sight by relying on his senses of smell, sound, and touch. In this role, Pacino expressed the importance of all of our senses and the rage that we feel when we are denied any of them. He also portrayed how these senses can become obsessed with carnal fixations.

When Al's sensual intensity is projected, we see the mannerisms of a Taurus bull. The usual features of Taurus are there. The most obvious is his thick curly hair.

Saturn conjoins Pacino's Sun and they both square his Ascendant. This may be why he is so small in height. It certainly explains why he frequently displays the mannerisms of a goat.

With Saturn's presence, Al has the gift for dramatizing how the human urge to "own and control" can turn into a drive for power. His performances have often examined this theme, as they gave us some disturbing insights into Taurus' darker side. Fortunately, most of them have incorporated a reoccurring Saturn theme: "In the end, we all receive what we have earned."

Moon: Sagittarius

This creature rarely finds contented pastures, for his emotions are instantly fired up and scattered by his Centaur Moon. This Moon trines Jupiter as it opposes Al's Mars and Venus (in airy Gemini). This keeps his emotions in a constant whirl. This erratic energy was masterly displayed in the emotional antics that we saw in Pacino's role in the film *Dog Day Afternoon*.

Ascendant: Leo

Like Jack Nicholson, Pacino's Pluto is in his 12th House conjoining his Leo Ascendant. The roaring fires of Leo also remain under the surface of his prideful mask—at least until his luminaries are activated.

As with Nicholson, Al has the close-set brow, wide and flat cheekbones and the large square chin of a lion. However, the bone structure of Al's jaw is much longer in height. This could be due to his Moon's trine to its ruling planet Jupiter and the giant planet's sextile to Venus (the ruler of his Sun). It explains why his features resemble those of a horse, as well as those of a bull.

Kirsten Dunst
4/30/1982, 1:00 P.M.
Point Pleasant, NJ

Remarkably, Kirsten had over 50 TV and film appearances under her belt by the age of 25. Moving between various genres of drama, comedy and art house fares, she become one of the few actresses to have succeeded as a child, adolescence and adult star. Her chart suggests why such a possibility was possible.

Taurus Sun

At the age of 12, Kirsten first attracted attention in the film *Interview with the Vampire*. There, she portrayed the non-ageing vampire *Claudia*—a grown woman trapped in a child's body. This role, which earned her a Golden Globe nod as "Best Supporting Actress" was immediately followed by her attention getting performances in *Little Women* and *Jumanji*. In her late teens, she received praise for her dramatic role in *The Virgin Suicides* and gained a teen audience in the cheerleader movie *Bring It On*. In her 20's, she gained enormous popularity in the hit franchise films *Spiderman I, II and III*.

Physically, Kirsten displays the fixed qualities of her Taurus Sun. The UR photo shows Taurus' square forehead, as well as Taurus' wide set nostrils and those easy going bovine eyes. Since the other key lights in her chart are both in the fixed sign of Leo, we also see the wide-set and cubical cheek bones of a lion.

Ascendant & Moon in LEO

With this abundance of fixity, Kirsten shows us what happens when the element changes, while the mode remains the same. The left photos show the anchored quality of Dunst's Sun at different ages. The middle left photo captures a moment when these earth and fire forces were in transition. The eyes are grounded but the tight lips are suggesting the confident snarl of a lion. The light of Leo glows brightly in the two lower photos. They show the folds that drop downward at the outer edges of the smile—to form the jowly cheeks and broad jaw of a lion.

Strong Saturn Influences

Longevity in any career often comes from strong Saturn connections. Dunst's Saturn sextiles her Moon and Pluto, while the ringed planet squares her karmic Lunar Nodes. This implies that her career would start young and she would recognition for her work for a long period of time. So far, so good.

Interestingly, child star Elizabeth Taylor's Saturn sextiled her Nodes. This regenerating aspect boosted her career, well into her later years in life.

Barbra Streisand

4/24/1942, 5:15 A.M.
Brooklyn NY

 Taurus Sun

Lights! Camera! Action! Whoa, let's get things in control—this lady is a Taurus! With her Sun in the 1st House (trine her Mars), there's an assertive practicality going on. However, with her other lights, there's also an incredible urge to present the content of her senses and feelings--and show them off to others.

The sensual content comes easy, for Barbra has four components in Taurus. This heavy fixity accounts for her legendary obsession with work—and the stubbornness she displayed, when she built her dense and rich creations.

Watch Streisand when she slows down to smell the roses. In these contented moments, her bovine eyes appear as she fixes onto the Earth. This contentment quickly disappears, when the fires of her other key components ignite!

Moon: Leo

"What's Up, Doc? Mostly me!"—says a Leo Moon. As we saw in many previous portraits, the lunar responses of a Lion will always attempt to outshine and upstage all of the other lights in the room. In Barbra's case, with every one of her reactions: *A Star is Born.*

These proud reactions were seen in the fixed and regal stance that appeared when Streisand reveled in the applause that she received from her fans.

With Pluto in her 5th House conjoined her Moon and sextiling Neptune (the ruler of Cinema), Barbra became obsessed with capturing every "sensual detail" in her films. This is why her films were filled with lush images, works of art, beautiful music and magnificently choreographed movements.

Ascendant: Aries

Save for a few reclusive periods of grazing, this lady has been a fiery comet blazing new paths! This can be attributed to her Leo Moon's trine to her Aries Ascendant. This enhances her strong sense of self, as it impels her to pursue her creative work.

In *Funny Girl*, *The Way We Were*, and *Yentl*, she lead the way in playing strong, independent women. She also charged through the glass ceiling and became one of Hollywood's first female producers and directors.

Notably, Aries stretches the normally cubical face of Taurus to form a bone structure that mocks the features of a Ram. Note the swept-back eyebrows and the convex face that is accented by the giant snout.

Add the Element of AIR

What we see here are two personalities with fiery Rising Signs and airy Moons. Their components are similar, but for each, a different planet dominates. This changes the nature of their comedy.

Stephen Colbert
5/13/1964, 9:03 P.M.
Washington, DC

Taurus Sun / Gemini Moon

Colbert's Taurus Mercury and Mars conjoins Jupiter. The latter two trine his 9th House Uranus/Pluto conjunction as they sextile his Saturn and Venus. Jupiter is his most aspected planet! His Moon's only aspect is its opposition to Neptune; his Sun has no aspects. Few guess him to be a Taurus Sun. Oddly, Stephen's only air is his Moon. However, its ruling planet Mercury is part of the Jupiterian aspects mentioned above. This is why Stephen is never "lost for words" and why he's so good at improvisation. This mercuric Moon also shows why he saw little emotion, when he interviewed quests on *The Colbert Report* or on *The Late Show*.

Tina Fey
5/18/1970, 10:42 A.M.
Upper Darby, PA

Taurus Sun / Libra Moon

The big difference between Tina and Stephen is that her Sun trines her Uranus/Pluto conjunction. This empowers her Sun with Uranus' outrageous view of reality. Oddly, Tina's Saturn and Mercury have no aspects, save for their conjunction with each other. With little Saturn, Tina lacks the political drive of Colbert. Also, her comedic skills have more emotional impact, since her Moon conjoins Jupiter. These two components trines her Venus and Mars in Gemini. These Air components gave her a incredible gift for words. Also, Saturn's conjunction (on her 10th House Mercury) gave her the tenacious drive to succeed as a writer. She became the first woman head-writer for *Saturday Night Live*, the executive producer of *30 Rock*, an author of several books, and a creator of several feature films.

Ascendants: Leo and Sagittarius

Tina's Leo Ascendant is the only fire in her chart. This mask enhances her fixed features, as it adds a dramatic flair to her luminaries and gives her an aura of confidence.

Colbert's Ascendant is also his only Fire, but it is in Sagittarius, the sign ruled by Jupiter. This kicks up the juices on his eight passive components, as it makes his Jupiterian nature even more obvious. It also gives his face many of the features of a Centaur.

Jay Leno

4/28/1950, 2:03 A.M.
New Rochelle, NY

As the host of The Tonight Show, Jay Leno gave us a "real time" view of his personality. (His reactions and views were usually his own, since he rarely followed a script). This provides us with a special opportunity, to see how astrology affects the personality.

Taurus Sun

At certain times, this bull seems almost immovable, as he relaxed in his "anchor chair". There, Leno's eyes would take on that "bovine gaze", as his voice deepened, and flowed ever so slowly, as he savored the stimulation from his receptive guests. In this state of Venusian contentment, Jay revealed the fixed and grounded qualities of his Taurus Sun. See two upper photos.

Physically, Leno has the large frame and shoulders seen in most Tauruses. Structurally, we also see the cubical skull and the flat (almost concave) facial plane—a shape further enhanced by the broad, horizontal eyebrows, the wide jaw and the stubby nose with its wide-set nostrils.

Ascendant: Aquarius

There's another fixed pattern going on here—the fixed air of Jay's Aquarius Ascendant! This Rising Sign affects his body's appearance and the general mannerisms that are apparent, when the Sun or Moon are not in operation.

In the Aquarius-ruled media world of television, Jay constantly presented his electronic mask to the world. Notably, when off stage, he often slipped back into the comfort zone of his more reserved solar and lunar energies.

With this Aquarius presence, Jay appeared restless and erratic. Oddly, his massive frame often seemed to be as light as air, as if he were hovering in an electrically charged cloud. There, he manifested those "out-of-the-blue surprises", that often contradicted the real world realities of his Taurus Sun. These contrasting fixations are the stuff from which his comedy was made.

Moon Sign: Virgo

When Leno's Virgo Moon is activated, Jay becomes noticeably analytical, as his thoughts become more detailed.

Like most Virgo Moons, he often responds by *"asking a question"*. This also gives him the annoying habit of reacting to his own jokes—by explaining the punch line several times! Now, he wouldn't want you to miss out on the ingenious play on words, or the detailed comic nuances or clever connections. Heck, to make it clear, he'll explain it one more time to be sure.

Jessica Lange
4/20/1949, 11:00 A.M.
Cloquet, Minnesota

 **Taurus Sun**

Jessica's Venus forms six aspects (including its conjunction to her Venus-ruled Sun in the 10th House). This inherent beauty won her a role in 1976's *King Kong*. There, it captured the heart of the beast, but many movie critics were not so kind. Jessica was typecast as an "object of beauty" and nothing more. Fortunately, this lady's 10th House Sun squares Saturn. She had bigger plans!

In 1981, she won critical acclaim, playing the murderous wife in *The Postman Always Rings Twice*. This was followed by her roles in the 1982 films *Frances* and *Tootsie*. The first won her an Oscar nod; The latter won her an Oscar. It was a great year for the light of this Venusian beauty to shine.

Moon: Aquarius

Jessica's Sun, Venus and Mars also form a sextile to Uranus. Since her Moon is ruled by Uranus, this gives Lange an emotional ability to intuitively understand and portray the *outer fringes of the human mind*. We saw this in her role as the actress and mental patient Frances Farmer. In 1994's *Blue Skies*, Lange played a seemingly mentally unbalanced wife, who faced the trials of domestic turmoil and the encroachment of age. This performance won her an Oscar for Best Actress. A year later, she played the delusional Blanche Dubois in the TV movie *A Streetcar Named Desire*.

In 2011, Lange continued to demonstrate her lunar gift by winning a Golden Globe and an Emmy for her role in TV miniseries *American Horror Story*. This series was a disturbing look at the dementia and dysfunction in the "All American Family". With her Aquarius Moon, Lange doesn't just flirt with life's mental aberrations—she revels in them. Blame it all on Uranus!

Ascendant: Leo

When Lange performs her work, she consistently shows the pattern of her three fixed personality components—her sensual Sun, electrical Moon and the radiant fire of her Leo Ascendant.

When her luminaries are in repose, the head rises as Lange's strong jaw and square chin locks into place. This gives her a glowing aura of confidence.

With her three fixed components, there is little change in the shape of Lange's features—only in their element of expression! The upper photos show how the flesh takes on a granular texture, when the Sun resumes control. When the lunar lights shine, the eyes sparkle with intensity. When Leo's fire rises, the bovine eyes turn into those of a cat.

Craig Ferguson

5/17/1962, 6:10 P.M.
Glasgow, Scotland

Craig's career started as a member of a punk band. By 1994, he became one of Great Britain's leading comedians. He is best known as the host on CBS's *Late Late Show* (2001 to 2012) and as the host of *Celebrity Name Game*. On these shows, he presented his unique blend of high brow humor, silly fantasy and suggestive bawdiness.

Taurus Sun

Craig's fixed Earth Sun squares Uranus in Leo. Uranus trines his Mars in Aries. This red planet also sextiles his airy Venus and Mercury. These expansive components account for Craig's keen, inventive and highly active mind.

Like we saw with **Jessica Lange**, Craig's Uranus/Mars aspect drives him to examine the mental irregularities and capabilities of others. In 2005, he won a Peabody Award for his profound interview with Archbishop Desmond Tutu. This ability to elicit information and converse with others is a product of Craig's Moon and Ascendant.

Scorpio Moon

Ferguson's Scorpio Moon conjoins Neptune and these components aspect Jupiter in Pisces. These two planets give him his unique gift for fantasy and humor, as well as an ability to show empathy for others. Many of the interviews on his *Late Late Show* were markedly sensitive and compassionate. As for his bawdy remarks, they can be attributed to his Moon's sextile to Pluto.

This Moon/Neptune conjunction may be why Craig felt "surrounded by confusion" in his younger years. This lead to excessive drug and alcohol abuse. Notably, with the maturing of his Sun, he brought it under control. In 2017, he celebrated his 25th year of sobriety.

Libra Ascendant

With his Libra Ascendant, Ferguson rarely appears as controlling and fixed as his luminaries suggest. His light persona is a product of this Venus—the planet that rules his Ascendant and Sun. With Venus' sextile to his Aries Mars, Craig easily disarms his guests as well as his audience with this open mask and his wide accepting smile. Any sexual/sensual innuendos implanted by his luminaries are often balanced by a reluctant apology: "Oh, I didn't really mean that—or did I?" Libra often has trouble deciding what side to take.

This friendly mask has served Craig well. For (as of the end of 2017), he has won two Daytime Emmys for being the "Outstanding Game Show Host" on *Celebrity Name Game*.

Michelle Pfieffer

4/29/1958, 8:11 A.M.
Santa Ana, CA.

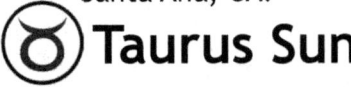 Taurus Sun

Check out the sensuous scene in the film *Witches of Eastwick* as Tauruses **Cher**, **Michelle** and **Jack Nicholson** all nibbled on cherries—and each others ears! Then, view Michelle as she croons and slithers in *The Fabulous Baker Boys*. In these sensual moments, this earthy creature's voice would become deep and resonant, as her bovine eyes fixed contentedly onto the pleasures in her surroundings.

Michelle's Mars joins Venus in her 10th House. To her public, she appears ethereal and fragile—like delicate porcelain. This look is accented by her Moon and Ascendant.

Moon: Virgo

With two key lights in Mercury-ruled mutable signs, it's hard to tell Michelle's Virgo Moon from her Ascendant. Still, her Moon stand out, when she becomes emotional, or reacts to others.

In these feminine lunar moments, the analytical energies become precise and grounded—as her Moon digests her sensual feelings and breaks them down into smaller, usable pieces.

In the performance of this task, her eyes are like shining crystals, seemingly lit from within. In the process, her hands hover close to the body.

In an interview, Michelle told us of the critical nature of her Virgo Moon, when she stated: "I tend to be unforgiving of people's imperfections." On the plus side, this Moon gives her the discriminating feelings and practical thoughts, that have served here so well in her acting career and personal life.

Ascendant: Gemini

In the film *Batman Returns*, Michelle played *Cat Woman*, a schizoid feline who constantly twitched, as if she was being treated by shock therapy. With each electrical charge, her eyes would spark and double blink, as her hands waved wildly out front.

Physically, this mercuric Ascendant gives her a translucent complexion and the lanky body frame and long arms and legs of Gemini.

When Mercury rises, Michelle floats away on her own mental plane. Her sister *Dee Dee* describes this phenomenon well: "When she enters a room, she walks through in her head".

This strong infatuation with ideas was seen in Michelle's films: *Up Close and Personal* and *Dangerous Minds*.

~~~

The Fixed Earth of Taurus is countered by the next sign in the Zodiac: Gemini

 Gemini

	Page
Introduction to Gemini Traits	129-131
Juliette Lewis & Gene Wilder	

The presence of Earth creates some dust

Michael Fox	132
Bob Dylan	133
Johnny Depp	134
Ian McKellen	135

Fire reigns, but it's still contained

Liam Neeson	136

The Fire spreads

Joan Rivers	137
Donald Trump	138
Neil Patrick Harris	139

The Air pressure is high

Marilyn Monroe	140
Venus Williams	141
Anderson Cooper	142
Bill Moyers	143

Water adds humidity to the Air

Mike Myers	144
Clint Eastwood	145
Nicole Kidman	146
Natalie Portman	147
Paul McCartney	148-148
Angelina Jolie	150

Gemini ♊ May 21 to June 20
Masculine Polarity, Mutable Air
Just think of the possibilities with your GEMINI friends!

Last month, the delights of **Taurus** piqued our curiosity. Now, as Nature's "quadrant of self-discovery" enters its final phase, the swirling winds of Spring are activated. With this stirring and expansive force, there is a need to reach out—and examine all things from both sides! This gives us the Mutable Air of **Gemini**: the sign that activates the bicameral minds of all living creatures, as well as the breath of Gaia (the living consciousness of the Earth).

With Gemini, the sensual input of Taurus is analyzed, so that individuals can understand and adapt to the contents in their environment. With these lessons, they can prepare for the new seasons that lies ahead.

If you're feeling curious about your world, head on out to your favorite gathering spot. Once there, listen for the "busiest buzz" in the room. It is likely coming from a hive of Geminis. Move closer and one of the Mercury Messengers will soon fly your way, introduce him/her self, and then proceed to solicit your observations on various subjects. The subject of concern is usually the one that is currently circulating in that person's inquisitive mind, but quickly it is likely to change.

In conversations, Geminis rapidly change their reference points, as they rearrange the order of their ideas. This makes it difficult to follow their thoughts. Fortunately, with the other Air signs, clarity arrives—when **Libra** keeps the thoughts in balance, and the Fixed Air of **Aquarius** brings defined resolutions.

With this array of ideas, these Gemini students learn to understand the content in their environment. This enables them to move out into the world—and begin their connection with their surroundings. This movement is driven by the emotions and feelings of **Cancer**, the next sign in the Zodiac.

☿ Rulerships and Associations for Gemini

Mercury is the ruling planet of Gemini. Thusly, it governs the nervous system, the mind and the way an individual thinks. The planet in which one's Mercury is placed defines the nature of one's thinking patterns.

In masculine Gemini, we find the expansive, inductive reasoning that assembles small ideas into larger concepts. The feminine act of deduction (the breaking down into smaller parts) is seen in **Virgo**, the other sign that is ruled by Mercury. The dueling between these two signs, operates the bicameral mind.

Geminis are the students, who learn words and language, to enhance their ever growing understanding of the world. These lessons began with their siblings, the ones with whom they made their first communication. Gemini is also associated with short personal journeys and the vehicles that take us there. These activities are triggered when planets transit the 3rd House.

Individuals with a Gemini Sun, Moon, and Ascendant, or a strongly aspected Mercury tend to exhibit the qualities of Mutable Air.

Gemini Physical Traits:

The swirling breezes of Mutable Air give these mercuric beings a light and vaporous appearance, as well as the "two faces" of the Gemini twins!

These dueling forces create twin folds above the sparkling eyes. This suggests that there is a double set of eyelids. Maybe so, for every flip of the lids appears to bring two blinks instead of one.

Note how the nose of Gemini tends to twist upward or downward as it "splits in two" at the tip. Also, the folds about and below the low-placed mouth suggest a double set of lips. The most obvious feature of Gemini is the rectangular box that is created by the cheekbones and Jaw. Note how it protrudes forward, at an unusual distance from the upper half of the face.

Juliette Lewis 6/21/1973, 4:50 A.M., Los Angeles, CA.
Gene Wilder 6/11/1933, 3:50 A.M., Milwaukee, WI.

With their Gemini Suns and Ascendants, *Juliette Lewis* and *Gene Wilder* give us a double douse of Mercury, as they show us how the Ascendant's bone structure skews the face, as it sends the cheekbones and jaws of Geminis protruding from the upper half of the face.

Gene's Aquarius Moon adds to his flighty nature and outrageous sense of humor. Juliette's Pisces Moon saturates the flesh and rounds her facial features. This water often short-circuits the mercuric energy of her Sun.

Gemini Body Language

With their Taurus-ruled throats, early humans uttered their first sounds and tones, to communicate simple thoughts. In time, these "words" became the language, that allowed us humans to describe a very complex range of concepts. All of this voicing is a product of the breath. It is generated by the lungs—the body part ruled by Gemini. These lungs supply the essential oxygen that gives all individuals the breath of life.

Gemini's rulership also extends to the arms, hands, and fingers. With these parts, humans find the ability to manipulate the contents of their surroundings. The rulership of these extremities explains why so many Geminis tend to "talk with their hands" as they express their ideas.

As Geminis fly about, their propeller-like hands carry them forward. Watch how the head acts like a rudder on a plane and how it flips from side to side—tracking Gemini's constantly changing mind. Every switch seems to change the course, and the direction of their pursuits.

Gemini rules the lungs, arms and hands

With their Earthy Moons, these first two portraits show how Taurus is the total opposite of Gemini.

Michael J. Fox
6/9/1961, 12:15 A.M.
Edmonton, Alberta

 Sun Sign: Gemini

In the TV series *Family Ties*, Michael played the role of the pragmatic child in a family with "hippy" parents. There, we saw the mercuric and interactive nature of his Gemini Sun. Ditto in his later TV series *Spin City* (1996 to 2002), where he played the deputy mayor and press agent for a city. In this job, he fluttered about, talked on the phone, and multi-tasked many projects. In his whimsical comedy, Fox's mercuric solar light shined brightly! It was embellished by his Air Sign Ascendant.

Ascendant: Aquarius

Fox's first major non-TV role was the giant hit movie *Back To The Future*. This was followed by the other worldly *Teen Wolf*. The reality-warping scenarios in these films are associated with Aquarius, the sign of Fox's Ascendant.

Uranus (the ruling planet of Aquarius) is in Leo, sitting near Fox's Mars. and opposing his Ascendant. Both of these planets oppose also sextile his Sun. This gives Fox a dynamic persona, but his Mercury (the ruler of his nervous system) is inconjunct to Jupiter (the closest planet to his Rising Sign). This suggests the connections between his nerves and body would be constantly scrambled. This may be a factor in the development of Fox's Parkinson's Disease. These aspects gave Fox many gifts, but also a heavy cross to bear.

In 2001, Michael left *Spin City* to begin his raising of funds to fight this disease.

Moon: Taurus

Michael's characters has always been mentally agile—and also noticeably bullheaded. This dichotomy is likely due to his Saturn's conjunction with Jupiter, and its T-square to Neptune and his Moon/Venus in Taurus.

This Moon's influence is seen when Fox becomes emotional. Not only is he firmly fixed in Earth, Saturn gives his bovine eyes a chilly and stoney gaze. In contrast, Jupiter injects an emotional sense of optimism. This hopeful attitude is reinforced by Uranus' sextile to his Sun and his hopeful Aquarius Ascendant. All of this likely inspired the title of his book: *Always Looking Up: The Adventures of an Incurable Optimist*.

With this positive attitude and his emotional determination, Fox was able to continue his career for many years, even though his disability was becoming more obvious.

"The times they are a-changing"
Bob Dylan
5/24/1941, 9:05 P.M.
Duluth, MN

Sun Sign: Gemini

In a *Newsweek* article, the interviewer noted: "As you sit across from him, his face keeps changing." This reporter surely must have known he was interviewing a Gemini. If not, Dylan's own comment should have given him a clue: "I don't think I'm tangible to myself. I mean, I think one thing today and think another thing tomorrow. I change during the course of a day. I wake and I'm one person, and when I go to sleep I know for certain I'm somebody else."

Bob's music changed a generation's way of thinking. His Sun's trine to Neptune (in Virgo) made his story-telling illusions precise and clear—as his Sun's square to Mars (in Pisces) gave his words a magical sense of rhythm. With his Sun conjoined Jupiter and Uranus, Bob's words covered a huge range of ideas.

Moon: Taurus

With his Moon, Saturn, Jupiter, and Uranus conjoined in Taurus (and the latter two conjunct this Gemini Sun), Dylan appears intensely focused. With his luminaries and these three planets also trining Neptune, Bob was given an intuitive gift for creating a constantly changing stream of thought-provoking images. With Saturn just one degree from his Moon, many of his works were biting commentaries on the ills of society.

With a touch of saturnine grey, Dylan paints his Taurian images by building masterfully constructed phrases. With the swiftness of Mercury, he delivers the tantalizing messages. The impact is real and it continues to alter our collective consciousness and souls.

Ascendant: Sagittarius

Sagittarius rising? Sure, there's the Centaur's domed head, the ball on the tip of the nose and the mutable face. However, the fire of this mask seems surprisingly stilled. This is due to the placement of his Ascendant's ruling planet Jupiter. It's in that huge cluster of Taurus Components. This alters his physical demeanor.

Watch Bob when he bounces on stage, displaying his Rising and Sun Sign's mutable energy—but note what happens when he finds his "spot on stage". Once there, Jupiter (and his Taurus Moon) quickly shifts his mask into a Fixed Earth mode. Note how his shoulders huddle over his guitar, as he locks himself into his focused and immovable stance.

Interestingly, all of Dylan's planets (except for Mars) are on the right side of his chart. This suggests that his work was created by powers higher than his own. It certainly seems that way.

Johnny Depp

6/9/1963, 8:44 A.M.
Owensboro, KY

 Sun Sign: Gemini

Watch how Depp's dark eyes sparkle with electricity, as he expresses the light of his Sun. His "gift for gab" was apparent when Depp became a teen idol on TV's *21 Jump Street*. However, from that beginning, his fans were attracted to something else in his nature—his inherent sensual intensity. This is not what we expect from a Gemini.

Examining his chart, you will see that his Mercury (the ruler of his Sun) is conjoined to Venus—in the easygoing sign of Taurus. These two personal planets form a T-square to his Saturn and a Mars/Uranus conjunction in his 1st House. These aspects explain his outrageous persona and his attraction to surreal action adventures like *Pirates of the Caribbean* and *The Lone Ranger*.

Moon: Capricorn

Capricorn Moons usually display somber emotions, as they interact with their physical world. However, Depp's Moon forms harmonious aspects to Neptune and Pluto. His emotional responses are not only cold and distant, they are also surreal and deeply mysterious.

We saw Neptune's influence in the films *Alice in Wonderland*, *Finding Netherland*, *Charlie and the Chocolate Factory* and the pirate movies.

Pluto's input was seen in Johnny's roles in the original *Nightmare on Elm Street*, *Sleepy Hollow*, *Dark Shadows* and *Sweeney Todd*. They all were quite unsettling—far beyond the conservative manners expected from a Capricorn Moon. Notably, Depp's Moon is in the Taurus decan. Add the Pluto aspect and a fixed Ascendant, and what you see is the cubical features of a Bull, rather than the Goat.

Ascendant: Leo

Johnny's Leo Ascendant gives him a flair for theater. With his 1st House Mars conjoined Uranus, and these two planets conjoined Pluto in the 2nd House, Depp gets lots of attention. With these three planets in Virgo, what we see is a disturbingly fussy persona.

This was displayed in the tightly wound nerves that he presented in his role as *Edward Scissorhands*. Then, consider the film *Ed Wood*, where Johnny played an extremely fussy, but totally inept film director, armed with only two talents: his overly confident Leo mask and Gemini's gift for "talking anyone into anything".

Physically, Depp's face mocks the features of a lion. Note the feline eyes, and bushy eyebrows, and how they are topped by the lion's mane.

Earth is rarely seen,
when Mutable Forces reign

Ian McKellen
5/25/1939, 9:30 P.M.
Burnley, UK

Unlike Dylan and Depp, Ian McKellen has no fixed key lights. He is a triple mutable sign. This makes the swirling Mobius patterns in his Gemini personality far more obvious.

 Sun Sign: Gemini

Notice the sparks of electricity, the rapidly blinking eyes, animated arms and hands, and the vaporous expressions when Ian attempts to communicate the array of ideas swirling in his head. These mercuric forces are enhanced by his Moon, which is also ruled by Mercury.

Moon: Virgo

With Ian's Virgo Moon, we see the feminine version of these mercuric qualities. They appear when McKellen emotionally interacts with others.

In these lunar moments, the mutable forces appear to be "grounded in the physical body" rather than in the mind. When the flying hands and arms of his Gemini Sun are restrained by the feminine force of Virgo, Ian's hands tend to pull things inward, closer to the body—often near the stomach region, the part of the body ruled by Virgo.

In reactive situations, Ian's reasoning often becomes deductive instead of inductive, as his Virgo Moon seeks the specific tidbits of information, that in their precise expression, will formulate his responses to others. As we saw in Taurus Jay Leno, this often results in more questions, than it does factual statements.

Ascendant: Sagittarius

Ian's fiery mutable Ascendant appears far more animated than Dylan's. This is due to the fact that both of Ian's luminaries are in the same mode as his Centaur mask. When filtered through this shield, the forces of Mercury widen in scope, as Ian attempts to present his giant philosophical and spiritual concepts. What we see is the image of a free spirited centaur, galloping to distant horizons, pursuing grander ideas and adventures. Appropriately, this swashbuckling, sage-like persona is what Ian presented to the world in his role as *Gandalf, the Gray* in *The Lord of the Rings* and *Hobbit* films.

*Our next portrait **Liam Neeson** is also a triple mutable sign. He has the same Sun and Ascendant as McKellen. His Moon is a mutable Fire Sign (not Earth), and he appears very "fixed and earthy" for a Gemini. Neeson shows us how planet positions can change one's personality.*

Air and Fire reign, but other factors restrain the conditions

Liam Neeson

6/7/1952, 9:55 P.M.
Ballymena, Ireland

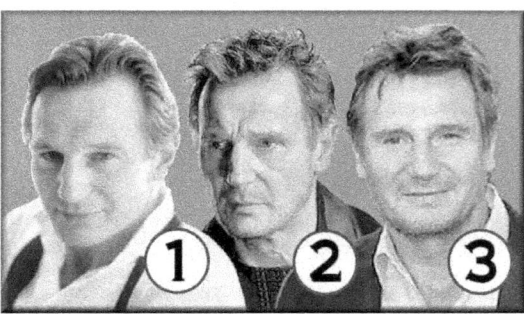

With Noel Tyl's rectification of the tragic death of Liam's wife, a probable birth time was established for this star. This birth time also sets up arrangements that explain why the fire and air of Liam's light is so reserved.

Gemini Sun

At the 2005 Golden Globe Awards, Liam lumbered onto the stage, sheepishly guarded and noticeably lost for words. Such mannerisms are not expected from someone with five air and three fire components in his chart. It contradicts his movie persona that give us the talkative master Jedi in *The Phantom Menace*, the smooth talking Oskar *in Schindler's List* and the buoyant Hannibal in *The A Team*.

Liam's Gemini Sun trines Neptune and his Libra Midheaven. His 10th House Mars (in Scorpio) also conjoins his Midheaven.

Neptune gave him the smooth voice to be Aslan's narrator in *The Chronicles of Narnia*. Mars (in Scorpio on the MC) shows why he often plays in intense, action films like those seen in his series of *Ransom* films.

Sagittarius Moon and Ascendant

Oddly, the mutable fire of Liam's Moon and Ascendant are well hidden. This may be why so many sources say that Liam's emotions are warmly and freely displayed in his private and personal interactions, but publicly it is a different story. This guarded persona is likely due to the fact that Liam's fiery Moon is imprisoned in his 12th House, just five degrees from his Ascendant. Also, this Moon sextiles his Saturn as it trines his Pluto in the 8th House. Another factor is his Jupiter in Taurus. This ruler of Ian's Ascendant and Moon opposes his Mars in fixed Scorpio. This dulls the light of his luminaries, while his Scorpio Mars explains his turgidly controlled physical movements.

Photo #1 reveals the high forehead, the long neck, and the pointed ears of a horse. However, since Ian's Moon and Ascendant are both in Sagittarius' second decan, they are influenced by the next Fire Sign to appear in the zodiac wheel—Aries! Thusly, many of the qualities of the Ram appear in his features—most noticeably in the forehead that tilts sharply to the back, the angled nose and the convex facial structure.

Photo #2 shows how these Aries features harden and intensify, when the force of Ian's Scorpio Mars goes into action. Notably, Aries and Scorpio are both ruled by Mars.

In **Photo #3**, we see the round, lunar features of a Cancer Crab. Since the Moon rules this sign, its placement near Ian's Ascendant infuses these features into his physical appearance. It also explains Liam's guarded entrance at the Golden Globes ceremony.

The Fire Spreads!
Joan Rivers
6/8/1933, 2:00 AM
Brooklyn, New York

 ## Sun Sign: Gemini

In her spirited "chats", Joan Rivers would often inject the quintessential Gemini line: *"Can We Talk?"* Why not? Geminis love to talk.

With Mercury and Venus also in Gemini, Joan had many other mental talents. She wrote most of her own material and she was one of the fastest, most agile minds in show biz! With Jupiter on her Virgo Mars forming a T-square to her luminaries, this lady operated like a mix-o-matic on full speed!

As a stand-up comedienne, Joan boggled our minds with her rapid fire mix of gossip and neuroses. She became America's top female comic, showing off her diversity in TV projects, sellout nightclub acts, books and records.

The UR photo show one of the few images of a Gemini with a nose that points upward at the tip. Likely, cosmetic surgery erased this unique feature.

Ascendant: Aries

Joan was the first female to have a TV late show, but it didn't survive its three year contract. One factor could have been her aggressive Aries rising.

When her Gemini Sun "ran out of words", this cardinal fire would kick in and send the conversation rushing in a new direction. It often appeared that the guests were being interrupted—just when things were getting substantive and/or emotionally interesting.

As Joan's chart shows, there were few moments of repose and little sensitivity for the feelings of others. Pluto in Cancer was her only water; Saturn, her only fixed planet, was in erratic Aquarius. Its ruler Uranus was in Aries, sextiling her Mercury and Venus. This aspect often scattered her thoughts, as it drove her mind to run off in another direction.

Physically, the swept-back eyebrows, upturned cheek bones and long chin suggest the features of a ram.

Moon: Sagittarius

Joan was making people laugh when she was 11. She likely was inspired by her jovial Sagittarius Moon, which so greatly influenced her younger years.

Born on the Full Moon, Joan's Sun/Moon path creates a straight-line highway between opposing points. Expressions and reactions easily race back and forth—to supply material from both sides of the Universe. This gave this Gemini a giant array of new ideas to pursue.

This lunar placement contributed to Joan's blunt and emotionally distant nature, but it also was the source of her boundless enthusiasm.

Donald Trump
6/6/1946, 10:54 A.M.
Queens, NY

Sun Sign: Gemini

The swirl of mutable air can be seen in Trump's sky-blue eyes—and in the cumulus clouds of hair that floats some distance from the surface. Oddly, there is more erratic energy here than what we'd expect from a typical Gemini. This is due to Donald's Sun. It forms a conjunction with Uranus on his MC, and both form harmonious aspects to expansive Jupiter. In addition, his Sun opposes his Centaur Moon and it sextiles his Ascendant. His Sun is the most energized component in his chart.

Interestingly, Donald's Sun, Mercury, Venus, and Saturn are the only feminine components in his chart. This is all he has to quell the expansive natures in his personality. Saturn's conjunction with Venus (in Cancer) may be why he relies on his "gut feelings" and it explains Donald's interest in real estate and the title of his book: *Art of the Deal*. Mercury's distant square from Jupiter may be why his thoughts are often expressed in short, simplistic sentences like: "You're fired"—the famous line from this TV show *Celebrity Apprentice*.

The light of Trump's Sun is focused thru the fixed fire of his Leo Ascendant.

Ascendant: Leo

With Mars on his Ascendant, supercharging his Sun and Moon, Donald sees himself was king of his domain. With Jupiter's aspects to both of these luminaries, he sees and feels everything on a big scale. With his Leo Mars, Donald boastfully proclaims that he can make everything "greater". This placement of Mars on an angle often portends an aggressive personality.

Transits at Donald's inauguration are notable. Saturn transited Trump's Moon and Uranus was squaring his natal Saturn—and transiting Pluto was in Capricorn. Pluto was not in Capricorn since the USA's revolutionary war (1776). With or without Donald, this was likely to be a period of revolutionary changes.

Moon: Sagittarius

Trump was born at a Full Moon in fiery Sagittarius. This Moon's sextile to Jupiter and trine to Mars explains why, with every emotional reaction, Donald instantly gallops in another direction—to chase a new train of thought.

Donald's Moon is the only planet on the right side of his chart. All of his other components are on the left side. This makes him self-driven, and less likely to seek the opinions of others.

When the lunar fires of his Moon are activated, Donald's eyes rise up on the outer edges, as the jaw extends forward and downward. This often mocks the face of a horse.

Neil Patrick Harris
6/15/1973, no time
Albuquerque, NM

Neil Patrick Harris had the title role as the prodigy teenage doctor in the 1990's TV series *Doogie Howser, M.D.* His recent work includes the 2015 TV series *How I Met Your Mother*, as well as frequent appearances as a master of ceremonies on multiple awards programs.

Sun in Gemini

Neil's Uranus forms a grand Air trine with his Sun and Jupiter. This raises Neil's flighty qualities, as it equalizes the mutable nature of his Sun. The expansive nature of his Sun is also restrained by its conjunction to Saturn and their square to his Mars in Pisces. Meanwhile, Neil's physical appearance is altered by his 24° Sun. (It's in the Aquarius decan and it trines Uranus). This makes Neil appear more Aquarius than Gemini. This fixed appearance is enhanced by his 23° Centaur Moon in the fixed decan of Leo.

Moon in Sagittarius

There are also several Aquarian ties with Neil's Moon. The strongest are Uranus' sextile to his Moon and its trine to his Moon's ruling planet Jupiter. The Air sign outer planets make, Neil's Centaur responses windy and wordy; There's little of the clownish reactions of the Centaur.

Another significant "suppressor" is that Neil's main personal planets (Mercury, Venus and Mars) are all in water signs. This water douses the expansive qualities of his luminaries. Still, the fiery and mutable forces of his Moon become apparent, when Neil becomes emotional.

Note how one eye curves up as the other drops downward—to form the wide set Centaur Eyes. Watch how his head rears up and how he tosses his head to the back, as his hands become very animated.

The Rhythms of Mars

Neil displays a sensitivity and calmness not expected from a person with just three passive components in his chart.* Much of this is due to his 12th House Pisces Mars and its inclusion in the powerful Grand Cross with his luminaries, Saturn and Pluto. In addition, there's the fact that Mercury (his Sun's ruler) conjoins Venus in Cancer.

Regardless of these amazing aspects, Neil's physical metabolism is driven by his Mars, and as noted, it's in the sign of Pisces. This gives Neil a rhythmical metabolism, that moves at a gentle pace.

Watch how his eyes and facial flesh swell and bubble, when he is preparing his creative tasks (and not performing). In the process, his mercuric hand gestures take on liquid, wave-like patterns, as his voice softens to express his inner feelings. This Pisces Mars makes him a delightful performer—and it gives him the gift of dance!

(His Ascendant is unknown, but it could also be in a feminine sign).

Look at what happens when Air dominates the personality

Marilyn Monroe
6/1/1926, 9:30 A.M.
Los Angeles, CA

 Sun Sign: Gemini

With her famous breathy voice, Marilyn would entangle bits of words with wisps of air. All the while, her eyes would dart about as her fingers and hands fanned the air, seemingly to generate the electrical voltage—that would light up and power her mercurial Gemini Sun.

Marilyn's Sun, Moon, Jupiter, and Mercury are all in Air signs! This is why this lady desired to be recognized for her mental capabilities, rather than just being a "physical object of beauty".

Oddly, this physically appealing lady had no Earth in her chart. There was no airport on which to land, or even a quiet place to relish the joys of her senses. With this, she was unable to build a base to gain recognition for her intellectual abilities. This lack of grounding was exacerbated by her Aquarius Moon.

Moon: Aquarius

With her Aquarius Moon trined to her airy Sun and conjunct Jupiter, Monroe was a markedly cerebral person, who had little ability to express her emotions. Her only water components were Saturn, Pluto and a Mars/Uranus conjunction in her 8th House. This made it hard for her to form close emotional relationships. Saturn's T-square to her idealistic Moon and Neptune brought on the delusions, that made it even more difficult.

When Monroe reacted or responded to others, her lower lip would pull tightly downward—to exhale an etherial phase or some wordy revelation. This reaction was often totally void of emotion.

Ascendant: Leo

With her entry into a crowded room (or onto a large movie set), Marilyn would instantly be in the spotlight, attracting attention from others. Why not? The Fixed Fire of her Leo Rising Sign was out front, warming up her breezy Sun and Moon. This mask gave her an appearance of confidence, as well as a glowing presence.

However, unbeknownst to the crowd, beneath this facade lie a surprisingly uncertain soul. After all, there was the tension of her Saturn's T-square to Neptune and her Moon-Jupiter conjunction in her 7th House. Furthermore, her Neptune's was placed in her 1st House, and this frequently doused the confidence of her Leo.

With this nebulous planet sitting by her window to the world, Monroe held on to the delusional vision that she would be recognized for her cerebral talents. Sadly, with Venus on her MC, all the world saw was her beauty.

Venus Williams
6/17/1980, 2:12 P.M.
Lynwood, CA

♊ Sun Sign: Gemini

On the tennis court, Williams' eyes would sparkle and dart about, as the Mercury Messenger quickly interpreted her every movement. With Mercury's rulership of her Sun, fingers and hands —and a Virgo Mars—we see why her movements are so nimble and precise.

Mercury places skill in Williams' hands and arms (the part of the body ruled by Gemini). These hands are empowered by her Mars—which conjoins Saturn in earthy Virgo. Her martial movements are precisely calculated, so that she can physically position herself, and counter her opponent's actions.

Off the court, Williams shows the intellectual curiosity of a Gemini. She speaks five languages, enjoys Russian history and Chinese culture and has an insatiable desire to obtain information from books on varied subjects. This multiplicity of interests is typical Gemini.

Physically, Venus shows the light and sprite qualities of her Air sign Sun. The UL photo shows how the rectangular jaw assembly projects forward from the upper half of the face.

including that wide, cherubic smile! In play, she is always fair and complimentary of her opponents. Any harshness is usually directed towards herself, as her Virgo Mars makes her critical of her own actions.

The position of Pluto on her Rising Sign allows Williams to see beyond the expected limitations and achieve the impossible. Somehow, she found the power to deliver the fastest serve in WTA history, clocked at 127 m.p.h.

Ascendant: Libra

William's Libra Ascendant conjoins Pluto. Both of these components trine Libra's ruling planet Venus. This gives this lady a strong desire to enhance the beauty of "others". This may be why Williams earned herself an Associate's Degree in Fashion Design, and why she regularly wore attractive necklaces and jewelry at her tournaments—many of which were her own creations.

Williams shows all the charms of Libra

Moon: Leo

With her Leo Moon (conjoined to Jupiter in Virgo and sextile her Sun), Williams' reactions and hand movements are instantaneous and precisely orchestrated. The fixed fire of her Moon brings instant reactions while her Virgo Mars brings precision to her Mercury-ruled hands. Coming and going, there is focus—as well as flexibility. This is the stuff that we find in tennis champions.

Anderson Cooper

6/3/1967, 3:46 P.M.
New York, NY

Mercury's wings fluttered in anticipation, when CNN began its 24 hour news format. When they added their rapid video edits, split-screen images and the constant scroll of news at the bottom of the screen, all of us Mortal Beings could get our daily "Mercury jolt" just by tuning in to the news! No doubt, the Winged Messenger was very ecstatic!

To top it off, CNN gave us a Gemini anchor, whose presentation clicked at a rapid pace, as the data flowed from his electric tongue. The Greek God Hermes was very pleased.

Sun: Gemini

Watch how Cooper's facial lines twist and how his eyes twinkle, as he dishes out the multi-sourced, cross-referenced questions to his bewildered guests.

In these interviews, Cooper's eyes seem to flicker incessantly. This gives the impression that every blink consists of two flaps, instead of one. In the process, Cooper's unemotional and breathy speech remains markedly calm, since it must be filtered thru his Libra mask.

Ascendant: Libra

When Cooper's luminaries are in repose, he presents the almond eyes, V-lined chin and the smile of his Libra Ascendant. With this pleasant persona, his guests are very receptive. However, this calm demeanor is not always pleasing surprise aggressive moments appear. This is due to Mars placement near his Ascendant.

Physically, Mars alters the balanced features of Libra and what we see is the vertically stretched image of a Ram.

Moon: Aries

As we saw in Anderson's reporting from the war lines of Iraq, the serene presence of his Libra Ascendant would suddenly intensify, when he became threatened by surrounding actions. In such emotional situations, the airy mass of Cooper's Sun and Rising Signs would suddenly become more stringent and aggressive. What you see is his Aries Moon. This Moon appears when guests avoid Cooper's question, or if someone accuses him of "fake news". The resulting anger has ignited the Cardinal Fire of his Moon. Watch how his eyebrows lift up on the outer edges as his head butts abruptly forward—to counter his opponent or enforce a point

Positively, Cooper's Cardinal Moon and Mars clears away the clutter. This makes his multi-layered questions clearer, simpler and easier to understand. However, when his Moon is riled, the calm mask is gone, and guests suddenly quit answering his questions.

Bill Moyers

6/5/1934, 11:15 P.M.
Hugo, OK

Bill Moyers was the press secretary for President Lyndon Johnson. Later, his career of journalism included a weekly show on PBS and the production of many documentaries and news programs. He has won many awards for his investigative journalism and civic activities and became known as a trenchant critic of the corporately structured U.S. news media. It all is reflected in his chart.

 Sun Sign: Gemini

Few communicated the complexities of our world as well as this Gemini—and he did it with a huge amount of care and compassion! Bill's Mercury, the ruling planet of his Sun, is placed in the compassionate sign of Cancer. Also, since his watery Mercury sextiles his earthy Taurus Venus and Virgo Neptune, his thoughts came across as substantial but also touching and filled with feelings.

Moyers displays many of the physical traits of Gemini, but what is special here is what we see in the two top photos. They clearly show how the cheeks and jaw create the oblong and angled box that protrudes forward from the eyes and forehead.

Aquarius Ascendant

Bill was the co-founder of *Movement for a New Society*. This organization envisions the improvement of social civic order by *changing the nature of personal values*. (This work was likely inspired by Bill's conjunction of Venus to Uranus).

Bill also sees this hopeful view of society thru the window of his Aquarius Rising Sign. A grand trine between his Sun, Ascendant and Jupiter (in Libra) inspires him to seek justice and fairness for all. This fixed mask helps him to present his complex social solutions and connect to his audience.

Since Aquarius also has a distinctly rectangular jaw, the placement of Bill's Ascendant in the Gemini Decan of Aquarius noticeably enlarges his lower face and jaw. This Rising Sign also makes the stubby nose, dimpled cheeks and square chin more prominent. His chin is not as pointed as we see in most Geminis.

Moon: Aries

In interviews, Moyer's interaction with his guests is far less aggressive than the Aries Moon that we see in **Anderson Cooper**. This may be due to the fact that Moyer's Mars is not on his Ascendant. (Instead, it forms a T-square to Saturn and Neptune). In addition, Bill's Moon forms a square to Pluto in watery Cancer. This certainly would douse the fires of any Aries Moon.

Add the Element of Water
Mike Myers
5/25/1963, 12:01 P.M.
Scarborough, Canada

 ## Sun Sign: Gemini

Mike first caught our attention on NBC's *Saturday Night Live*, most memorably as the partner of fellow Gemini Dana Carvey in *Wayne's World*. There, these Gemini twins exhibited the animated gyrations, flying hands and mercuric chatter we'd expect from Mutable Air.

Unlike Carvey, Myers' animated mannerisms are constantly countered by forces of containment. I.E., his expressions seem to rapidly alter between an expansive stir and a holding pattern.

This split-personality is likely due to the fact that Myers has six components in fixed signs and six in feminine signs. Fixed signs include his Sun's ruling planet Mercury in Taurus. With his Sun and Mercury T-squaring Saturn and his Mars on his Fixed Leo Ascendant, the fixed forces are solidified. Meanwhile, his Sun's square to his Uranus and Pluto (in Mutable Virgo) empowers the alternating current of his expansive Gemini Sun. The energy changes again, when his watery Moon floods the light of his Sun.

Moon: Cancer

Watch how Myers' expansive solar expressions suddenly shift and "go into reverse", as he withdraws into his shell. This "tidal shift" is often observed in masculine Suns, who have a Cancer Moon.

When Mike withdraws into these lunar waters, his clutched hands pull tightly into his chest. As the head tilts forward, the chin recedes as the eye sockets sink down on the face. This pressurizes the facial flesh and inflates the temples and cheeks into bloated curves. In this swell of cardinal water, the Crab gathers in its emotions, as it nurtures its new found sense of comfort.

This lunar placement soothes Myers' flighty energies, as it gives him a gift for expressing his emotions and feelings. Nowhere was this more apparent than in Mike's voicing of the bubbly and compassionate character *Shrek*.

Ascendant: Leo

Myer's characters are also dramatic, self confident, markedly quirky and noticeably aggressive. All of these traits were seen in *Austin Powers*—a character who displayed the essence of someone who would have Mars and Uranus on his or her Leo Ascendant.

When Mike's luminaries recede, the facial flesh reshapes, to mold into the proudly fixed mask of Leo. Note the bushy brows, the broad bridged nose and how the flat cheek bones drop directly downward, to create the jowly jaw of a Lion.

Clint Eastwood
5/31/1930, 5:25 PM
San Francisco, CA

 Sun Sign: Gemini

Eastwood's eyes twinkled and his face twisted into a smile, when he received his Oscar for Best Director for *Unforgiven*. In this electric moment, this Gemini was floating on cloud nine.

In lighter films like *Pink Cadillac* and *Every Which Way But Loose*, we saw Clint's looser side, as his mutable Sun dispensed ideas—in every which way!

In such moments of solar expression, Eastwood's hands fan the air, as his eyes sparkle and dart about. In the mutable atmosphere of his Air-sign Sun, Clint multi-tasks, as he stars, produces, writes and directs his film projects.

Clint's analytical abilities run at full tilt when he's behind the camera. However, in front of the camera, most people see him as an "action star". His Aries Mars trines Neptune, the ruler of cinema, and this oceanic planet is just three degrees from his Midheaven.

Ascendant: Scorpio

With Neptune on his M.C., Clint should be publicly recognized as a caring and sensitive soul. Not So! His Neptune trines his Aries Mars and his Scorpio Ascendant forms a snug trine to his Pluto in the 8th House. What the world saw was Clint's hypnotic stare and his overpowering and mysterious physical presence. This tough persona was seen in Clint's first major role as the unflappable and secretive *Man-With-No-Name* in his legendary *spaghetti westerns*. There was also his *Dirty Harry* films and the 2008 *Grand Torino*, movies that showed off the Scorpion's need to keep everything in control.

Moon: Leo

When Eastwood interacts with others, the prideful reaction of a Lion appears. Watch how his chest swells, as he takes on his royal stance to dramatically acclaim his authority: "Go ahead, make my day!"

In these lunar moments, the shape of Clint's face creates an impression of fixity that is similar to what we saw in **Mike Myers**. Note how they both display the fixed brows, jowly cheeks and the anchored upper lip of a lion. However, Clints' emotional reactions appear to be far more fixed, since his Ascendant is not in a cardinal sign.

With his Venus in Cancer, Clint also has his softer side. As we saw in *The Bridges of Madison County*, Clint can also becomes warm and playfully romantic. With this Neptune on his Midheaven in Leo (trining his Aries Mars), Clint has a keen understanding of show business, its scintillating ideas and power plays.

"Even from a very early age, I knew I didn't want to miss out on anything ... just because it might be considered dangerous."

Nicole Kidman on her love for scuba diving, skydiving and race cars.

Nicole Kidman
Sun Sign: Gemini
Moon: Sagittarius
6/20/1967, 3:15 P.M.
Honolulu, HA

With a Mutable Sun to feed her a stream of fleeting ideas and a fiery Centaur Moon to inspire her to pursue them all—Nicole is a daring lady. This desire to "not miss out on anything" is enhanced by Jupiter's placement on her Leo Midheaven.

Kidman's mercuric Sun brings an electric spark to her darting eyes, as it animates her hands and fingers, which often fan the air with a swirling twist. The reactions of her fiery Sagittarius Moon bring a release of inhibitions and her free spirited daredevil attitude. Bring it on!

Scorpio Ascendant

With these expansive mutable lights, Kidman often appears void of feelings. The emotions that we see are often tightly controlled and covered by the mask of her Scorpio Ascendant.

Nicole's Mercury is placed in the water sign of Cancer. It trines Neptune as it sextiles a Pluto/Uranus conjunction in Mercury-ruled Virgo. This gives her the appearance of liquid Mercury. She appears to be from another world.

As we saw in *Batman Forever, Moulin Rouge* and *Cold Mountain*, this liquid mask gives Nicole a mysterious and etherial persona. Neptune, her singular 1st House planet, adds to the illusion.

Be it comedy, fantasy or an intense drama, the real nature of her emotions and thoughts are rarely revealed, for they are often kept secret from our view.

Planet Placements Effect the Shape of the Physical Body

Interestingly, Nicole's torso (from the shoulders to the top of the hips) seems to be markedly small—while her highly placed and vertically stretched hips make her appear to be "all arms and legs"!

This enlarged lower half may be due to the fact that seven of her planets lie in the signs Leo through Sagittarius—the signs that rule the body parts from the heart to the thighs. Significantly, Jupiter (the ruler of Sagittarius) squares her Ascendant and trines her 2nd House Centaur Moon. This makes her Moon the most aspected component in her chart. This may be why this area of Kidman's body is enlarged.

Saturn, the planet of "shrinkage" sits alone on the other side of this grouping. It is in Aries, the sign that rules the head. Kidman's head appears quite small for someone with Scorpio Rising and prominent Sagittarius in her chart.

Natalie Portman
6/9/1981, 3:42 p.m.
Jerusalem, Israel

"I never had that fire in me, ever.... I'd rather be smart than a movie star.... I don't think I'd be able to deal with just acting, because I don't know if you get to use your brain that much." — **Natalie Portman**

These quotes reflect the content in Portman's chart. She has only one fire sign and five Air Sign components.

Gemini Sun
Virgo Moon

Portman's Mercury-ruled Gemini Sun and Virgo Moon accounts for her highly mercuric and intellectual nature. She was valedictorian for her high school class and was voted "Most likely to be on *Jeopardy*."

Interestingly, Portman skipped the premiere of *Star Wars Episode I: The Phantom Menace*. It was her first major motion picture role but she "had to study for her high school final exams". Indeed, Portman was a very dedicated Gemini student. Later, as her studies continued, she learned to carry on conversations in six languages. In 2003, she earned her degree in psychology from Harvard.

In Natalie's personality, these mercuric forces take on two distinctly separate qualities. The upper photos display the expansive, outward projecting energies of her masculine Sun. The upper right one shows the billowy Gemini jaw assembly that was described previously.

The bottom photo demonstrates how this jaw area changes, when Natalie reacts with the passive emotions of her Virgo Moon. Note how the face appears internally grounded, as the lower cheeks drop down on the sides to display the swelled jowls of Virgo.

Ascendant: Scorpio
The effects of planets in the 1st House

Portman has the same Ascendant as **Nicole Kidman**. Previously, we noted that Neptune was the only planet in Nicole's 1st House. So, let's compare that to Natalie, who has Uranus as the only planet in her 1st House.

Both display the flat cheek bones and large liquid pupils of Scorpio. Kidman's persona projects the dreamy and soft lit illusions of Neptune. In contrast, Portman appears to be locked into the mental world of Uranus. This is why she is such a dedicated student.

Scorpio Ascendants often have heavy bones, but the mutable luminaries of Portman and Kidman give them both lanky and slender frames. However, as the image in the box demonstrates, Portman readily takes on the body stance of Scorpio. This image from *The Black Swain* shows how the protruding hips send the upper back swaying to the rear and how the neck juts forward to create the profile of an eagle.

A Comprehensive Look at Luminary Progressions

Most of us Baby Boomers witnessed the life passages of Paul McCartney. Here, using a progression of "one day for each year in his life", we will illustrate how the progressed sign changes in Paul's Sun and Moon redefined his appearance, as well as the major creative changes and events in his life.

♊ Paul McCartney
6/18/1942, 2:00 A.M.
Liverpool, England

Sun in Gemini
The Sun's Progression into a New Sign Brings Creative Redirection

Paul's Gemini Sun progressed into Cancer when he was five years old. For the next 30 years, the sensitive water of Cancer was present, while the flighty energies of Gemini were noticeably restrained. Cancer's tidal rhythms showed in Paul's feel-good lyrics and vocals and in the streaming bass guitar riffs that he created for *The Beatles* and *Wings*.

In 1970, Paul quit *The Beatles*. The music of his new band *Wings* was similar in sound to what we heard before. However, eight year's later, when Paul's Sun progressed into Leo, he was given a surge of confidence—to move beyond his Cancer comfort zone—to create grander musical works! *Wings* disbanded in 1981 and Paul soon released a series of solo albums. Later, he created the unsuccessful movie *Give My Regards to Broad Street* and his 1991 commission to create a piece for Liverpool's Philharmonic Society received negative reviews. However, Paul's work soon became richer and more complex, after he learned that creative excellence is more than a product of confidence.

By 2009, as Paul's Sun progressed into Virgo, it was clear that Paul had mastered and perfected a diverse array of musical skills. It showed in his successful classical albums, the experimental *Electric Arguments* and his dance score for New York City Ballet. Significantly, at this stage in his life, Paul was also determined to offer Virgo's service to others—by initiating and performing in charity concerts around the world.

Moon: Leo

From the beginning, Paul was a natural showman. Emotionally, he was always comfortable performing on stage. So it is with most people who have Leo Moons.

Below, on the left, we see young and old examples of McCartney's Leo Moon—i.e., the glowing face he displays, when he reacts to others. When this fixed energy presents its light, we see the warm confidence and aura of a lion. This fixed fire became stronger after 1978, when Paul's Sun progressed into Leo.

Ascendant: Pisces

The mutable water of Paul's Pisces Ascendant accounts for his skewed and obtuse shaped bone structure. This off-sets his eye sockets and sends the jaw drifting off to the side.

When his luminaries recede, the facial flesh loses its surface tension. Consequently, one eye floats upward, some distance from the other. The right photos below show us how this mask, resembles the features of a fish. Up to his 36th birthday, Paul's progressed Cancer Sun make these water qualities more obvious.

Moon Progressions Indicate Major Life Events

Astrologer Marc Robertson wrote that the true significance of progressions can be seen in the Moon. Since the Moon progresses into a new sign about every 2.5 years, its aspects and House placement in a person's natal chart can frequently indicate the content of any major event that will occur in a person's life. So, it was with Paul.

When Paul met Linda Eastman in 1967, his progressed Leo Sun was in his 5th House of romance, sextiling his natal Venus—a time to meet "the love of his life". When they married two years later, Paul's progressed Moon was conjoining his natal Moon, Mars and Pluto (also in the 5th House). This coupling brought the world the highly driven and powerful creative team and band, known as *Wings*.

Sadly, when Linda lost her battle with Cancer in 1998, Paul's progressed Mars was in orb of his 7th House (Descendant) while it was squaring his natal Saturn. His progressed Moon was also squaring his natal Uranus and his progressed Sun was squaring his natal Venus.

Angelina Jolie

6/04/1975, 9:09 A.M.
Los Angeles, CA

♊ Sun Sign: Gemini

Angelina shows the restlessness and combustibility of someone who has eight chart components in Air and Fire—and no Earth to keep it grounded. The mercuric nature of her Sun is made ever more vaporous by the trine of her Sun's ruler Mercury to Uranus and its sextile to Jupiter on her Midheaven.

With her inherited Gemini curiosity, Jolie rarely stays focused on any one subject, for too long. The upper photos capture the mercuric nature of this Sun. Note how the eyes become translucent and electric, when she projects her solar beliefs. In conversation, Jolie's electric eyes will blink repeatedly, darting here and there as her hands animate the thoughts that are running through her head. The energy intensifies when she becomes emotional.

Moon: Aries

The energies of most Geminis seem abstract and dispersed, but this lady is often "right in your face"! Jolie's Moon, Jupiter and Mars are conjoined in Aries, and all three sextile her Sun!

This lady is an unstoppable force—and a real ball of fire! With these reinforced martian energies, we see why Jolie plays many action roles on the silver screen. She was the adventurous *Tomb Raider*, the femme fatale in *Sky Captain and the World of Tomorrow* and the power driven mother in *Alexander*.

The lower left picture shows the head strong qualities of Aries, as it hints of the dualistic nature of Angelina's Sun. The picture shows how individuals are frequently caught in this ambivalent moment, that lies between the Sun projections and their Moon reactions.

Ascendant: Cancer

Jolie's Venus, Saturn, and Ascendant are in Cancer, and they are the only feminine items in her chart. Notably, Angelina's watery Venus conjoins her Ascendant and they both square her Uranus. The outer planet explains her eclectic curiosity, and restless nature. This was captured in her description of "blue window tattoo on her back. Angelina claims that it symbolizes the fact that "no matter where she is (in any point in her life), she always finds herself looking out a window, wishing to be somewhere else." Indeed, this domestic Cancerian window is not providing much comfort, for her Aries Moon (the ruler of Cancer) is constantly driving her to seek new adventures.

Positively, this Cancer persona quiets the luminary energies, while Venus inspires her to improve the lives of children around the world.

♋ Cancer

	Page
Introduction to Cancer Traits	151-153
Ross Perot & Karen Black	

The waters flow with the Lunar Tides

Courtney Love & Liv Tyler	154
Harrison Ford	155
Dali Lama	156
Arianna Huffington	157
Robin Williams	158

Water is contained by the Earth

Will Ferrell	159
Della Reese	160
Kathy Bates	161

Add a little Fire & things get warmer

Tom Hanks	162
Forest Whitaker	163
Meryl Streep	164

Fire and Air inflates the bubble

Willem Dafoe	165
Lady Diana Spencer	166
Jesse Ventura	167
Sylvester Stallone	168
Benedict Cumberbatch	169

Making the transition to Leo

Jane Lynch	170-171
Tobey Maquire	172

Cancer ♋ June 21 to July 22
Feminine Polarity, Cardinal Water
Find Your Comfort Zone with your CANCER Friends!

On the first day of **Spring**, a new adventure of self-discovery began with **Aries**. With the shift to passive **Taurus**, the senses of every individual were enhanced, to enjoy the delights of Mother Earth. The understanding of this content was defined in the Sun's transit through **Gemini**.

At the **Summer Solstice**, when the Sun reaches its highest point in the sky, there is a massive polar shift, as the Sun (the light-of-self) begins its downward movement into night. It is here (in the **2nd Quadrant**) that individuals begin their interaction with their surroundings (**Cancer**), envision ways to enrich the environment (**Leo**) and serve others with their contributions (**Virgo**).

Cancers know that the bright summer light will not last. Perhaps that's why the craws of these Crabs are constantly gathering in "goodies" to fill their closets to the brim. Why not? These are the resources they need, to sustain their families.

All of the previously experienced movements, sensations and rearrangements are felt on every level by the Cancer Crab. With their intuitive feelings, these sensitive souls are keenly aware that everything is following a regular cadence—be it the daily reversal of lunar tides, the monthly Moon phases or the polar shifts that come, when the Sun enters another sign. Our Cancer friends feel ALL of Nature's rhythms—that is why they rarely leave the comfort of their homes.

In stormy weather, some crabs lose their sense of direction, and this makes them extremely emotional. In such moments, they withdraw into their shells. Still, all is well—for it is in this base where they regain their amazing "sense of timing" and the "inner confidence" to begin another round of interaction with the world. Watch how they stand at their front doors, as they wait for the right moment—to slide into the stream, and surf the cresting wave to distant shores, where precious treasures lie in wait. When the tide shifts, they'll ride the returning waves back to their homes—arms filled with treasured booty. This confidence is instilled by **Leo**, the next sign in the zodiac.

☾ Rulerships and Associations for Cancer

The Moon is the Goddess of instincts and the controller of one's habits and emotional reactions. It is also associated with menstrual cycles and motherhood. It rules the upper digestive tract that pulls the nourishment out of food.

This Moon also regulates the body's Parasympathetic Nervous System, the process that stimulates the body's need to "rest-and-digest" and "feed and breed". These feminine lunar impulses are countered by the masculine "fight or flight" urges of the Sun; those seen in the body's Sympathetic Nervous System. This is why Cancers are directed to sustain the home, the family and the memory of ancestors.

Cancer Physical Traits:

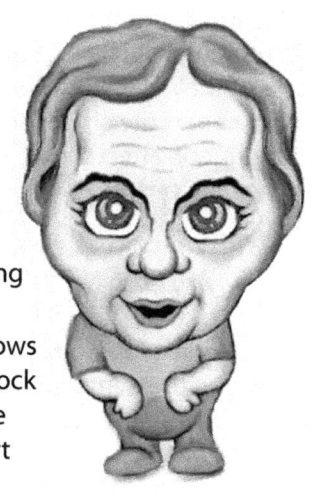

Since the Moon rules Cancer, this sign's translucent skin appears to reflect the blue-silvery light of a full beaming Moon. Structurally, this oval is seen in the Crab's giant, round temples. The facial components are centered in this circle, and they appear to swell in synch to the daily tides, or with the waxing and waning of this sign's emotions.

Interestingly, the furrows in the forehead, the eyebrows and the wavy triangle between the eyes appear to mock the lines on the back of the crab's shell. The rest of the body is full and round, save for the four lean and short extremities.

Ross Perot 6/27/1920, 5:34 A.M., Texarkana, TX
Karen Black 7/1/1939, 5:00 A.M., Chicago, IL

Let's begin by looking at two crabs with Cancer Rising. *Ross Perot*'s New Moon makes him a triple Cancer. *Karen Black* (with her Moon in Capricorn) is a Full Moon Crab. These significance of these Moon placements is illustrated in our first Cancer portrait.

Cancer Body Language

When the rulership of body areas progresses from Gemini's lungs down to the breasts, the energies are contained in the upper torso shell. The accumulation of feminine forces in the largest mass in the body, dynamically alters the body language.

When the Crab rests on the floor of the sea, the extremities are pulled in tightly to the body—to anchor the Crab securely in its present home of occupation. However, when the tides shift in a new direction, the crab begins its cautious move.

Watch how the crab tilts its heavy shell to the side, then shuffles its feet to the back—to push the tilted torso to the front. This off-balanced weight propels this creature forward, on its intended course of direction. Amazingly, the feet will then skitter to the front to regain the balance and bring the body back into an upright position. The above process is then repeated, to move the body a little further down the road.

Cancer Rules Breasts and Upper Digestive Track

The first four portraits in this section feature individuals who have more than one of their key lights in Cancer. They show us how the phases and lunar tides of the Moon affect the personality.

Courtney Love
(New Moon /Libra Rising)
7/9/1964, 2:08 P.M.
San Francisco, CA

New Moon people tend to be right out front with their emotional expressions, since both luminaries are usually in the same sign. Since Courtney's Sun is just 6 degrees before a New Moon, little or no light reflects off of its lunar surface. Like most New Moons, Courtney rarely reflects—she just constantly acts!

With Jupiter and Neptune aspecting both of her luminaries, Love's emotions often become exaggerated and ever so delusional. With her Pluto sextile her Sun, Courtney emotional outbursts are often disturbing.

Love's Libra Ascendant places her two luminaries at the top of her chart; only two planets rest in the lower half. This implies their is little time spent on "internal reflection". Furthermore, this cardinal mask squares her Moon. Her emotions are rarely presented in a pleasing manner.

Liv Tyler
(Full Moon / Cancer Rising)
7/1/1977, 6:08 A.M.
Portland, Maine

In contrast, Liv Tyler's components are dispersed throughout her chart. Her Cancer Sun opposes her Full Moon in Capricorn. This places her earthy Moon in the 6th House, and this accounts for the hints of Virgo in her personality that we saw in her role as Arwin in the film *Lord of the Rings*. In that role (and in her personality), Liv's emotional responses are slow to appear, and they seem cool and distance. Why not? The light of her Sun has to travel all the way to her distant Moon and then bounce back, to find its emotional expression.

The LR photo shows the bone structure of Liv's Cancer Ascendant, as well as the crystallizing force of her goat reactions. Note how the rounded flesh of the Sun removes the chiseled features of her Moon. This rarely happens in other Sun signs—but quite often in the one that is ruled by the Moon.

This effect of the Moon will be shown in the next three portraits, all of whom have a Cancer Moon or Ascendant to accent their Suns. There, we'll attempt to show how their different aspects and chart configurations color the delightful lunar projections and reactions of all Cancer Crabs.

~ ~ ~

Most people with a Cancer Moon often shows physical traits of the crab, regardless of their Sun Sign. Check out the Cancer Moons in this book's index, to see how a Cancer Moon affects the physical appearance of ALL Sun signs.

Harrison Ford
7/13/1942, 11:41 A.M.
Chicago Heights, IL

Sun & Moon: Cancer

Harrison's Sun, Moon, Mercury and Jupiter are in Cancer, but he has four components in Air Signs! This concentration of just two elements gives him a soft spoken manner as well as an ability to verbalize his thoughts and feelings (often in a natural, rhythmic manner). Perhaps that's why he usually plays quiet but quick-witted characters who have to think on their feet.

The upper photos show how Ford's cardinal waters tend to replicate the waxing and waning flow of the ocean tides. In the left photo, we see how the internal pressures push the facial features up and out—from within! The right photo captures the receding tides, as the waters rush back to return to their base.

Ascendant: Libra

Like **Courtney Love**, Ford has both of his luminaries in Cancer—but his emotional makeup is totally different! This is because the only aspect to his luminaries is his Moon's sextile to Neptune. In contrast (as noted), Love's luminaries forms multiple aspects to Neptune, Jupiter and Uranus. These aspects super-charge the churn of Love's Neptune. Also, her emotions are rarely presented in a pleasant manner, since her Moon squares her Ascendant!

With his Cancer Moon's harmonious sextile to his Libra Ascendant, Ford's waters rise gently to the surface. Note how the bulging facial features stretch into the symmetrically balanced lines when his V-shaped Libra smile appears.

Ford's Rising Sign trines Saturn and Uranus. These aspects account for his dual-edged public persona. In his roles in *Bladerunner* and *Star Wars*, the futuristic images of Uranus appeared. The serious Saturn influences prevailed in *The Fugitive*, *Witness* and *Patriot Games*.

Mars in Leo

In his role in the *Indiana Jones* films, Ford always appeared to be physical self-assured. He was always focused on task, save for when he became overly theatrical and/or demonstrative. Such physicality is common for individuals with a Mars in Leo!

It was this Mars that gave Harrison the physical demeanor that proved so attractive to his fans. Pluto (the higher octave of the force of Mars) is also in Leo. It sextiles Ford's Ascendant and also the previously mentioned Saturn/Uranus conjunction. This gave Ford the daring confidence to perform many of his own stunts.

Dalai Lama
7/6/1935, 4:38 A.M.
Takster, Tibet

According to Tibetan tradition, the Dalai Lama reincarnates from one life to the next. At the time of the last transition, it is believed that Buddhist spiritual leaders chose the fourteenth Dalai Lama by viewing the content in his birth chart. The signs were very clear, even when interpreted in the language of western astrology.

A Grand Spirit in Exile

The Dalai Lama's chart shows the gifts of a spiritual leader. His Sun and Ascendant form a grand trine to Jupiter and Saturn (the latter being in mystical Pisces in the 9th House of Religion). This water trine denotes a mastery of inner silence and a wisdom of the greater world—that he sees through the window of his compassionate Cancer Ascendant.

Mars in the 4th House suggests warfare in the home. (China invaded Tibet long before his birth and it was totally conquered in 1959). This Libra Mars squares his South Node and Pluto in Dalai Lama's 1st House. This suggests a karmic link with his nation's past and that he would become the frontal spokesman for his struggling nation that was his home.

Pluto in the 1st House gives him a strong sense of self-determination, while his 9th House Saturn indicates his religious teachings would be suppressed. Fortunately, this exile made the world conscious of his nation's fate, as well as the teachings of his Buddhist faith.

Sun & Ascendant: Cancer

The soft tidal waters flow gracefully, when this teacher presents his spiritual messages to the world. With a Cancer Sun and Ascendant, the Dalai Lama wears his heart on his sleeve. What he says and feels is right up front and unfiltered, since his beliefs and mask are one and the same.

Moon: Virgo

In more compassionate moments, the Dalai Lama's temples round as they beam the light of the Moon. With his Moon in Virgo (in the 3rd House of Communication) conjoined Neptune and sextile Jupiter, this spirit was given the gift, to find the words that would help others to pursue their spiritual path.

Watch what happens when his emotions build. Instead of the round face of a Crab, what we see is the long and skewed features of Virgo. Note how, when he becomes tangled up in his mercuric feelings, his stomach shifts to the front, as his hands point and count and diagram the thoughts in his head.

Arianna Huffington

7/15/1950, 3:00 PM
Athens, Greece

Sun & Moon: Cancer

As the namesake of *The Huffington Post*, Arianna became a regular on talk shows across America. With six of her components (including her three key lights) in water signs, you'd expect a more introverted and protective personality. However, Leo is on her Midheaven and all of her planets (save for Jupiter in the 4th House) are in the upper "sunlit portion" of her chart. This crab feels right at home, skittering about in the public light.

Like **Harrison Ford**, Huffington's next biggest grouping is her Air planets. She has three: Venus (in chatty Gemini) trines her Libra Mars and Neptune. The latter two are in her 11th House of "social communication". This (and her Saturn in Virgo in her 10th House of career) makes Mercury the dominate planet in her cart. It shows why she gained public recognition, gathering data and serving it to the world.

Physically, Arianna displays many traits of the Cancer Crab. She shows the usual swelling of the temples, and she also shows us how a Cancer's claw-like fingers often behave like the pincers on a crab. As the photos show, she seems to be grasping at as unseen treasures and pulling them near her chest.

Ascendant: Scorpio

Arianna's Scorpio Ascendant trines her Sun and Moon and it also squares Pluto. This gives her a powerful and controlling persona—as well as a window to the world that allows her to grasp the valuable resources—and discard the trash. This gift likely contributed to her website's success.

Transits Bring Big Changes

When Arianna sold "the baby that she created" to AOL (February 7, 2011), Uranus, the planet of abrupt disruption was about to enter her 5th House. Jupiter was also transiting this House, conjoining her natal North Node. This portended a huge gamble and a big payoff for Arianna, since Jupiter is the ruler of her 2nd House. *The Huffington Post* sold for $315 million!

Negatively, Jupiter's square to transiting Pluto (in her 2nd House) suggested a power struggle over "who would control what". With Uranus' pending entrance into her 5th House, it was likely that she could lose creative control. She did on many levels, and the site was soon filled with disruptive ads and commercials. Arianna resigned her role as its chief editor in 2016.

Robin Williams
**7/21/1951, 1:34 P.M.
Chicago, IL**

Like Arianna, Robin is a triple water sign. However, his three key lights exhibit all three modal patterns, as his waters surge, crest and splash on the shore.

♋ Sun: Cancer

In his more expressive moments, the water of Robin's Cancer Sun gushed up from within—to bulge his eyes and swell his temples. Still, there were many calmer moments, since his Sun's only aspect was its sextile to Saturn.

In these moments, the caring side of the Cancer Crap appeared. We saw it in his work with children. In *Mrs. Doubtfire*, he showed us how difficult it was for a male crab to let go of his "cast of young ones". In *Hook*, he was an adult Peter Pan, who held on to his childlike sense of wonder. In *Jack*, he played a child in an adult's body. In real life, he was a devoted father and family man.

Robin's Midheaven Mercury conjoins Pluto, trines Jupiter and sextiles Neptune. Jupiter gives Robin his gift for comedy and his mercuric chatter—as well as his attraction to the professorial roles that we saw in *Dead Poets's Society* and *Good Will Hunting*. Neptune gave him the ability to create delightful fantasies for all ages, be it the genie's voice in *Aladdin*, or the magical *What Dreams May Come*. Pluto's conjunction was likely the root of his frequent bouts with depression.

Moon: Pisces

Robin's Pisces Moon forms a grand trine with his Ascendant and a Mars/Uranus conjunction in his 8th House. These two planets form a T-Square to Jupiter and Neptune (the ancient and current rulers of the sign of Pisces). This accounts for his quixotic actions and over reactive emotions.

Scorpio Ascendant

Robin's Mars (in Cancer) was the most aspected planet in his chart. As noted, this ancient ruler of Scorpio trined his Ascendant. Also, Pluto (Scorpio's current ruler) squared his Ascendant.

With this, it is no surprise that Robin's persona was powerful. With Uranus trine his Ascendant, he also appeared outrageously bizarre. Uranus' impact was seen in his performance as the goofy space alien in *Mork and Mindy*, the role that launched his career. The deeper mysteries of Scorpio were revealed in his films: *The Fisher King, Jumanji* and *Awakenings*.

In those rare moments when Robin was not in an expressive or reactive mode, what we saw was the subterranean elements of his stocky body structure—i.e., the square skull and jaw, and the hooked eagle's beak of his Scorpio Ascendant.

Will Ferrell
7/16/1967, 10:09 A.M.
Irvine, CA.

Sun: Cancer

With his delightfully expressive face, Will Ferrell shows us the steps that Crabs go through, when they express the four phases or steps in Cardinal Water's wave of emotion.

As these Crabs rest comfortably in their shells, they are always anticipating the arrival of any upcoming tidal change. At the right time, they will make their move! What follows are the dynamic actions, that are pictured here:

1. When the eyes of the crab take on a lunar glow and the face rounds and swells (most noticeably in the temples), this is your hint that another wave of water is building within. This bubbly excitement often produces Cancer's warbling cackle.

2. With the increasing pressure, the wave of water builds within. This pushes the head and the facial features upward, as the water climbs to its tidal crest.

3. Once past the peak, the waters crash onto the shore—inundating everything and everyone in a tsunami of emotions.

4. After the crash, the water stills—as the tides reverse their flow. This returns the crab to its home on the ocean's floor. Once again, in this anchored space, it can feel the changing currents, and begin the preparation for the next onslaught of tidal surges.

Moon: Scorpio

This holding point (#4) demonstrates the fixed energies of Will's Scorpio Moon. Note how his eyebrows turn down to focus the laser-like eyes, so that they can examine the current conditions in his surroundings.

As we see in all of Ferrell's solar projections and lunar reactions, there is a delightful sense of fantasy and lunacy. This can be attributed to his Moon's conjunction with Neptune and the trine of these two components to his Sun.

Ascendant: Virgo

Ferrell's Virgo Ascendant explains the mercuric mask and nervous energy that he frequently presents to the world. It also explains why his long face lacks the expected circular shape of the Crab.

Uranus and Pluto sit near Will's Ascendant and these two planets sextile both of his water luminaries. This brings Will's liquid antics to the surface.

Uranus explains the goofy characters we saw on *Saturday Night Live*, in the film *Zoolander* and in his role as Santa's giant *Elf*. Pluto on the Ascendant brought us the hilarious power trips of the legendary *Anchorman,* and the daredevil antics of *Talladega Nights: The Ballad of Ricky Bobby.*

Della Reese
7/6/1931 10:00 A.M.
Detroit, Michigan

As a teenager, Della joined *Mahalia Jackson's Touring Choir*. This led to her two "million seller" records, her years of successful night club shows and her best selling book: *Angels Along the Way*. This biographical book was inspired by hit TV show *Touched By An Angel*. In this show (that ran from 1994 to 2003), Della played the mothering angel who guided her children with heart, substance and reverence. All of this is embraced in the contents in her chart.

 Sun: Cancer

Della's 10th House Cancer Sun conjoins Venus on her MC. This gave Della the graceful light to inspire her family, friends and the world. Of even more importance was her Sun's conjunction to Mercury and Pluto—the planet with the most connected component in her chart! (It has too many aspects to list). We see why this lady had such a connection with a power far greater than her own!

The UL photo shows how Della's temples swelled, when she projected her solar light to others. The UR photo shows her in a reflective state. Both photos show how the tidal forces of Cancer runs back and forth, rather than in one direction. That is why it is difficult to distinguish a Cancer's solar light from that of his or her Moon.

Moon: Pisces

Della's Jupiter conjoins her Mercury, and both planets trine her Moon. All the while, Uranus is forming a T-square to Saturn and her Mercury. We see why this lady used her talents to bring her friends and humanity together through the use of religious messages.

In her book, Della credited the miracles in her life to her faith in God and the goodness of humanity. With her compassionate Pisces Moon, Della was able to plant this belief in the hearts of millions of people. With this, the world gained a giant crop of earthly angels.

Ascendant: Virgo

Question this lady's faith or her intent, and this Crab would quickly raise her crystalline Virgo shield—defending her beliefs with a mix of facts and figures. Watch how her round facial lines would skew and stiffened, when she served her information to others.

With her mercuric persona, Della had a nonthreatening physical presence. However, with her Mars and Neptune in the 12th House of Religion and Pluto on her Sun, when Della became riled, she could instill the fear of God into anyone. When this woman spoke (or sang), people listened!

Kathy Bates

6/28/1948, 11:12 A.M.
Memphis, TN

 ## Sun: Cancer

The characters played by this actress run the gamut—from psychopathic murderess to sophisticated comedy. Her true nature was best seen in her motherly figure and homebody roles in *Fried Green Tomatoes* and *The Waterboy*.

Kathy's rounded lunar temples give her face a luminous glow and a silvery sheen. With her heavy-lidded eyes, she draws us into her cinematic characters. Before we realize what is happening, the undertow carries us away, on an unsuspected emotional ride.

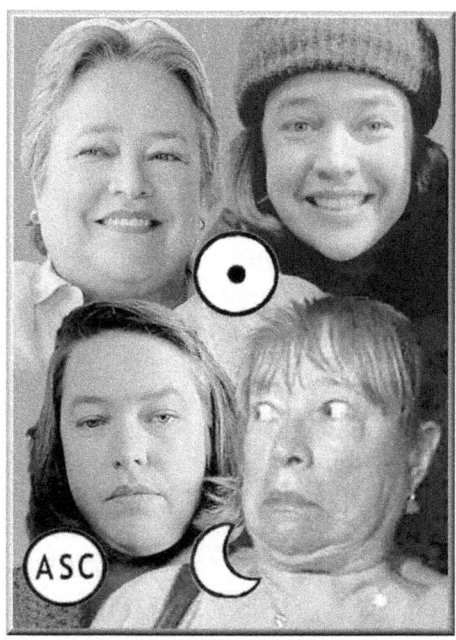

Kathy has given the world some of the most memorable scenes in cinema, and rightfully, she has received numerous awards for her performances.

Ascendant: Virgo

Often, Kathy appears tightly wound and nervous. That's appropriate, since all of those emotions have to pass through the precisely constructed mental mesh of her Virgo Ascendant.

Mars sits near her Ascendant, as it is opposed by her Moon. This gives her mercuric mask and forceful presence, that we saw in her stunning performance in *Misery*, the film that won her an Oscar for Best Actress in a Leading Role.

There, Kathy showed us the worst of Virgo, as she played a fanatical fan who fussed over the most trivial of details, as she tried to serve and cater to her captured victim's needs.

When the waters of Kathy's luminaries recede, Bates' liquid flesh solidifies as it takes on the smooth cast of porcelain. In the process, the twisting patterns of mutability skew the face. This sends one eye some distance up from the other as it gives the appearance that she is scornful of what she is seeing before her eyes. (This is a common trait for many Virgo Risings). This disdain is precisely registered in the tightly curled lips.

Moon: Pisces

Kathy's Moon stands alone, in the right hemisphere of her chart. However, this isolated Moon is glowing in direct opposition to her Ascendant—and this allows her to pour her emotions out through this window—and weave her audience into her worlds of illusion.

Bates' Moon also forms a T-Square to Uranus and Jupiter. This accounts for her many involvements in protests, and the social issues in her films.

In *Primary Colors*, Kathy's portrayal of a disillusioned lesbian feminist brought her audience to tears.

In *About Schmidt*, Kathy's sense of wonder hit the mark. Playing a new-age hippy mother, she did the impossible—she upstaged Jack Nicholson!

Add a little Fire and things get warmer

Tom Hanks
7/9/1956, 11:17 A.M.
Concord, CA

♋ Sun: Cancer

In the film *Splash*, Hanks introduced us to the liquid world of his Sun's home element. With his Sun's sextile to Mars (in Pisces) and his Neptune as the most aspected planet in his chart, Tom is given a non-aggressive nature but an ability to completely adapt his emotions. This allowed him to present to create many cinematic treasures—some fantastical (*Forrest Gump*) and comedic (*Sleepless in Seattle*). Some like *Philadelphia* and *Saving Private Ryan* were also emotionally wrenching, since his Sun is in the decan of Scorpio. With this, Hanks presents several of the physical features of the Crab, and also hints of Scorpio.

Ascendant: Virgo

Tom is the fourth of five Cancers who have Virgo Rising—and like the others, his face is longer and more angled than what we'd expect from a Crab. Oddly, Tom has a larger than normal head and torso, and small limbs—the features often seen in many Crabs. (It may be Saturn's trine to his Sun that is infusing these Crab features into his body).

Otherwise, Hanks truly displays Virgo's meticulous image, for his Mercury sextiles Jupiter (in the sign of Virgo). This makes him a very methodical crab.

Since the Rising Sign defines the "immediate space around the body", it often determines how people view the world before their eyes. Hanks was the crew member in *Apollo 13* who found the right stuff (Virgo's mutable Earth) to work out the details for a safe return. This obsession for detail was also seen, as he tried to unravel the hidden mysteries in *The Di Vinci Code*.

People with this Ascendant can be highly critical of everything that they encounter. Fortunately, Hanks shows little of Virgo's tendency to worry. His Moon is in playful Leo!

Moon: Leo

Hanks broke onto the national scene in the TV series *Bosom Buddies*. There, his sensitive Sun was often overridden by his loud and boisterous Leo Moon. In Tom's film *Big*, we saw how these lionized lunar emotions can reveal "the inner child" that is in all of us. That is why most people with this lunar placement are warm and playful, for they seem to remain "children at heart"—late into their lives.

You'll see Tom's Moon in its fullness, when his head lifts up out of the sea, to fix onto the glory of the moment. Ah, life is grand!

Forest Whitaker
7/15/1961, 10:30 A.M.
Longview, TX

Though born five years apart, Whitaker and Hanks have the same components and similar charts! The major difference is the decans of their Suns, the sign of their Mars and the planet(s) in the nearly vacate right side of their charts.

Sun: Cancer

Hank's 24° Sun is the Scorpio decan. As seen in his role of *Sully*, he shows the controlled emotions of a scorpion.

In contrast, Forest's 22° Sun is in the decan of Pisces. He looks "tough" but his characters are often soft spoken, timid and naive. This has earned him the name "The Gentle Giant".

Virgo Ascendant

Tom and Forest's Suns sextile their "Taurus Decan" Ascendants. This gives both men stocky frames, rather than the lean and lanky one of Virgo. Also, their Mars are in different hemispheres of their charts. Their physical drives seem to be empowered by "opposite forces".

Hank's Pisces Mars sits alone in the right hemisphere. As we saw in *Forrest Gump*, his physical actions are not "self directed", they just seem "to be operated by *other forces* beyond his control".

In contrast, Forest's Virgo Mars conjoins Pluto on the left-side of his chart. He acquired his physical skills through personal training. (He earned a black belt in *Kenpo*, a Japanese form of martial arts).

Forest's right hemisphere contains just three planets: Venus, Jupiter and Saturn. Saturn's snug trine to his Ascendant makes his skewed features all the more irregular. This "odd appearance" got him his role as Big Harold in *Platoon*. Venus gave him his musical talent, that in turn, brought him the lead role as Charlie Parker in the biological film *Bird*. The chilling effect of Saturn was seen in Forest's Oscar winning role in *The Last King of Scotland*, where he played the dictator *Idi Amin*. More recently, the passages of Saturn unfolded in his lead role in *Lee Daniels' The Butler*.

These successes all took personal effort, but these three right hemisphere planets had a great influence on his destiny.

Moon in Leo

Amazingly, Forest and Tom Hanks Moons have no major aspects, save for their conjunctions to Uranus. This outer planet makes both men emotionally distant, yet incredibly idealistic.

Uranus brings an electrical spark to their eyes, as their Leo Moons make both of them whimsical and playful. Positively, this socially conscious force of Uranus overrides Leo's tendency for self-aggrandizement. Both support many humanitarian causes. Hanks has contributed to a wide range of charities. Forest is a cofounder of "The International Institute for Peace".

Meryl Streep
6/22/1949, 8:05 A.M.
Summit, NJ

Sun: Cancer

Meryl's face displays many of the Crab's physical traits. The most noticeable features are her low-placed lunar temples and the bulging triangle between the brows. What is different is her demeanor. Meryl has her Sun conjunct Uranus and sextiling Saturn. It suggests the following scenario:

Imagine a crab scooting cautiously across the ocean's floor. Beneath the sand lies an array of randomly placed Uranian land-mines. Every so often contact is made. Zap! Crackle! The crab gets jolted with electricity. These jolts are physically harmless, but the static electricity remains—to alter the neurological circuitry and throw this crab's sense of rhythm out of balance.

This gives Meryl her delightfully irregular expressions—and they are never too bizarre, for Saturn's sextile quickly brings her back to normal—to reassume her regular routine. This produces a crab who is totally in control, but also playful and inventive.

As we saw in *Sophie's Choice* and *Out of Africa*, this arrangement contributes to Meryl's gift for articulating the irregular patterns, dialects and structural tones in various language and cultures. This is aided by her Mercury and Mars conjunction in Gemini, and her Venus' sextile to her Taurus Moon.

Moon: Taurus

Meryl's Taurus Moon contains the churning waters of Cancer, as it relaxes and grounds her emotions. These slow moving and earthy emotions stood out in her role in *Bridges Of Madison County*.

Meryl's interactions with others are often firmly fixed and markedly sensual. Note how the nostrils widen, as the eyes drop down on the outer edges to create the look of a contented bovine. These sensual emotions are further stabilized by her Moon's exact square to Pluto (in Leo and in her 1st House). This gives her a powerful range of emotions. All of them are mastered and totally controlled, as they're dramatically presented through the screen of her Leo Ascendant.

Ascendant: Leo

Meryl's Rising Sign is Leo. In *French Lieutenant's Women*, we saw Leo's theatrical facade in this "movie within a movie". This film asked the question: "Is this the real person, or are we seeing her 'Leo act'—out front, outshining her timid Cancer Sun?" In the film *Prada*, there was no question, as Meryl's Leo mask was firmly placed on center stage—constantly displaying her aura of confidence, while she was dispersing her royal decrees!

Air & Fire Inflates the Bubble
Willem Dafoe
7/22/1955, 7:30 P.M.
Appleton, WI

Sun: Cancer

Like **Meryl Streep**, Dafoe's Sun also conjoins Uranus. The big difference is that Willem's Sun is also conjoined by Mars and Jupiter in fiery Leo. This raises the electricity 1000 volts, and it doubles the amperage!

Streep's Saturn sextile's her Sun. Willem's ringed planet squares his Mars and Jupiter. For Dafoe, the stabilizing forces of Saturn are pulling his martial energies off in "another direction". Thusly, his physical movements are broad and expansive, not as contained as we see in Streep. These exaggerated gestures were seen in his disturbing performance as the Green Goblin in *Spiderman*.

All of Willem's planets are in his chart's right hemisphere. Leo Mars and Jupiter are placed near his Descendant (in his 6th House of Work), This placement of Mars accounts for his athletic motor skills, his giant sense of daring and his attraction to machismo roles like *Once Upon A Time in Mexico*. This is why he often does his own stunts in his films.

The upper photos show how the flooding waters of Willem's Sun inflate and round his facial features. The UR photo likely caught Dafoe in a moment when the electrical juices of his Uranus were also activated. This look of surprise appears quite often, since his Ascendant is ruled by Uranus.

Aquarius Rising

When air is injected into Willem's physical container, the pressured water percolates to the surface, so that it can escape its containment. The force of expression becomes more intense and ever more outrageous.

Dafoe's Aquarius Ascendant opposes all of those planets that surround his Sun. Thusly, they appear to be lying far to the back of this statically charged screen. The first impression that we see is someone who appears distant and other worldly. This eerie reality was seen in *Shadow of the Vampire*, a film that many believe to be Willem's finest role. (It won him his second Oscar nod after *Platoon*). In this film about the movie *Nosferatu*, Willem's vampire creature was disturbingly cold and distant—a creature living in the bone chilling, surreal atmosphere of Uranus.

Moon: Virgo

Willem's lunar light sparkles in the mutable Earth of Virgo. Since his Moon sextiles its ruling planet Mercury, his emotions are overly analytical and scarce of feeling. In contrast, Meryl's Fixed Earth emotions appear more anchored, and not so likely to fuss and worry over the smaller details.

In emotional moments, Dafoe's flesh crystallizes—to form the oblong face and the twisted lines of mutability. Mercury's square to Saturn likely contributes to the gap between his front teeth. That is a common trait seen in people who have Virgo Rising.

Diana Spencer
Princess of Wales
7/1/1961, 7:45 P.M.
London, England

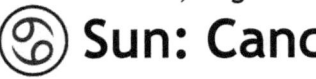 Sun: Cancer

With her afflicted Moon, Princess Diana was exposed to turbulent tides that could have shattered the shell of any other sensitive crab.

The upper photos show the round and low-set temples of the Crab. The UL photo shows how her head rises upward, as she peeks out of her shell. The UR photo shows the Princess in a protective mode. There, her arms are clutching tightly to her torso. This pulls her chest in and her head down. In this stance, she looks up at her subjects from that "peculiar angle".

Diana's caring and nurturing nature was best seen when she was working with or mothering children—her own or those in far away countries. However, there were stronger forces tugging on her sleeve, to draw this princess away from her castle.

Moon: Aquarius

Royal decorum flies out the window when an Aquarius Moon reacts! With her Venus T-squaring her Aquarius Moon and a Mars/Uranus conjunction, it is clear that strong actions and impulsive reactions were inevitable. With Mars conjoining Pluto in her 8th House, some nasty secrets were likely to be revealed.

When Saturn transited her Moon and squared her Venus in 1993, the romantic fairy tale was over, as Diane became more erratic, surprising many with her shocking responses. The Queen didn't know what to expect! Her royal astrologers should have known that Aquarius Moons are highly independent—and when their emotional attachments are shattered, they will resist all restrictions! With this royal divorce, Uranus brought radical changes to another institution.

Ascendant: Sagittarius

Those royal astrologers made another mistake. They should have known that you can never bridle a Centaur Rising Sign—particularly one that trines the quixotic planet of Uranus. It was clear that this Cancer Crab was not suited for household, much less royal duties.

This struggle was captured in the symbolic interpretation of Diane's 18° Ascendant: *"As it tries to escape from a burning house, a snake is stopped by a circle of fire."* (Janduz version).

With Jupiter (her Ascendant's ruler) square Neptune, this princess was impelled to chase one dream after another. Sadly, the chase ended and the candle light was extinguished on 8/31/1997 in a tragic car crash.

Jesse Ventura

7/15/1951, 3:00 A.M.
Minneapolis, Mn

♋ Sun: Cancer

It's hard to believe that this outlandish exhibitionist is a Cancer Crab, but let's look a little closer. Cancer is the only sign that could strike a sympathetic cord, push other people's emotional buttons and instill such a feeling of trust. This Crab was able to express his deeper feelings and win the votes to become his state's Governor.

In moments of solar expression, Jesse's face shows few hints of this watery Sun. Sure, the face rounds somewhat, but the eyes barely reveal the large pools of water that we see in most Crabs. This is due to his Moon and Ascendant.

Moon: Sagittarius

Sagittarius Moon Signs reveal their emotions in a brutally honest way. With Jesse, his impulsive reactions resulted in many politically incorrect comments, but people still liked him—because "he says what he feels". (There are likely few politicians with this lunar placement).

While Governor, Jesse often visited talk shows and traveled to distant places. Critics say this interfered with his job. His supporters say that it only allowed him to see "the bigger picture."

Like **Diana** and **Willem**, Jesse's Mars conjoins his Uranus in Leo. The big difference is that Willem's and Jesse's Moons form no aspects with these two planets, and both men also have their Moons sextile to Saturn. Both of them were far more stable and content with their positions in life. There is much unrest when the Moon, Mars and Uranus interact together.

Ascendant: Gemini

Mercury, the ruler of Jesse's Gemini Ascendant conjoins Pluto in Leo—as it forms a grand trine with his Moon. This explains Jesse's giant barrel chest and why he lacks the lanky body of Gemini. This Gemini mask also accounts for his gift for verbal chatter and theatrical sound bites.

Notably, Jesse's Mars and Uranus are in Cancer (in his 1st House). This accounts for his ability to be comfortable while he interacts and reaches out to others. With this gift, he went from being the mayor of a medium sized city to become the Governor of Minnesota. He was the highest elected official to ever win an election on a Reform Party ticket.

Like **Willem Dafoe**, Jesse has Mars on one of the angles of his chart. As noted, this position indicates that a person will have a high probability of being exceptionally athletic. Ventura was a Navy Seal and also a colorfully outrageous WWF wrestler.

Sylvester Stallone

7/6/1946, 7:20 P.M.
New York, NY

 Sun: Cancer

Stallone is best known for his boxing roles in the films *Rocky* through *Creed*. He also was a action star in multiple *Rambo* and *Expendables* films. Who'd ever think he's a sensitive Crab?

Sly's Sun and Saturn are his only water, and Mars is his only Earth. Still, Sly's demeanor is markedly reserved and far less aggressive than what we'd expect from someone with seven masculine components in his chart. This is likely due to his Sun's sextile to his Mars in earthy Virgo. (Saturn's square to his Moon is also a factor).

As viewed in the UR photo, we are shown how the "crest of a wave" pulls Sly's skull upward and to the right. When you view his chart, you will see that most of his components are clustered in this UR (third quadrant) of his chart. The arrangements in his chart are replicated in his physical appearance.

Libra Moon

Sly's Venus-ruled Moon snugly sextiles his natal Venus. This likely gave him the dreamy, heavy lidded and sleepy eyes that were so obvious in his younger years. The LL photo shows how Sly's air sign Moon lightens his facial energies, as it brings his features into balance.

Sly's Moon conjoins the planet Jupiter on his Midheaven. This giant planet is the ruler of Sagittarius, the sign associated with athletics. This explains why Stallone won public attention playing sports and action figures. Stallone was never a pro athlete. He just played one.

Sagittarius Rising

When Sly's fiery Sagittarius Ascendant rises to the surface, the water soaked flesh deflates, and this reveals the out-of-kilter underlying skeletal structure. Sly's LR profile photo shows how the long and thick horse neck trusts the head as well as the jaw to the front. Oddly, his Centaur jaw appears cubical in shape and the rear of the head does not "bulge to the back" like we see with most Centaurs. This is likely due to the fact that Sly's Sun is in the decan of Scorpio, his Rising Sign is in the decan of Leo and its ruling planet Jupiter is in the decan of Aquarius. All three are fixed signs!

Notably, it was not Mars that made Sly an action hero. Rather, it was his exercise of mental will that made Sly a star. This may be because the ruling planet of his Virgo Mars is Mercury. It conjoins Pluto. This gave Sly the where-with-all to perfect and build strength in every part of his body. Sly's real power came through this mind, and not in his physical actions.

Benedict Cumberbatch
7/19/1976, 12:00 P.M.
London, UK

Sun: Cancer

With six masculine components, Benedict shows little hints of what we'd expect from a Cancer Sun. Sure, there's the rounded flesh and cheekbones, but his eyes reflect little of the liquidity and depth of water. Also, instead of showing the reserved qualities of the Crab, Cumberbatch often appears electric and markedly quixotic.

Attribute this restlessness to Benedict's key components: they're all in cardinal signs! Also, his Sun conjoins Mercury, Venus and Saturn in Leo, and these four planets all form a T-square to his Moon and Uranus, while Mercury and his Sun also sextile Jupiter. These massive mercuric forces permeate every layer of his personality! These cerebral energies of Mercury reigned in his sharp tongued performances in BBC's *Sherlock Holmes* (and in his role as Julian Assange in *The Fifth Estate*).

Aries Moon

With his Moon's square to Saturn and Mercury, this crab's emotions are often calculated and analytical. With his Moon in Aries and his Mars in Virgo, his reactions become assertive—but also questioning at the same time.

Benedict was the officer in *War Horse* and the secret agent in *Tinter Taylor Soldier Spy*. With his Moon's opposition to Uranus, several of his roles also took us to some strange and futuristic worlds. He played the young Khan in *Star Trek into Darkness* and voiced the evil Smaug in *The Hobbit*.

Libra Ascendant

In his role in *Dr. Strange*, Cumberbatch activated all three cardinal components in his chart. His character was driven by the raging desires of his Aries Moon. With Pluto on his Libra Ascendant (in sextile to Mercury and Neptune), he found the balancing secrets of eastern religions to calm his mind and find a state of pure acceptance. Once there, he found a comforting place for his Cancer Sun. With those insights, all sorts of magical events began to happen.

Notably, this film's goal was to explore the impact of mind-over-matter. It was a great role for someone who has an empowered mercury in his chart.

When Benedict's luminaries are in repose, his facial lines come into balance, to present the squinted sparkling eyes and Libra's wide V-shaped smile. In such times, he appears lighter and markedly more pleasant.

When Fire components dominate, the water of Cancer evaporates
Jane Lynch
7/14/1960, 6:17 A.M.
Evergreen Park, IL

In her Emmy and Golden Globe winning role in *Glee*, Jane played Sue Sylvester, a tyrannical cheer leading coach who showed little sensitivity to the feelings of others. Many others also saw Lynch as being abrasive and arrogant, and few would expect her to be a sensitive Cancer Crab. Naturally, this is due to the other components in her chart.

Sun: Cancer

When Jane appears on interviews and talk shows, she is often aggressive and strong opinionated. She rarely appears emotional, for she has a point to make. This is not what we'd expect from a Cancer Sun. Astrologically, this may be why:

First of all, Jane's Sun is hidden in the 12th House and her Sun opposes Saturn in chilly Capricorn. Saturn also trines Jane's fixed and earthy Taurus Mars. This gives her the controlled poker-face that she presented as Charlie's sarcastic therapist in *Two and A Half Men*. It also accounts for gift for the dry humor we saw in her comedic roles in the films *The 40 Year Old Virgin* and *The Three Stooges;* It also helped her hone the unflappable demeanor that she perfected in *Glee*.

However, when Jane projects the mothering light of her Sun, her stony crust liquefies into swelling bubbles of flesh, as her voice takes on a sympathetic vibration. This is the voice that we heard in her massive array of children's films: *Wreck-It-Ralph, Shrek: Forever After, Ice Age: Dawn of the Dinosaurs* and *Alvin and the Chipmunks* were the most popular. This body of youth-oriented films was likely enhanced by Jane's Cancer Mercury and Venus, both of which conjoin her Sun. Lynch also showed the character of her Sun when she proclaimed that the best thing about her Sue Sylvester character was "she was a strong protector of the innocent".

Unlike **Benedict Cumberbatch**, Jane's Mercury and Venus are in Cancer, not in Leo. Also, Mercury does not form any other aspects, save for an inconjunct to Jupiter. She lacks the mercuric and analytical intensity that we saw in his portrait.

As been noted many times, the Moon is the ruler of Cancer and it has an abnormal influence on all people with this Sun Sign. With her Aries Moon near the Midheaven, we see why Lynch has received more recognition for her aggressive impulses rather than for the protective and kinder nature of her Sun.

Aries Moon

There is something strange about a Cancer Sun with an Aries Moon. Perhaps, it can be explained this way: Cancers often shy from the bright lights, as they withdraw from confrontation into their comfort zones. As the previous photos show, Cancer's cardinal waters are drawn inward—and down to the bottom of the sea, only to be pulled in different directions by the orbiting Moon. This explains the Moon's rulership of Cancer.

With her Moon in Aries, Jane's lunar emotions are tugged in a right-angle direction to her Sun. This changes their polarity and quality—as it turns her sensitive solar feelings into those of an expansive, straight-shooting Ram! (Fortunately, these fiery emotional outbursts dissipate as rapidly as they appear).

As with Cumberbatch, this lunar force gives Jane her clipped manner of speaking, a powerful sense of independence and an undeniable ability to say "what she really feels".

Ascendant: Leo

An astrologer must have been present to record Jane's birth time, of if she was born just 4 minutes earlier, Jane would be Virgo, rather than Leo Rising. The time must be correct, for Jane's often projects Leo's fixed aura of confidence, rather than a worried and mercuric one. Still, we could be fooled by her self-oriented Aries Moon.

Jane's own words support the presence of the lion: "I love being on stage. I love performing. I love the immediate response from the audience. I love theater people. I love theater."

Interestingly, this dramatic Ascendant trines Jane's Aries Moon, as it places her personal planets (Sun, Mercury and Venus) in her 12th House of healing, and her Saturn in the 6th House of health. Perhaps that is why Jane is attracted to roles that deal with therapy and counseling.

Along with her roles in *Glee* and *Two and a Half Men,* Lynch also starred in several episodes as Reid's schizophrenic mother on *Criminal Minds*. She also played a sex therapist on *Boston Legal* and starred in three segments of Lisa Kudrow's TV series *Web Therapy*. Jane also married a clinical psychologist.

Fortunately, with her Moon in the jovial 9th House and Jupiter in the sign of Sagittarius, Jane finds that comedy is the best therapy: "Making people laugh is a really fabulous thing because it means you're getting deep inside somebody, into their psyche, and their ability to look at themselves."

Astrology can also bring a chuckle, as it reveals amusing insights into our personal creative impulses and foibles.

Tobey Maguire
6/27/1975, 9:09 A.M.
Inglewood, CA

Sun: Cancer

Tobey won early acclaim in *Cider House Rules*, playing a misplaced orphan who was determined to find his place in the world. Later, in *Seabiscuit*, he portrayed a jockey who found his dreams and a new family in an underdog horse racing team. Many believe that Tobey was chosen for his role as *Spider Man* because he was able to show the hero's insecurities without being overly emotional. Tobey did it well, perhaps because he has no Earth, and his Sun and Saturn are the only water in his chart. With his five fire components, this Cancer Crab rarely shows his emotions.

The top left photo shows Toby in "full crab mode"—as if he was being pulled by distant tides. The second photo captures him relaxing in quiet waters. There, the tidal waters swell his facial flesh, to create a look of pure contentment.

In many of his films, Tobey's emotions had to be more than an expression of feelings. His Moon insisted that they serve a more altruistic purpose.

Moon in Aquarius

Maguire's Aquarius Moon forms a grand trine with his Sun and Uranus. Uranus (the ruling planet of Aquarius) opposes his Mars and Jupiter in fiery Aries. Jupiter also sextiles his Moon. Thusly, Tobey's emotional reactions were often presented with surprising force, but little feeling.

As mentioned in previous portraits, anyone who is missing an element often takes on the qualities of that element. This explains Tobey's desire to "connect with Earth" so that he can contain the water of his Sun and ground the electricity of his Moon. In these attempts "at finding Earth", Maquire appears to smother the fiery force of his Ascendant and Mars. This may account for his "monotone" voice and the lack of dramatic flair, that he showed in several of his performances.

Leo Rising

Toby's Venus exactly opposes his Moon and it is the closest planet to his Rising Sign. This directs his lunar qualities out through his Venus, rather than through his Ascendant. This 1st House Venus calms the surface tension. Consequently, the fires rarely appear to ignite.

Physically, this Rising Sign gives him the wide spread brows, the flat cheekbones and the fixed eyes of the lion. With Venus' presence, these feline eyes appear ready to drift off into sleep.

~~

*This abundance of fire and fixity takes us into **Leo**, the next sign in the Zodiac.*

♌ Leo

	Page
Introduction to Leo	173-175
Hulk Hogan & Patrick Swayze	

Step onto the stage of Leo
Three Film Directors	176
Alfred Hitchcock, Stanley Kubrick, Roman Polanski	
Joan Allen	177
Halle Berry	178
Charlize Theron	179

Combinations of Cancer and Leo
Lisa Kudrow and "Friends"	180-181
Robert De Niro	182

Fire turns the Water into steam
Whitney Houston	183
Sean Penn	184
Martha Stewart	185

The addition of Air feeds the Fire
Sandra Bullock	186
Barrack Obama	187
Amy Adams & Jennifer Lawrence	188-189

Earth cools the heat
Hilary Swank	190
William J. Clinton	191
Steve Carel	192
Dustin Hoffman	193
J.K. Rowling	194

Leo ♌ July 23 to August 22
Masculine Polarity, Fixed Fire
Step out into the world—and let your light shine!

Last month, Cancer took us on a ride with Nature's shifting tides. It helped us to find our inner base of comfort, and a place to call home! Now, in the warm, radiant light of Midsummer, many of Nature's creatures are inspired to move beyond their nests—to find their personal "spot" in the world that lies beyond their front door! In this spotlight, the expansive and masculine polarity of **Leo** glows. This gives every individual the courage and confidence—to strut about in their newly found kingdoms.

With the Fixed Fire of their Suns, these kingly Lions are inspired to focus on their surroundings. At every turn, they envision ways to make their world grander and brighter: "Let's build a gazebo in the park, paint city hall and create a theater for the arts!" Of course, all of these creative visions will be done with elegance and class—and yes, usually way over budget.

With every pronouncement, these dramatic souls will use their theatrical gifts to divert the course of a charging Aries Ram, arouse the sensations of a herd of Taurus Bulls, activate the minds of a gaggle of Geminis and torque the emotions of a pod of Cancer Crabs. Amazingly, everyone wants to be part of Leo's show!

Sadly, some lions believe that they are the creators of everything in their domain. However, the wiser Lions know that any success requires the creative support of others—and the inner lights of these co-creators also need to shine, so that they can provide the service that will bring any project to completion.

This giving of this service becomes the work of **Virgo**, the next sign in the Zodiac. The recognition and gathering of the collective ideas of others is symbolized in **Aquarius**, the sign that opposes **Leo** on the Zodiac wheel.

Rulerships and Associations for Leo

The Sun (the fixed ball of fire at the center of our solar system) is the ruler of Leo. Perhaps that's why some Lions believe "everything revolves around them—and they are the source of ALL creation!" Aside from that, the true gift of these felines is their ability to light up the confidence of all of the people in their presence. That is why Leo traditionally symbolizes the masculine influence of the father, the person who inspires children to be confident and courageous, so that they can become creative contributors to their communities. (This vision is made whole by the feminine contributions of the mothering Moon).

Like the coat of a Lion, Leos are often surrounded by the color of yellow-red or Orange. (Royal Purple is also popular). Appropriately, their metal is Gold and the Ruby is their stone. Sunflowers, rosemary, oranges and all citrus trees compliment their energies. Leo finds its home in the 5th House of creativity. Individuals with highly aspected Suns (as well as a dominance of masculine and fixed signs) tend to exhibit the qualities that are seen in these Leo portraits.

Traits of the Leo Lion:

With each entry into a new sign, the polarity shifts as nature attempts to create the opposite of what was created before. This concept is well illustrated in the transition from Cancer to Leo. The Crab sits on the ocean's floor, watching the reflecting beams of the evening Moon. This urge is countered by the Lion, who parades about, in the bright light of day.

When Leos enter the room, they instantly attract attention, as the spotlight is aimed in their direction. In this fixed light, everyone sees the royal presence of a lion, with his high cubical forehead, bushy wide set brows, fiery feline eyes and the large protruding ears. Note how the upper half of the face appears to rise high above the cheekbones. Below we see the wide bridged nose, the flat upper lip plate, the jowly jaw and square chin.

Hulk Hogan 8/1/1953, 6:13 A.M., Augusta, GA
Patrick Swayze 8/19/1952, 8:10 A.M., Houston, TX

The fixed fire is obvious in these lions, more so with *Hulk Hogan,* since he has a Leo Sun and Ascendant. His Virgo Moon accounts for his barrage of chatter.

With a Leo Moon, *Patrick* Swayze's lion shines in his expressions and reactions. With Virgo Rising, he appears more thoughtful and grounded than Hogan.

Body Language of Leo

Leo Rules the Heart also the Upper Back & Spine

In our fire-red blood, Gemini's oxygen and the nourishments of Cancer are pumped to all parts of our body by the heart. This fuel becomes the energy that circulates up and down the upper back, as it infuses the nerves of the spine with the life-giving force of spirit. All of these parts of the body are ruled and governed by the fixed fire of Leo.

With this "backbone", these lion's have the confidence to present their desires to others. Watch how their hearts lead them forward, as they strut onto the stage. Once there, their barrel-like chests will swell and expand as they revel in the adulation. (When they receive more strokes, the fires are stoked!) This incipient heat is stored in the glowing coals of Leo's internal furnace. It will soon erupt in a burst of theatrical flares.

Leo Film Directors:

Since Leo is the ruler of theater, it's appropriate that we start with three Leo directors. And since Neptune is the ruler of the cinema, we'll show how this planet influenced the celluloid visions and illusions that these masters put on film.

Alfred Hitchcock 8/13/1899, 3:15 A.M. Leytonstone, England

Hitchcock's Neptune (in Gemini) conjoins Pluto and opposes Saturn. This suggests that Hitchcock's film work would have a reverence for writing and the spoken word. Saturn implies that he would honor every word, as Pluto would get rid of the excess. Alfred was recognized as a genius who carefully story boarded every scene to create its own psychological effect—with the least amount of words!

With this Gemini Neptune sextile his Sun and trine his Scorpio Moon, Alfred was drawn to create cerebral murder mysteries. In *Dial M for Murder* and *Rear Window*, he used precise dialogue to develop the complex plots. In his masterpiece *Psycho*, the efficient and limited dialogue ensnared us in this film's web of terrifying visions.

Stanley Kubrick 7/26/1928, 1:41 P.M. Bronx, NY

This visionary has his Neptune in Leo. That figures! To him, every scene was an orchestration of movement and visual elements, designed to keep his audiences totally immersed in his created environments. In *Dr. Strangelove*, we laughed but were also terrified by the insanity of military politics. In *Barry Lyndon*, we all became mere specks in history. In *2001, A Space Odyssey*, we all became one with the universe.

Kubrick's Neptune squares his Scorpio Moon as it opposes his Taurus Mars. We see why he obsessively shot hundreds of takes of each scene, just to "capture the right moment", that would make the scene appear real, as well as transcendental.

Roman Polanski 8/18/1933, 10:30 A.M., Paris, France

Roman's Virgo Neptune gives his films a cerebral, clinical tone. That's likely why he calls film "a landscape of the mind," adding: "The only way to seduce people into believing you is to take painstaking care with the details of your film. Sloppiness destroys emotional impact."

Roman's Cancer Moon conjoins Pluto, as it sextiles Venus and Jupiter in Virgo. His Virgo (and his harrowing childhood during WWII) makes him overtly critical of human nature, but it also gave this Lion a talent for working small details into a bigger picture. In *Rosemary's Baby*, a seemingly pleasant urban setting changed bit by bit—to become a place of unspeakable horror. In *China Town*, we saw the grisly details of corruption in a big American city. Later in his career, in *The Pianist*, Roman tells the story of a Jewish pianist whose "fixation on every note and beat" helped him to survive the holocaust. It won him his only Oscar.

Joan Allen has the same components as our last Cancer portrait **Tobey Maguire**. However, their Ascendants and Suns are switched. Joan's Leo Sun and the rest of her chart components are summed up in her own words:

"...the stage was the perfect place to be outrageous, to be sad, to be angry, to be all different things." — **Joan Allen**

Joan Allen
8/20/1956, 12:45 A.M.
Rochelle, IL

Ascendant: Cancer

Many actors are typecast by the mask of their Ascendants, for this is the persona that is seen by producers and readily remembered by the public.

This may be why Joan's film work included many roles as a suffering mother or wife. The public identifies with the quieter emotions and compassion of her Cancer Ascendant, not her Leo Sun.

In *Pleasantville*, Joan was the colorless housewife who slowly evolved into a liberated woman. In *The Crucible*, her touching performance shined amidst a plethora of excessive theatrics. In the film *Nixon*, Joan received an Oscar nod for her nuanced role of Pat, the President's wife. Notably, it is her comment on this role that reveals the true nature of her Leo Sun and Aquarius Moon:

"....If Oliver Stone {the director} had wanted Pat Nixon to wear a G-string and swing from a chandelier, I would have played it that way." That bizarre image is what we'd expect from a Leo, with an Aquarius Moon.

Sun: Leo

Joan began her career in live theater, the place where Leo's fire truly shines. In her 1988 Broadway debut, she won a Tony Award for Best Actress in the play *Burn This*. This led to many roles in film.

With Joan's Leo Sun, the element of Fire quickly evaporates Cancer's watery mask, as it reshapes her face into a holding pattern. This gives us the lion's fixed eyebrows, feline eyes and uplifted cheeks. The two left photos show a unique Leo trait. Note how the lion's upper lip edge dips down on the sides, to create the distinct folds on the outer edges of the mouth.

Moon: Aquarius

In *The Bourne Supremacy* and *The Bourne Ultimatum*, Joan played the agent who was Bourne's most persistent pursuer. With her cool emotions, her character was constantly analyzing technical demands and plans of action, many times reacting intuitively, rather than logically. This cerebral focus is often seen in Aquarius Moons.

With this optimistic Moon and compassionate Ascendant, this lady is not just focused on her "Leo Self". She is deeply concerned for her nation, her community and the needs of others.

Halle Berry
8/14/1966, 11:59 P.M.
Cleveland, OH

Sun & Moon: Leo

In the 1999 film *Introducing Dorothy Dandridge*, Berry played the first African-American actress to be nominated for an Academy Award for Best Actress. (Dandridge's film *Carmen Jones* was released in 1954). Berry's performance as Dandridge won her a Golden Globe. With this, Halle's star status rose. Just two years later, in the film *Monster's Ball*, she became the first Afro-American to win the coveted Oscar for Best Actress.

With a Venus in Cancer, this Leo graciously shared the spotlight with others when she received the award: "This moment is so much bigger than me. It's for every nameless and faceless woman of color who now has a chance because this door, tonight, has been opened." Yes, lions can be warm and generous.

Like a true Leo, this lady loves to be in the spotlight. She began her film career flaunting the physical sensuality of her Taurus Ascendant, while showing off the physical force and athletic skills of her Mars and Jupiter conjunction in Cancer. She was one of the campy martial arts heroines in *X-Men*. She outmaneuvered the authorities in the caper *Swordfish* and also kicked butt in the 2002 James Bond movie: *Die Another Day*.

With her Leo Sun and Moon, Halle displays the proud bearing and physical features of the Lion. The best way to distinguish these two Leo luminaries from each other is to recognize the circumstance that activates the Leo fires. The upper left photo shows the fixed glow of this lion intensely projecting her solar light. On the right we see the

beaming and feminine reactions (i.e., reflections) of her Moon. In such moments as this, she becomes noticeably emotional. Naturally, with her Moon in Leo, these feelings are expressed in dramatic bursts of fire.

Ascendant: Taurus

When Berry's luminaries are inactive, the force of her Leo fires subside, as if they were being contained in a stone-layered fireplace. Allegorically they are, for Berry's Ascendant is in Taurus, the sign of fixed Earth.

When Taurus rises, Berry's feline eyes take on a bovine appearance as she appears more relaxed and contented. This softness can be attributed to Halle's Venus, for this ruling planet of Taurus joins her Mars in watery Cancer—and they both trine Saturn in the dreamy sign of Pisces! These liquid qualities are more obvious in Halle's sensual moments.

With her three key components in fixed signs, the lady desires to keep everything in tight control.

Charlize Theron
8/7/1975, 8:23 A.M.
Benoni, South Africa

Charlize's first major studio film was 1997's The Devil's Advocate. There she played a wife, who (with devilish interference) progressively descended into madness. This performance inspired film director Patty Jenkins to cast Theron as the serial killer Aileen Wuornos in the film Monster. This role won her an Oscar as Best Actress.

Sun and Moon: Leo

Oddly, this double Leo doesn't "like the spotlight to be about me." For this lady realizes: "Looks alone won't get you far....There's always someone younger, somebody prettier. You have to relay on something else." The desire to be "out of the spotlight"—and that finding of "something else"—are likely products of Pluto's sextile to her Moon, and her luminaries trines to Neptune. She knows what is real and what is a mere illusion.

The fixed features and focused eyes of the lion are seen in the UL photo. The UR photo shows the beaming reaction and glowing temples of Theron's Leo Moon. Folks who have conjoined Suns and Moons will often show these features.

Theron rarely shows the drama of Leo. Her mannerisms appear grounded, rather than expansive and fiery. Every physical movement is rigidly controlled and carefully orchestrated. Her Ascendant and Mars are in Earth signs.

Ascendant in Virgo

In the previous portrait, we illustrated what happens when one's Leo luminaries go on hold. With **Halle Berry**, her underlying bones resembles the cubical shape of her fixed Ascendent. However, with Charlize, we see the structure of her mutable Virgo Ascendant.

Notice how her one eye and brow shifts up from the other, as the jaw drops down and juts off to the side.

These skewed features may also be enhanced by Charlize's Sun and Moon. They both are in the Sagittarius decadent. This accounts for her long "horse neck".

Mars in Taurus

After Monster, Theron's film roles became more physically demanding, reaching new heights in Mad Max, Fury Road. This peak was quickly exceeded by her actions in 2017's Atomic Blonde, a film in which she fought villains in one of the longest single-take action scenes in recent cinema history. The strength and physical endurance she showed can be attributed to her Saturn and its sextile to her Taurus Mars. Notably, Mars is also in the Capricorn decan, and it is the closest planet to her Midheaven. This may be why Theron won fame as a female action star.

We get by with a little help from our *Friends!*

The TV show *Friends* was a wonderful look at human nature. With its six characters, it also provided a way to use astrology—to understand the nature of *your* friends.

In this show's six leading stars, *David Schwimmer* was the only Water sign. His Scorpio Sun made him the most reserved and quiet member of the group.

The chatter and electricity came from the two Air signs: Gemini *Courteney Cox* and Aquarius *Jennifer Aniston*.

The remaining three were all Leos!

Matthew Perry's Leo Sun and Ascendant made him appear to be the most confident of the lot. *Matt LeBlanc* and *Lisa Kudrow* both have Cancer Rising and water Moons, and this makes them keenly aware of the feelings of their companions. This compassion was apparent in Lisa's TV role and also in her other endeavors.

Lisa Kudrow
7/30/1963, 4:37 A.M.
Encino, CA

Leo Sun
Scorpio Moon

The fiery qualities of Lisa's Sun were rarely seen. What we usually saw was an easy going "flower child" who always seemed to be concerned about the deeper feelings of her friends, rather than herself.

This is likely a product of Lisa's Moon being the most aspected component in her chart. Another key factor is that her Mars is in Venus-ruled Libra—and this red planet sextiles her Sun and Moon. For her, other people really matter!

It is interesting to watch how this Cardinal Air drives and balances the fixed nature of her two luminaries. With its Venusian influences, Lisa would gently slide into every conversation to express her concerns about others. There, Kudrow would keep her emotions "well balanced" and in control. She rarely got angry or showed the intensity that is seen in most Scorpio Moons. Many considered her to be the most friendly person in the group.

In her expressive moments, Lisa would display the confidence and fixed Fire of her Sun. The UL photo captures her eyes in full feline mode. The UR photo shows the radiant glow of her projecting Leo Sun, the thick mane of a lion, the high forehead and the wide-set and flat cheekbones. Notably, the airy smile of Libra and the pleasantry of Venus are also present.

With her expansive Sun, Leo beams its light, as this confident lioness expresses her visions to her friends. However, when things get emotional, there is a noticeable change in polarity as Lisa's "show it all" Sun suddenly dims and she locks herself into the inner and private world of her Scorpio Moon. This injection of water douses the fire, as it anchors her facial flesh into fixed, cubical patterns.

Cancer Ascendant

In *Friends*, Lisa played the sensitive artist/folk singer Phoebe. She was the dreamer as well as the idealist who presented her visions of fairness and harmony. She was the one who constantly consulted her friends, as she attempted to calm their emotions.

Notably, Lisa's 1st House Venus is in Cancer—and it is the closest planet to her Cancer Ascendant. Since this sign is ruled by the Moon, it gives an extra boost to Lisa's already strong lunar tendencies.

Unlike the other ladies, Lisa became the mothering hen for the group. We saw this in her nurturing moments, when her feline eyes would widen and her temples would swell—to present the caring mask of the Cancer Crab. This was aided by her introspective Scorpio Moon, which enabled her to uncover her friends' deeper secrets.

Body Language of Leo & Cancer

Since Leo rules the heart, Lions often lead with their chest proudly jutting forward, as they march in their own parade! This confident body language appears when Lisa shows her solar light. However, when her Moon dominates, the polarity shifts to the feminine. This pulls the chest back and downward. The full-body photo (above) shows how the body tilts to the side, as this crab shuffles across the shore. This cardinal movement rolls like the tides. It surges forward, then pulls back. It lacks the regal stance of the lion.

Mars Changes Body Language

With its sextile, Lisa's Libra Mars feeds regular injections of oxygen (air) to fuel her luminaries. This infusion makes her Sun effervescent and pleasantly chatty, while its aeration of her Scorpio Moon opens her up, to recognize the deeper secrets of her friends and associates.

This Libra Mars was seen in Lisa's work on *Web Therapy*, (her online show that soon turned into a regular cable show). There, the mannerisms of Libra were apparent—as her hands moved from one side and then to the other—as she tried to weave her thoughts into both sides of the conversation. Just watch someone's physical motions as they work, and this will give you a clue on the sign in which their Mars is placed.

~~~

Aquarius Jennifer Aniston's has Libra Rising but little water in her chart. (Her portrait is on page 56).

Gemini Courteney Cox has Sagittarius Rising and a Virgo Moon. Both of these ladies often explored the ideas of their friends, not their emotions.

Let's jump into the Water!

Robert De Niro
8/17/1943, 3:00 A.M.
Brooklyn, NY

 Sun: Leo

As one of the consummate actors of his generation, Robert De Niro shows the flare you'd expect from a Leo Sun. He also played characters with a disturbing edge. In the '70's, us budding astrologers were guessing that this star of *Taxi Driver* and *Deer Hunter* had lots of components in Scorpio. It was a total surprise when his birth data was found, and he had no Scorpio components. However, this data showed that Pluto and Jupiter conjoined his Leo Sun and they both square his fixed his Taurus Mars. Add a Water Ascendant and Moon to this, and our Scorpio guess becomes "symbolically correct".

Ascendant: Cancer

Oddly, Robert's characters often presented a "caring side", even if they were totally deranged. In the film *King of Comedy*, Robert played an obsessed comic who kidnaps a popular talk show host—so that he could become famous! Throughout the movie, this loud mouthed King threw his childish tantrums, as he hovered over his victim like a mothering hen. This disturbingly protective presence was also seen in Robert's relationship with Jody Foster in *Taxi Driver*.

Robert's family friendly mask was at its best when he played the eccentric father in the series of three *Meet The Fockers* films.

Moon: Pisces

In his role in *Raging Bull*, Robert showed the stuff of his Taurus Mars, as he set a new performance standard by totally changing his physical appearance—turning from lean to muscular, and then back to pudgy and overweight. It was an amazing physical transformation likely made possible by DeNiro's Cancer Ascendant's trine to its ruling Moon, his Moon's square to Uranus and his Mars trine to Neptune. These aspects gave Robert a profound ability to alter his physical appearance.

NOTE: Jared Leto has similar aspects and similar results. See page 22.

This world of Neptune was seen in Robert's film *Awakenings*, where he portrayed one of his quieter roles as a patient who was emerging from the unconscious world of Neptune. Unhampered by physical desires or ego, we saw a person who expressed his feelings by openly reacting to the world with bewilderment, amazement and joy. Note how in his reactions, his rounded Water features were distorted. The resulting skewed facial lines often gave him the dreamy appearance of a Pisces fish.

Add more heat & things get steamy
Whitney Houston
8/9 /1963, 8:55 A.M.
Newark, NJ

 ## Sun: Leo

Whitney's first big hit song was the Leo anthem: *"The Greatest Love of All."* It is the lesson that Leo teaches. All love begins when you learn to love yourself.

When Whitney basked in the spotlight, she displayed Leo's "fixing of fire". On the stage, her mane and head would toss up and to the back, as she assumed her pose of royalty. As she moved about, her hands pawed the air with an intensity simulating rapid flicks of fire. She also exhibited many of the lion's physical traits that were illustrated previously.

Moon: Aries

The Moon is a reaction—a momentary step back in time, to gather memories to illicit an emotional response. The quality of this response is indicated by the sign in which the Moon is placed.

With her Moon in Aries, this backward step immediately ignites a forward explosion—that abruptly sends out a shot of returning fire! The good news is that the blast ends as quickly as it starts. The bad news was that her protective mask was in Pisces. It was difficult for her to avoid the returning fire, that she received from others.

Ascendant: Pisces

On stage, Whitney appeared confident, but there always was a sense that she was a vulnerable diva, just like the one she played in the movie *Body Guard*.

Early on, tabloids made it worse, as they revealed the turbulence in her marriage and how her career was controlled by her mother. Later on, they exposed the sordid details of how her explosive lunar temper got her removed from an Academy Awards show. This sensitive Pisces Ascendant provided little protection from the ravages of fame.

Positively, when Whitney was just "being herself" and not performing, the mutable waters of this mask would douse the heat of her fiery Sun and Moon. The resulting sensitive and caring persona enhanced her connection with her audience.

But that was not enough, for in Houston's chart, Neptune (the ruler of her Rising Sign) formed a T-square to her Sun and Saturn. This hard angle distanced Whitney from her sense of self (Sun) and reality (Saturn). All the while, Neptune's trine to her Ascendant enhanced the dreamy and illusionary world she saw through the window of her Pisces Ascendant. It was hard for her to handle reality.

Sadly, she died of an overdose of drugs on February 11, 2012.

Sean Penn
8/17/1960, 3:17 P.M.
Burbank, CA

♌ Sun: Leo

Sean doesn't appear to be a typical Leo Sun. This can be due to his Decans. As noted earlier, the first 10° (or decan) accents *the sign that the component is in*. With his Leo Sun, the next decan in Fire would be Sagittarius. With Penn's Sun (at 24° Leo), his Sun is in the third or Aries decan of Leo.

The top photos shows some hints of the features of the Ram, namely the concave face and the prominent snout. The cubical features of the Lion are weak, and his decan also makes Penn more aggressive than the average lion.

As we saw in *Dead Man Walking* and in his Oscar role in *Mystic River*, his work often deals with life's darker realities. This may be due to his Sun's placement in his 8th House—or perhaps Pluto and Uranus' conjunction with his Sun. This explains his tendency to end up in surprising and hellish situations, I.E., his fights with tabloid photographers, his visit to Baghdad just before the Iraq war, and his 2016 interview with the Mexican drug lord *El Chapo*, who had just escaped from a U.S. prison.

Ascendant: Sagittarius

The latest data on Sean's birth time gives him a 16° Sagittarius Ascendant. The Aries decan appears once again, to kick up his Martian energies another notch. However, since Jupiter (the ruler of Sagittarius) sits near his Ascendant, the features of the Centaur are quite apparent. The underlying bone structure is the strongest clue. Note how the domed skull gets wider at the top. There's also the long horsey neck, twisted nose and pointed horse ears.

The free spirited persona of Sagittarius was apparent in Sean's early role in *Fast Times at Ridgemont High*, but his later works rarely display the jovial mask of the Centaur. Also, when Sean attempts a simple laugh, it seems forced and he appears intense and secretive. This may be due to his 8th House Sun, Pluto's conjunction with his Sun, its sextile to Saturn and/or its trine to his Moon. It can also be the Aries decan of his Sun and his Mars' opposition to his Ascendant—or likely, all of these!

Moon: Cancer

Sean's Cancer Moon trines Neptune. This makes him very sensitive to events in his surroundings. This accounts for his persistent campaigning to reduce the toxins from our environment. In 2015, he produced the film *The Human Experiment*. It went head-to-head with the powerful chemical industry, as it showed what they were doing to the environment and our bodies.

Martha Stewart
8/3/1941. 1:33 P.M.
Jersey City, NJ

Sun Sign: Leo

She's been called the "Empress of Life Style" and the "Duchess of Domesticity". These names are appropriate for a royal lion whose goal is to "fill her audience's minds with good things every day."

Martha made her mark with her 1983 book *Entertaining*. It told people how to decorate, garden and get married—*in the best way possible!* These concepts became a 200 million dollar empire!

Lions are often very extravagant, but this lady promotes penny pinching principles. In a tour of her royal castle and garden, she proudly shows us the; gorgeous chandelier she made out of egg cartons and broken bottles. Later, she'll brag about the birdbath she created with an inverted hubcap. This flea market mentality is not the stuff of Leo. The fact that it's done with class, is.

Martha shows us the importance of the planets Mercury and Venus. Leos love to create, but every vision has to begin with thought. In Martha's case, that thought is shaped by her Mercury in Cancer. Her homebody mind tells her to discard nothing, as she reworks useless items into artistic creations.

Martha's art style is clear. She loves details and she wants everything to be perfect. Her Venus is in Virgo! This may be why Martha once offered a website plan to *"organize everybody's day."* With her Scorpio Rising, many folks also saw her as a control freak.

Ascendant: Scorpio

Stewart's Sun conjoins Pluto, while it squares her Scorpio Ascendant. This Fixed Water is the damper gate that keeps Martha's fiery luminaries in control. Yep, this adds to the image that she is indeed a "control freak".

Physically, this Ascendant gives Martha her wide, flat cheek bones and the eagle's beak. However, the intensity of Scorpio is lacking, for Venus sextiles her Ascendant, and this gives her persona a charming disposition.

Moon: Sagittarius

When emotions appear here, they all too quickly evaporate—for Centaur Moons are seldom moody or weepy, as they run with the moment and take their giant leaps of faith!

This Sagittarius Moon is also seen in Martha's sister TV hosts: *Oprah Winfrey* and *Joan Rivers*. All three share the Centaur's unbridled sense of optimism!

These three media moguls reached for the stars to build their empires. Each one found their success in a manner that expressed the qualities and desires of their Sun signs. The expansive lunar feelings gave them the desire to reach for higher goals.

The Addition of Air Feeds the Fire
Sandra Bullock
7/26/1964, 3:15 A.M.
Arlington, VA

Sun: Leo

In 1994, this lion burst onto the scene with her hit film *Speed*. Saturn was on her chart's midheaven—and ready or not—her star had risen! A few years later, as Saturn descended down her chart, the public attention diminished.

It isn't that Bullock hadn't tried, for she worked steadily, but her box office successes were few. On the plus side, she acquired a Golden Globe nod for her comedic role in *Ms. Congeniality* and turned heads playing a recovering alcoholic in *28 Days*. In her 2004 *Crash*, the film won Best Picture, but Sandra's performance was diminished by the movie's huge ensemble cast.

With Hollywood's obsession with youthful actresses and the dearth of older roles, this 14+ year downward cycle of career restriction occurred at the wrong time in Sandra's life. However, this was a period for her to hone her skills and acquire Saturn's deeper lessons. The rewards came after 2012, when Saturn began its upward swing in her chart. Amazingly, just 2 years later, Bullock won an Oscar for her role in the movie *The Blind Side*.

Sandra displays the regal qualities of the lion as well as the gangly mane, bushy brows and the wide flat cheekbones. The most recognizable feature is the intensely focused eyes. They seem to be lit from behind, by internal burning embers. The UR photo shows this powerful look. It's one that appears many times in this Leo collection.

Moon: Aquarius

With her Aquarius Moon, Sandra's emotions mimic the force of static electricity. Things cling together, then are abruptly released—so that they can quickly attach to something else. There is little sense of permanence.

The LR photo shows how the inside of the eyes lift upward, as the outer eyelids drop down to focus on distant points. It also shows how the outer edges of the lower lips pull sharply downward, to form fixed air's expression of surprise.

Ascendant: Gemini

When Bullock holds up her mutable Gemini mask, all signs of fixity are scattered in the swirling winds.

In moments when her Sun and Moon are inactive, Sandra's flesh takes on the consistency of fluffy clouds, as it lies on the underlining bone structure. This reveals the protruding rectangular jaw as well as the skewed features of mutability. Note how the nose points in one direction as the chin skews to the other side.

Barack Obama

8/4/1961, 7:24 P.M.
Honolulu, HI

When this portrait was created, Barrack Obama had just wrapped up his second term as President of the United States. This inspired this author to research the signs of the USA's leaders.

The "top elected signs" are Scorpio and Aquarius—with five for each sign. Taurus, Leo and Pisces have 4 each. 18 of 44 Presidents were fixed signs! This tells us this country likes a "fixed and stable anchor" to run the country.

 Sun: Leo

Barrack's sense of showmanship was seen when he was an off night speaker at the 2004 Democratic convention. There, he showed the proud stance of a Lion, as he presented his vision on how to build a better America. Four years later, he became the Democratic candidate and then POTUS.

As President, Obama held frequent press conferences and major national speeches. In many, he was able to emotionally connect to a large base of supporters. His Leo Mercury conjoins his Sun and sextiles his Moon.

Gemini Moon

Obama's Mercury/Moon sextile has significant consequences, for it enables him to find the right words to describe the visions in his mind—and present them in a manner that is emotionally comfortable to others. This was abetted by his Jupiter/Saturn conjunction in Aquarius and Saturn's trine to his Moon. This gave his words the scope and substance he needed to communicate with a large and diverse audience.

The creative work of Mercury is often assisted by one's Venus. Obama's Venus is in Cancer and it sextiles Pluto and trines Neptune. These aspects gave him a voice of clarity, that was often powerful and also emotionally convincing.

Ascendant: Aquarius

"Hope" was the word that became the symbol of Obama's first campaign, as he presented his dream for the future. "Hope" is a key word associated with Aquarius—the sign of his Ascendant. Notably, Uranus (the ruling sign of Aquarius) and his Sun are in opposition to this Rising Sign, straddling his 7th House cusp. This may have been why it was so difficult for him to correct the political divide in the country. On the other hand, his hopeful persona helped him find the right people to reverse a very tough economic crash. He finished his second term with a very high approval rating.

~~~

Obama was followed by Donald Trump, who joins JFK, as one of only two Gemini Presidents. Trump's portrait is on page 138. Fellow Leo Bill Clinton's is on page 191

Amy Adams   Jennifer Lawrence
8/20/1974, 12:00 A.M.   8/15/1990, 3:20 P.M.
Vicenza, Italy   Louisville, KY

These two stars were both Oscar contenders for their leading and supporting roles in the 2013 film *American Hustle*. In that movie, they showed their flamboyant Leo Suns, as well as other markedly similar personality traits. This is due to the fact that they both share Mercury-ruled Moons and mutable Ascendants. Here, we will show how the aspects and sign placements of these components define their differences in personality.

♌ Suns in Leo

Amy and Jennifer display many traits of the lion. They include the high forehead and broad brows that lock the feline eyes high on the face. Below, there's the wide bridged nose and nostrils and the wide-set cheek bones that drop sharply downward on the outer edges, to create the facial structure of a lion.

It is interesting that these two ladies often appear markedly animated, and noticeably more talkative than what we'd expect from a fixed Leo Sun. This can be attributed to their Mercury-ruled Moons and mutable Ascendants.

Moons in Virgo and Gemini

Amy Adams' Moon is in Virgo. Watch how the fixed confidence of her Leo Sun disintegrates when she gets emotional. Suddenly, she appears uncertain and worried. As she tries to express her feelings, she also becomes obsessed with the smallest of details. Positively, as we saw in *American Hustle*, it gives her a grounded and precise gift for manipulating words—to "explain" her feelings!

Amy's earthy Virgo Moon has no aspects, but her Mercury (the ruler of her Moon and Ascendant) conjoins her Sun, squares Neptune and sextiles Uranus. Meanwhile, Neptune trines her Venus and sextiles Pluto. These empowered creative planets give Amy an enhanced imagination, and we saw in her role as the influential wife in the film *The Master*, it also gives her a powerful gift for persuasion. These multiple aspects give Amy a quixotic and mercuric energy and a very inventive mind. With her Mercury and Venus in Leo, Amy is drawn to theater, the art of Venus, and the fantasies of Neptune. This was seen in her role was the princess in the animated/live action musical *Enchanted,* and in her portrayal of the artist Margaret Keane in *Big Eyes*.

Jennifer Lawrence's Gemini Moon constantly provides a swirling stream of air—to feed the fire of her flamboyant Sun! With her Moon's sextile to her fiery Sun, Lawrence's expansive and airy emotional reactions are flashier, and ever more instantaneous than what we see in Adams. In addition, Jennifer's Jupiter conjoins her Leo Venus and this enables her to view her surroundings on a giant scale. However, Jennifer's Mercury is in Virgo and it forms a grand trine with Saturn and Mars. Her Earth-bound Mercury mind runs at a slower speed. This (and her obsession with small details) often makes it difficult for her to find "the words" to express the expansive visions and feelings of her luminaries and Venus.

When the Mercury-ruled Moons of these ladies are activated, the twisting lines of mutability skew their facial features. Lawrence's hands scatter about, while Adam's hover close to the body. The main differences in their "physical energy" can be determined by looking at the signs in which their Mars are placed.

Placement of Mars

Mars tells us the nature of a person's physical metabolism, or the manner in which one performs any physical action. Adams' Mars is in Virgo and it sextiles Saturn. Her movements appear precise, calculated, yet noticeably delicate. This explains why, at a young age, Amy found the discipline to become a ballerina. This Virgo precision was seen in her singing and dancing role in *Enchanted*.

Lawrence also has an Earth Mars, but it is in fixed Taurus, trining Saturn and opposing Pluto. Jennifer's body runs at a steady pace and it is markedly controlled and powerful. This strength was seen in her physical activities, displayed in her role in *The Hunger Games* and its sequels. These skills were enlivened by the athletic fire of her Centaur Ascendant.

Ascendants in Gemini & Sagittarius

It is difficult to distinguish the differences in the Moons of these ladies, since they both have Mutable Ascendants in masculine signs. However, differences can still be seen in their physical appearances.

Amy's airy Gemini Ascendant gives her the sparkling off-set eyes, the pixie nose and the rectangular jaw assembly that protrudes out from the upper half of the face. This mask gives her an appearance that is similar to what we see in Lawrence's Gemini lunar reactions.

In contrast, Jennifer's persona is wild and unrestrained—that of a galloping Centaur! Physically, we see a high domed head that sweeps to the back. She also has the long angled jaw of a horse and the physical presence of a person who refuses to be corralled in any manner.

In 2005, when Swank's "Snapshot" was originally created, the article attempted to show a method to determine her then unknown birth time. It has been updated here.

Hilary Swank
7/30/1974, 5:28 P.M.
Lincoln, Nebraska

Sun: Leo

Physically, Swank shows the large mouth and the fixed feline eyes of a Lion. However, her eyes are intense and her personality is very introspective for a Leo. This is due to her Sun's sextile to Pluto and the fact that her personal planets (save for her Leo Sun) are all in feminine signs. With that in mind, we will try to guess her Ascendant. Amazingly, her Moon gave us a clue!

Moon: Capricorn

It was known that around 2 P.M. on Swank's birthday, the Moon switched from Sagittarius to Capricorn. After looking at several videos, the one that piqued our interest was the rather prosaic speech she gave at the 2005 Academy Awards. With Oscar in hand, Swank began her dialogue with: "I'm just a girl from a trailer park who had a dream." (This reference to her upward struggle is the emotional stuff of Capricorn). Hilary then went on to thank many of the functional contributors in her life. Rushed for time, in a moment of pure reaction, her final praise went to her publicist. There was none of the expansive sense of joy or wonder expected from Sagittarius. At this highly emotion lunar moment, all we saw was the practical reactions of the goat. We picked Capricorn as her Moon—and we were right!

Ascendant: Sagittarius

With this Moon choice, Hilary's birth time has to be after 2 P.M.—the time the Moon entered Capricorn. This means that her Ascendant could be anything between Scorpio and Aries.

To determine the Ascendant, one first has to look at her "body type". Swank's long neck and lanky structure suggests Aries or Sagittarius. This eliminates stocky Pisces and bony Capricorn. This author then concluded that her wide shoulders eliminated the Centaur—leaving Aquarius. To support this claim, I noted that she had "rapidly blinking eyes" and her "solar glow and earthy emotions seem to be electrically charged". (This also fits Sagittarius). I picked Aquarius, and I was wrong.

Wrong, but also Correct

We got the right Moon and a Centaur Ascendant was in the final three!

Another factor is that she has Uranus sextile the Ascendant. At the time of the original writing, this author did not consider aspects, but the angled horse chin (shown in the newly placed LR photo) should have been a clue.

This error is valuable because it gives the reader another thing to consider, when guessing a person's unknown Ascendant.

William J. Clinton
8/19/1946, 8:51 A.M.
Hope, Arkansas

 Sun: Leo

President Bill Clinton was always at ease in the spotlight. He has four components in Leo, including his glowing Leo Sun. This bestowed him a warm presence and a theatrical flair to present his dynamic visions to the world.

Oddly, Clinton shows few of the lion's physical attributes, save for his barrel-chested physique. This is likely due to the strong Libra stellium in his chart. It frequently redirects the fixed light of his Sun off to both sides, and this eliminates the square features of fixity.

Ascendant: Libra

Bill's Libra Ascendant conjoins Mars, Neptune and Venus. Jupiter is also in his 1st House. With those five Libra components, we see why he's so "long winded".

Clinton's Uranus is in Gemini and it is the nearest planet to his Midheaven. Thusly, he was publicly recognized for his wonky techno-babble and his inventive gift for gab. This 1st House cluster of planets gives Bill a extraordinary drive, a determined will, a strong sense of purpose—and a charming Libra smile to sell his political goals!

In his teens, Bill knew where he was headed. These Libra planets also gave "The Comeback Kid" a remarkable resiliency, for he was constantly weighing situations and shifting sides to keep his world in balance. This gave Clinton a gift for the give-and-take world of politics.

Clinton's opponents were often fooled by his indecisive appearance. They soon discovered that when he made up his mind, he could be very stubborn.

Moon: Taurus

Bill's Moon is the only feminine sign in his chart and it joins Uranus in being the only components on the right side of his chart. This explains his self-driven obsessions and the stubbornness we witnessed in the budget battle that led to one of the few government shutdowns in the history of the USA.

Clinton's earthy Moon (and lack of water) may also be why he showed little emotion and why any showing of compassion often used the phase: "I feel your pain." Clinton's Moon is in the 8th House.

When Clinton's bovine Moon glows, he often escapes to greener pastures, to graze and relax in contented reflection. Since Venus is the co-ruler of Taurus (and it's part of the group of planets on his Libra Ascendent), most of Bill's responses came only after slow deliberation—only after he determined that he had everything is in control!

Steve Carell
8/16/1962, 8:59 A.M.
Concord, MA

♌ Sun: Leo

In his role in *The Office*, Steve strutted through his corporate kingdom, radiating the confidence of his Leo Sun, as he assured his servant minions that he had everything in control. In these moments, Steve's chest would swell as it pushed the head high above the shoulders. His Leo Sun was in full play!

Uranus sits near Steve's Sun and this accounts for much of his outrageous demeanor. In *Evan Almighty*, *Little Miss Sunshine* and *Anchorman*, Steve gave us three famously bizarre characters—who saw visions of a coming flood, the nonexistent talent in a precocious child and emotional insecurity in his job as a weatherman. In all of these roles, Steve's confident Sun carried him forward in a world of chaos. This is what makes Carell such a unique performer.

When guessing Steve's Sun Sign, Leo would not be one's first choice. He is not a "roaring Lion", for he often appears analytical and emotionally confused. This is a product of his Ascendant and Moon.

Virgo Ascendant

Steve's Virgo Ascendant alters his solar features. Note how the long face, thin bridged nose and the skewed features create this earthy mutable mask. This fussy and worrisome persona was seen in Carell's roles in *The 40 Year Old Virgin* and *Get Smart*.

Steve's Ascendant forms a square to his Midheaven Mars in mercuric Gemini. Also, his Virgo Mercury sextiles Neptune, as it opposes his Moon and Jupiter. These aspects explain Carell's gift for writing comedy and fantasy. He was

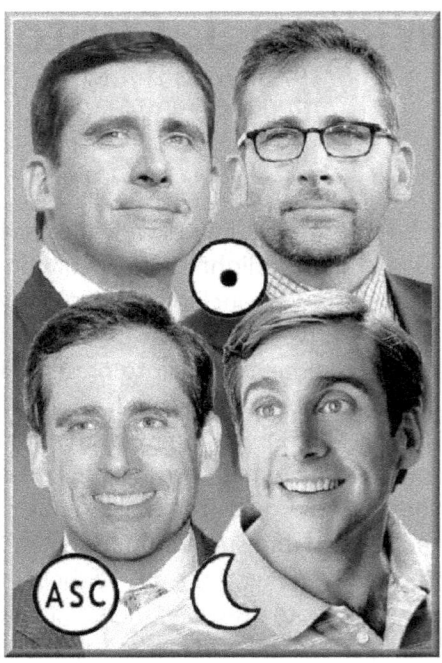

the co-writer on the script for the *Virgin* movie. He also won a Writer's Guild award for his work on *The Office*.

Moon: Pisces

When Carell reacts with his watery Pisces Moon, the fiery solar light of Leo noticeably dampens. Positively, this Moon's trine to its ruling planet Neptune (and its placement next to jovial Jupiter) gives him a giant gift for creating comical illusions. His Leo theatrics aren't all show—they are also imaginative and delightfully comedic.

This Moon also forms a trine with Carell's Gemini Mars. This gave him the boundless energy he needed to create his highly mercurial works.

In Steve's emotional moments, his face rounds and swells, as his eyes turn into deep pools of water. All the while, his fussiness of his Virgo Ascendant is adding to look of bewilderment. It is this contrast of vulnerability and indelible confidence that makes his comedy so unique.

Dustin Hoffman
8/8/1937, 5:07 P.M.
Los Angeles, CA

 Sun: Leo

This talented actor exhibits several of Leo's physical traits: the fixed eyebrows, the block-shaped skull and the hair that frames his face like a mane.

Dustin is such a disciplined actor, it is difficult to see any expressions that project the true light of his Leo Sun. In *The Graduate* and *Little Big Man*, a youthful and less controlled Hoffman let his Sun dominate, as he strutted like a peacock and filled the silver screen with his self-assured presence. Another exception was his role in *Lenny*, where he played the comic Lenny Bruce. Oddly, his most acclaimed performances were for the down-to-earth roles that we saw in *Kramer Vs. Kramer*, *Death of a Salesman*, and *Rain Man*. This can be attributed to the two Earth components in his chart.

Ascendant: Capricorn

Hoffman reached star status in his second film, *Midnight Cowboy*. There, he displayed his Capricorn Ascendant —the physical mask that no acting can hide! Ratzo's diminutive stature and bony features were etched into our minds as we watched this runty, goat-like creature carp and whine, while he scrambled for a buck.

Fortunately, Hoffman has expansive Jupiter on his Ascendant and this coupling forms a Grand Earth Trine with his Taurus Uranus and his Moon, Mercury and Neptune conjunction in Virgo. This powerful aspect give him the tenacity and discipline to perfect his craft, control his emotions and bring them to the surface in his body and facial gestures.

This gift was celebrated in Tom Cruise's remarks that were given at the 1997 Golden Globe Awards: "Dustin has the ability to capture the absolute truth in every character."

Moon: Virgo

The duality of Virgo often brings masculine as well as feminine qualities to the surface. This was apparent in Dustin's role as *Tootsie*.

In this cross-gender role, Hoffman was sensitive, analytical, and prissy—just what we'd expect from a meticulous Virgo Moon. There, we frequently saw his mutable lunar forces, skewing his facial flesh.

As noted, Dustin's Mercury (Virgo's ruling planet) is part of his Moon's Grand Trine. This gives Dustin a remarkable gift to remember and recite long passages of words. This was seen in his Oscar winning role as the savant in *Rainman*.

J. K. Rowling

7/31/1965, 9:10 P.M.
Yate, England

Sun in Leo

The writings of J. K. Rowling's *Harry Potter* are filled with many humorous and eccentric characters. Her word includes mythology and self-empowering themes. The latter shows the light of her Leo Sun, and it all was done in a manner that excited the creative spirit and playfulness of children.

Rowling rarely projects the expansive and prideful glow of Leo, for her Sun has no aspects and it is the only fire in her chart. However, there are a few Leo traits. The top photos show the wide and flat cheekbones that drop down to create the jowls on the sides of the jaw. There's also the strong, wide chin, but it appears abnormally skewed. These is due to the heavy influences of Mercury in her chart.

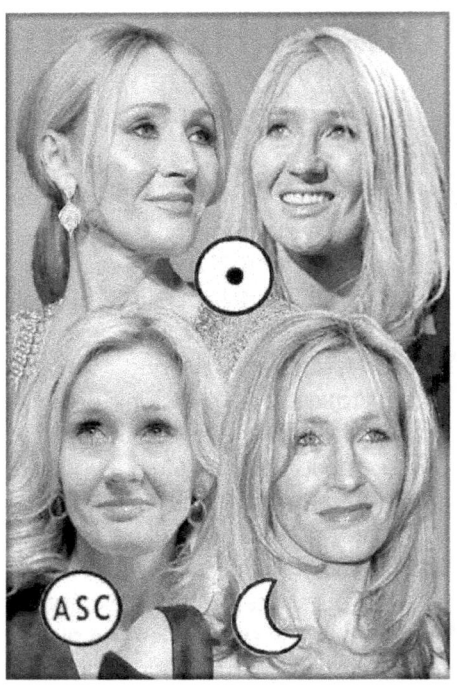

Virgo Moon

Rowling's Moon, Mercury, Venus, Pluto and Uranus are all in Virgo. All, save for Mercury, oppose her Saturn. In addition, Jupiter (in Mercury-ruled Gemini) T-squares her Moon and Pluto. With all of these links, the Mercury Messenger was able to give this lady just the right words—to show youngsters the true lesson of Leo: "One's creative power lies within one's self".

Virgo's critical nature was seen in the imperfections of the characters in her novels. Saturn brought lessons on ethics, student rivalry and institutional incompetency. Fortunately, with her Saturn's placement in Pisces (and its trine to Uranus), Rowling was able to coat all criticism in a blanket of compassion and hope. This hope was aided by her Aquarius Ascendant.

Ascendant: Aquarius

Rowling was born just after sunset. The resulting Aquarius Rising places the setting Sun in her 6th House. This suggests that Rowling would find her glory in her work!

This Ascendant also places all of J.K.'s planets (save for Saturn) on the right side of her chart. This lady is not "self-driven"—she is guided by other magical forces beyond her control!

When Rowling's fiery solar lights and mercuric lunar emotions recede, the facial flesh becomes inactive, as her vibrant eyes focus onto a distance place in space. The resulting facial molding makes the wide, square jaw assembly and broad chin of Aquarius more obvious. Oddly, even with a fixed Sun and Rising Sign, J.K.'s physical appearance is irregular. That cluster of Virgo planets constantly overwhelms the fixed force of her Sun and Ascendant.

This mutable force manifests in the next sign in the Zodiac: Virgo.

♍ Virgo

	Page
Introduction to Virgo	
Lyndon B. Johnson, Agatha Christie	195-197
Portraits of double Virgos	
Sean Connery	198
Mark Harmon	199
Keanu Reeve/Adam Sandler	200
Add some water to wet the Earth	
Cameron Diaz	201
Dr. Phil McGraw	202
Colin Firth	203
Jimmy Fallon	204
Melissa McCarthy	205
Add the heat of Fire	
Lily Tomlin	206
James Coburn	207
The Centaur gallops on to the field	
Richard Gere	208
Jane Curtin	209
—to hear the music of Neptune	
Pink	210-211
Breezes of air stir up a storm	
Amy Poehler	212-213
Jeff Foxworthy & Jack Black	214
Charlie Sheen	215
Tyler Perry	216

Virgo  August 23 to September 22

Feminine Polarity, Mutable Earth
It is time to be a steward of the Earth

At the end of Summer, a earthy maiden stands in the field, holding Nature's harvest in her hands. This maiden has learned to use the emotions of **Cancer** (as well as the visions of **Leo**) to embellish her understanding of her surroundings. Now, as she feels the chill in the air and sees the changing colors in Nature's foliage, she knows it is time to prepare for the wintery months that lie ahead.

Here, Mercury takes on its feminine polarity—as the mind examines the smaller bits within the complex ideas of **Gemini**. With this obsession with detail, our **Virgo** friends begin the work—of breaking apart, sorting and then reassembling their collection of physical objects into precise arrangements. With these actions, Virgo provides the first act of selfless service—the pure (virginal) offering of love to others! With this, the visions of **Leo** can become a reality!

Check out the head offices of any major organization, business or project. Look for the room with shelves filled with research materials or engineering plans. Find the desk that is stacked with piles of papers. It is likely that a Virgo will be sitting in the chair, busily organizing the stuff into neater arrangements.

To counter Leo's expansive overview, our Virgo friends analyze every detail, from every view. In excess, these energies can bring on nervousness, worry and hypochondria. Fortunately, these dueling ideas are brought into balance and given creative direction by the Cardinal Air of **Libra**, the next sign in the Zodiac.

Individuals with a Virgo Sun, Moon, or Rising Sign (or a strongly aspected Mercury in a feminine sign) will often express the analytical qualities of Mutable Earth.

Rulerships and Associations for Virgo

The two functions of the bicameral mind are captured in the duel rulerships of Mercury. Masculine Gemini is the act of induction. In contrast, feminine Virgo's task is one of deduction—the separation of small pieces from a larger whole.

Virgo rules the stomach and the massive array of nerves in the Solar Plexus. This part of the body is where our "subconsciousness mental processes" and "gut senses" operate. This provides the communication within the body—to sort, digest and transport the needed bits of physical material to specific areas of the body. This keeps the physical health of the body in order.

Pisces (the opposite sign to Virgo) intertwines the mind, body, mind, emotions and spirit into the wholeness—that makes healing possible!

The feminine force of Mercury increases when planets transit the 6th House or any component in one's chart. Many Virgos serve as scientists, engineers, statisticians, gardeners and any job that deals with health and hygiene. Their deductive skills also make them masters of criminal forensics.

Virgo Physical Traits:

In moments of self-expression, the long face and skewed facial features of Virgo appear—as their fingers sort through all of the objects within arm's reach.

Watch how one eye rises far above the other and how the mouth twists into a thin-lipped smile, when this mercuric creature discovers the tiny detail—the one that he/she deems to be substantially significant!

In these moments of discovery, Mobius trails of electricity spin in Virgo's crystalline eyes. Miraculously, these sparks of light appear to animate the changing thoughts that are formulating inside their mercuric minds.

Lyndon B. Johnson 8/27/1908
5 A.M., Johnson City, TX
Agatha Christie 9/15/1890, 4 A.M., Torquay, UK

Lyndon Baines Johnson and *Agatha Christie* are legendary Virgos with Virgo rising. LBJ also has his Moon in Virgo! They both had Virgo's squinted offset eyes, the thin bridged, drooping nose, the jowly jaw and the noticeable gap in the front teeth.

Virgo Body Language
Virgo rules the upper digestive track, stomach & solar plexus

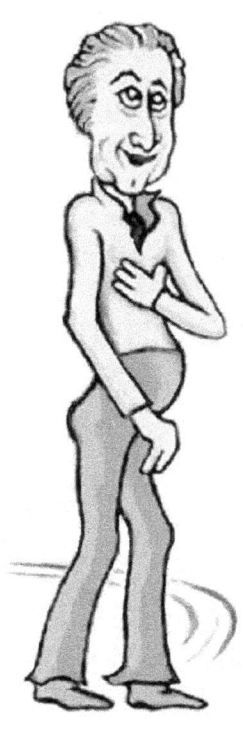

From Leo's Heart, body rulership progresses downward into the upper digestive track, the stomach and the solar plexus. This solar plexus contains well over 100 billion neuro-transmitters. It is the body's "second brain" that creates the non-verbal "gut feelings" that communicate any disorder in the body. These feelings tell the body what it needs to eat (and digest), so that it can extract the missing substances that will keep every cell in optimal order.

When your Virgo friends step forward to offer their service, you may notice that their rounded tummies protrude to the front. This sways the upper spine and chest to the back. The resulting lift in the "rear section" gives these people a stilted walk. Note how, with every alternating step, the stomach and the buttock will sway in opposite (left to right) directions!

Since Mercury is restrained here by feminine force of Virgo, the hands tend to hover close to the body—to shield its private "virginal areas".

Double Virgos show their stuff
Sean Connery
8/25/1930, 6:05 P.M.
Edinburgh, Scotland

The dictionary says that *"deduction is the act of logic where reasoning moves from the general to the particular"*. It is also the analytical process that brings *"given premises to their necessary conclusion."*

This gives us people who are very precise and particular in their thinking —i.e., Virgos, the deductive detectives of the Zodiac! As noted previously, expansive Gemini (the other Mercury-ruled sign) uses induction to bring in more facts to support a wider view.

Sun & Moon: Virgo

Interestingly, many of Hollywood's most successful detectives have been played by Virgo Sun signs: **Robert Blake** and **Peter Falk** were TV's *Baretta* and *Columbo*. In the movies, **Elliot Gould**, **James Coburn** and **Peters Sellers** gave us some offbeat gumshoes. Connery was the "super detective"—*James Bond, Agent 007*.

Connery's character was clever and sophisticated. Even with the latest technology, he'd still find a simple solution to neutralize his enemies. His Virgo-esque obsession for precision was noticeable in the simple ordering of a martini: "Shaken, not stirred."

Sean's Sun and Moon are both in Virgo! Consequently, his solar expressions and lunar emotions are markedly consistent. This allowed him to play characters with "high mental capacities". He was the medieval monk in *The Name of The Rose*. In *Medicine Man*, he was the jungle scientist searching for a cure for cancer. In *The Last Crusade*, his archeological knowledge surpassed those of his son *Indiana Jones*.

Physically, the Mobius patterns of mutability are most noticeable in this sign, since Virgo has the solidity of Earth to hold these patterns in place. This separation of sides often leaves a large gap in the frontal teeth, and this malleable clay allows others to "read every thought" in a Virgo's facial lines. Also, when they're sorting data, you might even see the messenger's wings fluttering in their crystal-like eyes.

Ascendant: Capricorn

Chatty? Ever changing? No way! This Virgo is made from more substantial stuff—since Capricorn rises and Saturn sits solidly on Connery's Ascendant.

Sean's heavy Saturn gives him a steely persona, and an aura of respect and authority. In life and in the movies, he has used this granite mask to convince others he was *The Man Who Would Be King*. In the film *The Untouchables*, he was the elder cop who knew where the real power lies. This role won him his first Oscar.

Mark Harmon
9/2/1951, 10:40 A.M.
Burbank Junction, CA

Virgo Sun and Moon

Mark Harmon's luminaries, Mercury and Venus are all in Virgo. The clinical side of Virgo was seen in his work in the medical dramas *St. Elsewhere* and *Chicago Hope*. The deductive logic of Virgo was seen in his role as a criminal investigator in *NCIS*, (2015's top rated TV show).

When Mark projects his Sun, the forces of mutable Virgo skew the facial lines by raising one brow up from the other, jutting the chin off to one side and twisting the lips and mouth. His lunar reactions bring similar expressions, as well as the inquisitive look displayed in the upper right photo. It suggests he is questioning the data or comments of others. This is a common response for Virgo Moons.

Ascendant: Scorpio
—or is it Libra?

AA rated data gives Harmon Scorpio Rising, but an eight minute error could give him Libra Rising. This is brought up since there are many photos of Mark that show the widespread smile and cherub cheeks associated with Libra and fewer that suggest the fixity and intensity of Scorpio. Fortunately, with today's internet videos, one can view the true nature of celebrities just "being themselves".

Watch Mark and you'll see a consistent shift in mode when his mutable luminaries recede. Watch how his mercuric eyes still and how his shoulders hunch forward as his hands clutch close to his body. If Libra was rising, the Cardinal Air would make Mark more outward and conversational. Instead, what we see is the protected persona of a Scorpion.

Physically, Mark has a large beak and a high, cubical forehead and heavy shoulders, features rarely seen in the well proportioned features of Libra.

Note: This Scorpio persona was seen in Mark's role as serial killer Ted Bundy in the television movie *The Deliberate Stranger* (1986).

Still, the question remains: why is the pleasant smile of Libra so prevalent in Harmon's appearance? Perhaps, it's due to the fact that his Moon conjoins Saturn in Libra and Venus (the ruling planet of Libra) conjoins his Sun!

Mars brings athlete skills

Mark was the starting quarterback for the UCLA Bruins (1972-73) and he received the National Football Foundation Award for All-Round Excellence. Mars, the definer of one's physical drive, is just 4 degrees from Mark's Leo Midheaven. This red planet also conjoins Pluto and trines Jupiter. This gave him powerful athletic skills.

Add a little water to the Earth
Keanu Reeves
9/2/1964, 5:18 A.M.
Beirut, Lebanon
Adam Sandler
9/9/1966, (no time)
Brooklyn, NY

Keanu and Adam both have Mercury, Uranus and Pluto conjunct their Virgo Suns. Their charts are markedly similar.

Suns: Virgo

Keanu Reeves has no Fire or Air in his chart. His three Virgo planets and Sun also conjoin his Ascendant, and they all are opposed by Saturn. This explains his cool and unexcitable demeanor.

This analytical perfection was seen in *Bill and Ted's Excellent Adventure* and later in *The Matrix*, a film where his precise and mercuric persona shined.

Adam Sandler's Sun also conjoins Mercury, Uranus and Pluto, but his Sun is out of orb to a Saturn Opposition. Adam's Leo Mars is his only Fire and he too has no Air in his chart. However, Adam's Neptune sextiles his Sun, as it forms a grand trine with Saturn and Jupiter in water signs. This makes his view of the world whimsical and filled with fantasy and comic illusions. He appears "far looser" than Mr. Reeves.

Moons: Cancer

Keanu and Adam both have Cancer Moons, but the aspects are different.

Reeve's Cancer Moon conjoins Venus and Mars—while it also trines his Neptune, as it sextiles Jupiter and his Virgo components (save for Pluto).

With his heavily aspected Mars, Keanu's physical movements seem to be controlled by forces outside himself. This may account for his mastering of the martial arts—and the highly physical roles we saw in his films *Speed*, *Point Break* and his series of *Matrix* films.

In contrast, Sandler's Moon has no major aspects (other than its sextile to his Virgo Venus). Also, his only fire is his lonely, unaspected Leo Mars. This fixed planet is overwhelmed by the six mutable components in his chart. This is why Sandler often appears awkward and physically uncoordinated (as we saw in his film role in *Water Boy*).

Fortunately, Sandler has his Jupiter in a grand water trine with Saturn and Neptune. With this, his mannerisms appear less analytical and far more compassionate. It also gives him his whimsical sense of fantasy and humor.

These energized water signs were seen in his film *The Wedding Singer*. There, in his reactions, Sandler's face would round and swell, as his soft voice took on a nasally and crabby tone.

Cameron Diaz

8/30/1972, 2:53 A.M.
San Diego, CA

 Sun: Virgo

In her breakthrough role in the film *Something About Mary*, Diaz played "the perfect woman" who was not only beautiful, but also kind and serving to others. In this role as a virginal figure and object of obsession, Diaz fully expressed the Virgo qualities of her Sun. It brought her many similar roles and a successful career.

Diaz shows the usual features of Virgo, all mentioned previously. What is unique in these photos is that Diaz shows us how the head of Virgo appears to be permanently planted at its base—at an angle that tilts it off from the line of the long neck!

Interestingly, Cameron's Virgo Mars conjoins her Sun and this gives her an earthy and mercuric physical energy. This Sun/Mars combination certainly was not suited for the kick butt, machismo role she played in *Charlie's Angels*. There, the misdirected energies became so obvious that Diaz was nominated for a "Razzie Award" as worst actress. This, and her Earth sign Moon, shows that she needed to stick to more substantial roles!

Moon: Taurus

When Diaz becomes emotional, her Taurus Moon takes control. In these lunar moments, the earthy demeanor of her Sun remains, but its mutable pattern is abruptly transformed into a holding pattern.

The LR photo captures Diaz in one of her lunar moments. There, her sensual bovine eyes draw us in—as her lush lips draw us closer. With Taurus Moons, it is hard to resist the temptation of their earthy responses.

Ascendant: Cancer

When Cameron's luminaries recede, the tidal waters of Cancer rise—to bring her emotional mask to the surface.

Since the Rising Sign shapes the underlying bone structure, Diaz's face is rounded by her "lunar temples". This gives her the bulging cheek bones, the wide delta between the brows and the facial lines that resemble the markings on the shell of a crab.

Venus (the ruler of Taurus) conjoins Diaz's Rising Sign. With this beautifying planet, the waters of Cancer round the rugged edges of Cameron's earthy Sun and Moon, as it models them into a pleasing smoothness. In addition, Venus' sextile to her Moon accounts for the pleasant mothering voice that we heard in Diaz's role as the gentle Fiona in the *Shrek* Film franchise.

Dr. Phil McGraw
9/1/1950, 7:15 P.M.
Vinita, OK

Earlier data give McGraw Scorpio Rising. In our initial photo search, the fixed reactions of Taurus were readily found, but it was difficult to find the bone structure of Scorpio. When we sought photos for his "Pisces Ascendant", the images of Pisces were far more plentiful.

 Sun: Virgo

With his self-help publications, Dr. Phil shows his life's purpose—creating a career fulfilling the needs of his 10th House Virgo Sun. In his daily "TV treatments", the doctor's mutable energies twist and spin every word, as he analyzes his guest's motivations—to correct the imperfections in their thinking and attitudes.

In his attempts to define every detail, Dr. Phil makes his solutions neat and orderly. Once done, he usually sums it up in one of his precise "ten second bits of wisdom". One of his Virgo-ish favorites is: "You either get it, or you don't". This shortness of words is likely a product of McGraw's Moon.

Moon: Taurus

When Dr. Phil makes a response or interacts emotionally with a guest, the mercuric force of his Sun often takes on a dynamic modal change. Watch how he becomes more focused and more stubborn and controlling.

In these moments, his earthy flesh takes on a cubical form and his eyes become firmly fixed. You might hear his utter his favorite line: "Get real!"

With his Moon opposing his Scorpio Mars, McGraw is driven to reveal the content of other people's secrets.

Ascendant: Pisces

Certainly, Dr. Phil didn't win his millions of fans being an analytical fuss putt. After all, McGraw is selling his image as a caring and "transformational agent". That is what we'd expect from someone who has a Pisces Ascendant.

Phil's books *Creating Your Life From the Inside Out* and *Life Strategies* affirm that there is "a process that can bring personal healing". The doctor sees the magic through this Pisces window. However, with his Virgo Sun, the magic often comes off as being too clinical.

When Phil ceases to express the force of his earthy luminaries, his flesh rounds as his eyes enlarge into reflecting pools of water. In the process, the earthy texture soften, as it is liquefied by Pisces' sea of water. As expected, the offset lines of mutability remain, as the chatter of his mercuric Sun quietly disappears. What we see is a compassionate and caring mask—the one that brought him his success.

"I have a kind of neutrality, physically, which has helped me. I have a face that can be made to look a lot better or a lot worse, depending on how I want it to look." — Colin Firth

Colin Firth
9/10/1960, 11:30 A.M.
Grayshott, England

In many of his film roles, Firth appears to take on the identity of a different person. In *Bridget Jones' Diary*, Colin was a likeable but rowdy bachelor. In his Oscar winning role in *The King's Speech*, Firth displayed the struggles of a speech impaired monarch. In *Tinker Tailor Soldier Spy*, we saw an articulate and cunning manipulator.

This gift for manipulating his appearance and personality is enhanced by the Grand Earth Trine between his Sun, Moon and form-inducing Saturn. Firth's malleable image is likely a product of his Mutable Sun and Neptune's placement on his Ascendant.

Sun: Virgo

With two fixed key components, Firth does not show the typical physical traits of a Virgo. However, when he projects his solar expressions, the divisional patterns of mutability kick in. As the top photos show, they push one side of his face above the other. This skews the facial flesh into twisted lines, as it tilts and narrows the openings of the eyes and juts the jaw off to the side. These features disappear when Colin's Ascendant and Moon dominate.

Moon: Taurus

The LR photo shows the intriguing elemental and modal changes that occur in the facial flesh, when Colin's Moon comes into play. Note how the dueling force of his Sun becomes firmly fixed, and how it transforms the smooth porcelain skin of Virgo into the lumpy fixed Earth of Taurus.

This transformation also instills the easy-going Venusian qualities associated with Taurus. This relaxed sense of stability and contentment is seen in the large pupils of Colin's bovine eyes.

These fixed features are enhanced by the fact that Colin's Sun is in the Taurus Decan and he has a fixed Ascendant.

Ascendant: Scorpio

When Colin's luminaries dim, his facial flesh settles on the underlying skeletal structure of his Scorpio Ascendant. The long and skewed structure of Virgo is missing. In its place we see the cubical forehead, the wide bridged beak-like nose, the rigid frontal cheek plane and square, firmly-set jaw. This Ascendant gives Firth his intense persona—the one we see, when his intense Scorpion eyes focus in our direction.

Jimmy Fallon

9/19/1974, 6:21 P.M.
Bay Ridge, NY

On February 18, 2015, Jimmy Fallon replaced Jay Leno as the host of NBC's *The Tonight Show*. Using this moment and nine other events, astrologer Isaac Starkman created a rectified chart to determine Jimmy's Ascendant. It appears valid, for it defines the missing quality that we see in his personality.

Sun in Virgo

Jimmy's Sun and Venus are both in Virgo and they are the only Earth in his chart. However, these two Virgo planets join four Libra planets in his Libra-ruled 7th House. When Fallon is not presenting the personal beliefs and desires of his mercuric Sun, the cardinal forces of Libra dominate! Note how his skewed facial lines align into horizontal balance, as he presents the effervescence smile of Libra!

Moon in Scorpio

Jimmy rarely shows the fixed intensity of a Scorpio Moon. This is likely due to the fact that his Moon forms a grand water trine with Saturn in Cancer and Jupiter in Pisces. Jupiter's placement in this triad of water allows Jimmy to present a free flowing range of emotions.

When these cardinal, fixed and mutable waters work in unison, Jimmy is able to voice the rhythmic cadences of others. That may be why he has a remarkable talent for mimicking the musical voice and personalities of others.

Fallon's Moon sextiles Venus. This adds to the previously noted Venus aspects, as it makes the focused emotions of Jimmy's Moon surprisingly serene. It also may be why Jimmy uses the word "love" so often in his descriptions.

Ascendant: Pisces

Amazingly, Venus also has more connections in Fallon's chart. This planet of love also opposes his Jupiter and Ascendant—and these components are T-shared by Neptune (the ruler of his Pisces Ascendant).

These Venus aspects made Jimmy the most pleasant of the 2017 "late night talk show hosts". His Neptune aspects also add to his "nice persona"—and his previously mentioned musical gifts. Jupiter's placement on this "front gate" accounts for Jimmy's gift for humor, and his caffeine driven persona.

With his Ascendant in the mutable water sign of Pisces, Jimmy's physical appearance (or body structure) is somewhat plump—and not what we'd expect from a normally lanky Virgo Sun. The mutable features appear at all levels in his face, since his Moon is in the Pisces decan and it trines his Ascendant and Saturn in Cancer.

Melissa McCarthy
8/26/1970, No Time
Plainfield, IL

 Sun: Virgo

McCarthy's career began with her role in *Gilmore Girls*. It was her enthusiastic but fussy nature in that role that inspired producers to cast her as a lead star in the hit CBS series *Mike and Molly*. This led to an array of successful comedy films such as *Identity Thief, Tammy* and *The Boss*.

In all of these photos, this lady projects an exuberance flair that is unexpected from someone with a earthy Sun and a watery Moon. Surprisingly, Melissa has only two air components and only one fire sign in her chart—her Leo Mars! However, this red planet conjoins her Sun and it also sextiles Jupiter. This is why her personality is so expansive and theatrical.

Moon in Cancer

Melissa's watery Moon is in its ruling sign of Cancer—and it also sextiles her Sun! Consequently, Melissa's tidal emotions are churned by the stirring forces of her Virgo Sun and exaggerated by its trine to Jupiter.

Melissa's Moon also squares Uranus. This explains why her quixotic characters tend to pursue distant windmills. In addition, Pluto conjoins her Sun's ruler Mercury. That may be why her comedy in films is far from "virginal", and why it's often filled with crude and off-color comments.

Mars in Leo

As noted, McCarthy's Mars is in Leo, and this shows in every step that she takes. As we saw in *Spy* and *The Heat*, Melissa often struts about—boasting of the magnificence of her accomplishments! The comedy comes from the fact that her awkward actions often have disastrous results. (This may be due to her Mars' square to Neptune, the most aspected planet in her chart).

The fire of Leo showed in her boisterous performances in *Mike and Molly* and in her Oscar nominated supporting role in *Bridesmaid*.

Ascendant: Aquarius?

Melissa began her role in *Gilmore Girls* when Saturn entered her 4th House and begin its upward climb in her chart. When it reached her Midheaven in 2016, McCarthy's first big budget movie *Ghostbusters* was released. From this, one could conclude that she was born around 6 P.M., when Aquarius was rising in her chart. This time would place Neptune on her Midheaven and Jupiter (the ruler of comedy) in her 9th House.

Add some Fire to the Water
Lily Tomlin
Sept. 1, 1939 / 1:45 A.M.
Detroit, MI

 Sun: Virgo

With a Virgo Sun in the third House, Lily has a gift for communicating the "nervous hilarities" in human nature. These Virgo mannerisms were seen in Lily's *Ernestine* (the condescending phone operator) and in the prudish consumer advisor *Judith Beasley*. Both of these characters illustrated Virgo's fastidious obsessions and how this sign tries to remain grounded, as its mind chases fleeting thoughts. The most obvious movement is seen in the flittering fingers and hands—which are trying to point out and sort the trivial details that others rarely see.

Moon: Aries

Action happens when an Aries Moon responds to the forces that are cast in their direction. Most of these reactions are curt, direct, and intense. Many are quick bursts of return fire, that disappear as quickly as they appear.

In her role in *All of Me*, we saw a bitter and dying woman with a determined will to start over again. This character was quintessential Virgo and she also showed the most negative side of an Aries Moon: the emotional abrasiveness that drives everyone away.

In real life, this lunar placement simplifies Lily's very complex Virgo nature, as it gives her an incredible sense of independence. With Jupiter conjunct her Aries Moon in the 10th House of career, Lily was emotionally driven to pursue her comedic career. Furthermore, this drive was reenforced by her Capricorn Mars. It gave her the tenacity to become an independent producer, create her own plays and videos—and pursue a very enduring career!

Ascendant: Cancer

Like most Cancer Ascendants, Lily is given their own "pressure release valve"—to regulate the outflow of their internal emotions. In Lily's calmer emotional moments, this water valve is slowly opened—to round and swell Lily's flesh and erode the stoney edges of her Earth. However, with her Aries Moon, the valve was often fully opened—to release an emotional tsunami!

Fortunately, with a 1st House Pluto, Lily' emotions are highly controlled. This gives Lily a sensitive and nurturing presence, as well as Cancer's gift for imitation and mimicry.

Physically, Lily's Cancer Ascendant is seen in her beaming lunar temples—the mask that she presented in her baby-faced character *Edith Ann*.

James Coburn
8/31/1928, 8:15 P.M.
Laurel, NE

Sun: Virgo

Coburn's first lead role was in the James Bond spoof *My Man Flint,* where he parodied the unflappable qualities of the other Virgo super spy—Sean Connery. Shortly after, he won a cult following by displaying "Virgo's penance for worry" in *The President's Analyst.*

Coburn's photo on the upper right captures the suave, mercurial qualities of Virgo, as well as other Virgo features. Ironically, James was often typecast as an "action tough guy". This is likely due to his Ascendant.

Ascendant: Aries

With the angular and muscular facial lines of his Aries Ascendant, Coburn had the "machismo image" which won him many action roles in TV and motion pictures. Coburn's first major action role was as the quirky, knife-throwing member of *"The Magnificent Seven".* Later, he played Pat Garrett in Sam Peckinpah's *Billy The Kid* saga and the cunning villain in Sergio Leone's *Fistful of Dynamite.*

In these films and others, James had a gift for combining the fiery drive of Aries with his cool, mental solar energies. Also, with his Natal Uranus conjunct this Ascendant, he was able to give his characters an "over the edge" quality. Perhaps this was why he never reached "major star" status. Many of his characters were too eerie to find mass appeal.

Moon: Pisces

Such edginess is a rarity for a Pisces Moon, but it is appropriate, when you look at its placement. Coburn's Moon is hidden in the 12th House. Uranus sits in-between his Moon and Ascendant. Uranus' electrical field often blocks the warm emotions that we'd expect from his watery Moon.

Hints of James' Piscean fantasies were seen in his comedic roles, but rarely did we see any real raw emotion. Then, in 1998, when Jupiter transited Coburn's Pisces Moon during the filming of *Affliction,* James was given the chance to "expand his emotional expression." There, in his role as a cruel, alcoholic father, he gave the most emotionally wrenching performance of his career. It won him an Oscar for Best Supporting Actor!

There was a story told at Colburn's Oscar party, where he was quoted that he was "shocked" that he won. In true Virgo fashion, James then went on to analyze his win and the events in his long career, and he concluded— "I finally got one right."

Richard Gere
8/31/1949. 12:00 P.M.
Philadelphia, PA

 Sun: Virgo

As Gere's chart indicates, he has the mental agility, philosophical world view and compassion to be more than an actor. With Saturn on his Sun and both components sextile Uranus, Gere became also known as a political activist and a spokesman for justice in Tibet.

This ringed planet also gave Gere the determination to pursue his personal goals. One was his youthful goal to become a musical performer. This dream lead to his role in the 2011 hit film *Chicago*.

Moon: Sagittarius

Gere's Sun is in square to his Moon. Thusly, when he expresses the Mobius patterns of his Virgo Sun, the force of expression spirals slowly, as it emulates the solidity of Earth. In contrast, in Richard's lunar reactions, the fires are ignited. This makes the mutable forces more intense and animated. These Earth and Fire variations of mutability were on center stage in Gere's performance in the film *Chicago*.

Richard's Moon also trines Pluto, as it squares a Venus/Neptune conjunction in Libra (in his 9th House). These four components (and the previously noted Uranus aspect) account for Gere's urge to seek justice and promote fairness in the world. His Centaur Moon suggests he would find the solutions through his spiritual pursuits.

These prominent Libra forces likely inspired Gere's lawyer roles in the films *Primal Fear*, *Red Corner* and *Chicago*. The balance was found in his life long study of Buddhism.

Richard's Jupiter-ruled Moon has kept him optimistic and positive. This expansive Moon also reduces his Virgo Sun's tendency to be worrisome and critical.

Ascendant: Scorpio

In the films *Days of Heaven*, *An Officer and a Gentlemen* and *Pretty Woman*, Gere's mysterious and protected persona was just what we'd expect from a Scorpio Ascendant. In these roles, his fixed presence cast the image of "an urban power figure", who appeared to have his world in total control.

When Gere's luminaries are in repose, the intense focus in his piercing eagle eyes are on full display. We also see Scorpio's bone and body structure in his heavy shoulders and the rounded features of Fixed Water in his face.

Of course, when Gere's solar and lunar lights are reignited, the mutable forces screw the facial features once again, and the intensity disappears.

Jane Curtin

Sept. 6, 1947 / 2:00 P.M.
Cambridge, MA

♍ Sun: Virgo

On *Saturday Night Live,* Jane and her fellow Virgo Bill Murray created many nervous and analytical characters by exaggerating Virgo's quirkier traits.

Later, Jane's Virgo found full expression in her role as Allie, in the sitcom *Kate and Allie*. Adorned in her high-collared blouse and a frilly apron, Jane would constantly fiddle in the kitchen and fuss over a variety of details—real and imagined! A decade later, this worrywart filled the airwaves once again, with her hit show *Third Rock From The Sun*. Whatever the situation, Jane's characters would always express their disgruntlement with a pained snarl.

With her Sun, Mercury and Venus in the 9th House of comedy, this Virgo torment is masterfully expressed—all to create the maximum laughter!

Ascendant: Sagittarius

With all that 9th House energy and an ebullient Sagittarius Ascendant, Jane was given an extraordinary gift for comedy. This Rising Sign makes this normally timid Virgo loud, animated, clumsy and incorrigibly blunt. With her 8th House Saturn trining her Ascendant, Jane easily puts on a dour and sarcastic exterior. For her, it's just part of the show, to add to the comedic effect.

You'll see her mutable fire rise when the Centaur rears its head, to break free from the constrictive reins of her earthy Sun and Moon. In these moments of unbridled optimism, the tight-lipped frown quickly turns into a wide-toothed smile, as a twinkle appears in her eyes. You might even hear a horsey laugh as she gallops away, to chase another comedic windmill.

Physically, this Ascendant gives Jane a wide jaw and chin, and broad hips.

Moon: Taurus

If you watch *Third Rock* again, you will observe how Jane reacts to John Lithgow's romantic advances. Note how her mercuric nature abruptly solidifies into an immovable mass, as her nostrils widen and her eyes steadily fix into a bovine-like gaze. Oddly, she'll be momentarily lost for words, and will only respond, when she feels some sense of control.

Like most Taurus Moons, Jane's first responses are insufferably inflexible, but watch that wall of resistance crumble, when her lusty Taurian lunar urges become overwhelming.

Neptune aspects create the music

In the previous portrait of Virgo **Jimmy Fallon**, it was noted that his five Neptune aspects contributed to his remarkable talent for "mimicking the music and personalities of others". Our subject here shows us what can happen with someone has nine Neptune aspects in her chart!

Neptune is the ruler of Pisces—the water sign that is known for its remarkable sense of rhythm. Thusly, many people with an empowered Neptune become gifted musicians. Pink's soulful and emotional voice has been compared to two other Earth sign ladies: Taurus *Adele* and Capricorn *Janice Joplin*. The luminaries of all three make connections with Neptune. Pink's Moon trines Neptune, while her Sun makes a square. Janis' and Adele's Suns both trine Neptune. Joplin's Moon is in square, while Adele's Moon makes a conjunction with Uranus, Saturn and Neptune—and this planet is on her Descendant. (See **Adele**'s portrait on page 110).

In addition, the Neptune of these three performers are also forming various aspects to Saturn. This gave them the tenacity to master their musical talents.

PINK
(Alecia Beth Moore)
9/8/1979. 3:00 P.M.
Doylestown, PA

Alecia Moore's musical career began in 1995 as a member of the teen R&B group *Choice*. Their record sales were disappointing, but her record label saw a greater potential and they offered "*Pink*" a solo deal! It was a wise move, for her debut album went double platinum. In 2009, Billboard named her "Pop Songs Artist of the Decade" and with her 2017 album *Beautiful Trauma*, her total album sales climbed to over 40 million copies.

Pink is known for her raspy and husky voice, her adventurous appearance, her humor, emotional rawness and infectious dance beats. Much of this can be attributed to the contents in her chart.

Virgo Sun

When this lady presents her big voiced and "tough chick" music on stage, the last thing that people see is a prissy Virgo Sun. That was also the case when this author searched for photos. Few showed the mercuric nature of Virgo, save for those that showed Pink when she was working on a task, composing lyrics or conversing with others on a late night talk show.

In the left photo above, Pink displays the cool and protected qualities seen in most Virgos. The 2nd photo shows the disgruntled look of puzzlement that often appears, when Virgos find themselves in "imperfect situations".

Pink shows little of the dueling force of Mercury. This likely due to the restraining power of Saturn—the planet that conjoins her Sun, Mercury and Venus! Amazingly, these components all square Neptune—and all (save for Mercury) sextile her Uranus and Mars.

These massive Neptune and Saturn connections account for Pink's rigid "tough girl" demeanor and powerful emotional presence. Uranus explains her fluorescent spiked hair and eccentric appearance. Mars' aspects (and her fiery Moon and Ascendant account for her energetic stage presence.

Aries Moon

Pink's Moon is in Aries and it is opposes Pluto. These two components are T-squared by Mars, the ruling planet of Aries. This Moon clears away the clutter of Pink's Neptune aspects, as it gives her a highly directed sense of self.

This keen sense of independence was seen at the end of her second album, when she demanded that she be given "total creative control of all her future musical projects". The empowered Mars is also seen in her athletic performances.

All of Pink's planets and Sun are on the top half of her chart, save for her Moon, that sits alone on the Nadir of her chart. With this distanced Moon, Pink's emotions are hidden below the surface, but when she makes an emotional decision—this lady takes action!

Pink was the one who proposed to her race car driver husband Cary Hart. She did it in the middle of a race—by writing "Marry Me" on the crew's pit board! He pulled out of the race to tell her "yes".

Sagittarius Rising

On stage, Pink has gained recognition for her highly acrobatic performances. This is a gift common for those who have

an athletic Archer Ascendant. What is unusual here is that Pink's Rising Sign is conjoined by that massively aspected Neptune, while it also forms a grand fire trine with Jupiter and her Moon. This gives Pink her expansive and emotionally riveting persona.

On a public scale, rather than personal, this lady is seen as a "tough and emotionally controlled performer". This fits, for Pluto sits one degree from her Midheaven. She also appears non-threatening, it is amazing what nine Neptune aspects can do. It was not the athletic show or the aura of toughness that made Pink a star. She succeeded by connecting with the emotions of her fans.

Physically, Pink shows the long neck and jaw of a horse, as well as the skull that sweeps sharply to the rear. She also displays the flat cheeks and high and square forehead of a Lion. Pink's Ascendant and Moon are both in the decan of Leo.

When Air is added to feed the Fire of a Leo Moon, mercuric Virgo becomes theatrical.

Amy Poehler

9/16/1971, 4:33 P.M.
Newton, MA

Amy gained her fame on *Saturday Night Live*. In 2001, on her first year in that show, she was quickly promoted from featured player to full cast member. She was only the third person to earn this distinction (after Harry Shearer and Eddy Murphy).

After departing *SNL* in 2008, Amy went on to star in the TV series *Parks and Recreation*. Her work on this show won her a Golden Globe as well as a Writer's Guild Award. In 2011, *Time* magazine listed her as one of the "Top 100 most influential people in the world."

In 2016, Amy's TV show ended, but her work in comedy continued. She became Executive Producer of Comedy Channel's *Broad City* and won acclaim for hosting the *Golden Globe Awards* with her friend Tina Fey. (See page 124).

Here, we will show how Amy's gifts for comedy, improvisation and showmanship are indicated in the components in her chart.

Sun in Virgo

With her Sun, Mercury, Venus and Pluto in Virgo, the energy of mutable Earth is seen in Amy's analytical mannerisms, as well as in her thinking process.

The nit-picky qualities of Virgo were a part of many of Amy's *SNL* characters, but the grounded energy of Earth was often overridden by more expansive forces. This is due to the fact that these four Virgo components are the only feminine elements in her chart. The other seven components of expansive Air and Fire dominate her personality!

Still, hints of Virgo remain. The UL photo shows the body language of Virgo and how Amy's chest pulls back, as her head and neck shift in one direction and her shoulders tilt in the other. The UR photo shows the "angled head" and how the force of Mercury skews and angles the features in her face.

Pluto conjoins Amy's Venus and Sun, and her Moon, Ascendant and Mars are in fixed masculine signs. We see why Amy exhibits many of the features and mannerisms of Leo.

Moon: Leo

When Amy becomes emotional, the mutable patterns of Amy's Sun become even more difficult to detect. In such moments, Amy's analytical nature ceases—as it's replaced by the fixed glow and unquestioning self-confidence of her Leo Moon.

Note how the head rises, as the hands cling to her proud, expanding chest. In this emotional reaction, the firmly set jaw lifts the chin upward; This shortens the long face we'd expect from Virgo. This action also pulls the flesh on the cheeks upward to form the wide, flat cheek plates of a lion. This occurs with most people who have a Leo Moon!

Ascendant: Aquarius

When her luminaries are deactivated, the starry-eyed mask of Amy's Aquarius Ascendant rise to the surface. This gives Amy a light and seemingly vaporous and electrified persona—as well as a fixed appearance that is similar to what we see in her lunar reactions.

Unlike her Moon (which seems to amplify Amy's inner light), the rising light of her Ascendant appears to be empowered from some distant source in outer space. This connection gives Amy a steady stream of inventive and intuitive ideas—and a fantastic gift for improvisation!

With a fixed Ascendant and Moon, we see little of the long and skewed physical traits of Virgo. After all, the Aquarius bone structure is compacting all of the facial elements into the center of Amy's large head. This gives her face a square and cubical shape.

There is something else that is unique about this lady: all of her components are joined by interconnected aspects! Amy's Gemini Saturn forms a rare "Double Grand Trine". One is with her Aquarius Mars and Libra Uranus; The other with her Ascendant and her conjoined Venus and Pluto!

Also, Amy's Saturn is in opposition to her Jupiter and Neptune conjunction, and these two planets also form a square to her Moon. This Jupiter/Neptune conjunction is on Amy's Midheaven. This explains Amy's fantastic gift for humor and fantasy. Their placement in jolly Sagittarius likely inspired her to pursue a career in comedy.

Many Virgo Portraits Lack Leo Components

Since most of our portraits are "stars of theater", Leo has been a common component. However, we were surprised to find that **Amy Poehler** and **Lauren Bacall** were the only Virgos who had Leo as one of their key components. In contrast, Virgo components reigned in our group of Leo Suns. This component question was also brought up in our discussion on Aries, when we noted that none of our Aries Suns had any of their other key lights in cardinal signs.

In this Virgo section, our portrait of **Charlie Sheen** (page 211) shows the difficulty one can have, when one's three key components are in the mode of mutability. *[See index for list of others who lack a Mode or Element].*

This "analysis of Mode and Element combinations" is beyond the scope of this book. It may be an area for readers to explore in their future studies on human nature.

Jeff Foxworthy
9/6/1958, no time, Alanta, GA

Jack Black
8/28/1969, 3:04 A.M., Redondo Beach, CA

Jeff Foxworthy shows many of Virgo's features; Jack Black's are less obvious. For both, these features appear when they express the convictions of his Sun.

In the activation of their Suns, these men's fingers precisely point and count —as they analyze the material in their surroundings and assemble their findings into orderly arrangements. These mannerisms are enhanced by their mutable Moons.

Moons: Gemini & Pisces

Jeff Foxworthy's Moon in masculine Gemini makes him highly cerebral and verbal. In emotional moments, this expansive Moon speeds up the pace of his speech, as well as the animated gestures of his mercuric hands and fingers.

Jeff's luminaries form hard angles to Saturn. This gives him a stable of words, to express his insights into the foibles of humanity. This was seen in his *Blue Collar Comedy Tour* and in his TV quiz show: *Are You Smarter than a Fifth Grader?*

In contrast, **Jack Black**'s emotional responses are stirred by the forces of a feminine Pisces Moon. When this mutable water permeates and rounds his facial flesh, its meandering currents erode his earthy facial features. In the process, the mercuric logic of his Sun is inundated by a flood of delusional feelings.

With his Moon's opposition to Pluto and its square his Sagittarius Mars, Jack's reactions are surprisingly fiery and exaggerated—not those of a reclusive fish. Positively, his lunar impulses give him an ability to feel the rhythms of the currents and this gives him his gift for music! His work with his rock band *Tenacious D* got him his break-through movie gig in *High Fidelity* and his first lead role in *The School of Rock*.

Ascendants

Jack has a large torso and short extremities, i.e., the body structure of a crab. This **Cancer Rising Sign** forms a grand trine with Jack's Moon and Neptune (the ruler of Pisces). Thusly, the element of water appears to dominate his appearance and expressions.

Jeff's redneck and conservative persona is far more caustic than we'd expect from someone with a Gemini Moon. This suggests that he may be born around 4:10 P.M., which gives him a Virgo Decan **Capricorn Rising**. This would explain the goat-like stance he often holds on stage. Or, it could be his Taurus Mars or those aspects of Saturn to his luminaries?

Charlie Sheen
9/3/1965, 10:48 P.M.
New York, NY

 Sun: Virgo

Virgos are the so called virgins of the Zodiac, who are often timid about their amorous natures. Charlie Sheen throws that archetype out the window!

Why you ask? Sheen's Virgo Sun conjoins Uranus and Pluto, as it sextiles his Mars and Neptune in Scorpio. Charlie is driven by lustful, delusional and impulsive forces.

Charlie's three Virgo planets showed their positive side when he prepared for his ultra-buff roles in *Hot Shots 1 & 2*. For the second film, Sheen developed a physical program that, in his words, was "Olympic in its intensity." To obtain this perfection, he combined yoga, physical regiment and a very restricted diet. His Mars trine to Saturn brought the discipline. Pluto enforced the obsession, but it was quickly destroyed by Uranus. Five years later, Charlie returned to his old habits and nearly died from a drug overdose. This instability can also be attributed to the triplication of Mutable forces in his three key lights. With this excessive mutability (and his Venus in indecisive Libra being his only cardinal sign), it is difficult for Charlie to maintain direction and focus in his life.

Moon: Sagittarius

Charlie's Moon is in Sagittarius. With this Mutable Fire, Sheen follows every emotional impulse. With his Leo Mercury trine his Moon and sextile Jupiter (the Centaur's ruling planet, Sheen's Mercury-ruled Sun and Ascendant are unbridled. This Leo Mercury explains Sheen's theatrical flair and "winning

confidence" that we saw in Sheen's role as the swinging womanizer in his hit TV series *Two and a Half Men*. These Centaur and Jupiterian energies also account for his success in comedy and sports roles. *Spin City*, the *Scary Movie* franchise, *Major League* and *Eight Men Out* are good examples.

Ascendant: Gemini

This Ascendant gives Charlie seven components in mutable signs! In 2011, Sheen showed us what can happen, when one's mutable forces get out of control. That year, transiting Jupiter was conjoining Uranus in late Pisces, squaring Sheen's Jupiter and Moon. This aspect injected "tiger blood" into his Centurion lunar emotions, as it heightened his delusions. After a period of very bizarre and crazy antics, he was fired from *Two and A Half Men*.

As shown in LL photo, this Rising Sign often forms a protruding box on the lower half of the face. It also skews the alignment in the skeletal structure.

Tyler Perry

9/14/1969, 12:01 A.M.
New Orleans, LA

Our previous two Virgos have Neptune in Scorpio. Tyler Perry was born just before Neptune entered Sagittarius. It was time to birth a new array of film directors and stars, to bring a little comic relief to the world of the cinema.

 Sun: Virgo

In live interviews, the earthy side of Mercury is apparent when Perry projects the rays of his Sun. Watch how his regulated speech moves in precise and steady steps—as he reveals the imperfections and foibles in our human nature.

Ironically, Tyler's physical features lack many of the mutable qualities of his Sun and Ascendant. This may be due to his Sun's placement in the Taurus Decan and his Ascendant and Moon's placement in the Aquarius Decan. This gives him a very fixed appearance. (See UR photo).

Moon: Libra

Tyler has a very unusual chart. Seven of his components are compacted into his chart's 4th quadrant. (Saturn is the only planet on its right side). What is fascinating is that his Leo Venus is the nearest planet to his Midheaven. Next in line, his Sun conjoins Pluto in Virgo. This is followed by a running string of five components in Libra.

With Uranus in the middle of this string of planets, Tyler was driven to communicate the social behavior and culture of the African-American church in which he was raised. In this community, Tyler began his career as a playwright, creating staged plays for his friends. With this 3rd House Sagittarius Mars trine his Leo Venus and sextile his Mercury, we see why Perry has a gift for words.

The abundance of 12th House components tells us why the theme of "forgiveness" permeates much of his work. It not only reflects the thoughts of his own culture, it also reveals truths that apply to all of humanity.

Ascendant: Gemini

Tyler's gender switching role as the chatty *Madea* displays the persona of his Gemini mask. This role elevates the mercuric vibrations of Tyler's Sun, as it frees him from the worrisome urges of his Mercury-ruled Sun.

Watch how Tyler's speech accelerates (and how his hands fly about) when he takes on this grandmotherly role.

Check out Tyler's presentation on Youtube: *I Can Do Bad All By Myself*. There, his character *Madea* shows her unrepressed Libra components, as she offers her delightful relationship advice to others".

This relationship with others begins in the next sign in the Zodiac: Libra

♎ Libra

	Page
Introduction to Libra	
Jimmy Carter, Barbara Walters	217-219
The breezes of Air run strong	220
Kate Winslet	221
Hilary Duff	222
Kelly Ripa & Fran Dreshler	223
Hugh Jackman	224
Gwyneth Paltrow	225
Ignition of Fire turns up the heat	
John Lennon	226
Christopher Reeves	227
James Caviezel	228
Tim Robbins	229
The addition of Earth stills the winds	
Matt Damon	230
Susan Sarandon	231
Sigourney Weaver	232
Water moisturizes all of the Elements	
Yo-Yo Ma & Jason Alexander	233
Bruno Mars	234
Deepak Chopra	235
Paul Simon	236
Julie Andrews	237
Michael Douglas	238
Will Smith	239

Libra ♎ September 23 to October 22
Masculine Polarity, Cardinal Air
Co-create a lovely world with your Libra friends

Six months ago at **Aries'** *Spring Equinox*, a new creative adventure was born. Then, in the waning light of **Cancer's** *Summer Solstice*, individuals began the task of interacting with their surroundings. At the Fall Equinox, the **Libra** Sun is now entering the **3rd Quadrant**, as it moves down into the darker half of the globe. Here, the Sun is lighting the other half, and the light-of-self is dimming. It is time to interact with the "other world" that lies beyond our personal reach!

With this movement, the Cardinal Air of Libra drives individuals to share their personal experiences with others. With this weighing of ideas and thoughts, they can recognize what has true value and meaning—and then discard all things of little worth (**Scorpio**). With this higher knowledge (**Sagittarius**), they can complete the lessons—and carry them forward into a New Year of creation.

If you're in a mood for some social interaction, then head on out to your nearby bakery or coffee shop—the one with elegant art, cushy chairs and classical music playing in the air. Look for tables that are filled with pleasant chatter. If you find one that has little dissension and few strongly-stated personal opinions, you can be sure that it is filled with a community of Libras!

Hire a Libra to start up your creative team and manage your human resources department. They will evaluate the Virgo service of every individual—to make sure that they are contributing to the greater goal. These charming diplomats know how to calm any personnel conflict and encourage cooperation. They can keep your projects functioning smoothly—and keep your budget in balance!

But take notice, for these defenders of justice will insist that you treat everyone fairly! Follow their wise advice—for it will be your "consideration of others" that will make your business grow and prosper!

♀ Rulerships and Associations for Libra

Earlier, Venus was associated with the personal sensual enjoyment that was relished in the feminine sign of Taurus. Here, in its masculine form, Venus' governance is expanded to encompass the embellished pleasures of art and beauty—those joyful sensations created in the mind. It is one's Venus that defines the appealing qualities that one sees in others. Therefore, it determines the nature of those that we desire to have in our partnerships and marriage. This activity is defined by the aspects, transits and planets in one's 7th House.

It is the weighting of Libra that determines "the value of all things". A similar function is seen in the Kidneys, the body part that determines what substances are needed, and those that must be removed. (This elimination is the job of **Scorpio**).

Libra is associated with justice, elegant art and love of love itself. This sign's colors are pale blue and pink. The stone is sapphire and the metal copper. Careers include lawyers, judges, beauticians, dress designers, welfare workers and any work that's carried on in surroundings where the arts are appreciated.

Libra Physical Traits:

In the Fall air, the fluffy cumulus clouds gently rise and bloom, as they spread to the sides, to keep the masses of air (and temperatures) in balance. This is why the expressions of Libra appear to spread in a horizontal direction. It is also why their demeanors and facial features appear to be in perpetual balance. With these gentle breezes, there is rarely a hint of a thunder storm.

This gives these souls the larger than normal head, that floats above the "pleasantly plumb" body frame. In the face, we see the perfectly leveled eyebrows and almond eyes. The most recognized feature is their wide, ever present V-shaped smile.

Jimmy Carter~10/1/1924, 7:00 A.M., Plains GA
Barbara Walters~9/25/1929, 6:50 A.M., Boston MA

Barbara Walters and *Jimmy Carter* are both Libras with Libra rising. In their bone structure and facial features, the archetypal shapes and qualities of Libra are enhanced, since the solar expressions and the mask are one and the same.

Body Language of Libra

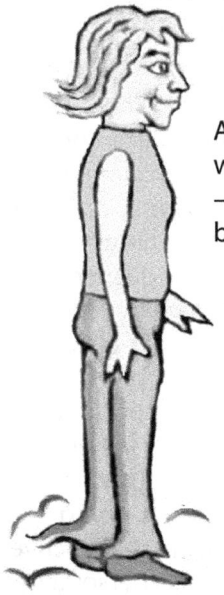

The rulership of body areas started at the head in Aries. Appropriately, at the midpoint between the head and the feet we find the body region ruled by the opposite sign of Aries —Libra! When these forces are placed in this center point, the body appears to take on a "perfectly erect position".

Watch how these Venusian creatures glide across the floor with their erect, vertical posture. It suggests that they are walking with a book on the head. That is what fashion models do, to enhance their careers. This may be why so many fashion models have Libra Sun signs.

When Libras begin their "scale weighing act", the hands are held low, as the fingers point to the sides. Watch how the arms move in and out and up and down—to keep the torso in perfect balance.

The lumbar and kidneys lie in this arena of rulership. It is in the kidneys that the body's liquids are weighed, to separate the waste from the material of worth. In some traditional listings, the body's skin is also ruled by Libra, since it also serves to keep the body fluids in balance.

Libra rules the kidneys & lumbar region

Kate Winslet
10/5/1975, 7:15 A.M.
Reading, UK

For years, Winslet was considered as a subject for the *Dell Horoscope* column, but she didn't seem to "fit the features of a triple Libra." This was before this author discovered the importance of Decans.

Sun, Moon and Ascendant: Libra

Winslet's Sun, Ascendant and Moon are respectively 10, 11 and 13 degrees—all in the second decan of Libra. The first decan presents the true essence of any Zodiac sign. The second decan (any degree from 10 to 19 degrees) alters the energies to reflect the next sign in the element's trilogy—in this case, Fixed Air. Thusly, Kate shows many of the traits and features associated with the bearer of focused light: Aquarius!

As demonstrated in her photos, Kate hints of the evenly proportioned facial lines illustrated in the Libra caricature. However, the funneling fixity of Aquarius also prevails. This gives her a large square skull, the delta between the brows and the nose—with its wide bridge, box-like tip and wide nostrils. Also, the cheek bones are drawn into the center, creating dimples high on the cheeks. The most noticeable difference is that her narrow, tightly drawn mouth. The wide smile of Libra is missing!

The upper photo captures Kate in her solar glow, as she projects the outward cardinal "push" of Air. The lower-left pic captures her surprised lunar reaction. The one to the right reveals a moment of neutral expression and the structural mask of her Ascendant. In all photos, the wide sweeping smile of Libra is missing, replaced by her rigid, tight lipped smile. The placement of her three key lights in the Aquarius decan alters the picture. The caricatures show the differences between the two.

Other Planetary Connections

Despite her huge fame in *Titanic*, Kate often chose to play in small "art house" films such as *Eternal Sunshine of the Spotless Mind, Quill* and *Iris*. (Blame this impulse on her Uranus' sextile to Venus). These roles lead to several deeper films, including 2008's *Revolutionary Road* and *The Reader*, which won her a Golden Globe, and her first Oscar.

Kate has six chart components in air signs, but Pluto conjoins her Sun, Moon and Ascendant. This accounts for her emotionally intense energy, as well as the mysterious and seductive scorpion qualities in her personality. This conjunction also impacts her appearance, as it locks in the fixed nature of her Aquarius Decans. It explains why the gentle breezes of Libra are rarely felt or seen.

In this portrait of a Libra with an Aquarius Ascendant, we see many of the features we observed in Kate Winslet.

Hilary Duff
9/28/1987, 3:56 A.M.
Houston, TX

Sun: Libra

In her title role in the Disney Channel's *Lizzie McGuire* (2001), Hilary Duff became a star at the age of 14. This successful TV show spawned *The Lizzie McGuire Movie* (2003). At the same time, Duff was storming the music charts with her top 40 singles "So Yesterday" and "Come Clean". Her first album "Metamorphosis" quickly ascended to #1 on the Billboard 200. *Rolling Stone Magazine* proclaimed her "Teenager of the Year" in 2003.

In he adolescence years, Duff pursued other films roles: *A Cinderella Story*, *The Perfect Man* and *Cheaper By The Dozen* (2005) were lightweight, family films that captured the vivacious and charming qualities of Duff's Libra Sun.

Physically, Duff shows the almond-shaped eyes and the wide smile of Libra. However, there's also the delta between the brows and the wide bridged nose, but the smile is not as pleasant, for it widens at the base, as it's pulled sharply downward. It's similar to what we saw in Kate Winslet. This can be attributed to Hilary's Aquarius Ascendant!

Ascendant: Aquarius

Look closely, and you will see marked similarities between these two ladies, notably in the skeletal structure. Both have the high set cheekbones and wide cubical chin and the wide shoulders of Aquarius. In Winslet, it is because of the Decans of her three key lights. With Duff, this structure is strong, because her Sun's only aspect is its trine to this fixed air Ascendant.

With this window to the world, Duff is involved in many altruistic and humanitarian projects. She served as the 2004 Official International Spokesperson for "Kids with a Cause", and has involved herself with various philanthropic activities, giving generous donations to the victims of Hurricane Katrina. This serving of humanitarian causes is emotionally supported by her Moon's conjunction to Uranus.

Moon: Sagittarius

It is in Duff's excitable reactions, where we see the greatest difference in the personalities of these two ladies.

Winslet is sultry, mysterious and reserved, for Pluto conjoins her three key lights. In contrast, Duff's Uranus conjoins her Centaur Moon—and this planet also trines Jupiter! Hilary's emotional reactions are whimsical and exuberant, and instantly projected out for all to see.

Hugh Jackman

10/12/1968, Time Unknown
Reading, UK

♎ Sun: Libra

Unlike our two introductory ladies, Hugh shows the well balanced facial features of Libra. (This may be why Jackman was placed on *People Magazine's Top-50 Beautiful People* five years in a role). Note how the lines run horizontally to form the wide-set almond eyes, the broad billowing smile and the V-shaped lines in the chin. (His birth time is unknown, but it is likely he does not have a fixed Ascendant).

Jackman is an accomplished singer and he won many awards (including a Tony). He also won a Golden Globe for his performance in the 2012 film version of *Les Misérables*, but he is best known for his role as Logan/Woverine in the four *X-Men* movies.

According to Hugh, he found it.... "difficult to summon up the rage and darkness of the character of Wolverine." He noted that once he found the tone, he said it was relatively easy to return to the role. This ability to identify with these "darker tones" likely comes from his Sun's ruler Venus' placement in Scorpio, and its sextile to Jupiter and Pluto.

Moon: Gemini

Notably, Hugh's Jupiter and Pluto are in mercuric Virgo, and they square his Mercury-ruled Moon. Mercury also conjoins Jack's Sun, and both of these components trine his Moon.

These multiple aspects give Jackman remarkable verbal skills. Pluto gives him a powerful other-worldly aura, while Jupiter brings a wide range of creative talents. Neptune's conjunction to his Venus contributes to his musical skills.

For those who have seen Jackman in unscripted moments, it is clear he has a heightened curiosity and a very aerated gift of gab. With his Libra Sun and Mercury trined his Gemini Moon, Hugh's solar and mental capacities run in synch with his airy "lunar memories". This gives Hugh an incredible memory!

When Jackman hosted the *Tony Awards* and *Saturday Night Live*, he memorized almost every line. He did it because he is terribly near-sighted and he struggled to read the cue cards.

Why the eyesight problem? Many say the Fixed Stars in the heavens and their placement in certain signs often suggest "physical irregularities". Notably, Hugh's Sun and Mercury are opposed by Saturn and the Fixed Star Vertex. Both are conjoined in Aries, the sign that rules the head and eyes. Saturn brings limitation, while Vertex portends eye weakness or blindness.

Kelly Ripa
10/2/1970, 5:23 A.M.
Stratford, NJ

Libra Sun & Moon

In 2011, Kelly replaced Regis Philben to become the new host of *Live!* This TV talk show was a perfect place for Kelly to present her charm and the gracious V-shaped smile.

Ripa's Sun and Moon's only aspect is their conjunction with Uranus. The spark of this planet is seen in her middle photo. There, the cardinal air spreads the almond-shaped eyes, as it drives them to shift from side to side to search for new ideas to explore. Kelly rarely expresses any of her deeper feelings.

Virgo Ascendant

Ripa's breezy persona is embellished by her Virgo mask. The obsession for details is enhanced by her Mercury, Mars and Pluto, which are also in Virgo. The lower photo shows how her mutable Rising Sign skews her bone structure. It has little of the balance shown in Fran's photo on the right.

Fran Drescher
9/30/1957, 7:28 A.M.
Flushing, NY

Libra Sun & Ascendant

In her hit TV show, Fran played *The Nanny*, a character who often took the side of every underdog who entered her life. Such actions can be expected from someone whose Uranus sextiles her Libra Sun, Ascendant and Jupiter!

In her career, this Libra pursued an array of offbeat diversions. The drive ran strong, since her three key lights are all in cardinal signs.

The upper photos show Libra's solar expression, but Fran's widely stretched horizontal eyes show what happens, when Cardinal Air finds an exhilarated state of expression.

Capricorn Moon

When Fran becomes emotional, the smooth lines of Libra harden, as her cheek bones rise to form the solemn image of a goat. It was in these lunar emotional outbursts that Fran would erupt with her famous and abrasive nasal laugh—the one that mimicked the bleating cry of a goat!

With her tenacious Capricorn Moon (and all of her components on the left side of her chart) Drescher was more than just a star. She was the producer of most of her projects.

Gwyneth Paltrow
9/27/1972, 5:25 P.M.
Los Angeles, CA

♎ Sun: Libra

Raised by two successful theatrical parents, Paltrow established herself as a star early in life, as she quickly achieved a sophistication atypical for thespians of her generation. This charm and poise was aided by her Libra Sun.

In many of Gwyneth's mannerisms, we see the weighing action of Libra. Most of the time, the weather appears markedly calm, but underneath the storms seem to be constantly churning. Paltrow's mutable Moon trines her Sun, as it conjoins her Mars and Pluto. These latter three components sextile her Neptune in Sagittarius, and they also square her Jupiter in Capricorn.

Moon in Gemini

With her Sun conjoined Mercury and Uranus (and all three trine her Moon), Paltrow's mercuric emotions fly all over the place. These swirling emotions are often prone to surprising interruptions. In these emotional moments, Paltrow's hands cease to teeter to the sides. Rather, they are waving out front in a Mobius pattern. The winged messenger has taken over flight control!

Just recall Paltrow's scattered "litany of words" when she received her Academy Award in 1999. Her Gemini reactions were so excited, there wasn't enough time to express all the words that were running through her head.

The LR photo shows how the mutable forces in these lunar moments skew the balanced lineage in her face. These mutable patterns are enhanced by her Moon's opposition to Neptune, the ruler of her Pisces' Ascendant.

Ascendant: Pisces

Interestingly, Paltrow's Neptune and Moon also forms a T-square with her Ascendant. Thusly, her airy luminaries quickly become a part of the frontal presence, that she displays to the world.

When the winds of Paltrow's Sun and Moon recede, the air pressure lowers, as the moisturized front of her Ascendant moves in, to fill the void. This rounds Gwyneth's flesh, as it turns her eyes into deep pools of water. Caught in the liquid net of her Pisces Ascendant, Paltrow's hands no loner flutter about. Rather, they appear to be engaged in the act of swimming.

Through this Pisces window, Gwyneth senses and feels the rhythmic patterns in her surroundings. This gave her the talent to create the accents and dialects in *Shakesphere in Love*, the film that won her an Oscar for Best Actress.

The Ignition of Fire turns up the heat!
John Lennon
10/9/1940, 6:30 P.M.
Liverpool, UK

"All we are saying is give peace a chance."

 Sun: Libra

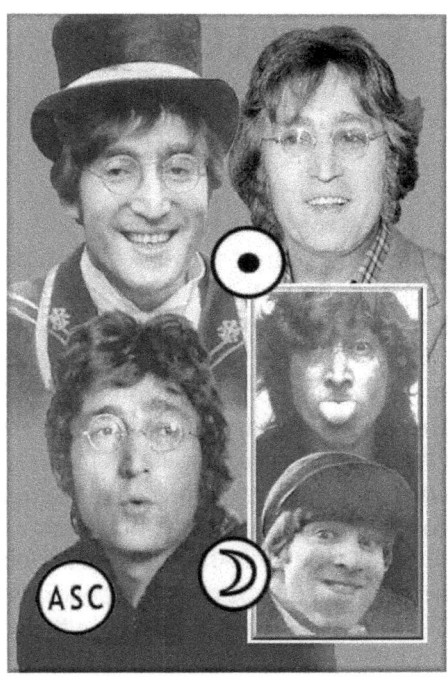

John Lennon's chart indicated that he would have "a lackadaisical sense of self". That is odd for someone who become one of the most "self-actualized" individuals in his generation. Let's explain:

With his Libra Sun, Lennon was highly capable of seeing, analyzing and judging the behavior of others. However, as his often untidy appearance suggested, he rarely directed his attentions on himself.

This is due to the fact that his Sun had no aspects—save for its inconjunction to a Saturn/Jupiter conjunction in Taurus—and its snug opposition to his Rising Sign! This placed his solar light in the background "on the other side", where it was busily relating to "other things".

John's solar light was seen and heard in his words and music. All of this was empowered by the aspects of his Moon.

Aquarius Moon

John's Uranus-ruled Aquarius Moon forms a grand trine with Uranus and the previously noted Neptune/Mars conjunction. Also, this Moon is opposed by Pluto and T-squared by Mercury. Mercury opposes a Jupiter/Saturn conjunction in Taurus. These incredible lunar aspects gave John a brilliant mind and a very active and inventive imagination. He was able to invent the powerful *Mind Games* that inspired others to join him, to create a more peaceful world!

In the '70's anti-war movement, John became a reluctant leader. In his 1969 "Bed-In for Peace with Yoko Ono", we saw the not-so-aggressive action you'd expect from a Libra Sun, with a Libra Mars conjoins his Neptune.

Another factor was that John's Moon and Mercury were the only components in the top half of his chart. Still, people expected him to "lead the charge" since they were seeing the fiery and martial mask of his Aries Ascendant.

Aries Rising

Lennon's Jupiter Saturn, Jupiter and Uranus are all in his 1st House—signs that suggest he would be a spokesman for a generation.

Physically, this mask vertically stretches the normally well proportioned features of Libra. This gave John the raised eyebrows, the large snout, the tall upper lip plate and the prominent chin—all features often seen in a Ram!

Christopher Reeve

9/24/1952, 3:12 A.M.
New York, NY

Sun: Libra

Fate takes strange turns. A life can be charmed, then stricken with adversity. Both test a person's character.

In 1977, with his charming Libra smile, Reeve won the coveted role of *Superman*. The last thing they wanted was an aggressive, war-like hero. They wanted someone who had a strong, commanding presence but also a twinkle in the eye. After all, comic book heroes shouldn't be taken too seriously. Reeve's chart reflected these qualities.

Chris had his Sun and four other planets in Libra. With these highly directed cardinal energies, he quickly moved beyond his "super role" which ended in 1987. It was time to reach out and play a diverse range of roles—from the periodical *Remains of The Day* to the farcical *Switching Channels*. He also found expression as a film director and an environmental spokesman.

Ascendant: Leo

As noted earlier, the creators of *Superman* needed someone with a commanding presence. Of course, they hired someone with Leo rising! This sign beams with confidence—as it presents its aura of royalty! Also, Pluto's conjunction on his Ascendant gave Reeve the stature of a powerful Lion. Pluto's darker side was seen in Reeve's films *Deathtrap* and *Street Smart*.

Then, there was the twist of fate—the tragic 1995 accident that left Chris paralysed from the neck down. Oddly, Chris' South Node's conjoins Pluto on his Ascendant. This implies that his physical body would be restricted, so that he could serve others through his 7th House North Node. Bravely, until his death, Reeve used his remaining strength to galvanize research in "nerve regeneration". This Plutonian medical research unveiled valuable lessons to serve mankind.

Moon: Sagittarius

Even with this tragedy, Chris reflected the ever optimistic glow of his Centaur Moon. In a 2011 interview on *"The Late Show"*, he constantly referred to his luck: "I have so many privileges and such good help.... I'm very lucky I can make a difference."

With his Centaur Moon conjoined his Mars, Reeve was a lover of sports, horses, the outdoors, as well as his unbridled enthusiasm. Even with his condition, Chris showed how the mind and spirit can soar, even when the body is immobile. Christopher Reeve showed the strength of a true hero.

James Caviezel

9/26/1968, 11:14 A.M.
Mt. Vernon, WA

 Sun: Libra

James' first lead role was in the movie *Frequency*, where he played a son who communicated with his deceased father on an old ham radio. This film was followed by *Deja Vue* (another time travel film) and *Outlander*. These films all contain the otherworldly Sci-fi themes that we associate with Uranus—the planet that conjoins James' Sun, Pluto and Jupiter! These Uranian aspects also contribute to James' charismatic nature, his strong moral and religious beliefs and his willingness to take on unorthodox roles.

When James projects the cardinal air of his Libra Sun, his eyes sparkle as the lines in the face stretch horizontally to form the broad billowing smile. This pleasant image contradicts James' public persona.

Ascendant: Scorpio

James breakthrough film was *The Passion of the Christ*. In this role, he conveyed the ideals of "The Prince of Peace" as well as the brutal nature of humanity. With Scorpio Rising, these disturbing realities are readily examined in much of the work that he presents to the world.

In his popular 2011-14 TV program *Person of Interest*, James played a highly controlled ex-spy and agent. Pluto's sextile to his Ascendant enables James to present this unflappable persona. However, Neptune also conjoins his Scorpio Ascendant, and it's in the decadent of Pisces decadent. This softens his hard Scorpio edges, as it infuses the dreamy qualities of Pisces into his appearance. These compassionate sensitivities were apparent in his work in *The Thin Red Line*, *Stoning of Soraya M.* and in the previously mentioned *Frequency*.

Moon: Sagittarius

James appears strong and muscular, but as we've seen in *The Count of Monte Cristo*, and in his TV series, he also is athletically skilled.

With his Sagittarius Moon and Mars at the top of his chart, James dreamed of becoming a professional NBA player. However, a foot injury turned him towards acting. Fortunately, with that Neptune conjunction to his Moon and Ascendant, he has a gift for expressing his emotions, as well as athletic abilities.

Note how James' Centurion reactions skew his facial features and how the top lip twists up on one side, to mock the shape of a horse's mouth.

Tim Robbins
10/16/1958, 2:12 A.M.
West Covina, CA

♎ Sun: Libra

The balancing forces of Libra are seen in Tim's solar expressions. Sometimes, as seen in the UL photo, the calm demeanor shows little outward motion. At other times (as the UR photo shows), the face is activated as the cardinal forces, as they gently shift the facial elements—to keep every expression in perfect balanced.

With this constant redirection, many Libras appear indecisive and ineffectual. However, Robbins has his Sun on his North Node and nine of his components on the left side of his chart. He is karmically driven to pursue a defined course of action. With Saturn sextile his Sun and its ruling planet Venus (and Mars in Gemini), Tim's Cardinal Air become highly political and rich with social commentary. This LIbra is a mover and a shaker-upper!

As we saw in his satirical *Bob Roberts* and his provocative *Dead Man Walking*, Robbins uses the full range of his Libra mental gifts—creating his art, not only by acting, but by also being the writer and director of these films.

Ascendant: Virgo

With a Virgo Ascendant, Robbins sees his surroundings as being filled with workable solutions and opportunities —all to be of service to others. With Pluto on this Ascendant, this window often presents an imperfect and disturbing view of the world. Positively, it shields his Sun's tendency to worry.

This grounded mask was masterfully expressed in Tim's role as the inmate in the film *Shawshank Redemption*. There, he diligently served as the warden's accountant, as he meticulously orchestrated his long range "plan of escape".

Even though Tim's birth time is uncertain, his demeanor in this film strongly supports the probability that he has Virgo rising.

Moon: Sagittarius

In reactive moments, Tim's Sagittarius Moon breaks through his crystalline persona, igniting his personality with an expansive and humorous energy. This Moon opposes his Mars, conjoins Saturn and trines Uranus. Mars activates and electrifies his lunar emotions. Uranus' connection adds a spark of quirkiness, as Saturn adds a tone of seriousness. When these lunar energies glow, one side of the face lifts up some distance from the other. This injection of mutable fire also makes his gestures more animated.

The addition of Earth stills the winds
Matt Damon
10/8/1970, 3:22 P.M.
Boston, MA

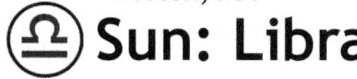 Sun: Libra

Matt Damon shows the easy going nature of Libra, but there is an extra sense of calmness here, for Venus (the ruling planet of Libra) conjoins Neptune on Damon's Midheaven.

For a double Air Sign, Damon is surprisingly reserved and grounded. His Moon and Mars are in Earth signs and they sextile Venus and Neptune in Scorpio. As we saw in *The Martian* and *Oceans Eleven*, Matt rarely gets excited. His airy nature appears well contained.

However, this restrained force escapes its grip, when Matt's expansive Libra smile appears. As the UR photo shows, when these cardinal winds of Libra accelerate, they stretch the mouth and eyes sharply off to each side.

Matt's Moon also adds a serious demeanor to his personality, notably when he encounters emotionally dire situations. These stoney reactions are enhanced by Saturn's trine to his Moon.

Moon: Capricorn

With their lethargic natures, Libras are pleasantly plump. With a grand Earth trine between his Capricorn Moon, Taurus Saturn and Virgo Mars, Matt's physique is more solid and muscular.

Matt's Mars also conjoins Pluto—and this powerful planet makes harmonious aspects to four of his other components! This gives Matt the emotional discipline and determination to rebuild himself into "the physical condition", he will need to play any role. With his Mars and Pluto in Virgo, he has been able to make these phenomenal physical changes. In *Courage Under Fire*, Matt lost 40 pounds to portray his emaciated character. Later, he buffed himself up for his roles in *The Talented Mr. Ripley* and his multiple *Bourne* identities.

Aquarius Rising

When Matt's cardinal luminaries dim, the friendly smile and serious emotions disappear, as he locks into the distantly focused persona of his Aquarius mask. This other-worldly connection runs strong, since Aquarius' ruling planet Uranus conjoins Matt's Sun.

With this fixed air, the creative mental impulses of his airy Sun become markedly inventive. This intuitive spark likely contributed to the creation of the script for *Good Will Hunting* (which Damon co-wrote with his friend Ben Affleck). This insightful work won the Oscar for *Best Original Screenplay* in 1997.

Uranus also explains Matt's attraction to highly technical and futuristic dramas like *Interstellar* and *The Martian*.

Susan Sarandon
10/4/1946, 2:25 P.M.
New York, NY

♎ Sun: Libra

With Venus on her Midheaven, Susan shows the world the sensual and pleasant qualities of her Venus-ruled Libra Sun. This sugary, cream-puff image is seen in most ex-models (and a lot of Libras). Susan also has Libra's insatiable drive to creative justice and fairness in the world. Like with **John Lennon** (another Libra with a Capricorn Moon), Susan is also a social activist.

Susan has five components in cardinal signs and this drives her to excel in her work as well as correct the imbalances in the social scales.

Susan first attracted a following as the cheerful suburbanite in *The Rocky Horror Picture Show* and followed with the provocative films *Pretty Baby* and *The Hunger*. Her gift for playing characters (who were caught up in greater turns of events) was also seen in *Atlantic City*. In this role, she received her first Oscar nod, playing a hapless casino worker.

Physically, Susan exhibits many of Libra's evenly proportioned features, but unlike most Libras, Susan does not have Libra's almond-shaped eyes. Her eyes are round and full, and they reflect the dreamy depths of water. Neptune conjoins her Sun! Hints of Pisces are seen in her appearance.

Ascendant & Moon: Capricorn

Sarandon's career seemed to magically progress ever more rapidly, as she becomes older. With a Capricorn Moon and Ascendant and Saturn conjoined Pluto, it's no surprise that this lady has the gift of improving with time—all so gracefully! When she entered her 40's, she turned the tables and successfully portrayed the rare roles of seductive older women in *White Palace* and *Bull Durham*. Then came *Thelma & Louise*, *Lorenso's Oil* and *The Client*—and three more Oscar nominations! Her creative powers reached a new high in 1995 with *Dead Man Walking*, a film directed by her Libra ex-companion Tim Robbins. On this film, Saturn rewarded Susan with her second Oscar for Best Actress!

Physically, Susan's Ascendant gives her the wide and high-placed cheek bones. This mask gives her the stolid presence of a goat. With her Moon conjoined the Ascendant, her emotions are quickly planted on the surface—and then "held in suspension", to reinforce her stoney and rigid persona.

This presence of Capricorn makes Susan appear emotionally cold and solemn. Positively, since it is the only Earth in her chart, it keeps her grounded, and it gives her an aura of authority.

Sigourney Weaver
10/8/1949, 6:15 P.M.
New York, NY

 ## Sun: Libra

In her roles in the comedy/drama *Dave* and in the original *Ghostbusters*. Weaver's curt one-liners showed how the breezy push of Cardinal Air could break through any wall of resistance. Still, there is something unique about Weaver's energy. There's little of the flighty and indecisive qualities of Libra, rather there's also a powerful and calm resilience that seems to get stronger then she is encountered by threatening forces. This was clearly seen in Weaver's legendary role as Ripley in the *Alien* films.

This unflappability is a product of Weaver's Venus, the ruler of her Sun, Moon and Ascendant. As you'd expect, her Venus is in Scorpio! In addition, Pluto conjoins her natal Mars in Leo and both planets sextile her Sun. This gives her an ability to physically display an aura of power. She is one tough lady. It is not what we'd expect from Libra!

In contrast, Weaver's personality regularly takes on a doe-like gentleness. Like **Susan Sarandon**, Weaver has Neptune conjoined her Sun. This serene nature is enhanced by her two key Venus-ruled Taurus components.

Ascendant & Moon: Taurus

With a Taurus Ascendant and Moon, Venus finds its earthy expression, as it gives Weaver a sensual and solid physical presence—and a stubborn, emotional makeup! This was seen In *Gorillas in The Mist*, as she displayed Taurus' obsessive nature, playing a primatologist, who was consumed, even love-struck, with her sensual simian friends.

This Ascendant places Capricorn on Weaver's Midheaven—suggesting that she would find success portraying steely cold and tenacious women. We saw it in her role in *Working Girl*, where she played a snooty and greedy executive. Notably, her image of unyielding strength was so recognized, she was hired to do ads for a Japanese steel company.

Notably, Jupiter is also in Weaver's 10th House and it sextiles her Venus. Even with this rather cool Capricorn public image, Weaver rejects such highly serious ambitions, claiming: "I think Al Pacino is a great actor, but I'd rather work with Kevin Kline or Bill Murray any day". There, Weaver follows her Venusian urges, creating thoughtful and light hearted comedies. Though she can show a "heart of steel", this Venus Goddess believes that life should be filled with joy and pleasure.

Water moisturizes the other elements
Libra Suns

The upper photos capture the light and airy expressions we'd expect from Libra Suns. However, here we have another opportunity to show how this solar light is altered by the Ascendant and Moon. This task is made easier, since both have their Moon and Ascendant in the same mode—and one for each is in water.

Yo-Yo Ma
Cancer Moon
Aries Ascendant
10/7/1955/6:00 P.M. Paris, France

Renowned cellist Yo-Yo Ma is a triple cardinal sign. Thusly, his personality components all appear to be moving in different directions.

With his Libra Sun, the forces appear to be moving in a horizontal direction. The photo clearly shows this trait.

With his Cancer Moon, the lunar tides bring in a gush of water. It rounds the face as it alters the direction in his body's stance. Here, Yo-Yo appears to be looking up from the bottom of the sea, as he gently moves with the tidal rhythms.

Yo-Yo's Ascendant is Aries, the sign that opposes Libra. In contrast to the horizontal push of Libra, Aries drives the cardinal force vertically and in a frontal direction. This pushes the forehead sharply to the back, as it instills the convex features and long jaw of a Ram.

Jason Alexander
Gemini Moon
Pisces Ascendant
9/23/1959, 6:04 P.M. Newark, NJ

Jason is known for his role as George Costanza in TV's *Seinfeld*. In this show, Jason's character humorously displayed the indecisive nature of Libra. With his mutable lunar and ascending lights, this wavering quality was made even more obvious.

Like **Gwyneth Paltrow**, Jason has a Gemini Moon and a Pisces Ascendant. In both of their emotional moments, their Moons divide their solar lights—as they spiral them in two directions. However, Paltrow's emotions are more stable, since Saturn conjoins her Moon.

When Jason's bewildered Pisces mask appears, the flesh sags as it hangs on to the underlying skeletal structure. This sculpts the flesh into in an array of obtuse and irregular patterns. Notably, Saturn's placement on his MC and its sextile to Neptune lowers the water pressure. Jason lacks the large and deep-pooled eyes, often seen in Pisces.

Bruno Mars
(Peter Gene Hernandez)
10/8/1985, 3:56 P.M. Waikiki, HA

Bruno Mars' career began as a member of a record producing/song writing team that created tunes for other stars (including Cee-Lo Green). They were named the "Biggest Songwriters of 2010" by *Music Week* magazine. In that same year, Bruno's first album *Doo-Wops & Hooligans* was completed with the help of his creative team. It made him a star!

Many of us were introduced to Mars' music at the 2015 Super Bowl, where he performed, showing his dynamic flare of Fire, his delightful mix of lyrics (Air) and the inspiring rhythms of Water.

Sun in Libra

Bruno's airy Libra Sun accounts for his need to create ideas and collaborate with others. These easy-going energies also explain why his music shows little of the aggression we'd expect in hip-hop. It became what some called "friendly-pop".

On his first album, the relaxed lights of Libra shined in his sleepy tune: *The Lazy Song*. The album also contained his hit homage to Venus: *Just The Way You Are*—a song in which we heard Bruno's high-pitched, airy and breathy voice, as well as the soothing, loving and melodic tones of Libra. Bruno also displays many of the regular physical features of Libra.

Moon in Leo

Youngsters with Leo Moons are often theatrical and desirous of attracting the attention of others. These lion impulses drove Bruno to perform at a very young age. There are some delightful videos on the internet of Bruno strutting on stage. One at just the age of four!

Bruno's Leo Moon beams in his performances, as it adds a flare of elegance to his show. It may also account for his many hats, which proudly serve as his emotional crown.

You'll see a hint of fixed fire, when Bruno struts onto the stage to preen and pose for his fans. However, these attention seeking desires of Leo quickly recede, as his Libra shifts attention to the other members of his band—so that they can share in the spotlight too. This consideration for others is enhanced by Bruno's compassionate and sensitive Ascendant.

Ascendant: Pisces

Bruno's Pisces Ascendant accounts for his dreamy and other-worldly appearance —a look accented by his large dreamy eyes and skewed facial expressions.

Bruno's astrological gifts give him an ability to bring people together, to share in his array of international and historical musical offerings. It is, as NPR music critic Ann Powers stated: "A part of the art that offers humanity....a glimpse of a better world, or at least a happier one." With this Pisces mask, Bruno presents to the world the joy that inspires people to dance together in harmony.

Deepak Chopra

10/22/1946, 3:46 P.M.
New Delhi, India

♎ Sun: Libra

In *The Book of Secrets*, Chopra states: "...wherever consciousness wants to go, the human brain will follow."

Chopra's teachings often describe such mental dynamics, as the cardinal air of his Sun weights the differences between body, mind and spirit.

With his Libra Sun in the 8th House (conjoined Jupiter) and his Mars conjoined Mercury (in Scorpio)—Chopra reveals life's magical secrets! With Pluto is in his 6th House of Health, he also has remarkable insights into healing.

Venus is the ruler of Deepak's Sun and it is placed in Sagittarius—and in the 9th House to boot! Thusly, his work aims to expand the minds of others into higher states of consciousness. With his Libra Sun's calm demeanor, Deepak attempts to recreate the balance that he sees in the wholeness of Spirit.

Ascendant: Pisces

Chopra believes: "When our thoughts, actions and feelings fuse in the one reality of Spirit, we can experience the flow of life without obstacles or resistance."

Chopra is seeing this idealized view of universal patterns through the window of his Pisces Ascendant. In reverse, this compassionate mask allows him to present these magical Pisces realities and illusions out to others.

Like Pisces **Edgar Caycee** and Leo **J. K. Rowling**, Chopra's Ascendant places most of his planets on the right side of his chart. Deepak also is not self-driven, rather he is guided by greater forces beyond his control. Chopra's only left hemisphere planet is Uranus. This planet of "Enlightenment" rests in his 3rd House near the 4th House gate. This planet guides him into the other side as it activates his intuition.

Moon: Virgo

With his watery window to the world, Chopra senses and feels the connections between all things. However, with a Virgo Moon, his gut emotional reaction is to question and rationalize the truth behind these feelings. The end result is often a complex examination, often filled with the smallest of details.

You can see Chopra's lunar emotions when he responds in his Q&A sessions. When challenged, he becomes noticeably nervous and mercuric. However, the message rings true, for his other components give him the patience and compassion to communicate the lessons, that will serve the emotional and spiritual health of others!

Paul Simon
10/13/1941, 2:33 A.M.,
Newark, N.J.

"...the people bowed and prayed, to the Neon God they made."

 Sun: Libra

Paul Simon, like John Lennon has Neptune trining Uranus, and both of their Venuses also form hard aspects to this planet. This accounts for their highly intuitive imaginations and abilities to "reach out" in their creative work.

Lennon's Uranus was in his 1st House, so his intuition drove him to "alter the attitudes of individuals." Simon's Uranus is in his ninth House, opposing his Sagittarius Venus. His work is more philosophical and multi-cultural in scope. I.E., he is intuitively inspired to communicate *The Rhythm of the Saints.*

Unlike Lennon, Paul's Mars does not conjoin Uranus—Saturn does! Paul's revolutionary sparks are far more restrained, and far less militant.

Cancer Moon

Paul's Cancer Moon forms a T-square with his Libra Sun and his Aries Mars. With his mellow Sun in opposition and his lunar tides pulling these martial forces off to the side, Simon shows little of the aggressiveness of an Aries Mars. Positively, this "drive in three directions" impelled Simon to produce a massive output of work.

In his emotional moments, Simon's face and temples swell and round. This creates a shape that resembled the shell of a crab, as the swelled flesh made the broad cherub cheeks of Libra ever more apparent. This watery presence also gives him a soft and melodic voice.

Virgo Ascendant

Another factor is Paul's earthy Virgo Ascendant. This mercuric persona accounts for Paul's obsession with perfection and his tidy and meticulous appearance. (Unlike the scruffy Lennon, Simon often wore a neatly pressed turtle neck or some form of suit).

When Paul's Sun is not stretching his face into "horizontal equilibrium", what we see is the oblong and angled shape of the underlying mutable bone structure. This places one eye higher than the other, as it sends the jowly jaw jutting off to the side. Noticeably, the hard edges of Earth are softened by the presence of dreamy Neptune in his 1st House.

Paul's gift for poetic words can be likely attributed to his 3rd House Mercury and its trine to his Cancer Moon. This enables him to and feel (and then communicate) the spiritual messages of his Sagittarius Venus.

Julie Andrews

10/1/1935, 6:00 AM
Walton on the Thames, England

♎ Sun: Libra

This British singer was the original Eliza in the stage performance of *My Fair Lady*. As the fairest of the fair, she brought our lives into balance with her grace, beauty, and gift for song. In *The Sound of Music*, good feelings abounded. In *The Americanization Of Emily*, love prevailed over cultural differences. In *Mary Poppins*, there was magic in the air and it was "lover-ly."

When her Sun radiates, Julie seems to tranquilize her audience. Her arrival in any scene calms the air as those soft-lit eyes, that broad, friendly smile and her soothing voice leave us feeling incredibly content. This is Libra's expression at its finest.

Ascendant: Virgo

Early in her career, Julies starred in many family friendly films, presenting her squeaky clean and fastidious image to the world. What we saw was the virginal mask of Julie's Virgo Ascendant.

In *Mary Poppins*, we saw a conservatively dressed nanny, with her high collared Victorian gown. Her bonnet and an umbrella added to the prissy image. This character would also fuss and analyze over every detail, as her Libra Sun attempted to keep things in harmonious balance.

Moon: Scorpio

Something is rotten in *Camelot*! With the beginning of 1980, the goodie two-shoes image was palling as Pluto left Julie's 1st House. When Pluto transits any House cusp, expect transformation!

In 1980, Julie began work on *S.O.B.*, sending shock waves as she bared her breasts. The next year, she went out on the edge again, playing a cross-sexual role in the film *Victor Victoria*.

This cathartic departure turned off many of Julie's stodgy fans, but it also revealed what most of us sensed all along—this lady is a strong willed and powerfully determined woman!

When Julie becomes emotional, her sparkling Libra eyes transform into the deeply focused eyes of an eagle. But, unlike other Scorpio Moons, Julie's eagle eyes are not so disturbing—for her Moon is conjoined by jovial Jupiter! There are no secrets to hide, for this emotionally optimistic lady is always willing to share her feelings with others.

When this lady communicates her cheery Libra ideas, this Moon serves a valuable purpose. There are few sugary solutions here, for her feelings are transforming her ideas, so that they can have real value and worth!

Michael Douglas

9/25/1944, 10:30 A.M.
New Brunswick, NJ

Neptune rules the Cinema

From 1942 to 1955, Neptune (the ruler of motion pictures) was in Libra. Films in this era gave us easy-going stars like Jimmy Stewart and Shirley Black.

In 1956, when Neptune entered Scorpio, *The Manchurian Candidate* exposed the evils of "brain washing". In the 70's, when Neptune moved into philosophical Sagittarius, Michael began his career as a producer, creating the provoking film: *One Flew Over The Cuckoo's Nest,* a film that questioned who is really insane. This Centaur period ended with Michael's two adventurous comedies: *Romancing the Stone* and *Jewel of the Nile*—two films about a writer (played by Kathleen Turner) who creates a fantasy world within her head.

In 1984, when Neptune entered the sign of Capricorn, many films became suddenly serious. In this era, Douglas created his biting salute to greed—the film: *Wall Street.*

Positively, Michael uses his lunar energies to succeed in a very complex and costly business. This Libra knows what ideas appeal to the public. With his Moon in the 2nd House and his Midheaven in Leo, Michael had a gift for producing financially successful films.

Sun in Libra

Michael's Neptune is in Libra and it conjoins his Sun. Mars is also in Libra and it trines Uranus in Gemini. The breezes of air run strong. We see it in his sparkling almond eyes and in the banter he freely presents to others.

Moon: Capricorn

In *Wall Street*, Michael's Moon cast a somber shadow when he uttered the words "Greed is good." In *Falling Down*, he played a recluse who (in his reaction to the world) becomes progressively colder, while failing to recognize the carnage he had created. This is the negative side of a Capricorn Moon.

Ascendant: Scorpio

When the cardinal forces subside, Michael's cherubic cheeks deflate, as they reveal the substructure below the surface. Magically, an intense presence fixes and forms, when Scorpio rises!

Through this window, Michael sees the darker obsessions in human nature. We saw them in his films: *Disclosure, Fatal Attraction* and *Basic Instinct.* In *The War of the Roses*, Michael showed us what happens when the reasoning element of Libra is consumed by Scorpio's need for control. In this film, he revealed how things become deadly, when people refuse to compromise.

Will Smith
9/25/1968, 1:46 A.M.
Philadelphia, PA

Sun in Libra

Will Smith was the successful musical performer named "Fresh Prince". His work soon became the center piece of the TV show *Fresh Prince of Bel-Air*. There, Smith introduced his edgy music with the charm of his Libra Sun. Some say this show made the genre of "rap music" acceptable across America.

When the cardinal force of Smith's Libra turns on, his face aligns into evenly proportioned arrangements. Still, the face is not quite in balance, for Smith has Mar, Jupiter, Uranus and Pluto clustered together in the mutable sign of Virgo—and that quirky Uranus conjoins his Sun!

This massive Virgo gives Smith his analytical verbal skills. His Virgo Mars accounts for his nervous and mercuric physical movements. Uranus explains Smith's impulsive energy and why he is attracted to Sci-Fi roles like *I-Robot*, *Independence Day* and those outrageous *Men in Black* movies.

Ascendant: Leo

There was no birth time when Smith's "Snapshot" was completed in 2002. His Rising Sign was unknown, but this author concluded it might be Leo.

This was based on Smith's hammy and theatrical persona in *Fresh Prince of Bel-Air* and the fact that Smith often entered the room with the flamboyant strut of a lion. It was a tough call, since Pluto conjoined Will's Uranus and he had a fixed Moon—but it was correct!

Will's new birth time also shows that his Leo Ascendant trines Neptune, a common aspect for movie stars with musical talents.

Moon: Scorpio

When the analytical breezes still, Will's Scorpio Moon reflects its dark shadow. In this dim light, Will's eyes become focused and intense, as the head tilts forward, arching the upper back. These fixed forces also keep Smith's creative forces in control!

Control was not there during the filming of 1999's *Wild, Wild West*, when Smith's "Leo demands" became overbearing. Also, his performance was criticized; the film was a box office dud.

Fortunately, the experience brought maturity, as it inspired Smith to do more serious work. Shortly after, he starred in the film *Ali* and followed that as the producer and star of *In Pursuit of Happiness*. Both films brought him rave reviews and Oscar nominations. Shortly after, *Newsweek Magazine* named Smith: "The most powerful actor in Hollywood".

The power of Scorpio is examined in the next series of Portraits.

♏ Scorpio

	Page
Introduction to Scorpio	239-241

Body language of Neil Young, Grace Kelly, Ed Asner and Michael Dukakis

The breezes of Air run strong

Whoppi Goldberg	242
Leonardo DeCapiro	243
Emma Stone	244-245
Roseanne Barr	246

The addition of Water raises the humidity

Condoleezza Rice	247

Earth contains the Water

Matthew McConaughey	248
Ryan Gosling	249
Walter Cronkite & Dan Rather	250
Joni Mitchell & K.D. Lang	251

Ignite the Fire

Martin Scorcese	252
Maria Shriver	253
Bill Gates	254
Julia Roberts	255

Feed the Fire with Air and stir the flames

Goldie Hawn	256
Ann Hathaway	257
Jodie Foster	258-259
Danny DeVito	260

Scorpio ♏ October 23 to November 21

Hold on to what is meaningful, with your Scorpio friends!

Feminine Polarity, Fixed Water

In the middle of the Fall season, the life force has gone on hold. The leafs have fallen from the trees and the grass has turned to brown. In this dimming light, the actions of **Libra** have helped us to evaluate what is valuable, and which of Nature's offerings will be needed, to help us through the long Winter nights.

In times of scarcity, the natural impulse is to "hold on to all possessions", even those that may prove to be burdensome. That is why you need to call a **Scorpio**, to determine which of these physical and emotional attachments need to be discarded. Only then, will you be free—to fly away on the wings of the Eagle!

You'll likely find these mysterious souls in your town's secretive gathering spot, the one that has heavily-framed furniture, deep red drapes and darkly colored walls. The atmosphere is misty and damp. You have entered a den of Scorpions!

In that room, you will be surprised that there's little chatter. Rather, the conversations are deliberate and focused. Look closely and you will see that many of these folks are intensely observing the other people in the room—deeply probing the nature of their feelings—so that they can determine the intent of their actions. (Perhaps that is why Mars used to be the feminine ruler of Scorpio?)

What is surprising about this group is how quickly they make their collective decisions. Why not? The true intents of everyone in the group have been exposed. "The Bull Shit has been transcended!" When truth is revealed, there are no secrets—and powerful transformations materialize.

Enlightened Scorpions know that these powerful insights only come to those who understand the meaning of the 12 steps in Nature's creative process. This divine wisdom is presented by **Sagittarius**, the next sign in the Zodiac.

♇ Rulerships & Associations for Scorpio

In ancient times, Mars was the ruling planet of masculine Aries, while Scorpio was assigned to be the ruler of the feminine side. With the discovery of the planet Pluto, astrologers found a new ruler for Scorpio—and a "long range" wave cycle to cover multi-generational interpretations. Some have noted that, since Pluto was the last planet in our solar system, it represents the totality of life cycles within this cosmic egg—i.e., sex and reproduction, birth, death, the after life and the transformations that occur throughout all time.

Scorpio is associated with hypnosis, hidden underworld forces, and catastrophic transformations (eruptions and earthquakes). Positively, it represents how we transcend physical limits by replicating our will and creative desires into other forms: children, writings, art, government, etc.

Careers for Scorpios include psychiatrists, detectives, police and military work, and psychic and spiritual healers. Many of the world's best surgeons are Scorpios.

Scorpio Physical Traits:

Scorpio's emotions are held deeply within, as they hide their feelings from the eyes of others. This sense of secrecy is seen in their anchored and hypnotic eyes. When you see a red light, glowing within these purple eyes, you know a secret will soon be revealed.

This internal focus affects Scorpio's physical appearance, as its forms the Scorpion's markedly square skeletal structure and molds the facial flesh into cubical blocks.

Note the wide rectangle plate on the forehead, the squarely set (and bushy) brows, the Eagle's beak, the broad and flat cheekbones, and the protruding ears with their large dangling lobes.

Scorpio Body Language
Scorpio rules the Pelvic Area & Reproductive Organs

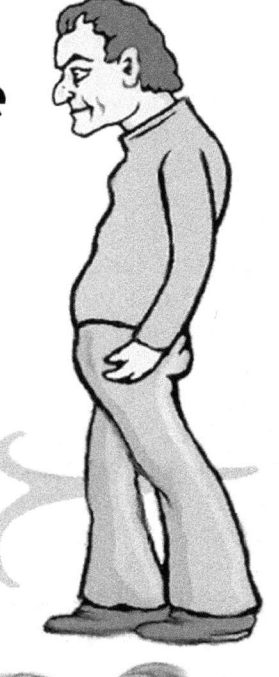

With Libra, the body was in perfect balance. Now, with Scorpio, the rulership progresses down into the lower pelvic area, the area where the toxic waste from Libra's kidneys are eliminated. Scorpio is also the ruler of the genitalia and reproduction organs.

The focus of power in this part of the body draws the pelvic region to the front. This tilts the upper spine sharply to the back. To compensate, the upper shoulders, neck and head jut sharply to the front— to create the profile of an eagle!

Watch how the heavy arms appear to flap slowly, as the Scorpion slithers steadily forward. This movement suggests that these arms are the feathered wings, that will soon will lift these creatures upward in magical flight. Since the forces are fixed and contained, the body language of a Scorpio may be the easiest to detect.

Neil Young, Grace Kelly and *Ed Asner* have Scorpio Suns and Ascendants. *Neil* best demonstrates how the flat back of the skull sweeps to the front. All four share the body language seen in the profile photo of Scorpio Sun *Michael Dukakis*. He shows us how the forward trust of the pelvis tilts the upper torso to the back, and how this tilts the neck and head sharply to the front.

Check the internet for birth data on on these celebrities.

Whoopi Goldberg

11/13/1955, 12:48 P.M.
New York, NY

Sun and Moon in Scorpio

Scorpio powers run strong with this lady. As co-host on TV's *The View*, Whoppi earned a reputation of saying "what she feels". Why not? Her Sun and Moon are both in Scorpio. This allows her to use her solar expressions and lunar reactions to reveal the nasty secrets, that others often try to ignore.

With her Sun in the 9th House (conjunct Saturn) and her Sagittarius Venus on the Midheaven, Whoopi uses comedy to lite up the dark side of reality. With her Sun's ruler Pluto conjoining jovial Jupiter in theatrical Leo, the dynamics go both ways. Some see her work as hilarious. Others find it disturbingly upsetting.

Whoppi's Moon conjoins Mercury and this planet forms conjoins her Neptune and Mars in Libra. This makes Goldberg emotionally bewildered and indecisive, when she attempts to express her personal thoughts. In contrast, when she connects with the creative ideas of others, her concepts flow freely, without hesitation. Her Venus trines Uranus.

Ascendant: Aquarius

When Whoopi floats through the gate of her Fixed Air Ascendant, the intense and probing force of her luminaries cease—as her mind focuses on finding a new source of ideas.

With the presence of the electric light of Aquarius, Whoopi's guests and friends now sense that her questions are no longer personal—they are seeking solutions to a greater concern! Everyone is ready to join in on the conversations.

In the movie *Ghost*, the forces of Scorpio and Aquarius were delightfully displayed as Whoopi's sparkling eyes transformed into deep pools of water. There, we saw the intuitive sparks and the idealized gestures of Aquarius, and how they were humorously countered by the defensive urges of Scorpio.

Like **Roseanne Barr** (pg. 242), Whoopi has Aquarius rising and both have their Venuses in Sagittarius. Both seem to have little concern about the image that they present to the public. With their Scorpio Suns, both often wore black or dark shaded attire. This dress was often embellished by some inappropriately outrageous decorative addition.

This combination of fixed Air and Water often gives us folks who are very private, but also very concerned about others. Whoppi and Roseanne both know that the collective actions of others are very valuable—for this involvement makes our society more secure, as it creates a better place to live.

Before we go further, let's review the qualities that were displayed in the previous chapter. and examine a star who has strong Libra in his chart.

Leonardo DiCaprio

11/11/1974, 2:47 A.M.
Hollywood, CA

 **Sun: Scorpio**

DiCaprio has three chart components in Scorpio, but he has five in the sign of Libra. All of these water and air components are clustered in his first two Houses. Saturn sits in his 10th House and Jupiter is the only one on the right side of his chart. This makes him tenacious and highly self driven.

With Mars conjoined his Sun and trine Jupiter, Leo made many daring leaps early in his career. The big breakthrough came with his Oscar nominated role as a troubled teen in *What's Eating Gilbert Grape*. Shortly after, he went into the darker side playing a pyromaniacal teen in *Marvin's Room*. This was followed by his role as a heroin addict in *The Basketball Diaries* and his controversial role as the gay poet Rimbaud in *Total Eclipse*.

With so many Libra components (and Uranus conjunct his Mercury and Mars), we see why Leonardo participated in so many non-mainstream "art films".

As Leonardo's career advanced, the power of his Scorpio Sun intensified, as did his roles in film. With *Gangs of New York*, *Django Unchained* and *The Revenant*, his public image became more brutal. This intensity was enforced by Pluto's conjunction with his Moon and Ascendant, and its sextile to Neptune.

Moon and Ascendant in Libra

With a Libra Ascendant and Moon DiCaprio was quick with a quip and a smile, as he began his career playing the cheery kid in TV's *Growing Pains*. This Libra charm was also apparent in William Shakespeare's *Romeo and Juliet* and in big hit *Titanic*—the film that proved he could bring teenage girls into the theaters in droves.

In *The Man In The Iron Mask*, we saw the solar and lunar dichotomy in his personality, when he played the duel roles of an evil king and his fair-minded twin brother.

~~
Historical Note:
With his 2015 role in *The Revenant*, Leo was nominated for the fifth time for an Oscar. Here, he immerged as the winner for the first time!

This long delayed reward came as transiting Saturn opposed his natal Saturn in the 10th House.

Emma Stone
11/6/1988. 12:50 A.M.
Scottsdale, AZ

Emma Stone's feature film debut was in the hilarious 2007 teen-angst saga: *Superbad*. This was followed by the comedies *Easy A* and *Crazy, Stupid, Love* and her coveted role as the new love interest in *The Amazing Spiderman*. Shortly after, she found acclaim and her first Oscar nod (as "Best Actress in a Supporting Role") for her performance in *Birdman or (The Unexpected Virtue of Ignorance)*. In 2017, she garnered more raves for her role in *La La Land*. In that year, she also was cast to portray a live-action version of the evil *Cruella de Vil* (Disney's villain from *101 Dalmatians*). In this role, she playfully showed the darker side of her Scorpio Sun.

 Sun: Scorpio

In talk show interviews, Emma projects the powerful intensity of the fixed water of her Sun. The upper photos shows how her facial elements fix and hold, as she expresses her strongly held feelings. This fixity is seen in the winged brows, that lift up on the outer edges, to focus her eagle eyes on distant prey. Note the large, deep-pooled eyes and how her "fully saturated flesh" solidifies the cubical features in her face. These fixed features are reinforced by the underlying bone structure of her Leo Ascendant.

With her Sun conjoined Pluto, the power is intensified and this gives Emma a gift for playing mysterious and powerful women. Fortunately, this conjunction's sextile to Neptune (and her Sun in the Pisces' decan) relieves the tension, as it provides her with a wonderful sense of fantasy. This was seen in her two *Spiderman* roles, and in her voicing of characters for the animated film *The Croods*.

Ascendant: Leo

In any luminary expression, we often see changes in the flesh—noticeably in the eyes. Naturally, there is little change in the bone structure since it is solid, save for the malleable jaw. It is this rigid underlying form that defines the shape of one's Ascendant.

Thusly, since Stone's Rising Sign is Leo, all of the photos above show the cubical skull, broad wide-set brow, stubby nose and wide chin of a lion. If you compare the LL photo with the two of her Scorpio Sun, the greatest difference is seen in the eyes. There, they appear feline-like, and seemingly lit within by fiery embers. The top photos of her Sun also appear fixed, but (in contrast) the eyes reveal the ocean depths below. With her Moon, we see bigger changes, since the flesh is activated by a mode of another making.

Moon: Libra

LR photo on the previous page, we see a totally different person. There, Stone's Cardinal Air Moon is reacting and this force spreads the facial lines off to the sides. This also produces the wide cherub smile of Libra, as it removes the fixed formations in her flesh.

When Stone's emotions are activated, the once saturated facial flesh suddenly appears light and translucent. Also, the anchored eyes now float freely on the surface. They seem to be held in place by her cloud-like billowing eyelids.

The square forehead and nose do not change, since they are locked in place. However, the horizontal forces have leveled the eyebrows and pulled the chin inward, an action that makes the broad jaw of the lion less obvious.

The Body Language of Emma's Components

Here, we will show how Emma's body language can help you recognize the astrological components of any person.

To do this, one needs to observe WHERE the power is concentrated in the body and HOW it is being activated. The "where" is determined by the part of the body that each sign rules. This all is described in the introductions on each sign.

Fixed Water: Scorpio Sun
(Body rulership: The Lower Hips)

In the left photo, you will notice that this force is passive, and centered in the lower hips (the part of the body ruled by Scorpio). When this area is projected forward, the chest and shoulders tilt to the rear. To compensate, the head angles sharply forward, and this gives us the recognized stance of a Scorpion. Note how the eyes appear to enlarge, to suggest the presence of water.

Cardinal Air: Libra Moon
(Body rulership: The Kidneys)

The center photo shows us the "change in Mode" as Emma's fixed components are loosened by the horizontally directed Air of her lunar reactions. Since Libra rules the midpoint in the body, the posture is vertically balanced. (No body part dominates over another.) The most obvious action is the arms that weigh up and down on each side, to maintain the balance.

Fixed Fire: Leo Ascendant
(Body rulership: The Heart)

With Leo, the mode is still fixed, but the force appears as expansive fire. All of this warmth is fixed in the giant hearth of the Lion's heart.

The right photo shows the masculine fire of Emma's Leo Ascendant as well as the feline eyes of a cat. Note how Leo's chest expands proudly outward, and how the head rises upward to create the illusion that royalty has just entered the room.

Roseanne Barr
11/3/1952, 1:21 P.M.
Salt Lake City, Utah

♏ Sun: Scorpio

Few have presented the cutting edge of comedy like Roseanne. Like **Whoppi Goldberg**, she tells it like it is! There is no subject that is taboo, not even on national television. Life has its dirty laundry and Barr made us laugh at it all.

When Roseanne expresses her true self, the gray skies of November cast their spell, as Scorpio take control. Watch how her facial expressions fix and hold, as her Eagle eyes search for a new array of nasty secrets to unveil.

With Uranus trine her Sun, Barr's TV character constantly stood up for any underdog—and for anyone who was being exploited. With her crude style of manipulation, she seemed to maintain control by helping others to find "their own sense of power". And they believed it was possible—thanks to the optimistic mask of Roseanne's Ascendant.

Ascendant: Aquarius

Normally, Scorpios hide their secrets, but not with Roseanne. Her Ascendant is Aquarius! Instantly, every thought in her head is broadcast over the public airwaves. This is exacerbated by Uranus (the ruler of her Ascendant). It trines her Sun and sextiles Jupiter. Everything is out front—for everyone to see.

This is "one strange lady" with a unique and unorthodox persona. Who else would have worn inappropriate attire at important social events, participated in mud-wrestling, sung the national anthem off-key and boastfully sported a tattoo (long before it became a social trend). Yes, Roseanne revolutionized our concept of how we think we should look. You didn't have to be thin and beautiful to be cool.

Moon: Gemini

Gemini Moons tend to release their emotions by talking. Since Barr's Moon opposes her Sagittarius Mercury (and trines her Ascendant), her chatter rarely ceases! This gift for gab was seen in Barr's TV show. There, in the family's interactions, her encyclopedic mind came alive—as she responded to others with her profuse array of facts and bits of trivia.

This mutable-air Moon scatters the normally fixed pattern of Barr's Sun and Ascendant. When her mercuric lunar urges were activated, her eyes would dart about, as they followed the scattering motions of her flying hands and fingers.

With her Centaur Mercury near her Midheaven, Roseanne was able to take the massive array of "comedic ideas" in her head and turn them into successful forms of entertainment.

More Water raises the humidity

Condoleezza Rice
11/14/1954, 11:30 A.M.
Birmingham, AL

 ## Sun: Scorpio

Growing up in Birmingham during the racial riots, Ms. Rice became tough and determined as she worked her way up the ladder of power. She was a National Security Advisor during 9/11 and then went on to become President Bush's Secretary of State.

Condi's Scorpio Sun sits on her MC, and it conjoins Venus and Saturn. Amazingly, this Sun also makes aspects to every other planet in her chart (save for Mercury and Neptune). These massive interlinks gave this lady a gift for dealing with the intrigue of international power plays—those that she saw through the window of her Aquarius Ascendant.

Ascendant: Aquarius

Jupiter and Uranus oppose Rice's Fixed Air Ascendant. This instilled a giant sense of hope, and it likely inspired Rice to pioneer her policy of "Transformational Diplomacy" (a US policy that tried to expand the number of responsible democratic governments in the world). Unfortunately, Neptune also forms a T-square to these three components. This idealistic outlook proved to be overly optimistic. Democracy is not easy to achieve.

In Condi, we see the heavy lidded eyes and the box-like jaw of Aquarius. Oddly, the electrical breezes of Air remain well hidden. This is likely due to the fact that seven of her chart components are in water signs. These are her only feminine signs, for she has no Earth in her chart.

Moon: Cancer

Like **Rosanne Barr**, Condi's Moon also conjoins Uranus. The difference is that Barr's Moon is in Gemini, while Rice's Moon is in the emotionally contained sign of Cancer. Condi's lunar reactions are also more disciplined. Saturn not only conjoins her Sun, it trines her Moon.

Like Barr, Condi shows the broad flat cheeks of the Scorpion, but what is unusual here is that Rice also shows the beaming lunar temples of a Cancer Crab. As noted many times before, a Cancer Moon often shows up in one's physical appearance. This lunar influence is more obvious here, since Rice's Sun is in the decan of Cancer.

NOTE: Condi was the second woman (after Taurus *Madeleine Albright*) to fill the fourth most powerful position in the United States government. The third woman was *Hillary Clinton*, who also is a Scorpio. These three fixed signs knew how to control power.

Earth contains the Water
Matthew McConaughey
11/4/1969, 7:34 P.M.
Uvalde, Texas

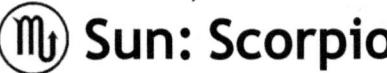 Sun: Scorpio

McConaughey's Scorpio Sun adds a sultry intensity to his personality. He also displays many of Scorpio's traits, but what is special here is the UL photo. It shows how the forward slope on the back of the skull combines with the back-tilted brow to create the narrow top on Scorpio's head. Add the large beak and the curved upper back—and you get the image an Eagle preparing to take off in flight.

Matthew has no fire signs and five of his components are in fixed signs. Furthermore, eight are crammed into the lower "night time" part of his chart. This is why Matthew often withdraws into his own private world—when he isn't interacting with others.

Moon: Virgo

Matthew's other key lights are both ruled by Mercury. However, rigid Saturn opposes his Scorpio Mercury and Sun, and this ringed planet also trines his Virgo Moon. Even when his Virgo Moon is "fully activated", he is emotionally rigid and markedly "short on words". Just recall "Alright, Alright, Alright", the catch phase in the film *Dazed and Confused* that launched his career.

When Matthew gets emotional, he often becomes obsessed with details, and this makes it even more difficult for him to find the right words to express his feelings. These analytical Virgo qualities were apparent in McConaughey's film roles. In *A Time To Kill*, he was the idealistic lawyer who carefully chose his words, as he assembled the facts to support his case. In the Sci-fi epic *Interstellar*, he was the questioning scientist, who matter-of-factly examined the complexities of time and space.

Ascendant: Gemini

Matthew's Gemini Rising gives him a curious view of his world. His Ascendant's trine to Uranus accounts for his love of traveling and why he became known as the "unkempt vagabond", who appeared in the strangest out-of-the-way places. These aspects also account for Matthew's rebellious and image-be-damned demeanor. This carefree persona, to some critics, comes across as a lack of passion (a charge rarely given to a Scorpio!) This could be due to the fact that his zero-degree Aquarius Mars aspects every planet in his chart except Jupiter. This greatly dilutes his martial energies.

Ryan Gosling

11/12/1980, 2:34 P.M.
London, Canada

♍ Sun: Scorpio

Gosling's 20+ degree Scorpio Sun is in its third decan of Cancer. With this, and other factors to be discussed momentarily, we will show why Gosling shows more traits of Cancer than Scorpio.

This Cancer decan defines Ryan's early career, which included a regular stint on Disney's *Mickey Mouse Club,* and several other family oriented TV shows. Hints of mothering Cancer were also in his 2007 film *Lars and the Real Girl.* However, his later works (*Ides of March, Drive* and *Blade Runner 2049*) are more riveting and powerful, for with aging, his Scorpio Sun has found its true expression.

The upper right photo shows Scorpio's cubical features, as well as the intense, focused eyes of the Eagle.

Ascendant: Pisces

Ryan easily senses what people are feeling, and in reverse, he also pours his feelings out to others. This may be due to his Pisces Rising Sign, which is also in the decan of Cancer.

This passionate persona prevailed in Ryan's role in the romantic drama *The Notebook*, a film in which his "Hey Girl" meme shot his career into stardom. Notably, it was this role and his proactive comments on women's rights that inspired *Ms. Magazine* to name him their "favorite sensitive movie dude for feminists". These Pisces forces also gave Ryan that gift for dance that we saw in his award winning film *La La Land*.

The left photos show how this mutable Ascendant skews the sectors in the face to give him the dreamy look of Pisces. (It was more obvious in his youth).

Moon in Capricorn

Ryan's Capricorn Moon sextiles his Sun and Ascendant. This merging of these three key lights (in different modes) gives Gosling a balanced array of creative energies.

Watch how the intensity of Ryan's fixed Sun ceases, when the directing force of his cardinal Moon is activated. This tenacious lunar drive is then rerouted and liquefied as it pours out of the portal of his Ascendant. This diverse range of expressions was apparent in Ryan's performance as a drug addicted teacher in *Half Nelson*.

In more emotional moments, the waters chill, as Ryan's steely eyes take on the cold lunar stare of a goat. As seen in the LR photo, this Moon instills a demeanor, that suggests the expressions seen in Nicholas Cage's Capricorn Sun.

Fortunately, Rylan's Sagittarius Mars conjoins Neptune on his Midheaven. This warms the water, as it brings comedic release to his lunar reactions.

Walter Cronkite
11/4/1916, 6:00 A.M.
Saint Joseph, MO

Dan Rather
10/31/1931, 6:13 P.M.
Wharton, TX

Suns: Scorpio

For 40+ years, these Scorpios Suns presented the news (and many traumatic events) to the world. In the process, they rarely revealed their personal feelings. After all, these fixed signs were our "anchors"—and we expected them to keep their emotions in control!

Physically, both show the intensely focused eyes, the bushy eyebrows and the large lobed ears of Scorpio.

Moons: Pisces & Cancer

These two men have water-sign Moons—to unlock the fixity of their Suns and help them deal with the tides of changing events. The manner in which they displayed their personal feelings often reflected the qualities of their Moon Signs.

Cronkite's Pisces Moon was rarely seen on the air, save for when he announced the death of President Kennedy. Later, we saw Pisces' look of awestruck wonder in full bloom, when the first spacecraft landed on the moon. In such moments, Walter's terse facial lines would relax and droop, to form the skewed and dreamy-eyed look of Pisces.

When **Rather's Cancer Moon** interacts with others, the tidal currents surge—to inflate his flesh and create the beaming face of the crab. This Moon makes Dan emotionally comfortable with his guests. However, when these cardinal tides surge, he often becomes noticeably "pushy and persistent", when he tries to pull secrets out of others.

Rising: Scorpio & Taurus

Both of this men have fixed Ascendants. It has served to gave them their well anchored personas.

Walter's Scorpio Rising gives him an underlying bone structure, that reinforces the features of his Sun. The elongated and square skull (with the forward-tilted plate on the back) is similar to the shape seen in Matthew McConaughey.

Dan's Taurus Rising shortens his face into a cube, as it broadens the bridge on his Eagle's beak. Note how it widens at the nostrils, to form what appears to be a stubby nose. His eyes appear markedly contented, and they suggest the presence of a Taurus Bull. Oddly, he has no Air in his chart.

Joni Mitchell
11/7/1943, 10:00 P.M.
Fort Macleod, Canada

K.D. Lang
11/2/1961, 2:03 A.M.
Edmonton, Canada

Suns in Scorpio

These musicians have their three main components in feminine signs, and like most musicians, they have strong aspects to Neptune.

K.D. Lang's Sun sextiles Pluto (the ruler of Scorpio) and her Mars is in Scorpio! Fixed Water dominates her chart, but her Sun conjoins Neptune. Her work is melodic and soulful, but it is also infused with power wrenching emotions.

Unlike Lang, **Joni Mitchell**'s Sun is in the Pisces decan, and Neptune forms the most aspects in her chart! With her Pisces Moon on the Midheaven (and all of this Neptune), we see why this optimistic flower child's music calmed the hearts of many, in the turbulent 1960's and '70's.

Virgo & Pisces Moons

K.D. Lang's Virgo Moon conjoins Uranus and Pluto. Thusly, in emotional moments, K.D. constantly questions the status quo, as she obsessively seeks deeper truths in her music. These Virgo components drove her to perfect her verbal presentation. With Pluto nearby, she was determined to connect emotionally and intellectually with her audience.

Joni Mitchell's Pisces Moon opposes its ruling planet Neptune. Also, this dreamy planet conjoins Venus, as it sextiles Pluto and trines Joni's Uranus. With all of this Neptune, Mitchell became a strong spokesman for the environment, while she inspired others to find their own connection with Nature. This sense of synergy was expressed in her hit songs: *The Circle Game* and *Both Sides Now*.

Virgo & Cancer Rising

Lang's ***Virgo Rising*** (and Moon) explains her long, lean and skewed facial features, and why she defines her music as being "an assembly of sounds and emotions...a healthy, whole body experience." The latter comment is likely due to her Pluto/Ascendant conjunction and its trine to her Sun and Neptune.

Joni's Cancer Rising can be seen in her underlying bone structure, which mocks the shape of a crab's shell. Like most Cancer risings, she has the large and circular face, and the large upper torso of the crab.

Joni was seen as the "Woodstock Songstress" who mothered and nurtured our common feeling for family and community.

Heat the Water with Fire
Martin Scorsese
11/17/1942, 12:24 A.M.
Flushing, New York

♏ Sun: Scorpio

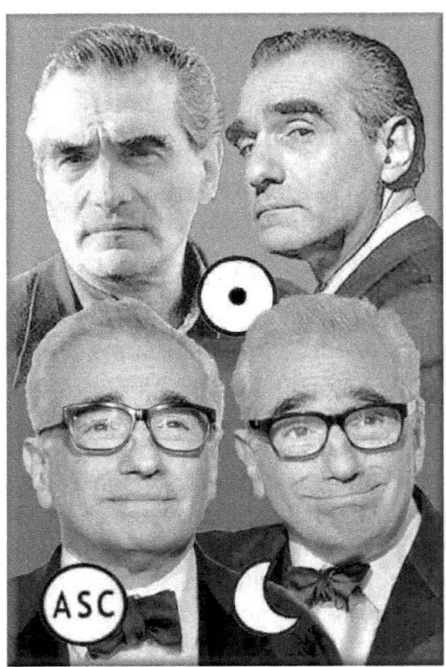

Martin Scorsese is considered to be his generation's greatest film director. His intense and energetic cinematic works often featured sociopathic loners struggling with their inner demons (i.e., *Taxi Driver* and *Cape Fear*). Even his comedies (*King of Comedy* and *After Hours*) dwell on the darker side. This Scorpio wants us to know that life isn't always pretty!

Scorpio's desire to "fix and hold" can be seen in Martin's creative impulses. He personally spurns the notion of a director's cut: "Once a film has been completed, it should not be further altered in any way". Martin is also is a vocal advocate for film preservation, and he has helped to save and restore many precious and endangered films.

Martin has the standard traits of Scorpio, but his broad and busy eyebrows are more obvious than what we seen in others (save for Walter Cronkite).

Moon: Pisces

With his Sun, Mercury, Venus and Mars in Scorpio, Martin's work often locks into the darker realms of reality. Fortunately, these fixed components all trine his Pisces Moon, and this supplements the lack of Earth in his chart. With his mutable lunar emotions, he also has an ability to escape the fixity—and present the uplifting views of the Eagle!

Pisces provides the universal solvent, as well as the solution, that bring all creation to completion. Since this mystic Moon is the "most connected component' in Martin's chart, we see why he once aspired to become a priest. This fascination with religion was the core of many of Scorsese's feature films. There was the controversial *Last Temptation of Christ*, which depicted the human doubts Christ faced in his final ordeal. There's also *Kundun*, Martin's film on the life of the Dalai Lama and the 2017 film *Silence*. Each examines a religion from a different region in the world.

When his lunar lights beam, Martin's facial lines often shift to present a look of amused delight. Since this Moon squares Saturn, the joy is usually well contained.

Ascendant: Leo

With a fixed fire Ascendant, Martin was given a lion's demeanor and the aura of confidence that helped him to succeed in the world of theater. However, Martin says he generally feels uncomfortable in front of the camera. That's understandable, since his Ascendant squares all those personal planets in Scorpio, while his Sun opposes Uranus on his Midheaven. He sees "others as being the stars", rather than himself.

Maria Shriver
11/6/1955, 5:12 P.M.
Chicago Heights, IL

With seven components (including her three key personality lights) in fixed signs, Maria displays the cubical features of fixity. She also shows us how the force in this Mode is altered, when it appears in a sign of a different Element.

Scorpio Sun (Water)

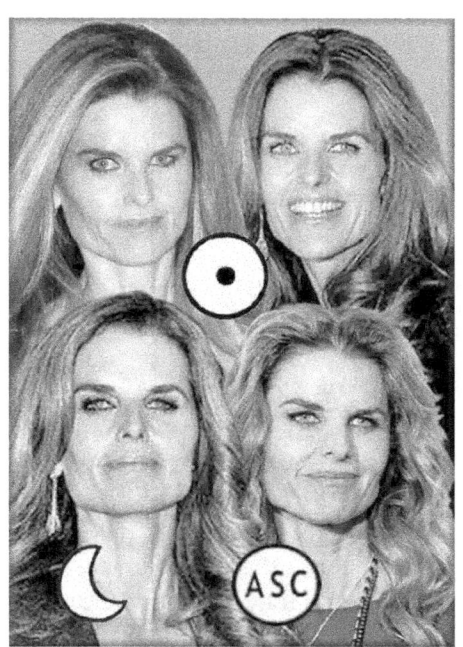

When Shriver projects the rays of her Water Sun, the blue-hued flesh rounds as the eyes enlarge into liquid pools of light. From deep within these watery lenses, a laser-like light emerges. Its intensity suggests the sting of a Scorpion, or the joy of an Eagle lifting off in flight.

Shriver's Scorpio Sun, Saturn and her Ascendant are the only feminine signs in her chart. With this abundance of expansive forces (and Jupiter's conjunction to her Sun's ruling planet Pluto in Leo), Maria shows few of the reclusive and secretive qualities of Scorpio. This may be why she became a journalist for NBC'S *Dateline*, CBS's *Morning News* and *Sunday Today*. Notably, her Moon, Pluto and Jupiter are all in Leo, in the 4th House (Cancer's home). That's why so much of Maria's work supported children and family causes.

Leo Moon (Fire)

When Maria's Leo Moon reflects the light from her watery Sun, there is a change in polarity, as well as a rise in temperature. This Moon's sextile to her Libra Mars and its square to Saturn gave Maria the charm, and the discipline to succeed in the competitive field of broadcast journalism.

When Maria's Leo fires ignite, her once liquid eyes take on a fiery glow, as the energy shifts to her heart. This placement in this part of the body gives her a stance of dignity and self confidence. In more heated emotional situations, they bring her solar waters to a boil. Still, with all of this drama, Maria's earthy persona remains, to keep her anchored.

Taurus Rising (Earth)

When her luminaries go into repose, Maria's fixed features appear more rugged, seemingly set in stone. What we are seeing is the mask of her Earth Ascendant. With its bovine eyes and firmly set features, this mask displays the contented sensuality of Venus.

With her Leo Uranus trine Venus and Aquarius on her MC, Shriver is an advocate of many causes. Perhaps that is why she received the *Pathfinders To Peace Award* for inspiring others to become their own "Architects-of-Change". This ability for to teach "the art of change to others" suggests that Maria has mastered the many fixed forces in her chart.

Bill Gates
10/28/1955, 10:00 P.M.
Seattle, WA

Sun: Scorpio

At the young age of twenty-five, Bill Gates convinced mighty IBM to use his computer operating system. After all, this Scorpio knew what his "hidden under-structure" was worth! In time, it became "Windows", the program that made PC's accessible to everyone.

More than anyone, Gates should know the purpose of an "operating base", for he has three planets and his Sun in his 4th House. There, his Sun conjoins Neptune and they both square Uranus on his Ascendant. Neptune also sextiles a Jupiter and Pluto conjunction in his 2nd House. (This portends massive personal wealth).

These Uranus aspects enabled Gates' solar-lit imagination to envision a giant array of technical innovations, while his Venus and Saturn conjunction in the 5th House gave him the creative discipline to get it done.

Ascendant: Cancer

On first glance, the seemingly vulnerable mask of Bill's timid Cancer Ascendant appears. This rounded face with its fully pooled eyes disarms the treat of his fixed Sun. With those four components in his Cancer-ruled 4th House, the water in this window is clear as glass. This gives him the capability to attract and surround himself with the right conditions and the right people —at the right time!

With Uranus conjunct his Ascendant, Gates was given an ability to see the future of computers and the internet —both are governed by Uranus!

Moon: Aries

Bill's Aries Moon stands alone, above the horizon on Gate's Midheaven. All of his planets are hidden in the nighttime portion of his chart. Thusly, little is known about his personal life, but the manner in which he interacts with others (and the world) has gained him huge public recognition. With his Moon in Aries, he is known for inspiring others to take action.

Bill's Libra Mars conjoin Mercury, and it opposes his Moon. This Aries Moon (and his four cardinal planets) gave Gates' the ability to clear the clutter, make quick decisions, and "drive his ideas forward"—to lead the way to new frontiers. All the while, Bill's Scorpio Venus (and its conjunction to Saturn) gave his a gift for knowing what was valuable, and what had to be discarded. These aspects helped to make him the richest man in the world.

Julia Roberts
10/28/1967, 12:16 A.M.
Atlanta, GA

Astrological patterns often show in the roles that movie stars play. For instance, it is amazing how Julia's portrayal as *Erin Brockovich* revealed her own chart components. There, we saw a foul mouthed "don't give me any crap" individual (Scorpio), who was constantly over-whelmed by the demands of motherhood (Cancer). In addition, this character also displayed the boisterous confidence of a lion.

♍ Sun: Scorpio

With a water Sun and Ascendant, Julia's projects a soft and sensitive nature. However, with a fixed Sun and Moon (and all of her components in the lower "dark half" of her chart), Julia's emotions are often placed on hold, and rarely seen in the public light.

As we saw in her first big hit *Pretty Woman*, Julia's emotions are secretive, and also lusty and seductive. In her role in *Erin Brockovich*, Julia demonstrated Scorpio's wonderful ability to persuade others to "hold on to her values".

With her Venus, Jupiter, Uranus and Pluto in analytical Virgo, the dueling energies of Mercury often appear in Robert's solar expressions. Just recall (in her role as *Erin*), how her eyes sparked and blinked, as her fingers sorted the "Virgo data". Also note how, in her pursuit of material, Julia's physical movements always appeared to be purposefully directed. Julia's Mars is in the earthy sign of Capricorn.

The UL photo shows the upward sweep, often seen in the eyes of an Eagle. The UR photo shows the piercing Scorpio eyes, as they lock onto a distant treasure!

Moon: Leo

The reactions of Julia's Leo Moon lift her eyes and brows, as they light her face with a glow of confidence. The resulting out-trusted chest creates the prideful stance of a Lion.

When Scorpios with a Leo Moon get emotional, there is a marked change in their disposition. When the fires of Leo flare up from within, they become expansive and fiery, and more playful and theatrical. Sometimes, to their own chagrin, many of their hidden solar secrets are exposed in the light.

Ascendant: Cancer

When Julia's fixed Sun and Moon are inactive, the tidal waters of Cancer rush in—to present the comforting mask of the Crab and cool the fiery embers of Leo. These cardinal waters loosen Julia's fixed luminaries. Suddenly, she appears softer, more caring and vulnerable. She becomes somebody we love and trust—not someone who wants to "be in control".

Goldie Hawn
11/21/1945, 9:20 A.M.
Washington Highlands, DC

"Astrology is nonsense"

That was what this author thought, years ago, when I read that Goldie was a Scorpio. All I saw was a giggling chatterbox. This was not the description the books gave of a Scorpio. Later (after I became aware that people are more than their Sun Signs), I looked at Goldie's chart and I was amazed at how well it described her personality. It showed me the magic of this ancient science. It made me a believer in astrology.

Sagittarius Rising

As the astrology books say: *a person's first impression is often their Ascendant*. This certainly fits the galloping filly (with the high-pitched whinny) that I saw on *Rowan and Martin's Laugh In*. There, I also saw Hawn's physical appearance—her large domed head, the long neck and the big horse-like eyes that swept back from the wide bridged snout. These traits are seen in most Centaurs.

Moon: Gemini

That chart also told me that Hawn had a Gemini Moon. It certainly explained the chatter that I saw in her role in *Private Benjamin*. There, we heard her high-pitched, breathy voice—as we saw her rapidly blinking eyes and her flying fingers animating her thoughts. These traits were obvious, when she *talked about her feelings*.

Later, I noticed that Jupiter was at the top of Goldie's chart and it was in trine to her Moon/Uranus conjunction. In addition, her Leo Mars trined her late degree Sun. This Jupiterized Mars explained this lady's expansive and theatrical physical metabolism. The other aspects fit the quirks in her personality—as well as her joyous and outrageous gift for comedy!

Still, there was little to convince me that she was a Scorpio.

Sun: Scorpio

In Hawn's 1969 Oscar-winning role in *Cactus Flower*, I saw my first true glimpse of this lady's emotional Sun. Later, in the film *Shampoo*, I saw her inner strength, as she played a rejected lover who found her own sense of personal power. A decade later, in *First Wife's Club*, Fixed Water dominated her revenge seeking character. This role showed me how Hawn's power was elevated by her Mars' trine to her Sun, while it also showed me why (in ancient times) Mars was also the ruler of Scorpio. With her Leo Mars, Hawn found the focus and drive, to become a successful film director and producer.

Hawn shows us how one's Sun Sign becomes stronger with age. The UR photo shows her younger years, when the Centaur features reigned. In later years (as the UL photo shows), the physical qualities of Scorpio are more distinct.

That's how Goldie Hawn made this author a believer in astrology!

Anne Hathaway
11/12/1987, 9:00 A.M.
Brooklyn, NY

 ## Sun: Scorpio

Anne's Mercury, Venus and Jupiter conjoins her Sun, but like **Goldie Hawn**, she still doesn't appear to be a typical Scorpio. Perhaps this is due to the fact that her Sun and Mercury are in the Pisces decan and her two other Scorpio planets are in the Cancer Decan. This softens her physical features and the tone of her voice, as it dilutes the intensity of her fixed Scorpio Sun. Her solar light is also loosened by her cardinal Libra Moon, and the fact that (like Goldie), she has a Centaur Ascendant.

Sagittarius Rising

Hathaway's breakthrough came in *The Princess Diaries*. There, she had to perform the adolescence awkwardness of a girl who was being "groomed for royalty". For Anne, the clumsy mannerisms of her character were easy to perform. She admits she "is a klutz". Astrologers would claim that this is due to her "I can trip over anything" Sagittarius Ascendant!

This mask makes Anne's bone structure similar to Goldies. What is obvious here is Anne's pointed ears and how her nose and chin twist in opposite directions.

In contrast to Hawn's "mercuric image", Anne appears more grounded, since her Mars is in Capricorn. In addition, Hathaway's presence has an etherial quality. She seems to be floating in her own dreamy world. Neptune conjoins her Ascendant as it sextiles Saturn and her Sun's ruler Pluto. (Also, eight of her components are in the third Quadrant, the home of Pisces).

Neptune's link to this Rising Sign gives Anne the gift for fantasy, that we saw in her two *Alice In Wonderland* roles, and in

the animated film *Rio*. The Centaur's comedy talents were seen in her film *Get Smart*, while *Colossal* and *The Dark Knight Rises* showed how Scorpio Sun became stronger, as she aged.

Moon in Libra

Anne is known for her easy going emotional nature. This is appropriate, since her Libra Moon sits on her MC, and it also sextiles her Ascendant. The charming emotions of this Libra Moon were clearly present in *The Devil Wears Prada*. There, Anne played the assistant to a demanding and overpowering fashion magnate. Even when treated badly, Anne would always respond with a cheerful smile. In this film, Anne showed how Libra's sense of fairness is what every business needs—to be successful!

Goldie and **Anne**'s *Air Moons and Centaur Ascendants make them light and cheery. With our final two "Centaur Risings", we will show how Pluto aspects and transits dim the fire—and make the light of Scorpio more mysterious.*

Transits of Pluto Bring Empowerment and Transformation

Jodie Foster's chart has a clutter of four Scorpio components in the 3rd quadrant. It was noticed that slow moving Pluto was transiting this area in her chart during much of her career. Amazingly, it was discovered the every time Pluto transited each component in this sector, her career was empowered—or she went through major personal transformations! This shows that the long range cycles in our solar system somehow influence or parallel the patterns in our lives.

Jodie Foster
November 19, 1962
8:14 A.M., Los Angeles, CA

Jodie's career began in a TV commercial at the age of 2. Soon after, this child actress had parts in many TV shows and several "coming-of-age" movies. However, it was at the tender age of 14 when she gained national attention, playing the young prostitute in Martin Scorsese's *Taxi Driver*. This was the beginning of a career that for years would reflect the steamy intensity of Jodie's Pluto-ruled Scorpio Sun.

Sun in Scorpio
Embellished by the Transits of Pluto

As noted, Jodie has four Scorpio components. What is unusual is that her Sun and Mercury rule the signs in which her Mars and Moon are placed. Also, Foster's 9th House Pluto and Uranus are the nearest planets to her Midheaven. Pluto dominates her chart!

Perhaps that is why the transits of Pluto appear to match virtually every key event in her career. So, let's take a look at those Pluto trigger points:

In 1976, when the film *Taxi Driver* was released, Pluto was transiting mid-Libra (in Jodie's 10th House of Career). Also, Saturn was transiting her 8th House, conjoining her Leo Mars. It is appropriate that Jodie's rise to fame came from such a sexually provocative role.

Foster's next breakthrough came in 1988, when transiting Pluto conjoined her natal Neptune. This empowerment of the ruling-planet-of-cinema won Jodie her first Oscar, for her role in the film *Accused*. Oddly, at this high point in her career, transiting Saturn and Uranus were conjoined in Foster's 1st House and both planets were squaring transiting Venus on her Libra MC. Apparently, this uplifted Venus placed Foster in public view again—to override the fact that Saturn was not transiting up the right half of her chart.

Next up (in 1991), when transiting Pluto was hovering over Foster's Venus and Mercury conjunction (in her 11th House), the film *The Silence of the Lambs* premiered. All of society was shocked by the evil of Hannibal, but impressed by Jodi's unflappable nature. At this time, Jodie also experienced a Saturn return in her Second

House. This was her biggest box office hit to date—and it won her another golden Oscar!

The next contact was in 1994, when transiting Pluto connected with Jodie's Sun—and also entered her 12th House. Here, in the film *Nell*, Foster give us what many consider to be her finest performance—playing a powerless soul imprisoned in her own self created world. This is the stuff we'd expect in the 12th House, the home of Pisces!

When Pluto entered Sagittarius in 1997, Jodie's film *Contact* pondered the existence of life in outer space. More thoughtful and humorous works followed, for Foster was now free to express the mutable lights of her Moon and Ascendant.

In 2002, when Pluto crossed over Jodie's Centaur Ascendant, she began a popular string of hits (from *Panic Room* to 2007's *The Brave One*). However, when Pluto transited into Capricorn in 2011, the run was over, as her film *The Beaver* became one of the year's biggest box office flops. Still things may turn around, for Pluto will enter her 2nd House in 2019. In 2028, Pluto's last contact will be with Saturn.

Moon in Virgo / Sagittarius Ascendant

The Ascendant is the mask that one sees, when the luminaries are in repose. In contrast, one's Lunar reactions tend to activate the facial flesh, and therefore, create more activity. This explains why it is difficult to separate the mannerism of someone who has a passive Moon and a masculine Ascendant. The Rising Sign appear to be more reactive or outward than the Moon.

Above, the left photos show the feminine reactions of Jodie's earthy Virgo Moon. When Jodie reacts, her passive lunar energies pull the upper neck and chest to the back, as it pushes the stomach forward, to create the stance of Virgo. Her reactions are contained in Earth, but hints of Mercury are seen in her animated fingers.

In contrast, Jodie's Centaur Ascendant seems to be constantly bouncing out front, spreading the heat of mutable fire, as it lights up the spirited persona that she presents to the world. This gives her Sun's moody eyes a needed sparkle!

Since both of these components are mutable, the skewed and offset features of mutability are obvious. However, the Ascendant's bone structure gives her the broad front teeth, the long neck and the protruding jaw of a horse. This eliminates many of the fixed features we'd expect from someone with prominent Scorpio and Pluto.

Danny Devito

11/17/1944, 10:20 A.M.
Neptune, N.J.

In his career, Danny has played many characters who live on the squeamish edge. Strangely, they all seemed so funny! That's what you can expect from a Scorpio with prominent Sagittarius.

♏ Sun: Scorpio

In the TV series *Taxi*, Devito was the dispatcher who regularly made his cohort's lives a living hell. Life dealt him a short deck (a shortness of height as well as hair) and he was ready to sting anyone, just to get even. In his moments of "demonic possession", Devito would fume and snarl as his eyes took on a hypnotic laser-like glare. The taxi crew knew the look, and as a running gag, they would just ignore and avoid him. This lack of control made him even more upset.

Mars conjoins Danny's Sun, and they both sextile Jupiter. Mars gives him the drive and determination to express his solar urges. Jupiter gave him his wicked sense of comedy.

As an actor, director and producer, Danny has created a prolific list of works that seem to be homages to his Scorpio Sun. There's the deadly obsession of *The War of the Roses*, the macabre sentimentality of *Throw Momma From The Train* and the cruel coldness of *Ruthless People*. Also, who can forget his creepy penguin character in *Return of Batman*?

The UL photo shows the knowing eyes of the Eagle. On the right, two Scorpions are seen in full sting mode. Fortunately, Danny's dark urges were often altered by the fiery lights of Sagittarius.

Moon & Ascendant: Sagittarius

When Danny bounces into the room, little of the staid qualities of Scorpio are seen. In this entrance, what we see are the expansive gestures of a clown—the fire of his Centaur Ascendant!

Oddly, this fiery light is harder to see in Danny's emotional reactions. His Moon opposes Uranus, trines Pluto and sextiles his 9th House Neptune near his MC. This may be the source of Danny's bizarre, mysterious and fantastical humor that was seen in the spy spoof: *"Austin Powers, Goldmember"*.

In conclusion, we must say that this Scorpio knows how to have fun! With his wonderful sense of humor, he wasn't "shorted" on anything!

This takes us to the last month in the year, and the final sign in this collection of portraits—Sagittarius

♐ Sagittarius

	Page
Physical Traits and Body Language of Sagittarius	
Introduction to Sagittarius	261-263
The Centaurs' comedic and athletic skills shine!	
Jon Stewart	264
Bruce Lee	265
Three Scorpio Moons show how Water Douses the Fire	
Scarlett Johannsen	266
Steven Spielberg	267
Bette Midler	268
Air Feeds the Fire	
Ben Stiller	269
Tina Turner	270
Jake Gyllenhaal	271
Julianne Moore	272
Britney Spears	273
The Element of Earth Smothers the Fire	
Jeff Bridges	274
Don Johnson	275
Steve Buscemi	276
Kiefer Sutherland	277
Sarah Silverman	278
Brad Pitt	279
Taylor Swift	280
Miley Cyrus	281
Jane Fonda	282
Dancing in the light	283

Sagittarius November 22 to December 21

 **Aim for the stars with the Archer's Bow!**
Masculine Polarity, Mutable Fire

In the final days of the Fall season, the dimming Sun is carrying us into the darkest day in the year. Fortunately, our past experiences have given us the wisdom to know—that very soon—the light will rise again! This brings an uplifting sense of joy and optimism, as it ignites the spirit of **Sagittarius**.

With Mutable Fire, we are freed from the bindings of our Scorpio emotions. Now, we can seek the knowledge that we will need, to complete the resolutions for the New Year ahead.

These *Archers* are often seen at local sporting events, often as the athletics who are playing on the field. This expansive fire is also recognized in the *Centaur*, the half-horse/half-man creatures, who can be found at the livelier hot spots in your community, dispensing their profundities out to others. They may be the comedian at the comedy club, the laughing hyena chuckling at the bar, or the DJ playing music on your local radio station. These ponies are often seen in wide-open spaces. If stuck inside, they will need a big window, to view the outside world.

The scattering force of Mutable Fire makes these restless souls very impulsive. This is why their thoughts take quantum leaps in logic, and why they often blurt out the first thoughts that appear in their head. This bluntness is irritating, but we must remember that the fiery arrow of the Archer are lighting the path ahead—to pass this knowledge on to others. This task of teaching others (and inducing a degree of discipline) comes in the new cycle of building light, that begins with the Sun's entry into earthy **Capricorn**.

♃ Rulerships & Associations

Jupiter is the largest planet in the solar system. It's a big ball of gas! Perhaps that's why it rules the sign of Sagittarius? In earlier days, Jupiter was also the ruler of Pisces and it became known as "The Greater Benefic", since it appears to open many doors to opportunity. These gates open wide, when planets transit the 9th House. A positive Jupiter transit can inspire the urge to pursue knowledge, higher education, or a speculative venture. This expansive outlook can inspire individuals to travel to distant lands, learn foreign languages and spread their ideas to the world, through teaching and publishing.

For the Romans, Jupiter was represented by Jove. For the Greeks, Zeus was ruler of this planet. Also, Jupiter's twelve year orbit gives each of the twelve animals signs in the Chinese Zodiac their own year of good fortune.

Careers for Sagittarius include teachers, lecturers, lawyers, interpreters, horse trainers, veterinary surgeons, travel agents, sportsmen, priests, writers and any work that doesn't reign in this creature's roaming spirit.

Sagittarius Physical Traits:

When the fires spread, Spirit expresses itself in its two distinct expressions of Mutable Fire: the Centaur and the Archer. This horse brings us the free spirited soul that we see in many comedians, creating joy and laughter wherever they go. In the Archer, we see the people with incredible athletic and sports skills.

Both show the high-domed forehead, the wide bridged nose with the bulbous tip, the long, angled neck and the horse eyes that sweep up and then to the back, on the sides of the face.

On the right, we see two celebrities with a Sagittarius Sun and Ascendant. *Joe Dimaggio* shows how the skull widens sharply at it progresses to the top. He also displays the large teeth and pointed ears of a horse. *Caroline Kennedy* shows the sparkling eyes and the joyful expression of Mutable Fire. Note how, when she smiles, the upper lip becomes thin as the lower lip narrows in width. Kennedy also shows how the lower jaw assembly projects forward, as the chin juts off to the side.

Joe DiMaggio: 11/25/1914, 7 A.M. Martinez, CA / **Caroline Kennedy** 11/27/1957, 8:15 A.M., New York, NY

Centaur Body Language
Sagittarius rules the Thighs

When the body forces shift into the thighs, the energy is divided, as one high-stepping thigh and then the other, pulls the lower body forward on the path ahead. Any change in attitude abruptly alters the course.

This placement of force in this body region defines this creature's body appearance. The upper chest, which sways to the back, seems abnormally small, compared to the lower pear-shaped hips and large thighs. The legs seem to become smaller and narrower as they progress down to the feet (which appear as diminutive hoofs). This half horse/half human creature illustrates the dynamics and body language of people who have strong components of Sagittarius in their charts.

This section begins with a portrait of the comedic side of Sagittarius—that of the free-spirited Centaur clown.

Jon Stewart
11/28/1962, No time
Trenton, NJ

Sun & Moon: Sagittarius

In his 16 years as the anchor of *"The Daily Show"*, Jon Stewart delivered his his tongue-in-cheek interpretation of political events and pop culture for cable's Comedy Channel. His show soon became the *real* source of news for the younger generation, for his "news" was more than comedy. Who can forget his moving monologue after the Charlie Hebdo killings, or his campaigning on behalf of the 9/11 first responders. These actions prompted the NY Times to compare Jon to Edward R. Murrow and Walter Cronkite, the most revered newscasters in American history. Jon's show also received 21 Emmys and 5 prestigious Peabody Awards.

The humor was what we'd expect from someone with a Centaur Sun and Moon—more so, when their Jupiter squares their Sun and Mercury. However, Jon also had a deeper side—the part in his personality that resonates to his Jupiter's square to a Uranus and Pluto conjunction in Virgo. Jupiter is the source of his giant sense of humor. Uranus provided him with his intuitive insights into political/social issues. Pluto gave him the extraordinary depth of perception, that enabled him to expose the power plays of others. The seriousness and discipline comes from his Sun's sextile to Saturn.

The lower left photo shows Jon's Leo Mars, as he proudly takes his confident Lion stance. The other photos show the

standard traits of Sagittarius. Note his large domed head and the long protruding jaw with the pointed chin. You'll see these features repeated again and again in the celebrities in this section.

(Jon's birth time is unknown, but he may also have a Centaur Ascendant).

Fixed Venus and Mars

With six mutable components in his chart, you expect Jon to be incapable of focusing on any task. His success shows that is not the case. This is likely due to the four fixed planets and their aspects: Jon's Scorpio Venus conjoins Neptune and these planets square his Mars in Leo; This red planet also trines his Moon.

Jon's theatrical Mars gave Jon the drive, while Neptune brought the compassion. His fixed components also helped him to stabilize his mutable energies, and focus on his work.

~~~

Our next portrait looks at Sagi's other side—that of the athletic Archer.

Bruce Lee
11/27/1940 / 7:12 A.M.
San Francisco, CA

Sun & Ascendant: Sagittarius

Bruce Lee's ability to take the physical capabilities of the human body to unimaginable levels made him a legend. From one inch from his chest, (without any swing or leverage), Lee could send an opponent flying across the room. His kicks and punches were so rapid, the cameras had to run at higher speeds to catch the movement. It is sad that he only made four films in his career.

Several astrological factors explain Lee's incredible physical skills. First of all, this Sun is just one degree before his Rising Sign. Lee's physical body (the Ascendant) is "one-with" the full athletic force of his Sagittarius Sun! Eight planets in the 3rd Quadrant enhance the connection, while these two key lights form a snug trine to Lee's Pluto—the planet that "stores power". Also, his Pluto was in his 8th House in the sign of Leo (the sign that rules the Heart). Somehow, Lee was able to control the empowered juices (adrenaline) in his body, so that he could perform his incredible feats of power.

Even with these key lights in the same sign, it is easily to distinguish one from the other. The UL photo shows how Lee's flesh lights up, when his Sun is activated. Note how it enhances the joy filled and mutable lines in his facial expressions. Meanwhile, the UR photo shows the Archer force in repose. Here, the underlying skeletal structure of the Ascendant is revealed. Both photos show the skewed features, offset eyes and the protruding chin that we see in most of the portraits in this section.

Scorpio Moon

Lee's Scorpio Moon makes six major aspects! It conjoins his Mercury, Venus and Mars—all in Scorpio! These five components also oppose a Jupiter and Saturn conjunction in Taurus, and all of them (save for Mercury) are T-squared by the powerful planet of Pluto.

The key planet here is Mars—for it is the driver of Lee's physical movement. It was Pluto's T-square to these planets, and its trine to his Sun, that gave Lee the strength and discipline to master his super human physical feats.

With these multiple Pluto connections and his Pluto ruled Scorpio Moon, it is no wonder that Lee often showed the dark intensity of Scorpio.

We suggest that readers spend some time marveling at Bruce Lee's chart. It captures a moment in time, when the Universe (and Nature) was able to induce incredible physical power into the body of a living soul.

Scarlett Johansson
11/22/1984, 7:00 A.M.
New York, NY

Scarlett's breakthrough came early with her role in the 1998 film *The Horse Whisperer*. In 2003, she was named "Best Actress" at the Venice Film Festival for her role in *Lost In Transition*. Thirty films later, she became the highest grossing actress of all time—thanks mostly to her earnings in her athletic role as "The Black Widow" in the Marvel Comic films: *Iron Man, Avengers* and *Captain America*. She also performed in several comedies and dramas, while she also established herself as a musical performer. Her song *Before My Time* received an Oscar nod for Best Original song. These diverse talents can be attributed to the mutable fire of her Sun and Ascendant.

Sun & Ascendant: Sagittarius

Bruce Lee and Scarlett's Suns are is just a few degrees from their Ascendants and they both have Scorpio Moons. The difference in these two is that Lee's Moon conjoins his Scorpio Mars—and both of them are opposed by a Saturn/Jupiter Conjunction. In contrast, Scarlett's Saturn conjoins her Sun and Moon, while Jupiter trines her MC and conjoins her Venus.

This gives her a natural, rugged quality. Bruce won fame for his athletic skills. Scarlett was named "Hollywood's most natural beauty".

As seen in most of the women archers in this section, few appear soft and cuddly. Rather, the attraction is the sparkle in their eyes and their athletic appearances. Like most Archers, Johansson displays the skewed facials features, the upswept eyes that sweep up on the outer edges, the broad frontal horse teeth and the long horse neck. The most obvious trait is the upper skull that sweeps sharply to the back. The sultry qualities come from the conjunction of her fiery Sun and magnetic Scorpio Moon.

Moon: Scorpio

In Bruce Lee's portrait, it was noted that his Scorpio Mars conjoined his Moon and squared Pluto. Scarlett's Aquarius Mars also squares Pluto, but her red planet also sextiles her "Saturnized" Sun and Moon. She shows many of the disciplined mannerisms that we saw in Bruce Lee, but her physical movements move at a far slower speed.

Since Scarlett's Mars sextiles her Sun and Ascendant, the static electricity of fixed Air fuels her fires, and it gives this lady an incredibly magnetic and powerful aura. It may be why *Esquire Magazine* named her "The Sexiest Woman Alive".

Centaur or Archer, or both?
Steven Spielberg
12/18/1946, 6:10 P.M.
Cincinnati, Ohio

Sun: Sagittarius

Sagittariuses are the eternally youthful *Peter Pans* of the zodiac, who send us flying off to *Never Never Land*! Few have taken us on as many fantasy trips as Steven Spielberg. And what productions they were—all "big in scope" or "epic in proportion". These Archers rarely think small, and with Steven, it was that way from the beginning. His first major film *Jaws* filled the theaters and cleared the world's beaches. Shortly after, he had every nation experiencing their own *Close Encounters of the Third Kind*. Later, we all acquired the Sagittarius urge to travel, galloping around the world with *Indiana Jones*. Wow, what fun!

Steven shows many of the physical traits of the Centaur. Most noticeable is the high domed forehead and broad-ridged nose with its bulbous tip.

In Steven's Sun expressions, the animated enthusiasm of mutable fire becomes apparent, but his physical energies change when he's in a "work mode". His Mars is in Capricorn and it conjoins his late degree Sun (in the 6th House of work and service). This reins in and directs his scattered solar fires. Steven is a tenacious work horse!

Moon: Scorpio

With a Scorpio Moon square to Pluto and Saturn and sextile his tenacious Capricorn Mars, Steven knows where to find the magic—and how to use it, to creative his Neptunian showbiz illusions! With his 5th House Venus conjoined Jupiter (also in Scorpio), his massive list of creative projects seems to never end.

These Scorpio powers allow Steven to "focus his energy" and keep his Archer arrows right on target.

Ascendant: Cancer

With his watery Moon, Steven feels the emotional reactions of his audience. With this Moon's trine to his Cancer Ascendant, he is also given a window—to view and feel how his work is being experienced by others.

When Steven is not interacting with, or directing his crew—he momentarily withdraws into his protective shell, so that he can identify and emphasize with the feelings of his imagined audience.

In these moments, he draws his hands and arms close to his chest, as he assumes the protective stance of a crab. In the process, his face swells and rounds as the eyes widen into deep puddles. Such moments are brief, for all to quickly, the Centaur returns, to once again play with his fantastic Neptunian toys.

Bette Midler

12/1/1945, 2:19 P.M
Honolulu, HI

Sun: Sagittarius

The sparks fly when this fun-seeking Centaur whinnies, snorts, and prances on stage. Midler's energetic actions and hilarious hoof-in-mouth comments bring instant excitement.

With five chart components in fire (including Mars in Leo), Bette is a real dynamo. The laughs are bountiful, the gestures animated and the spirit restless. With no earth to ground her, this lady is constantly fired up, as her high-stepping thighs carry her across the room, to interrupt a nearby conversation, or just create commotion. This is exacerbated by her Aries Ascendant.

Ascendant: Aries

Bette always seems to be caught in the proverbial frying pan. To escape the heat, she jumps into the fire.

Allegorically, this shows how people with an Aries Ascendant "instantly act" —as they charge forward to pursue their newly perceived adventures.

When Bette's Sun kicks in, the energies scatter like buckshot, but with the cardinal fire of this Ascendant, these fiery forces are highly directed. This gives her the drive to vehemently defend her many personal causes. It also gives her the power to belt out a torch song with ease.

As we saw in the films *Ruthless People* and *Outrageous Fortune*, Bette often uses the frontal assault of her Rising Sign in her comedic routines. The combination of these abrasive Aries qualities with her delightfully blunt Sun is what made her a star.

Moon: Scorpio

Like all of our other Scorpio Moons, Bette's fiery Sun is doused, when she reacts to others. You'll see it when this lady becomes emotional, as her eyes enlarge and transform into deep pools of water. You'd also swear there are fiery embers glowing at the bottom of the pool. Bette's fiery Ascendant draws this inner glow to the surface.

When Bette's Moon casts its impish glow, the fires are contained as her animated face fixes into a semi-liquid holding pattern. This solidification is enhanced by Bette's Pluto. It squares her Moon, trines her Sun and conjoins her Mars. That's why Bette's emotional responses are often steamy and racy.

Bette and the others in this opening section all had strong Pluto aspects. We believe that Pluto did not ordain them an empowered position in life. Rather, Pluto gives each individual the will and strength to persist. That is the magical gift of Pluto.

Air feeds the Fire!
Ben Stiller
11/30/1965, 5:35 P.M.
New York, NY

Sun: Sagittarius

Up to this point, no one has fully matched the mutable nature of **Jon Stewart**, save for Ben Stiller. Ben also has six mutable components, but unlike Jon, we know his Sun, Moon and Ascendant are all in Mutable signs.

When Ben projects his scattered and enthusiastic energy, the fire of his Sun spreads in all directions. In these exuberant moments, the sparkling eyes ignite, as his face projects the big mouthed smile of a very restless horse.

Ascendant: Gemini

With Mutable Signs on his three key lights, there is little change in Ben's pattern of expression. However, when each one surfaces, we see the force of a different element.

Thusly, when Ben's Ascendant rises to the surface, his persona takes on the nature of mutable Air. Stiller's expansive nature remains, but now he is noticeably more windy and chatty. This presence of billowing clouds creates the twin dimpled cheeks and the cumulous features of Gemini.

Moon: Pisces

The biggest change is seen when Ben's lunar emotions are activated. For here, there is a change in polarity, as the expansive force of his fiery Sun and Air Ascendant is replaced by the feminine energy of water.

When Stiller responds to others, watch how how the mutable water rounds his flesh as it turns his his eyes into liquid puddles. This gives his face a dreamy and sometimes bewildered appearance. It also makes Ben more intuitive and sensitive.

Mars, Venus in Capricorn

With all of this mutable energy, Ben's actions regularly take on the qualities of a goat. Why not? His Mars and Venus are in Capricorn—and his Mars sextiles his Saturn in Virgo. This red planet also joins his Venus in a trine to his Pluto/Uranus conjunction in Virgo.

The influence of these outer planets brought Ben many absurd, but also serious roles. Just recall *Night at the Museum* and *Meet the Parents,* or his roles in *What about Mary* and *Along Came Polly.* [The latter film's ads promoted him as "the most cautious man on Earth"].

Positively, these Saturn connections make Ben's characters believable, grounded and real.

Tina Turner
11/26/1939, 10:10 P.M.
Nutbush, TN

Sun: Sagittarius

Tina Turner is a genuine Centurion thoroughbred. The animal nature of her sign becomes apparent when Tina gallops on stage, kicks the air, rears her head and tosses her red-hued mane.

Tina has her Sun, Mercury and Venus in Sagittarius; also Saturn, Pluto and her Ascendant are in fire signs—and six planets and her Moon are in mutable signs. Her "wild fire" outshines that of **Jon Stewart** and **Ben Stiller**.

When Tina gyrates on state, she shows how Centaur fires burn in a crisscrossing "Mobius" pattern. They can be seen in the rotating movements of her hands, arms and legs. A hand gesture on the right may shimmer and shake, then flare up in a countering left-handed surge of fire. A high step to the right is followed by a skip to the left. A upturned smile on the left raises the right eyebrow. Unlike the blowtorch of Aries or the concentrated heat of Leo, Tina's fires are divided —and they spread in all directions!

Tina shows several physical traits that are associated with Sagittarius. The UL photo shows the Centaur's horsey eyes and broad frontal teeth. The LL photo shows the lanky and large thighs, and the body stance of Sagittarius.

Moon: Gemini

Turner was born on a Full Moon and this places her Moon in Gemini. This Moon is the only air in her chart, but Its fullness provides ample oxygen, to fuel the fire of her Sun.

Watch Tina in any interview, and you will soon discover that she has a tendency to chatter. Watch her hands fly about, as she diagrams the thoughts in her head. These light and mercuric gestures becomes obvious, when she gets emotional.

The two top photos show the mutable patterns of Sagittarius and Gemini. The left one shows the "fire" in Tina's eyes. The right one appears to have captured "a moment of mercuric reaction". There, the expression is less forceful, seemingly more electric. Tina's Gemini Moon has eclipsed the fire of her Sun.

Ascendant: Leo

With Leo Rising, Tina shines on stage, as she puts on her dynamic show! At other times, what we see is the cubical facial structure and noble mask of a lion, proudly fixed on center stage.

Since Pluto is the closest planet to Tina's Ascendant, it gives her a raw and magnetic persona. The fires are always cooking inside this fiery furnace.

Jake Gyllenhaal
12/19/1980, 8:06 P.M.
Los Angeles, CA

Sagittarius Sun

With five components in Fire and four in Air, Gyllenhaal often displays an expansive personality. However, Jake is best known for his performances in *Brokeback Mountain* and *Love and Other Drugs*—roles that showed the sensitive and vulnerable side in his nature. These unexpected character traits can be attributed to the aspects in his chart.

Neptune (the ruler of dreamy Pisces) conjoins Jake's Sun and both of them sextile Pluto. This contributes to Jake's controlled and restrained demeanor—traits that we rarely associate with a free spirited stallion. In addition, Jake is grounded by his Capricorn Mars. It is the only Earth planet in his chart, and its forms a snug square to Pluto. This accounts for his stolid physical metabolism, and the tenacious timbre and determination that he displayed in the films *Zodiac* and *Source Code*.

Jake shows most of the features outlined in previous Centaurs. What stands out is his large bulbous-tipped snout and the high domed forehead.

Moon: Gemini

With a Gemini Moon (like **Tina Turner**), Jake becomes very verbal when he's emotional. However, Jake's lunar reactions are odd, for they either run at "full chatter" or in a state of quiet suspension. This may be due to Gemini's ruler: Gemini. It conjoins his Sun and Neptune. All the while, Jake's Moon is trining a Saturn/Jupiter conjunction in his 3rd House. He talks a lot, or doesn't at all. Saturn's sextile to his Ascendant enforces this pattern.

Leo Ascendant

Jake and Tina share the same three Key Lights, but Jake appears far less fiery and showy. What we often see on first impression is a surprisingly relaxed individual. This could be due to the noted Saturn aspects to his Ascendant and Moon, or the fact that Saturn and Jupiter are both conjoined in the Venus-ruled sign of Libra. Another factor may be Jake's Moon. It is the only component above the horizon on his chart. Such individuals are often introverts.

When presenting his Leo mask, Jake displays the wide-set brows and cheek bones, the cubical skull and the mane of the lion. However, this Ascendant's sextile to those Libra planets injects Venusian qualities into his physical features. When the fixed Leo forces rise, we see hints of Taurus (the feminine sign ruled by Venus). Note how Jake's heavy lashed and sleepy eyes appear bovinely, rather than feline in nature.

Julianne Moore

12/3/1960, 5:53 A.M.
Fayetteville, NC

Moore's film breakthrough was 1997's *Boogie Nights*, where she earned her first Oscar nod. Her huge box office hits came later in *Jurassic Park II* and *Hunger Games I* and *II*. In 2015, she won her first Oscar for her role in the film *Still Alice*.

Sun: Sagittarius

Moore is the third Centaur subject with a Gemini Moon, but the first with her key lights in masculine and mutable signs. This makes it difficult to separate her three components from each other.

Still, traits of the Centaur can be seen when Moore expresses the fire of her Sun. The upper photos show how her jaw drops down and forward, to lengthen the face. They also show how the eyes lift up on the outer edges, to mock those seen in a horse. Oddly, the only aspect of Moore's Sun (other than the one to her Moon) is its square to Pluto. This outer planet trines Jupiter (the ruler of her Sun ruler). This may be why she rarely performs in whimsical or comedic roles. Many of her films were very Plutonic, dark and emotionally demanding.

Gemini Moon and Ascendant

The verbal skills of Gemini are seen in many of Moore's characters. In *The Hours*, she was an avid reader, swayed by the suicide of novelist Virginia Woolf. In *Still Alice*, Moore played a linguistics professor struggling with Alzheimers. Few of her roles were light or comedic. Exceptions included her role as the artsy daughter in *The Big Lebowski* and her role as Sarah Palin in the TV ministry *Game Change*. (This wonky retelling of the 2008 Presidential campaign won her an Emmy).

On the right in the center box, the photo of Sarah Palin closely resembles Julianne's image. This is why:

Moore's Gemini Ascendant and Moon are both in the Aquarius Decan. Also, Uranus sextiles her Moon and Ascendant. The Fixed Air of Aquarius often overrides the mutable force of Gemini.

Notably, Palin has an Aquarius Sun and Moon, and she also has Mercury Rising (but it is in the sign of Virgo).

Thusly, both ladies display the tensely locked smile of Aquarius. Note how the lower lip is drawn sharply downward, to expose the upper and lower teeth. This trait becomes more obvious when Julianne's lunar emotions are activated. There, her skewed facial features disappear, as the fixed force molds her flesh into the rectangular shapes, often seen in Aquarius.

Britney Spears

12/2/1981, 1:30 A.M.
Mahon, MS

Sun: Sagittarius

Britney began dance training at the age of 8. At the age of 11, she joined Disney's *Mickey Mouse Club*. Two years later, when Pluto entered Sagittarius (and transited over her Uranus) Spears signed her first record contract. From then on, every time Pluto transited one of her three other Centaur components, her career made a major transformation.

In 1999, Speers released her first LP *Baby One More Time*. At that time, Pluto was transiting her Sun, as Uranus transited her Aquarius Moon. The record was a massive hit, the best-selling album ever released by a teenage girl.

Alas, fame is only transitory. In 2005, transiting Pluto began its conjunction with Speer's natal Neptune, as transiting Neptune was wobbling around her Moon. In this period, the tabloids were hinting of Britney's drug problems.

A few years later, Saturn began its transit over this cluster of planets in Britney's first quadrant. Her popularity waned and there were many challenges in her career. It was a period to pull back, work hard and build new creations.

Speers persisted. In 2013, as Saturn transited over Britney's Jupiter, and Pluto ended its long run in Sagittarius, she released her 8th album *Britney Jean*. The song *Work Bitch* was a huge hit—and critics called it her best work in years. Whew! The drought was over.

Moon: Aquarius

Spears' Aquarius Moon is in her 5th House of creativity, shining its light in harmonious sextile to her radiant Sun. Notably, Saturn also trines this Moon as makes aspects with Britney's Venus, Pluto and Neptune. This combination of Aquarius and Saturn gives Speers the intuitive focus to be inventive and creative. Saturn gives her the drive to persist at her creative projects. Her Moon's trine to this ringed planet makes her emotionally chilly and distant.

Ascendant: Libra

Britney has Venus's beauty, as well as the pleasant persona of her Libra Ascendant. This Rising Sign shined in her adolescence years—and it certainly pleased the producers at Disney. Then, as we saw in Pluto's transit into Sagittarius (and its contact with Uranus), Britney image became more outrageous.

Later, in 2012, when Spear's Ascendant progressed into Scorpio, Britney's image went from bizarre to sulky. In this period, she began her career's resurrection, perfecting her dance, as well as her physical appearance for her sexy *Work Bitch* video. Indeed, her career (like all things on this Earth) had followed the astrological cycles of Nature.

Bring in the Earth.
Jeff Bridges
12/4/1949, 11:58 P.M.
Los Angeles, CA

With a trilogy of mutable signs in his chart, Bridges was given the flexibility to adapt to over 30 years of changing trends in the motion picture business.

Sun: Sagittarius

Jeff's films cover a gamut of genres. Early on, there was the rebellious comedy of *Rancho Deluxe* and the futuristic *Tron* and *Starman*. Later, we saw the psychological dramas *Jagged Edge* and *Against All Odds,* the metaphysical philosophy in *Fisher King* and *Fearless*—and the oddball views of *The Great Lebowski*. Such diversity and scope of material is what we can expect from a Sagittarius.

In his career, Jeff also learned to master the altruistic nature of his solar light. In 1997, he made the TV movie *Hidden in America*. It's a must see for anyone who questions the lack of hunger in our so-called secure economic system. Jeff took on this issue and became one of the key organizers of the worldwide "End Hunger Network". Sagittariuses have a gift for seeing the bigger picture!

Jeff shows many of the standard Centaur traits. The most obvious is his horse mane, which seems to scatter in all directions. This is likely due to the fact that all three of his key lights are in mutable signs.

Ascendant: Virgo

Surprisingly, Jeff is not as fiery as we'd expect from a Centaur. He appears serious, well grounded and seemingly driven by a steady hand. This can be attributed to the fact that Saturn and Mars are all conjoined on his Capricorn Decan Ascendant—in the earthy sign of Virgo. All of them form a T-square to his Sun and Mercury, and his Moon.

These heavy Saturn aspects restrain the expansive stirring force of his Sun and Moon, while his Virgo Mars makes his physical movements appear rigid and mechanical. This Mars also drives Jeff to serve others. It is what we saw in his *Hunger Project*.

Moon: Gemini

In emotional moments, the expansive forces of Bridge's Gemini Moon are activated. Abruptly, the restrains of his Virgo components disappear, as his masculine lunar forces send his hands and fingers fluttering out front—to animate and illustrate the content of his thoughts.

With this new burst of curiosity, Jeff tends to ask a lot of questions—as he attempts to "describe the feelings in his head".

Don Johnson
12/15/1949, 10:30 PM
Flatcreek, MI

Sun Sign: Sagittarius

In his life as well as in his TV roles, Don Johnson has displayed the restless character of a Sagittarius. In *Miami Vice* he played a free-spirited cop, running about in Florida's jet-set social scene, living a lavish life-style with flashy clothes and spiffy cars.

Nearly a decade later, Don returned with his hit show *Nash Bridges* and his movie *Tin Cup*. His newfound popularity and power came in 1996, just as Saturn entered his 8th House. During the previous two years, he was less fortunate, for Saturn had traveled through his 7th House and it brought his long marriage with Melanie Griffith to an end.

Don's *Nash Bridges* character reflected many of the conditions in his real life at the time. His new character was recently divorced and trying to be a responsible parent. The show's theme suggested that Johnson has become more philosophical with age, as he learned the lessons of Saturn and began to disseminate the wisdom of his Sun.

Ascendant: Virgo

Johnson was born just 11 days earlier than **Jeff Bridges** and both men have similar charts. Don's Mars also conjoins Saturn in Virgo, both planets square his Sun—and he also has Virgo Rising!

The big difference is that Don's Saturn does not conjoin his Ascendant, and his Rising Sign is in the Virgo decan (unlike Bridge's decan of Capricorn).

Don's Virgo decadent strengthens his mutable features. It also explains his well dressed style and his meticulous appearance. In contrast, Bridge's persona is often grubby and utilitarian.

With his Virgo decan, Johnson shows about the same "mutable traits" as Mr. Bridges, even though Don is not a triple mutable sign. This explains why these men look so similar. It is obvious when you view both of these set of photos.

Moon: Scorpio

The real difference in these two men can be seen in the patterns and force of their lunar reactions.

Jeff's airy reactions are as expansive and almost as animated as the force of this fiery Sun. In contrast, when Don emotions appear, his rigidly set eyebrows focus his eyes to the front. as his facial flesh liquefies and rounds into a holding pattern. His natural reaction is to pull back and become still and secretive. This gives the impression that Don he is trying to keep things in control. He is. His Moon is in the fixed water sign of Scorpio.

Steve Buscemi
12/13/1957, 11:30 A.M.?
Brooklyn, NY

Sun in Sagittarius

Unlike **Jeff Bridges** and **Don Johnson**, Steve's Saturn conjoins his Sun, rather than his Ascendant. This explains the chilly aura that Buscemi casts, and why he rarely displays the joy of his Sagittarius Sun. Positively, it was this gray demeanor that earned Steve a huge following of fans, and 100+ supporting movie roles. It made him the leading character actor in the new millennium.

Buscemi was born on Friday the 13th, an ominous day that suggests why Steve often plays characters who quickly find their demise. In his six films with the Cohen brothers, he dies in three—most famously in their macabre comedy *Fargo*. Steve also was executed by Tony, the mafia boss in HBO's *The Sopranos*. Buscemi jokes that when he reads a script, he must first check to see how long his character survives. This dark sense of humor is not expected from a Sagittarius Sun.

Virgo Moon

Saturn not only conjoins Buscemi's Sun, it also squares his Moon. This Moon is in the same Capricorn decan of Virgo that we saw in the Ascendants of our two previous portraits. Steve's Moon trines Virgo's ruling planet Mercury, and it also sits in the sign of Capricorn.

These Saturn aspects to his luminaries gives Buscemi the chilly, calloused and cruel emotions that we saw in his lead role as Nucky Thompson, the powerbroker who built the *Board Walk Empire*. (Yep, it's that UR photo).

With his Virgo Moon, Steve was able to display the twitching and mercuric mannerisms that were needed, for him to portray his nervous, fast-talking and overtly worried characters.

Pisces Ascendant?

With an unknown birth time, Steve's only water is his Scorpio Mars. Oddly, his most striking feature is his large and bulging eyes. This goggle-eyed persona suggests the presence of more water.

If born around 11:30 A.M., Steve would have a Pisces Ascendant. This places his Sun and Saturn on his Midheaven. Pluto also sits in opposition to his Ascendant, as Mars, Neptune and Jupiter (the ruler of his Sun) are anchored in his 8th House of Scorpio. With his Scorpio Mars and Neptune in the 8th House, we see why Steve's film career was filled with roles that ended up in his demise.

With Pisces Rising, Steve joins **Ben Stiller**, **Julianne Moore** and **Jeff Bridges** to give us the largest group with triplicated modes. This may be something to explore in future works.

Kiefer Sutherland
12/21/1966, 9:00 A.M.
Marylebone, UK

Sun in Sagittarius

Save for his *The Three Musketeers* role, there have been few films in which Kiefer displayed the jovial and humorous side of his Sun. However, it was in his earlier personal actions, where his centaur's rambunctious nature ran wild, as it earned him reputation for being a party animal. These actions likely accounted for his two short termed marriages.

And speaking of actions: shortly after learning to rope for his role in *Young Guns*, Kiefer quit acting to pursue a rodeo career. His Sun's T-square to Pluto and Uranus likely inspired this daring athletic endeavor.

Physically, Kiefer also displays many of the Centaur traits that were seen in previous subjects.

Capricorn Rising

Capricorn Rising certainly fits Kiefer's public persona. As we've seen in his roles, in *24* and *Designated Survivor*, he is serious, calculating, tenacious and highly directed, i.e., he's always on "duty". Ditto in his film role: *A Few Good Men*.

Kiefer is also known for his villainous roles, notably for his performance as the KKK fanatic in *A Time To Kill*. With his Mars square his Ascendant and Venus, he's comfortable projecting this cold and unlikable persona. Why not? It got him lots of work.

When Kiefer's fiery luminaries are in repose, his eyes take on the gray shade of smoked glass, as the flesh settles to expose the low and wide set cheek bones. This gives him the gaze and appearance of a goat.

Aries Moon

Kiefer's short fused temper has made him a frequent subject for the tabloids. He was even accused (but acquitted) of breaking a person's nose, by butting the victim with his head. Such an reaction certainly fits an Aries Moon!

Sutherland's Mars is in serene Libra, but it opposes his Moon and trines his Mercury and Jupiter. These aspects imply that his emotions and thoughts will be pumped with a giant boost of adrenalin—every time that he has a strong emotional interaction with others. These reactions are abrupt and forcefully driven, but they quickly recede. However, all too often, the damage is already done.

With four personal components in cardinal signs (his Moon, Venus, Mars and Ascendant), the mutable energies of Kiefer's Sun are often overridden by his pushy mannerisms. Positively, this drive (during the run of *24)*, made him the highest paid actor on television.

We conclude by looking at five more Centaurs with Earth components in their charts. In four, that component is Capricorn. This takes us back into the New Year cycle, where these portraits began.

Sarah Silverman
12/1/1970, 6:30 A.M.
Bedford, NH

Sun & Ascendant: Sagittarius

Sarah is a comedian, writer, singer and actress. Her writing stint on *Saturday Night Live* lasted just one season, because none of her sketches made it past dress rehearsal. A co-writer said her sketches didn't work at SNL "because she's got her own voice, she's very much Sarah Silverman all the time. She can play a character but she doesn't disappear into the character; She makes the character her". That happens often in folks who have the same mask (i.e., Rising Sign) as their Sun.

After SNL, it took nearly a decade of various gigs for Sarah to find her fan base. In 2005, her standup comedy act became a feature length movie. In 2007, she began her own Comedy Central program and hosted the MTV musical video awards. (On the latter, Sarah was criticized for mocking the musical stars). Also, as a guest on network talk shows, her comments were regularly censored, so most of her appearances were on the cable channels. Like many Centaurs, this lady was inflicted by this sign's infamous "hoof in mouth" disease.

The outrageousness can be attributed to her Sun's sextile to Uranus. This naughtiness may be due to Neptune's placement on her Ascendant and Sun and their square to Pluto in Scorpio. Furthermore, this Pluto is on Sarah's

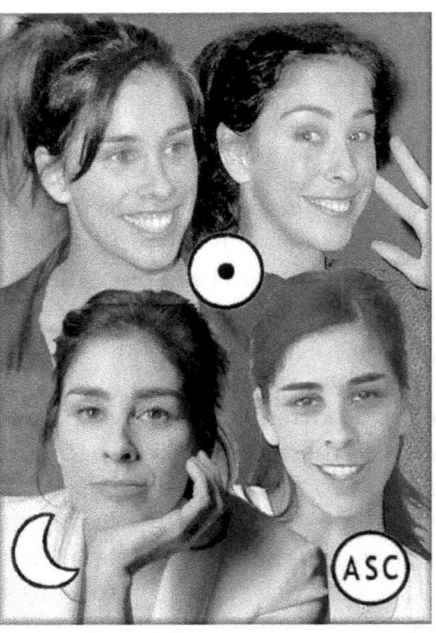

Midheaven. That is why she has gained public recognition for her often ribald comedy. It is rare for someone with a conservative Capricorn to push the boundaries of traditional conventions.

Capricorn Moon

Not only is Sarah's Moon in pragmatic Capricorn, it also trines Saturn and sextiles her Venus in Scorpio. This Moon explains why her comebacks and reactions are bitter and sarcastic. Venus accounts for the dark tone in her comedy.

Notably, Sarah's Moon forms a square to Uranus. This, and her previously noted Sun's sextile to Uranus, gives Sarah has a gift for understanding political and social realities.

With her Uranus in Libra (as it is with many born in this period), Sarah has gained recognition for challenging the unfairness within the existing social system. It earned her a speaking segment at the 2016 Democratic Convention! That is a rare occurrence for a comedian.

Brad Pitt

12/18/1963, 6:31 A.M.
Shawnee, OK

Sun and Ascendant: Sagittarius

The wild spirit of the Centaur ran freely in Brad's first major film role as the rebellious son in *A River Runs Through It*. This was the beginning of a career that grew in Jupiterian proportions—and it made him one of the super stars of our time! We saw the Archer's attraction to sports in Brad's ingenious baseball film: *Money Ball*. The Centaur's philosophical questions of life were examined in *Seven Years in Tibet* and *The Tree of Life*

The upper photos show how the head rears up, when this Centaur kicks into action. What stands out is the seemingly unconstrained exuberance and the facial lines that express the act of pure joy.

Oddly, Brad has rarely performed in a truly humorous role, showing little of the animated silliness that we see in folks like **Sarah Silverman**. Instead, Brad was often the cool and restrained "straight man" who feed practical observations back to others. (Just recall his roles in *Ocean's 11, 12 and 13*). This nature is likely due to that Brad has six Earth Components in his chart, including his Moon.

Moon: Capricorn

Pitt's Moon conjoins Mercury and Venus in the sign of Capricorn. His Moon and Mercury sextile Neptune in Scorpio; while his Capricorn Mars trines Pluto in earthy Virgo.

Thusly, Brad is mentally and creatively attracted to films with strong Pluto and Neptunian overtones. He was the tale teller in *Interview with the Vampire*, the obsessed detective in *Seven*, the institutionalized patient in *Twelve Monkeys* and the leader of *Inglorious Basterds*.

This presence of six components in Earth signs explains Brad's grounded and staid disposition. However, it is his Moon and Mars in Capricorn that gives him shows the emotional reactions and physical movements of a goat.

The LL photo shows what happens when Brad becomes emotional. Note how the flesh on the upper cheek bones builds into the stoney mounds that push his eyes upward, tightly placing them under the rigid ledge of the brow. It gives him a very serious appearance.

When Brad becomes physical, his Cardinal Mars drives him in an upward direction. This red planet's square to Jupiter (his Sun's ruling planet) gives him the extra physical stamina, to climb to the top of any mountain!

With all his Capricorn components and Saturn's square to Neptune, we see why Brad was attracted to the age-reversing lead role in the magical film *The Curious Case of Benjamin Button*.

The fires ignite when these two gals perform on stage, but surprisingly, both of their Suns are the only fire in their charts! Most of their components (including their Water Moons, Earth Ascendants and a Neptune/Uranus conjunction in Capricorn are in feminine signs. Here, we will look at the astrological arrangements that make these ladies similar, as well as unique and different.

Miley Cyrus
11/23/1992, 4:19 P.M. Franklin, TN

Sun in Sagittarius

Miley Cyrus is an American actress and singer-songwriter, who is best known for her role as Miley Stewart/Hannah Montana in Disney's TV series *Hannah Montana*. A 2007 sound track from that show was a huge hit. It made Cyrus one of "Forbes Top Superstar Earners under the age of 25".

Like Taylor, Miley displays the long chin, the wide frontal teeth and the skewed features of the Centaur. Also, the impulsive and animated force of mutable Fire is obvious. However, as we saw in her TV character (and in her later musical career), Miley appears more lackadaisical and less motivated than Taylor. This is because all of Miley's components (excluding Mars and Saturn) are on the RIGHT SIDE of her chart! Miley's seems to be directed by forces beyond her control, not by her own actions. This drive is also suppressed by her other key lights.

New Moon in Scorpio

Cyrus' Moon is close to her Sun, but it sits in the water sign of Scorpio. Her Sun, Ascendant, Moon and Mercury also conjoin Pluto—and Pluto trines her Cancer Mars. We see why Miley's eyes appear as deep pools of water and they lack the sparkle seen in Taylor Swift. .

These Pluto aspects explain Cyrus' bizarre and sexually provocative performances, which are orchestrated by her Saturn—that is placed in Aquarius on her Midheaven! In contrast, Swift's Saturn is in earthy Capricorn, near her Ascendant. Taylor's public image is far more pragmatic and conventional.

Ascendant: Taurus

When Miley's fixed persona appears, this Venus-ruled Earth sign presents its relaxed and bovinely features. They are markedly different than the rugged and chiselled goat features that we see in Taylor Swift.

Taylor Swift
12/13/1989, 8:36 P.M.
Wyomissing, PA

Sun in Sagittarius

In their 2017 review of Taylor Swift's music, the *New York Times* stated that Swift appears to be "more in touch with her inner life than most adults". Such philosophical pursuits are expected in most Sagittarius Suns, but rarely in someone this young.

As noted above, Swift's Centaur Sun is her only fire sign. In addition, her Sun makes no aspects to other components. So why does she have this incredible drive to "understand her self"? This may be due to the fact that all of Taylor's components, except for her Moon and Jupiter are on the LEFT SIDE of her chart. (In contrast, most of Miley's planets are on the right side.)

On this side of the chart, the Sun (the light of one's self) is building—as it makes its rise to high Noon. People with concentrated components on this side are driven to bring this light of self to full brightness.

That NY Times article also described Swift as being "one of pop's finest songwriters and country's foremost pragmatist." This tenacious sense of determination can be attributed to her five Capricorn components.

Capricorn Ascendant

On her work on the album *Speak Now*, Taylor maintained that she stated "nothing is finished, until it's written about", while adding: "I think about my next move 10 steps ahead". This sounds like someone with their Ascendant, Mercury, Saturn, Neptune and Uranus, all conjoined in Capricorn. This is also why she is incredibly organized and constantly creating new material. (This urge to put her words and music into "solid form" is likely a product of her Capricorn Mercury). The creative magic comes from her Scorpio Mars' sextile to Venus and its conjunction with Pluto. The gift of musical rhythm come from her Water Moon

Full Moon in Cancer

Taylor Swift was born on a Full Moon in Cancer. This lunar sphere opposes 3 of her 4 Capricorn planets and Ascendant.

As noted, this Moon conjoins Jupiter, and they are the only components on the right side of her chart. Both are barely in the 6th House, while Jupiter is the closest to the Descendent. Swift is emotionally attached to her work, and open to all of her fans. It is difficult for her to be close to individuals.

Jane Fonda
12/21/1937, 9:14 A.M.
New York, NY

Sun: Sagittarius

The expansive and humorous side of the Centaur was seen in Fonda's earlier work. Her first big hit was the delightful film *Cat Ballou*. This was followed by the chirpy *Barefoot in the Park* and the futuristic romp *Barbarella*. Thereafter, her work became increasingly serious, as her social awareness grew. This all was foreknown by the heavy Aquarius and Capricorn forces in her chart.

Jane's Sun trines her Moon and sextiles her Mars (in the late degrees of Aquarius). Also, her Sun and Venus are in Aquarius' 11th House, and her Jupiter in Aquarius conjoins her late degree Capricorn Ascendant. Uranus also trines her Mercury. With these links, Jane soon became known more for her activities, more so than her film work. This zeal was supported by Jane's Saturn (the most aspected planet in her chart).

Capricorn Rising

Jane shows little of the Centaur's traits. This may be due to the fact that Jupiter (the ruling planet of Sagittarius) sits on her Ascendant—less than one degree into earthy Capricorn. Furthermore, her Ascendant sextiles Saturn, opposes Pluto in Cancer—and trines Neptune.

These aspects dim the spark of Fonda's fiery Sun and the expansive qualities of Jupiter, but they also empower the altruistic spirit that makes Jane a real *shaker and mover*! Saturn's multiple links explain her long and enduring career and why Jane's films have examined so many important social issues.

There's her harrowing depression era film *They Shoot Horses Don't They*, her Oscar winning role in *Klute*, the nuclear fears of *China Syndrome*, the powerful anti-war drama of *Coming Home* and the insights into aging in her film *On Golden Pond*. Fonda always seemed to be ahead of the time curve, viewing society's struggles through the door of her Capricorn Ascendant.

Leo Moon

Jane's protests against the Vietnam war drew many angry responses, and she admitted there were errors in her behavior—but Jane proudly defended the core of her actions. Jane's Moon is in the fixed sign of Leo.

These fiery holding patterns (and the lion's showy gestures) appear, when Jane emotionally responses to others. Since Jane's Moon trines her Sun, and her Sun is in the Leo Decan, her features appear to be closer to those of a lion, rather than a horse.

~~
Sagittarius completes these portraits and the cycle that began with Capricorn.

The "Light Wave" of Creation

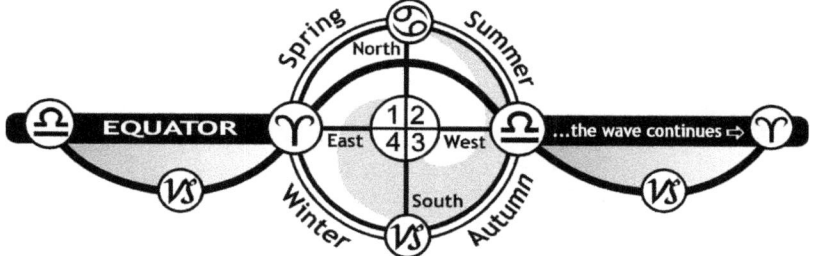

In **Sagittarius**, we witnessed the darkest days of the year. Now, things are looking brighter, for the Sun is now rising in the sky—and we have acquired a higher understanding of our world, by gaining insights into Nature's *Divine Process of Creation*, and the patterns that make all things in the Universe possible.

These insights are explored in science, philosophy, religion and in the language of astrology. Astrology is the only one to proclaim that *"there is a time for every purpose under heaven—and this purpose is ingrained into the makeup of our being".*

With these insights, it is time to review the lessons we have learned, and use them to begin a new round of creative pursuits. This takes us into a New Year, and the month of **Capricorn**—the point where these portraits began.

In the opening of each section in this book, the qualities and conditions of the four seasons and 12 months were described. With each Zodiac sign, we showed how the Sun's movement from the previous sign brought a shift in polarity, as well as a different elemental condition and modal activity. With this, the 12 steps in the *Dance of the Seasons* were defined, as they illustrated how the monthly and daily alterations in light, and the turning of the seasons and planets—all regulated the rhythms and patterns within our physical bodies.

This *Pulse of Nature* was visibly illustrated in the Earth's three key cycles of light. It was seen In the awakening of every morning's light, and deeply felt in the four phases in the monthly lunar cycles, more so at every Full Moon. Its power of manifestation was fully sensed, when the Sun turned in a new direction, to bring the Earth a new season—and its array of new creations!

Here, with the conclusion of this photographic evidence, it is hoped that this book have shown how the language of astrology can help individuals to find their connection with Nature—so they can run in synch with the rhythms of greater forces, and make their contributions to create a better world.

In this journey, it should be noted that these astrological forces do not dictate our destiny. Rather, they only serve as a guide—to tell us of the next step to take—and when it is time to make our move.

www.ingramcontent.com/pod-product-compliance
Lightning Source LLC
Chambersburg PA
CBHW060458090426
42735CB00011B/2033